PERSONALITY DISORDERS AND SUICIDE: THEORY AND RESEARCH

PERSONALITY DISORDERS AND SUICIDE: THEORY AND RESEARCH

HILARIO BLASCO-FONTECILLA
ENRIQUE BACA-GARCIA
AND
JERONIMO SAIZ-RUIZ

Nova Science Publishers, Inc.
New York

NOTICE TO THE READER

The Publisher has taken reasonable care in the preparation of this book, but makes no expressed or implied warranty of any kind and assumes no responsibility for any errors or omissions. No liability is assumed for incidental or consequential damages in connection with or arising out of information contained in this book. The Publisher shall not be liable for any special, consequential, or exemplary damages resulting, in whole or in part, from the readers' use of, or reliance upon, this material. Any parts of this book based on government reports are so indicated and copyright is claimed for those parts to the extent applicable to compilations of such works.

Independent verification should be sought for any data, advice or recommendations contained in this book. In addition, no responsibility is assumed by the publisher for any injury and/or damage to persons or property arising from any methods, products, instructions, ideas or otherwise contained in this publication.

This publication is designed to provide accurate and authoritative information with regard to the subject matter covered herein. It is sold with the clear understanding that the Publisher is not engaged in rendering legal or any other professional services. If legal or any other expert assistance is required, the services of a competent person should be sought. FROM A DECLARATION OF PARTICIPANTS JOINTLY ADOPTED BY A COMMITTEE OF THE AMERICAN BAR ASSOCIATION AND A COMMITTEE OF PUBLISHERS.

LIBRARY OF CONGRESS CATALOGING-IN-PUBLICATION DATA

Blasco-Fontecilla, Hilario.
 Personality disorders and suicide : theory and research / Hilario Blasco-Fontecilla, Enrique Baca-Garcia, and Jeronimo Saiz-Ruiz.
    p. ; cm.
Includes bibliographical references and index.
ISBN-13: 978-1-60021-753-1 (hardcover)
ISBN-10: 1-60021-753-2 (hardcover)
1. Suicidal behavior--Psychological aspects. 2. Personality disorders--Complications. I. Baca-Garcia, Enrique. II. Sáiz Ruiz, Jerónimo. III. Title.
[DNLM: 1. Personality Disorders--psychology. 2. Suicide, Attempted--psychology. WM 190 B644p 2007]
RC569.B583   2007
616.85'8445--dc22   2007017817

Published by Nova Science Publishers, Inc. ✦ New York

To Manuela Fontecilla Redondo, teacher, beloved mother

Hilario M. Blasco Fontecilla

CONTENTS

PREFACE

Although suicidal behaviors are common in a vast array of psychopathologies, the attention paid to suicide risk in personality disorders has remained scant. This book, with its focus on suicidal behavior in personality disorders provides an important step forward in terms of scientific knowledge from not only a theoretical and research perspective, but also from a clinical point of view.

The first part of the book addresses several key theoretical considerations that have important clinical implications for the treatment of these patients. The book addresses basic concepts regarding the constructs of temperament, character, and personality with special attention to the problems of reliability, validity and clinical utility. The coverage of topics ranging from cultural determinants of "normal" personality functioning as well as data regarding gene-environment interactions and their influence on suicide risk for personality disordered individuals reflects the comprehensive nature of the material presented herein.

The problem of suicidal acts is addressed from two different conceptualizations of personality functioning. Suicidal behavior in the context of categorical descriptions of personality disorders, put forth by diagnostic classification systems, last updated in the 1990s is addressed thoroughly. Particularly commendable is the extensive material presented on two of the Personality Disorder Clusters least represented in the literature. Compared to the still relatively modest number of studies focusing on Cluster B Personality Disorders and suicidal behavior, which generally focus on Borderline Personality Disorder, the number of theoretical and original scientific studies that address this problem in Cluster A and C Disorders is vanishingly small. In addition, the book also focuses on more modern, dimensional conceptualizations of personality functioning and their relationship to suicidal acts. Thus, the approach in this book is both comprehensive and up-to-date.

This book will serve as a solid, groundbreaking manual of utility to clinicians and researchers alike. The wealth of information provided will not only enhance the reader's fund of knowledge: this book is poised to provoke consideration of ethical and legal ramifications of the work that occurs in the clinic on a daily basis and to stimulate novel ideas for addressing the problem of suicidal behavior associated with personality disorders and traits.

Maria A. Oquendo, M.D. and J. John Mann, M.D.

ACKNOWLEDGEMENTS

We are most grateful to all the patients who helped us to carry out our research on suicide. Also, we would like to thank all the contributors for their great effort in this project.

PART I: PERSONALITY, PERSONALITY DISORDERS AND SUICIDE: THEORY

INTRODUCTION

H. Blasco Fontecilla

Personality disorders (PDs) are characterized by an important social burden, social, job and familial disordered relationships, and a high economic cost for developed countries (Oldham, 1994). The prevalence of PDs is estimated to be between 10 to 13% in general adult population, and between 36 to 67% in hospital samples (NIMHE, 2003). The diagnosis of PDs is related to a lower educational level, to a longer time being jobless, to marital problems – with high prevalence of separation and divorce- and alcohol use (Samuels et al., 1994). Moreover, it is associated to high comorbidity in both axis I and axis II disorders, worsening axis I prognosis (Reich & Rusell, 1993; Patience et al., 1995).

Despite the impact of PDs in the National Health Services of developed countries is not well establish, Smith et al. (1995) calculated its cost £61.3 millions to the *National Health Service (NHS)* in 1986. In a one year follow-up in a primary care setting, the diagnosis of a PDs increased the cost per patient only when associated to other mental disorders (axis I diagnosis), but not alone (Rendu et al., 2002). It must be taken into account that when a diagnosis of a PDs is made, comorbidity is the rule and also, that the majority of patients diagnosed with a PDs are seen at a primary care setting (NIMHE, 2003), where *cluster* C PDs are the most prevalent (Moran, 2000). However, in the mental health services, cluster A or B PDs are more frequent, and their diagnosis is probably associated with a higher cost. Nowadays, subjects diagnosed with a PD are the new "revolving door" patients. Studies addressing the question whether or not psychotherapy is more cost-effective than the current hospitalization based treatment should be implemented.

On the other hand, nowadays the topic of PDs is one of the most controversial among mental health workers. Currently, there is no a clear response to whether they should or not be considered a medical condition and if so, whether they should or not be treated by the mental health professionals. Furthermore, in spite of the emergence evidence that some treatments might be useful, the idea of PDs as disorders with no demonstrated effective treatment is widespread among mental health workers (Sanislow & McGlasham, 1998). Moreover, some clinicians do not want to treat subjects diagnosed with a PD (NIMHE, 2003). This might have to do with firstly, with the peculiar characteristics of these subjects and secondly, with the inner lack of specific skills to treat them. Some reasons can be argued to treat them: some patients do improve with treatment, there is increasing evidence that some changes can be exerted on personality in adult people, and the increasing pressure of governs of developed countries, where just a legal or forensic approach is not anymore justified. On the other hand, treating subjects diagnosed with a PD may have to do with the currently blurred limits of Psychiatry as a medical science, leading to an abusive medicalization of "normal" life events –are the abnormal behaviors of these subjects "symptoms" of the human condition or just only signs of our Society that do not allow them more?-. The lack of reliability of current categorical classifications, the lack of highly specialized professionals and resources, and its high cost are also reasons that make the ground to avoid treating subjects diagnosed with a PD.

Finally, it should also be stressed the increasing interest on this field (Medina & Moreno, 1998). This might have to do with the inner necessity of industrialized countries to face its social and economic consequences. However, it is also surprising that, currently PDs are a very poorly studied area in Psychiatry, particularly aetiology (Coid, 1999).

On the other hand, *suicide* is a complex phenomenon secondary to the interacting of genetic, biological, psychiatric, familial and socio-cultural factors. It is a public health issue of prior importance, particularly when considering that suicide rates have increased in industrialized countries, and are one of the leading causes of death at developed countries (La Vecchia et al., 1994). Around 750.000 people attempted suicide in the US (American Association of Suicidology, 2000; American Foundation for Suicide Prevention, 1996) and a million of people die every year of suicide. Suicide and suicide attempts are two closely related phenomenons. Thus, 3 to 7% of patients who attempt suicide eventually complete it, while 50% of subjects who suicide have at least one previous suicide attempt. Moreover, it is usually found a pronounced family history of suicide behaviors – independent of their own suicide history- (Samuels JF et al., 1994). The relatives of people who suicide have up to 8 times greater risk of suicide (Roy, 1986; Roy et al., 1997; Tsuang, 1983).

In the WHO/EURO multicentric study was found that suicide attempts are more frequent among women between 15 to 24 years; in men, the rate of suicide attempts was greater between 25 to 34 years (Platt et al., 1992). In the US, epidemiological data are found in the *Epidemiological Catchment's Area* (ECA) study (Weissman et al., 1999), and in the *National Comorbidity Survey* (NCS) (Kessler et al., 1999).

Regarding the relationship between *personality disorders* (PD) and *suicide*, it should be taken into account that mental illness is the most important risk factor for suicide, as nearly 95% of subjects who suicide have at least one mental disorder. Traditionally, major depressive disorder (related to 80% of all suicides) and schizophrenia (10% of all suicides) are the diagnosis more closely related to suicide. However, depression might be *necessary* but not *sufficient* to explain suicidal behavior, as the majority of depressive patients will never neither attempt suicide nor suicide (Brodsky et al., 2001). This might have to do with the presence of a PD. Some authors have suggested that the presence of a PD is at least at the level of importance of major depression or schizophrenia, but little research has been carried out (Linehan et al., 1986). It is calculated that at least one third of all suicides and around 70% of suicide attempts take place in subjects with the diagnosis of a PD. Subjects diagnosed with a PD have the highest rate of suicide repetition and they also are the ones with a greater prior history of suicide attempts and psychiatric treatment (Suominen KH et al., 2000).

The commonest PD associated with suicide attempts are *borderline PD* (BPD) and *antisocial PD*, both characterized by impulsivity. Another issue to be borne in mind is that of comorbidity: the majority of suicide attempts take place in people with comorbidity, particularly between BPD and major depressive disorder/substance use. Moreover, the so-call manipulative suicide attempts typical of subjects with BPD might be minimizing the real risk of suicide of these subjects. Their suicide attempts might be seriously considered and actively treated, something that seems not to be happening (Samuels JF et al., 1994).

The main objective of the present book is to give a clear and profound review of the role of PD on suicide behavior. Data on PDs different of BPD and antisocial PD are scarce. We are of the opinion that readers will appreciate to find information not only on these PD but also on the remaining PD to set the basis for their research or clinical work.

Contributors are all clinicians and researchers focused on the study of suicide. We have tried to give a comprehensive but clear overview of the main topics in this area. The book has two well-differentiated parts: the *first one* is an introduction to some theoretical issues that we considered basic to set the ground when approaching the *second part*, which is devoted to research on the influence of personality, and particularly, PDs on suicide behavior. In addition to the extensive review carried out, we present also data on some of the research that our research group and other groups are carrying out in this area. Some of them have a clear use into the daily activity of clinicians. We hope that they are one-step more to help in lowering the rate of suicide behaviors and suicides.

PERSONALITY AND PERSONALITY DISORDERS

1.2.1. BASIC CONCEPTS: TEMPERAMENT, CHARACTER, PERSONALITY

H. Blasco-Fontecilla

Despite Hippocrates began the study of personality with his *four basic temperaments*, there is still an outstanding lack of uniformity and agreement regarding the terms of *temperament, personality* and *personality disorder* (Rutter, 1987). Though, the majority of authors have used the term temperament as constitutional while character was widely used as a concept secondary to external influences (Baca Baldomero & Roca Bennasar, 2004). Kretschmer was probably the first author who tried to fix the meaning of temperament and character, pointing out temperament was the neuroendocrine basis that determined sensibility to external stimulus and psychological function among others, while character had to do more with the vital evolution of each human being (Kretschmer, 1954).

Temperament

> "Temperamental dimensions in infancy are the ´personality` of the newborn [...]"
> Caspi (2000)

Allport (1937, 1961) defined temperament as the set of inner characteristics of a human being that depend on the constitutional development and genetic background. Buss & Plomin (1975, 1986) said it was the group of behaviour characteristics – especially the ones related to the *style of behaviour*- present in the early childhood and stable across individual development. They established five criteria for dimensions of temperament: genetic component -the most important-, stability, presence in adults, adaptativeness and survival function, and presence in animals. A number of theories back the biological basis and different dimensions of *temperament* (Allport, 1961; Buss & Plomin, 1986; Eysenck, 1967; Gray, 1983; Kagan et al., 1987; Millon, 1993).

It is the part of personality whose components are hereditary, stable, based in emotions and non-influential by sociocultural learning (Goldsmith et al., 1987). In general, early psychologist considered temperament as the "congenital emotional predisposition" of human beings (Cloninger, 1994). However, Rutter (1987) criticised Buss & Plomin´s temperament characteristics, and suggested that the main difference between temperament and other personality aspects was temperament having to do with the *style* of behaviour. He pointed out temperament heritability was not very high - Cloninger (1988) would later establish inheritance accounts for a 50% of the variance of temperament-. Rutter defined *temperament* as "a relatively small number of simple, non-motivational, non-cognitive, stylistic features of which emotionality, activity and sociability are the best validated" that represent predictable modes of response, appear early in childhood, are quite stable after pre-school years and have probably neurobiological correlates. He pointed out that used in this way it could be applied to both children and adults.

Cloninger (1994) considered *temperament* is the part of personality that has to do with the unconscious automatic reactions and associative habit learning perceptually based, present not only in humans but in nearly all vertebrates. He also stressed its moderately heritability, stability from childhood through adulthood and consistency across different cultures and ethnic groups. Finally, he suggested four dimensions of temperament (harm avoidance, novelty seeking, reward dependence and persistence).

Character

According to Cloninger (1994), character "was what people made of themselves intentionally". In other words, the term character is related to voluntary directed impulses, it means *directionality* (Baca Baldomero & Roca Bennasar, 2004). Character would be the result of the interaction of temperament characteristics with the world, society and culture (Medina & Moreno, 1998). It is the part of personality that has to do with volition and cognition.

Cloninger (1994) distinguished two different major neural systems for *temperament* and *character*. He defined *character* as "the self-aware concepts that influence our voluntary intentions and attitudes" that has to do with propositional learning and abstract symbolic processes. In contrast to *temperament*, it would be weakly heritable, sociocultural learning would be more important in its development, and it would mature at a rate depending on the basal dimensions of temperament and sociocultural education (Cloninger, 1994). He postulated three dimensions of character -*self-directedness, self-cooperativeness, self-transcendence*- that could be achieved by insight learning and would have to do respectively with the extent to which an individual identifies the self with an autonomous person, an integral part of humanity and an integral part of the universe (Cloninger et al., 1993).

Personality

Currently, there is a rather good consensus regarding its meaning (Moran, 2000). Allport (1937) – considered the father of the modern *personology* (Baca Baldomero & Roca Bennasar, 2004)- thought that personality was a dynamic organisation about the way an individual relates with himself and others, and deal with the traits he is endowed with and the experiences that go through. As Rutter (1987) said, different authors have emphasized the integrative and organising function of personality. He pointed out that the main difference between *personality* and *temperament* has to do with the non-behavioural aspects of personality -cognitive processing and motivation-.

Cloninger (1987), based in his own previous studies, stated that personality could be defined in terms of the "individual differences in the adaptive systems involved in the reception, processing, and storing of information about the environment" and defended its multidimensional structure. Later on, Cloninger (1994) said that personality results of the interaction between multiple processes related with the different dimensions of temperament and character, and stated that personality was "a complex hierarchic system that can be naturally decomposed into distinct psychobiological dimensions of temperament and character" (Cloninger et al., 1993). It is also important to consider that personality "actively organizes, integrates, and regulates experiences and behavior to enable individuals to reach their goals"; as assessment of these processes is not possible, it must be inferred from overt behaviour (Livesley et al., 1994).

Personality traits are shown to be stable over time (Stalenheim, 1997). An important characteristic of *personality* is its temporal stability, though certain circumstances can produce major changes and it's not immutable (Livesley et al., 1994).

Cloninger et al. (1993) suggested "a seven dimensional model of personality; four temperament factors and three character factors" where *dimensions of temperament* have a stronger neurobiological and genetic basis and are related to susceptibility to neurotic syndromes – i.e. anxiety and somatoform disorders-, while *dimensions of character* mature in adulthood enhancing better personal and social effectiveness. In this model, *personality* would be the result of interaction of temperament and character (Cloninger, 1994). *Personality* implies "differences between individuals in the adaptative systems involved in the reception, processing, and storing of information about experience" (Cloninger et al., 1993).

Table 1. Differences between temperament and character based on Cloninger´s model of personality (Cloninger et al., 1993; Cloninger, 1994)

Personality	
Temperament	Character
Perception	Conception
Emotion	Volition
Instinct	Will
Habit	Cognition
Unconscious automatic reactions	Conscious self-aware plans
Procedural learning (associative conditioning)	Propositional learning (conceptual insight)
Unconscious memories (percept driven)	Conscious memories (concept-based)

Personality Disorders

As Livesley et al. (1994) stressed, in order to differentiate between *personality* and *personality disorder* (PD), it is basic to define what a *disorder*. They considered DMS-III-R concept of disorder as dysfunction as the starting point. It has been suggested that dysfunction should be measured apart from PD itself (Widiger, 1993). This model was probably based on Schneider´s vision of PD, considering them apart from mental illness and differentiating between abnormal personalities and PD, in the latest stressing its own suffering and making others suffer, where surrounding culture and socioeconomic structure should be considered (Baca Baldomero & Roca Bennasar, 2004). Livesley et al. (1994) are of the opinion that an evolutionary perspective is needed to develop a culture-free definition of PD and gave the example of the four universal tasks basic to adaptation given by Plutchik (1980) –*hierarchy, territoriality, identity* and *temporality* (problems of loss and separation)-.

The concept of *personality disorder* is hard to pin down, controversial and has to do with not only deviant traits but also pervasively maladaptive functioning (Rutter, 1984; Rusell & Hersov 1983). Prins (1991) referred to them as the `Achilles´ heel of Psychiatry, and despite its controversy, the term is widely used as it is a helpful category. The origin of the concept is not on a model of normal *personality* (Hill, 2002), though as Berrios said it appeared unwillingly in the nineteen century after the definition of what character and personality was (Baca Baldomero & Roca Bennasar, 2004). Kretschmer (1936) linked particular personality types to specific types of mental illness. Kurt Schneider (1980) was the first one to offer a psychiatric model of *PD* based in abnormal personality traits as obsessionality and the current *anankastic, schizoid* and *schizotypal* PD are derived from his descriptive classification.

The concept of Axis II (PD) was first introduced in the third edition of the Diagnostic and Statistical Manual of Mental Disorders (DMS-III) to allow clinicians to diagnose both Axis I and Axis II disorders in one subject at the same time (Millon, 1993). In the fourth edition of the Diagnostic and Statistical Manual of Mental Disorders (DSM-IV) (American Psychiatric Association, 1994), PD are defined as enduring, inflexible and maladaptive patterns of perceiving, relating to and thinking about the environment and oneself, which cause significant functional impairment or subjective distress. They characterize the extreme end of the broad personality dimensional scales, which characteristically involve maladaptive patterns of behaviour that cause friction or distress to the subject or those with whom they interact (Stone, 1993). From an evolutionary point of view and accepting a rather simple definition of personality as the way a life organism gets adapted to its environment, PD could be defined as a particular way of disadaptative functioning (Millon, 1993). Livesley et al. (1994) used a "working definition" of PD "as extreme personality variation associated with the failure to attain the universal tasks of identity, attachment, intimacy, or affiliation" and reminded its proximity to "Freud's definition of mental health as the ability to work and to love".

Personality-disordered subjects have poorer coping strategies in response to stress, and manifest a tendency to resist treatment and to dismiss responsibility for their own behaviours, preferring instead to externalise them by shifting blame onto other (Blaszczynski, Steel & McConaghy, 1997). They also have a higher risk of aggressive behaviours directed toward others or oneself, particularly under stress, due to their inability to manage stressful situations and their less adequate interpersonal skills in resolving difficulties.

Coid (1999) reminds that PDs are secondary to both constitutional and environmental influences, and that their aetiology seems to be multifactorial. The traditional assumption is that PD have their onset in childhood or adolescence, however they are not usually diagnosed until adulthood (Zocolillo, 1992). In the DSM-IV (American Psychiatric Association, 1994) PD are defined as "an enduring pattern of inner experience and behaviour that deviates markedly from the expectations of the individual's culture, is pervasive and inflexible, has an onset in adolescence or early adulthood, is stable over time, and leads to distress or impairment". The International Classification of Mental and Behavioural Disorders (ICD-10) (World Health Organisation, 1992) defines a PD as "a severe disturbance in the characterological condition and behavioural tendencies of the individual, usually involving several areas of the personality, and nearly always associated with considerable personal and social disruption´ and it is stressed that the age of onset is in the childhood or adolescence".

Table 2. Basic characteristics of PD. Based in Rutter (1987)

1. Onset in childhood/adolescence.
2. Pervasive abnormalities of functioning that influence their social relationships.
3. Longstanding persistence over time with no marked changes (not episodic).

Conclusion

Temperament can be defined as a group of relatively few individual characteristics present since childhood, reasonably stable after the first years, and has to do with behavior style and unconscious automatic responses; it is be the biological part of personality (Millon, 1993). In contrast, *character* is more determined by social learning and environmental interaction would. It refers to the way human beings are and get adapted to the social environment they have to live in. Finally, the concept of *personality* results of the mix of *temperament* and *character* dispositions where the individual becomes aware of himself as a differentiated individual –self-consciousness- and knows who he is –self-identity-, being consistent and coherent. It is an abstract concept, which includes thoughts, reasons, emotions, interests, attitudes, abilities and other similar (Davidoff, 1984). A scientific definition of personality must include feelings, cognitions, behaviors and morality/ethics. Given the way we think, we are, we behave and that is unique and particular, it is supposed these characteristics to be stable across time, making people rather previsible. Thus, personality could be defined as the set of characteristics defining the way of being and functioning as a person, perceiving, thinking, feeling and behaving, fairly consistent and that allows our differentiation between people not only as individuals but as social, cultural and species group, having a rather good stability across time and evolutionary consistency. Analysis of the differences would allow behavior – i.e. suicide behavior- predictions about one specific person in a specific situation.

1.2.2. CURRENT PERSPECTIVES: CLASSIFICATIONS OF PERSONALITY DISORDERS AND THE PROBLEMS OF RELIABILITY, VALIDITY AND CLINICAL UTILITY

F. Cañas de Paz and B. Franco

While classifications in psychiatry, as in any other field of medicine, may serve many purposes (clinical decision-making, communication, teaching, management, legal, etc.) (Jablensky & Kennedy, 2002), its main interest probably arises from the fact that they reflect a synthesis of the current knowledge in a given area. They can be taken, so to say, as a quick test about how deep, comprehensive and coherently organized is the information available about the phenomena studied... and from this point of view personality disorders offer a very problematic panorama (Parker & Hadzi-Pavlovic, 2001).

Since the publication of the DSM-III in 1980 - that can be considered the starting-point of the present classification system in psychiatry- the studies in the field of personality disorders have experienced an extraordinary "jump forward" from almost any possible point of view. And this unprecedented success is aiming to the paradox that, probably, the most extended conclusion from all the evidences collected up to now could be that this system is unsatisfactory for any of the purposes it has to serve, or at least that the pitfalls are so important that it have to undergo deep changes (Paris, 2005; Widiger, 2005; Vedeul, 2005). We will try to briefly review the main issues at play in this field and summarize the likely alternatives in the near future.

Classifying PD's

To build a classification means making groups or sets or objects (called *classes, categories* or *taxa*) based on their attributes or relationships, and using that classification implies the explicit assignation of an object to one class or category following some principles or rules for identification. Following a classic work from Robert Sokal, "the paramount purpose of a classification is to describe the structure and relationship of the constituent objects to each other and to similar objects, and to simplify these relationships in such a way that general statements can be made about classes of objects" (Sokal, 1974). The process is aimed to achieve economy of memory, ease of manipulation of information and, ideally, describe what is known as the *"natural system"* so to say displaying the "true" relationships between objects. As a consequence, a clear set of necessary and sufficient criteria may be defined as a rule to assign additional candidates to the correct class (monothetic definition).

This model is thought to be easily applied to physical entities or "substances" that can be stripped of all "accidental" characteristics so to reveal its "essence". But even in natural sciences, this "essentialist" model can be confronted with the very difficulty of determining which are the essential components of an object, so other models have been set up. One of them, derived from "folk" or "natural" thinking is the prototype-matching strategy that makes a correspondence between each class and an "ideal" type, the *prototype*, which is formed from a set of the most common features presented by typical members of the category. The process of identification goes through a comparison between the actual object and the prototype to assess how close they are, even using in some cases statistical measures, to give an estimate of the degree of similarity (Cantor, 1986) (procedure that can be further operationalized using "fuzzy" logic). Other model puts the emphasis on the systematic description of all the attributes of the objects (its phenotype), giving equal weight to all of them (thus avoiding the problem of determining its "essence"); the classes are formed using statistical algorithms to select the individuals that share the maximum number of characters, so it is called "numerical taxonomy" (1999). In both models, prototypical or numerical, there are no necessary or sufficient conditions to be ascribed to a class and the process of identification is based on the proportion of properties shared with the defined category (polythetic definition).

The subjects to be classified are another source of concern. Personality disorders are explanatory constructs of a high level of inference (patterns of behavior that are persistent, pervasive, desadaptative, and dysfunctional). These disorders are clinically heterogeneous, descriptively multidimensional and arise from complex adaptive systems and multifactorial ethiologies (Cloninger, 2002). Therefore, no single way or criterion can be selected to guide categorical assignment of these syndromes and there are authors that consider they do not even exist as valid clinical entities (Lewis & Appleby, 1988).

With this background, it is not surprising that personality disorders constitute a field of continuing debate and controversies, and this, of course, is reflected in the evolving concepts, taxonomic position, and suggested management they have received in clinical psychiatry. As it has been shown in recent reviews from an European (Baca & Roca, 2004) and an north American (Oldham, 2005) perspective, in the early years of XX century, when the basement of modern psychiatric nosology were placed, there were prominent authors who viewed personality or temperament pathology as intermediate conditions between normality and more severe forms of mental disorders (the functional psychoses) in a kind of what now is known as the "spectrum model" –in this group could be Kraepelin, Bleuler and Kretschmer –while a rather opposing view was held by Schneider, who's influence in the field of what he called "psychopathic personalities" has been long lasting, and considered them to be deviations from normality and not illnesses in the narrow medical sense in a kind of "dimensional" definition while he set up many of the prototypical categories that still persist in the classifications.

The most widely used classificatory systems in our days, the tenth edition of the WHO International Classification of mental and behavioural disorders (ICD-10, 1992), and the fourth edition (with the later "text revision") of the American Psychiatric Association Diagnostic and Statistical Manual of Mental Disorders (DSM-IV-TR) (APA, 2000) are the result of a convergent evolution (see Table 3) that cannot be analyzed here with great detail due to space limitations (for that purpose we recommend the before mentioned reviews and also the study from Perez Urdaniz et al. (2005). Both of them follow the categorical model (as in the other mental disorders) with a polythetic set of criteria with identical weight in order to make a diagnosis, but they grossly differ in two important ways: the existence of a separate axis for personality disorders in the American system and the transference of the schizotypic personality disorder to the schizophrenia and other delusional disorders in the ICD, and both differences will point to one of the issues at debate: is there any scientific based ground for the separation of personality disorders from the other clinical syndromes? But before going further in this direction, it will be convenient to clarify some other properties of good classificatory systems.

Table 3. Personality disorder categories in ICD-10 and
DSM-IV-TR classificatory systems

ICD-10	DSM-IV-TR
Paranoid PD	Paranoid PD
Schizoid PD	Schizoid PD
	Schizotypic PD
Disocial PD	Antisocial PD
Emotionally unstable PD Impulsive type Borderline type	Borderline PD
Histrionic PD	Histrionic PD
	Narcissistic PD
Anxious (with avoidant behaviour) PD	Avoidant PD
Dependent PD	Dependent PD
Anankastic PD	Obsessive-compulsive PD
Other PD	PD not otherwise specified (PDNOS)

Validity, Reliability and Clinical Utility

Classifications, in order to be successful instruments in clinical practice and research, must fulfil some requisites and can be evaluated with respect to three classes of criteria (Westen et al, 2006): 1) *Internal criteria,* such are *comprehensiveness* (do the classes cover all the relevant objects in the field of study?), *coherence* (are the syndromes described conceptually meaningful?), and *parsimony* (is the classificatory system capable of integrating diverse observations with the minimal redundancy and using few assumptions, concepts and terms?) (Millon, 1991). 2) *External criteria,* that link the constructs of the system to relevant variables (dysfunction, treatment response, laboratory tests, family aggregation, etc.), and 3) *Clinical criteria,* which refer mainly to the extent the system is found relevant and useful by clinicians in everyday practice (later on addressed as "*clinical utility*") (First et al., 2004). The resulting taxa or classes must represent adequately the features of studied objects (i.e. be *valid*), and allow consistent results when used by different persons or in different moments (i.e. be *reliable*). It is common sense that an unreliable measure cannot give valid results, so reliability has become a forced "first step" of any classification that claims to be valid.

Variability in diagnosis can originate from three main sources:

a) Variation arising from the nature and course of the disorder itself (patient and occasional variance).
b) Variation derived from the information gathering procedures (observation and information variance).
c) Variation due to the method followed to elaborate diagnosis (criterion variance).

The first source is out of our possibilities of modification as it belongs to the inherent variability of bio-medical phenomena. The second one can be clearly reduced through the use of standardized instruments to get the relevant clinical information (self-administered questionnaires, checklists, and structured interviews) which increase the completeness and homogeneity of data gathered from patients. Another way of increasing the quality of information at this level in some cases consists in the utilization of additional informants to avoid biases in mostly subjective data. The third source of variability can be reduced introducing operational definitions with diagnostic criteria and decision algorithms for each category. This, together with the multiaxial system, was probably the main change brought by the third edition of DSM. But very soon after its publication it became clear that, while the reliability of "personality disorder" diagnosis as a whole was acceptable and comparable to other axis I disorders, when specific PD categories were compared the agreement was much lower and frequently far from acceptable levels (kappa < 0.4), also depending on the type of instruments used: the lowest values were for unstructured clinical interviews and increased when using self-administered questionnaires, checklists or structured interviews –in this order –in parallel to the time consumed and the need for qualified and trained staff (Bronish & Mombour, 1998).

Other untoward result has been a very high rate of co-occurrence of more than one PD diagnosis in the same patient as it was very soon pointed out by Widiger et al. using DSM-III categories (Widiger et al., 1991). This problem was, at last partially, attributed to an extensive amount of overlap of many specific criteria across different PD diagnosis (Pfhol et al., 1986), something that happened even at higher rates in DSM-III-R (Morey, 1998). If we add to that the lack of clear differentiation between normal functioning and pathology which entails the arbitrary definition of cut-off points to make a diagnosis and a rather heterogeneous result in some of them (Oldham, 2005; Westen et al., 2006), together with the frustrating absence of consistent findings in neurobiological research and treatment of specific PD disorders, it is not surprising that a feeling of disappointment and criticism pervades this field and numerous voices claim for a deep review of the present model (Jablensky, 2002). And one of the reasons frequently mentioned is the need for developing taxa that are more valid as reliability, although being important, by itself does not produce good classificatory systems. Otherwise, the opposite can be postulated, as non-valid classes very likely would render unreliable results.

Diagnostic validity is a complex construct taken from the field of psychological testing (Blacker & Endicott, 2000; Oldham, 1991). It includes different facets as:

- *Face validity*: how accurately a category and its diagnostic criteria describe a syndrome or disorder.
- *Descriptive or construct validity*: degree of uniqueness of the features characterizing a category when compared to others; it is related to other facets known as *convergent* and *discriminant validity*, i.e. how well criteria from different categories relate within and between them, allowing differential allocation of patients with minimal overlapping or mixed cases.
- *Predictive validity*: strength of the likely relationship between a given category and future clinical course, response to treatment or complications.

- *Concurrent or external validity*: level of correlation with external features accepted as validators (neurobiological markers, family history, etc.)
- *Assessment validity*; existence of an efficient method to assess the presence or absence of the disorder.

In the field of mental disorders, there is a lack of external criteria that can serve as a "gold standard" against which diagnostic concepts can be validated. Robins & Guze (1970) proposed a set of five steps to provide the highest level of validation for mental disorders: 1) clinical description; 2) laboratory studies (today it would include neuroimaging and other newly developed neurophysiologic tests); 3) delimitation from other disorders; 4) follow-up studies, and 5) family studies. If we try to apply this program to personality disorders as a group we should find discouraging results from the very first step as has been shown by Blashfield & Breen (Blashfield & Breen, 1989) with a rather low face validity for DSM-III-R PD categories, mostly due to overlap in meaning among the criteria for three pairs of them: histrionic / narcissistic, avoidant / dependent, and schizotypal / paranoid.

The results already available from the Collaborative Longitudinal Personality Disorder Study (CLPS) (Skodol et al., 2005), probably the most ambitious prospective study undertaken up to now with the aim of providing reliable empirical knowledge about the nature, course and impact of PDs, give some confirmation of this as the authors decided to focus the design on four specific disorders (schizotypal, borderline, avoidant, and obsessive-compulsive) that are considered the most prevalent of the three DSM PD-clusters plus the OCPD which, in spite of having been ascribed to cluster C, is clearly separable from these clusters. The selection of those categories may be, at least in part, the explanation of the acceptable to good levels of reliability, internal consistency and diagnostic efficiency of diagnostic criteria found in the study, as it avoids the "blurring" effect of the use of other categories not so well delimited as the mentioned in the previous paragraph.

Related but not identical to diagnostic validity is the construct of *clinical utility* as formulated by First at al. (2004). For these authors, a classificatory system has to be evaluated with regard to the degree it assists its users in:

1. conceptualizing diagnostic entities
2. communicating clinical information to all participants in the health care system (practitioners, patients and their families, managers, etc.)
3. applying diagnostic categories and criteria sets in practice
4. choosing effective interventions, and
5. predicting future needs

When we look to DSM PD categories from this perspective, it is discouraging that in some studies less than half of patients treated in clinical practice are diagnosable with DSM categories (Westen & Arkowitz-Westen, 1998), and also there is a very high frequency (between 21 and 49%) of use of the residual category of personality disorder not otherwise specified (PDNOS), this being the single diagnosis most found in many studies (Verheul & Widiger, 2004; Shedler & Westen, 2004).

Conflicting Issues in Classifying PD's

All the data presented up to now and the alternatives suggested by the many workers in this field can be grouped under some rubrics that have attracted most of the debates in recent literature about PDs (see Table 4).

Table 4. Conflicting issues in the classification of PD's

Axis II vs axis I
Categories vs dimensions
Stability vs change
Instruments for PD evaluation
Atheoretical vs theory driven

Distinction vs Continuity between Axis I and Axis II Disorders

As it has been already mentioned, DSM-III introduced a multiaxial system of classification for mental disorders, with personality disorders included in axis II together with mental retardation, given that these conditions had an early onset and were persistent; the main reason to explain this decision was to ensure that "consideration was given to the possible presence of disorders that are frequently overlooked when attention is directed to the usually more florid axis I disorders" (APA, 1980). Also there was a kind of assumption of a more "psychological" ethiology (Oldham, 2005), and consequently a lower likelihood of response to biological treatments.

Undoubtedly, this major modification in the way personality disorders were handled in classifications led to an impressive increase in interest and research work in this area. Nevertheless, the data gathered in the years elapsed since this moment challenge the very foundations of this decision, as there is increasing evidence that PDs may have a late onset, a remitting course, and can respond, to some extent, to biological therapies (Fountoulakis & Kaprini, 2006; Ruocco, 2005). The Collaborative Longitudinal Personality Study (Skodol et al., 2005) have also provided some data about the existence of fundamental underlying dimensions of psychopathology between borderline PD and major depressive disorder and PTSD, as well as between avoidant PD and social phobia. Krueger (2005), in a very documented review, makes a strong case for the suppression of this distinction as it seems that the inconvenients of its maintenance overcome the advantages, even in fields so distant from "science" as are public opinion and health care management.

Categories vs Dimensions

It has been suggested by many authors that a dimensional model of PDs would improve reliability and validity of diagnosis and be more clinically useful than the current categorical model (Widiger, 2005; Verheul, 2005; Cloninger, 2002; Trull et al., 2007). A strong support for that point of view can be taken from Hempel, who almost half a century ago stated that although most sciences start with a categorical classification, they often replace them with dimensions as more accurate measurement can be developed (Henmpell, 1961). This implies moving from a present/absent dichotomy to a continuous score on a variable called factor o dimension that overcomes the problem of artificial boundaries, overlapping categories, and conveys more information about patients than a reduced yes/no decision.

But the term "dimensional" is far from being univocal and, when applied to PDs, may describe quite different approaches of quantifying personality and personality pathology, being more or less akin to the classical model. One can be simply derived by rating the number of criteria a patient fulfil for every category of DSM classification, a kind of "dimensionalization" of the categories that can be rated, as Widiger & Sanderson (1995) suggested, in levels of "absent, traits, subthreshold, threshold, moderate and extreme" and that show a better correlation with other variables as functional impairment (Skodol et al., 2005). In the same line can be considered the proposal of a "level of severity" measure as proposed by Tyrer (2005) or the degree of matching of a given individual presentation to a prototypic DSM PD category (Westen et al., 2006).

Another step can be to use factor analysis ratings (top-down strategy) to identify the personality traits underlying personality disorders or cluster analysis (bottom-up strategy) to find groups of patients who share some features of disordered personality. Applying this method, some authors have identified four factors that account for a significant amount of variability in the domain of PD traits and symptoms: *emotional dysregulation*, *inhibition*, *dissocial behavior* and *compulsivity* (Livesley et al., 1998).

Finally, other alternative is to start from existing trait models of normal personality that have been built independently from diagnostic classificatory systems. Underlying this approach is the assumption that personality disorders are not qualitatively different from normal personalities, but extreme variants that can be adequately explained using the same dimensional constructs than in general personality assessment. There are many of this models, from circumflex to three, four, five and seven-factors (see reference 39 for additional data), but all of them share a drawback: they usually produce a non-specific profile of higher order dimensions for all PDs that can only be distinguished at a lower facet level. This is the case, for instance, with the Five Factor Model (FFM) (Widiger & Costa, 2002), that shows an association between most PDs and a combination of high neuroticism and introversion with low agreeableness and conscientiousness not being possible a more detailed differentiation at this level.

But the widespread use of a dimensional system for diagnosing PDs is far from being easy to reach. Firstly, it cannot be said simply that personality pathology is only the elevation of certain personality traits. Statistical deviance alone is neither a necessary nor a sufficient criterion to diagnosing a disorder, a limitation connected more clearly to the systems coming from normal personality models (Livesley & Jang, 2000). As Wakefield pointed out, "dimensionalization" can bring the risk of "pathologization" due to the lack of adequate conceptual constraints (Wakefield, 2006), and since the times of Schneider, it has been widely accepted that a deviant personality by itself is not pathological unless it causes significant distress or impairment. The measure of such distress is far from satisfactory and the level that can be considered "significant" is highly subjective. This is the reason of the proposal of complementary constructs as "harmful dysfunction" (Wakefield) to help in this issue but not everybody agrees on its utility. Probably all this debate, that is related to the general definition of "disorder", is also linked with the rather arbitrary determination of cut-off points, a problem not new in medicine but specially complex in PDs.

Secondly, there remains the problem of choosing between the dimensional models available at present, which will be the one that best fits all available data. It is increasingly assumed that many models share a similar group of dimensions although they have assigned them different names (Widiger & Simonsen, 2005). In most systems we can find a dimension of *neuroticism* (also called *emotional dysregulation / negative affectivity*), other related to *extraversion* (or *positive affectivity*), a third one linked to interpersonal functioning *dissocial* (or *antagonistic behavior*), and finally a dimension of *constraint* (also named *compulsivity / conscientiousness*). This basic schema of high-level factors may be the basement for a more fruitful search in specific neurobiological and genetic etiologic factors, but much work is still needed in this area to overcome the disagreements.

Thirdly, our language and, at a certain extent our thoughts, works with categories in a more efficient way that with dimensions, and in clinical work decisions are often on a yes / no basis. Even if a dimensional model is generally accepted, some degree of categorization will be necessary for medical, legal and administrative purposes (Verheul, 2005). So, the development of a system to transform dimensional into categorical information fitting al these needs is crucial and still missing.

Other Conflicting Issues

The list of other problematic topics in the field of PDs can be very long, but due to space limitation we should mention only some of them we think are of higher interest. We shall begin with the controversy around *stability* of personality disorders. It is clear from its very definition that PDs are "enduring and pervasive" patterns of behavior, and as it was mentioned previously, its persistency in time was one of the reasons for their allocation in a different axis in DSM classifications. This conception was also responsible for the "therapeutic pessimism" that overshadowed this field, with only minor expectancies of change in the long run following prolonged psychotherapeutic efforts. But the findings of some recent outcome studies are rather conflicting with this perspective, as many forms of personality pathology decline over time. Analyzing the data from the CLPS and other outcome studies on PDs, Paris (2005) concludes that "personality disorder categories, as currently defined, are unstable" and he puts the alternative that either personality disorders are more benign and episodic than previously believed or the apparent remission of PDs is an artefact of how they are classified (invalidating present PDs categories). For this author, the explanation for this contradiction comes from the hybrid way of defining PDs, as they are a mix of traits (more stable) and symptoms (which tend to vary over time). While symptoms may remit, traits (abnormal in the case of personality-disordered patients) will persist, perhaps in a more adapted way of functioning..., but in this case, what is a personality disorder?

And linked to this topic is another polemic issue: what are the best *instruments* to detect /diagnose personality disorders? It has been repeatedly said that simple trait deviation is not enough to make a diagnosis (although it will be very likely), and that a measure of impairment is needed. As Paris points, "at present we lack criteria to determine whether high levels of any personality trait actually lead to harmful dysfunction and can therefore be defined as disorders".

Finally, we would like to mention a more general topic that, for us, pervades all the conflicting issues already mentioned. From the third edition of DSM onwards, it has been repeatedly said that this classificatory system is *"atheoretical"* trying to find a basement in purely empirical data (whatever that would mean...). But to make sense of complex findings is very important to follow some guidance as the aim is not only describing, but also explaining, and this is completely impossible without a theoretical framework. Of course, it does not mean "any" theory, but in the recent years there have been intents to link personality pathology with neurobiology and genetics (mainly through some dimensions that seem to fit better as endophenotypes), pointing to a fruitful future in this area.

Final Comments

It may be clear by now that the classification of personality disorders is a gauge that signals the very high complexity of this field of mental disorders. The present situation is evaluated as very unsatisfactory from almost everybody, given the many problems derived from how PDs are defined and classified: they are unreliably diagnosed, show high levels of comorbidity, research on its neurobiology or genetics is discouraging, and have a rather low utility to guide specific treatments. The alternatives are not yet much more satisfactory, a situation that has played in favour of a "conservative" stance, but we think that a kind of "stepwise" transformation will take place in the near future, refining the distinction between such an heterogeneous group of disorders between the more "symptomatic" or "spectrum like" and the other more "trait like" disorders, rediscovering old concepts as "temperament" in the way Akiskal (2005) proposes and developing a sound theory of (deviant) personality.

1.2.3. PERSONALITY AND CULTURE

E. Barbudo del Cura

What do we Mean when we Say '*Culture*'?

Definitions of Culture

Culture (from the Latin *cultura* stemming, from *colere*, that means 'to cultivate'), generally refers to patterns of human activity and symbolic structures that give such activity significance. The many different definitions of 'culture' reflect not only different theoretical criteria for evaluating human activity, but also different philosophical points of view on human nature. Anthropologists most commonly use the term *Culture* to name the universal human capacity to codify and symbollically the individual experience; since such wide sense has allowed some primatologists, like Jane Goodall (1986), to identify aspects of *culture* among human's closest genres of apes, the definition of this capacity should be specified to remain as the distinctive feature of the human being.

In 1952, Alfred Kroeber and Clyde Kluckhohn compiled a list of more than 100 definitions of 'culture' (Kroeber & Kluckhohn, 1952). Nevertheless, the definition of *Culture* made in 1871 by the British cultural anthropologist Edward Tylor (1958) still encompasses the great many aspects of the term and is frecuently quoted in contemporary books:

'Culture or *civilization*, taken in its wide *ethnographic* sense, is that complex whole which includes knowledge, belief, art, morals, law, custom, and any other capabilities and habits acquired by man as a member of society'.

Tylor's definition specifies that human being has to be conceptualized as a social being, stressesing that people do not carry their beliefs or worldview in their biological inheritance, but develop them within particular societies by means of exposure to specific cultural traditions. Such process of children learning their culture is named enculturation (Kottack, 1994), undestanding that cultural learning is not merely to acquire sets of distinctively human forms of adaptation, and organization of lifes, nor simple patterns of behaviour, but overall the exclusive human ability to use symbols and incorporate the baby´s mind, since his/her very birth, within a pre-existing symbolic structure.

Every personality disorder is defined, explicitly or implicitly, in terms of relational disfunction by means of finding out determined symptoms that are in fact symptomatic relational behaviours. The DSM-IV diagnostic criteria are shown as though these were absolute cualitative findings to be checked over by the clinician, but the clinician must be warned (and de DSM-IV enphasizes separately) that such criteria are outlined against a background made of what is considered socially and culturally normal during a determined stable historical period. A proper, non-overlapping definition of historical, social and cultural factors must be done. Since cultural learning not only takes part in the environmental circumstances around the individual, but also determines the assembly of the Self as the child grows up, an understanding of Culture as the fundamental human symbolic ability (not just the knowledge of an assortment of picturesque ethnographic anecdotes) is needed in order to accurately diagnose, prevent cultural bias and planify specific psychotherapies for every single patient.

The clinician should be aware of the particular sense given to the word 'culture' when interpreting clinical study results and psychiatric texts. Many culturally concerned psychiatric texts do not use the word 'culture' corresponding with the sense given by anthropologists, neither with an agreed operational definition for clinical research: the acquired behavioural characteristics that can vary from one population to another, defined against the background of the physical and biological environment a human population must adapt to for surviving, often referred as the *socialization process* (Levine, 1973). Sometimes, the word `culture´ operates as a diffuse allusion to what is not measurable during the positivist psychiactric research, amalgamating a mixture of social, historical, cultural and even unclear biological ideas, regarded as 'confusion factors', 'environment" or ' nurture', used as though these were a same *factual* thing instead of a variety of *ideological constructs* (becoming at worst into a veiled, implicit use of the post-World War II outmoded sense of race). The idea of *Culture* itself has been subjected to criticism from different disciplines, as I will expose below.

Contemporary Meaning of Culture

At the following points I summarize the contemporary meanings of 'culture', as shown in ordinary university handbooks (Kottack, 1994; Harris, 1988; White, 1959):

- *Culture* takes in everything, including the means of material production. In contrast with the medieval idea of *Culture*, which always signified the-cultivation-of-something (some specific art, agri-culture, the 'cultivation of the Soul', etc.), and today's romanticist, yet *essentialized,* idea of *Culture*, which means taste, education, refinement and appreciation of fine arts, the most meaningful aspects of Culture from an Anthropological point of view are those related with common people during their daily lifes, no matters if ordinary, particularly those affecting children during their *enculturation* process.

- *Culture* (capital *C*) is a general feature of the *Homo* animal genre. This is a shared faculty of the *hominids* to symbolize. Anthropologist use the word *culture* (small *c*) to describe the specificity of different cultural traditions across diverse societies. Human evolution suggests that there is not a human *Nature* independent of *Culture*, which is not an aggregate to a finished animal, but a fundamental element for the generation of such animal (White, 1959). Cultural Anthropology is the discipline that takes in theories about *Culture*. Ethnology theorizes on *Culture* comparing what is found out in *cultures*. Ethnography describes particular *cultures*. We tend to use the terms '*trans-cultural*' and '*cross-cultural*' to designate diagnostic and therapeutic psyquiatric matters when treating people who come from foreign nations and Non-Westen *cultures* (small *c*). If we are impelled by a theoretic interest on human *Nature*, the aetiology and the diagnosis of mental illness, and the recovery process throw culturally-oriented psychotherapies, we would better use the terms '*metha-cultural*' or '*metha-ethnographic*', since these imply that we are thinking about a general human function named *Culture* (capital *C*) that operates within the *Self* of everybody, everywhere and everytime. George Devereux, a psychiatrist and an ethnologist, wrote from a psychoanalytical perspective (Devereux, 1973):

  > 'The practice of a metha-cultural psychotherapy demands to the analyst a sort of neutrality analogous with that affective neutrality hoped of him during the analytical situation, with regard to his own infantile and residual neurotic needs' (Pp. 103-124).

- *Culture* is symbolic, and symbolic thinking is a process as exclusive as fundamental to humans. The main feature of *hominid* evolution is its dependence on *Cultural Learning*, which is the main consequence of human ability to symbolize; it permits us to build our individuality and our way to perceive the world within a symbolic system or structure weaved by our social group along its History. Some theories of *Culture* theories advocate for its mainly lingüistic nature, enphasizing that verbal language is the actual, unique and distinctive trait of *Homo sapiens* when compared to animals. American anthropologist Leslie White (1959) thought that *Culture* began when our ancestors got the capacity to symbolize, that is to say when they freely and arbitrarily provided any thing or any fact with meaning and respectively got and appreciated such meaning. A *symbol* is whatever, verbal or non-verbal, fitted within a particular language or *Culture*, that represents another thing without any obvious, or natural, or necessary connection between the symbol and the symbolized thing. The connection is arbitrarily agreed. Sometimes *Culture* is tought directly (for example, when parents show to their children how to say 'thanks'), but it develops consciously or unconsciously, verbally or nonverbally, through continuous interaction with others. It cannot be mistaken, as so many psychiatrists and psychologists do, with two other learning processes that are not exclusively to humans: first, *Situational Individual Learning* that occurs when the animal readjusts future behaviours based on its own experience (it could be, for example, the *conditioning* described by behaviourists); second, *Situational Social Learning*, that occurs when the individual learns from other members of the social group, not necessarily by language, like wolves learn hunting strategies from other members of the pack. Clifford Geertz (1973) writes on that matter:

> '(...)Culture is best seen not as complexes of concrete behavior patterns - customs, usages, traditions, habit clusters- as has by and large been the case up to now, but as a set of control mechanisms -plans, prescriptions, formula, rules, instructions (what computerization engineers name "programs")- for the governing of behaviors. '
>
> '(...)Believing, like Max Weber, that man is an animal suspended in webs of significance he himself has spun, I take culture to be those webs, and the analysis of it to be therefore not an experimental science in search of law but an interpretive one in search of meaning. ' (Pp. 19-117).

I suggest that parallel ideas about learning processes were developed by developed by the Systemic Therapy theorist Gregory Bateson (1972) with regard to the aforementioned learning processes: his 'learning I' concept resembles the *Situational Individual* one, his 'learnig II' concept resembles the *Situational Social* one, and 'learning III' connects to *Culture*, since it requires profound changes of self-perception that shows the person as one supra-individual piece fitted in with a symbolic system given by *Culture*.

- *Culture* prevails over *Nature*, it takes our animal biological needs to encode them into particular symbolic forms that will be subsequently tought through *Cultural Learning*. That is to say our shared human *Nature* is subdued and shaped by cultural systems into many different directions. Innate universal dispositions are culturally transformed into a variety of customs. Human being creates himself through *Culture*. The boundaries between what is innately controlled and what is culturally controlled in human behavior constitute a fluctuating and poorly defined line (Geertz, 1973). There is a shared human instinct of hunger, and we could even hypothesize common basic innate perceptual categories that condition the acceptance or rejection of determined eatable things, but above all every specific *culture* will determine if such things are tasty or disgusting, healthy or poisonous, sinful or sacred, reserved for feast, ritual or daily life..., depending on the symbolic position within the system assigned for it within the symbolic system. The same reasoning can be extended onto *emotion*, a core idea for Western *culture*, as well as a meeting point for two contemporary Western myths on human *Nature*: the biological one and the (individualistic) psychological one. Clifford Geertz (1973) writes on this question:
  > '(...) Not only thoughts but also emotions are cultural devices within the human being. (...)It is for sure that within human being neither prevalent fields nor mental series can be generated accurately enough without the guidance of a symbolic model of emotion. (...)Human nervous system unavoidably depends on the access to public symbolic structures to be able of making its own autonomous patterns of activity'.

It is noteworthy that similar ideas have emerged simultaneously among Systemic Therapy thinkers (Papp, 1983):

'(…) The therapist must focuse on the function played by feelings, and the form these are shown. (…) It is difficult to point out this concept as it opposes the spread notion that shows feelings as sacred things, as though these were the actual sign of "who-we-really-are" and "where-we-really-place"(…). This cult of open communication overlooks the politics of feelings within a social context. Feelings do not come from an individual psyche that is in communion with itself, but these are stimulated and conditioned by an audience made of others, regardless if such audience is just foreseen or remembered. The expression of feelings, like that of behavior, programmes others and is programmed by them'.

- *Culture* is not itself an attribute of the individual. It belongs to individual as a group member, it passes within society, generating an individuality that fits in the common experience. It is a shared schematic experience. *Culture* changes constantly, but determined *core* beliefs, values, world views and rearing practices do remain.

- *Culture* has got a pattern, and *cultures* are not accidental collections of customs and beliefs, but structured systems. Institutions, rules, rites and values are interrelated, so the change of one element affects all the other elements. The *cultures* are made up not just with economic activities and dominant social rules (Materialistic Anthropology representatives refer to these, respectively, as *superstructure* and *infrastructure*), but as well with a characteristic whole of *Core Values* that are basic, key principles that interlace each *culture*, making it distinctive. Individuals learn to share certain personality traits that are in fact shared cultural *Core Values*. For instance, rational pursuit of economic gain and worldly activities as a human tendency burdened with positive spiritual and moral connotations, enterprising character, individualism and the will to achievement and self-confidence (Max Weber's 'work ethics') are *Core Values* for most U.S. citizens – at least if considering their explicit *Emics* perspective (see later)-.

- People cope creatively with *Culture*: we do not always obey the rules. We can learn, misinterpret and handle the same rule in different ways. Some anthropologists distinguish between *Ideal Culture* and *Actual Culture*; the first consists in what people say that must be do and what they say that they do; the second is the actual behavior as the athropologist sees it. Most anthropologists prefer the terms *Emics* perspective (from the lingüistic term 'phonemics') and *Etics* perspective (from 'phonetics'). An *Emics* assessment describes one aspect of the *culture* from the perspective of a participant who is member of that *culture*; it may be refuted if contradicts facts perceptible by the participant. An *Etics* assessment depends on the phenomenic distinctions considered as appropiated by a community of scientific observers; it can not be refuted if disagrees with the participant's point of view, but will be refuted if empirical evidences given by the observers are eventually shown as false (Harris, 1989). *Etics* perspective is in fact the observers' *Emics* perspective, so it must be (cautiously) accepted that such community of scientific observers has got a more privileged way for knowing than the community of participants, that is to say Science is a privileged perspective in order to make predictions. This *axiom* makes possible empirical research but this is considered out-of-date by contemporary *hermeneutic* and postmodern *Culture* theorists, who only accept an encounter of diverse *Emics* perspectives, being the observer's one equally privileged than the participant's; this attitude disdains any behavioral analysis of *culture* and questions the very principle of objectiveness. Let us clarify the matter with an example: most contemporary U.S. citizens describe thenselves as monogamous, according to laws and strong religious or ethical principles (*Emics* perspective of the participants). But some anthropologists (Kottack, 1994) describe the actual situation as a 'serial monogamy' close to poligamy, due to high divorce rates parallelled by an appropriate rate of not-too-much socially condemned marital infidelity, and subsequent marriages, as unmarried stable couples do not enjoy complete social acceptance (*Etics* perspective of the observer). Nevertheless, this U.S. marriage puzzle may have catched the attention of the foreigner anthropologist to the point of receiving a biased interpretation, as it touches his own nation's increasing (but not yet stardardized) marital problems: that is *Emics* perspective of the observer. Marvin Harris is firmly opposed to postmodernists like Geertz, accusing them for platonism, mentalism, ideationalism and anti-scientifism, and he tries to rescue the classical empiricist attitude distinguishing between mental *Emics/Etics* and behavioral *Emics/Etics*. From Harris' point of view, the analysis of behaviours from *Etics* perspective is the key tool to assess any cultural phenomenon.

> 'Definitions should not be the substitutes for empirical research aimed to test particular theories (…). It can be concluded that the so praised simplicity of the Platonic kingdom exists nowhere else than inside the imagination of ideationalists. In real life all the rules are surrounded with a half-light of "cancellation and trigger clauses" (that is to say rules to infringe the rules), that in turn contain more rules to infringe the rules ad infinitum (…). There are many evidences proving that cultural information treasured within the brain contains contradictory instructions. (…) Our ideational and behavioral repertoires can not be reduced into a set of stable and permanent programmes, human social life implies unceasing changes (…)' (Harris, 1989, pp. 29-47).

- *Culture* is not always adaptative in the long term (our faith in the idea of "progress", a *Core Value* for Western societies, could destroy the Planet), but *enculturation* is always adaptative for the individual in the short term.
- A *culture* is not a hermetically sealed up entity. Every culture influences and is influenced by the rest. Even if contemporary rhetoric makes believe that each culture constitutes an original entity, there are many evidences that prove the ubiquitous, subtle blend of native and foreign influences within all the *cultures*. A thorough historical examination of a *culture* always yields the presence of sets of imported foreign elements, which may be eventually seen as a genuine part of one's own *culture*.
- Biopsychological equality among human populations is assumed today by most anthropologists, and *race* is considered today a socially and culturally constructed *Emics* perspective concept, without any scientific basis. Phenotypical differences among the peoples are not denied (as commonsense does not deny phenotypical differences among individuals), but these are statistical, not deterministical neither absolute. What is more: there is not any clear physiognomic cutpoint for separating populations in terms of racial traits.

- There are *UniversalTtraits* shared by all *Homo sapiens* that distinguish them from other species. *Biological Universals* are our long child dependency period, sexual activity during all months of the year instead of seasonal, and an extremely complex brain allowing the use of symbols, language and tools. *Psychological Universals* come up from human biology-environment interaction and 'programmed' child development experiencies; it is not clear in what proportion such developmental programmes are genetically or culturally determined. It is not completely synonimous to Cloninger´s concept of *Temperament* (Cloninger & Svravick, 1997), which includes basic neurobiological conditions and excludes others that are acquired through child development; these last are considered a part of the concept of *Character,* an acquired set of traits that are in fact definetely fixed as bio-psycological composites by the earliest attachment experiences. *Social Universals* are acquired through interactions within family as well as society; the most outstanding examples are the human tendency to *exogamy*, linked to the *incest taboo*, which is clearly prescribed from *Emics* perspective in every *culture*, but not so clearly fulfilled when evaluated from *Etics* perspective (and certainly a fact in our own *Emics* perspective psychiatric daily practice). Between what is *Universal* and what is *Particular*, there are *Generals* like the 'nuclear family', a structure that operates in many societies, but not all of them. Such discovering led the anthropologist Bronislav Malinowski (1927-2001) to argue during the 1930s that the Oedipus complex was absent in the Trobriand Islands, where he found the 'nuclear' or 'matrilineal complex' to consist of a psychological constellation where the boy loves his sister and hates his mother's brother. The evidence of that book is the cornerstone for the claim of relativists that the existence of the Oedipus complex is a cultural product of the Western patriarchal family structure, despite it has been tried to contradict by subsequent field work (Spiro, 1983). Nowadays most cultural anthropologists reject the Oedipus Complex to be a Universal (Harris, 1988).

Ways of Looking at Culture

There are different ways of looking at *Culture*. Only some of them are accepted by today's anthropologists, while the others belong to the *Emics* perspectives of Werstern peoples, especially if they are politicians and other non-anthropological thinkers:

Culture as Civilization

This idea of *Culture* developed in Europe during the 18th and early 19th centuries. It identifies *Culture* with *Civilization* and contrasts it with *Nature*. Some theorists attached the Western ideological constructs of *Progress* and *Evolution*, a way of thinking that permits classifying some countries as more civilized than others, and some people as more cultured than others. Today most social scientists reject the monadic conception of *Culture*, and the opposition of *Culture* to *Nature*. Social thinkers contrast the 'high' *culture* of *elites* to 'popular' *culture* and analyse the continuous swapping of incons, themes and other cultural materials between them, as though these were in fact mere *subcultures*.

Culture as Worldview

This is the most inclusive way to think *Culture*. Historians and philosophers agree today that this perspective started during de Enlightment and thrived during the Romanticist Era among scholars in Germany, as some of them were openly concerned with the nationalist movements that would originate unified nations in Central Europe (Bueno, 1996). Terms as abstract as influential like *Volksgeist* ('the spirit of a people'), *Zeitgeist* ('the spirit of a time') and *Kulturkampf* ('struggle for culture', the Bismarckian's *leitmotiv* for secularization of the young Germany) spread during the 19th Century. Despite their underlying criticism of *Rationalism*, yet hidden under euphemisms, these weird German ideas still operate within many current academic discourses and political sermons. A distinct and incommensurable world view characterizes each ethnic group, romanticists thought: this approach to *Culture* still separates *civilized* and *primitive cultures*, but its most dramatic creation is the idea of *national culture*. Despite its obscure, and therefore potentially racist use (as it unfortunately would happen), 19th Century anthropologists like the aforementioned Tylor adopted the term to be applied to a wider variety of societies discovered within the imperial colonies. As tribal cultures were rapidly disappearing and great flows of inmigrants began to arrive into Western countries since the 1950s, *Subcultures* (groups with distinctive symbol patterns within a larger *culture*) became the subject of study, raising the question of how cultural sciences can *reify* social problems, obscuring up facts like inequalities of wealth, political unfairness and power struggles. When Psychiatrists and Psychologists make use of the words 'culture', 'nation', 'ethnicity' or 'race', they should be warned about the poor denotative properties of these terms and their history, the dangers of their vague connotations and the consequencies of their *reification* on research, diagnosis, treatment and Ethics with regard to Personality Disorders. Popular believes concerning foreign groups, derived from such *reification*, tend to be stereotyped, exaggerated and highly evaluative: group stereotypes are then *psicologyzed* in the sense that they reduce complex national societies into the portrait of an individual (the Spaniard, the Englishman...), and attribute to such mental image derogatory qualities as though these would characterize a single person: 'the Spaniard is lazy, sensuous, liar...' Such characterizations are false, dangerous and irresponsible oversimplifications that have nothing to do with *Culture*, but with *Emics* perspective, neurotic complexes and prejudices of the observer who makes use of them.

Culture as Symbols

Symbolic view of culture has been set out in the preceding paragraphs. It dominates contemporary academic discussion. Symbols are both the practices of social actors and the context (Max Weber's 'webs of significance') that gives such practices meaning. Members of a culture rely on these symbols to frame their thoughts and expressions in intelligible terms, and what is more: their feelings.

Culture as an Evolutionary Stabilizing System

Along the last decades we witness how biologicism revives as a presumptive social science with a suposedly stronger empirical basis. Evolutionary psychologists argue that the mind is a system of neurocognitive modules produced by natural selection to solve the adaptive problems of the evolving hominids, so the diversity of forms that human *cultures* take are constrained by innate information processing mechanisms underlying behaviors. Adaptive innate neurocognitive modules include language acquisition modules, incest avoidance mechanisms, intelligence and sex-specific mating preferences, alliance-tracking mechanisms and so on. These mechanisms are hypothesized to be the psychobiological foundations of *Culture*.

Other theories also consider *Culture* itself, as a whole, a product of stabilization tendencies inherent in evolutionary pressures toward self-similarity and self-cognition of societies, through the 'differential reproductive success'. Such view of culture as an operating mechanism has been tried to be reproduced by means of computerized iterative algorithms, and connects with Richard Dawkins' (1982) theory of *memes*. Dawkins proposes that *memes* are units of cultural information transferable from one mind to another, analogous to genes. There would be a *memetic evolution* that alternates change with stability over time through feedback mechanisms. Nevertheless these theories can explain in a very abstract way *Universals of culture*, but fail when tackle the problem of *Generals* and *Particulars*, *reifying* specific cultural findigs instead of questioning their history and nature.

Some Criticism at the Idea of Culture

Instead of those who question a particular definition of *Culture* and the specific searching methods derived from it, the Spanish philosopher Gustavo Bueno questions the very idea of *Culture*. The contemporary idea of *Culture*, he states, is as much abstract as *reified,* and it is an apparently *substantialized* idea that paradoxically takes its prestige from its very conceptual obscurity, vast connotative field and confusionism. So he calls it a *myth* (Bueno, 1996), venturing that our contemporary *Myth of Culture* has come to replace that social function played by medieval myth of *God's Grace* at mobilizing and *alienating* individuals. Joining an empiricist and materialistic point of view, he states (Bueno, 1991):

'The modern idea of culture –we may say the German Idea of Culture *par excellence*-considers culture above all as some sort of supraindividual organism (…), whose subject is no longer exactly an individualized psycological subject, but a People; it is in such a way that culture will be said as the People's spirit, the Volksgeist. Of course that culture reaches the individual too, but shaping him, personalizing him ("culture and personality", we say) and elevating him over his merely animal or natural condition. That is why, from now onwards, objective culture will never again be reduced into a fact: it is a value, too. Culture is spirit, so it is not reducible into "soul" or into psychology. This is the great contradiction inaugurated by the modern idea of culture: the contradiction of an expected, impersonal objective entity that however is shaping an individual subject (…). Cultural sciences will then replace the old Theology because, amongst other things, "Science of Religion" will come to be a great part of those cultural sciences' (Pp. 53-56).

Most anthropologists (but not surely many other professionals like psychiatrists or politicians) agree that culture does not exist as something actual-within-the-real-world. In fact, it is an intellectual construction available to describe and explain a complex set of findings. In that sense the empiricist view of *Culture* (understood as an operative way of studying human behaviours within social context) meets by chance with the symbolist view of Clifford Geertz (1973), as he estates:

'Understood as interacting systems of interpretable signs (…), culture is not an entity, is not the thing where to attribute, in a causal way, behaviours, institutions or social processes. Culture is a context within those phenomena can be described in an intelligible way' (Pp. 19-117).

The dangers of *Culture reification* are not coming from either Materialistic Empiricism nor from Symbolism, but from outlying fields like the self-designated Sociobiology and other Neo-Darwinian tendencies that progressively permeate psychiatric discourse. The fundament of these, the so-called *differential reproductive success* has been proved by controlled experiments on animals and it is partially supported by statistical (but non-experimental) analysis of some human populations, but has never been proved in regard with social or cultural facts. Thus, Neo-Darwinian positions remain hypothetical despite its self-proclaimed scientificity. What is more, cultural anthropologists are not against Darwinian theories, they simply refuse to apply its bio-evolutive principles onto *Culture* because these belong to different fields of knowledge, manageable by incommensurable paradigms, in T.S. Kuhn's sense. Marvin Harris (1989) warns about the political use of *Culture reification* as a bio-evolutive static entity:

'Looking back on it, we see that racial, hereditary and biological approaches for the explanation of social and cultural differences and similarities had just been silenced or remained latent. Their appeal as a way to justify and explain disparities with regard to income and prosperity matters, as well as growth of a disadvantaged class, crime and other social pathologies, augured their return' (P.77).

Basic Questions about Personality with regard to Culture

There are Two Meanings for the Word 'Personality'

The problem of diverse meanings for the term *Personality* looks like that one of the two main contemporary senses for the term *Culture*: the symbolic one *versus* the behavioral one. We can use the term *Personality* in two distinct, but related senses (Harris, 1989). In the first meaning, *Personality* refers to the complex psychological processes occurring in a human being as he/she acts in daily life, directed by internal and external forces; this intertwining between environmental conditions and behavioral response is distinctively organized toward the goals of self-regulation and social adaptation, leading the individual to respond to environmental stimulation with distinctive patterns of responses; this is a symbolic schemes view. In the second, narrower meaning *Personality* refers to the internally determined consistencies underlying a person's behaviour, the enduring differences among people insofar as they are attributable to stable internal characteristics rather than the differences in their life situation; this is an empiricist behavioral view. This second sense, however, is based on the observation of consistencies in the behaviour of the individual across diverse situations, rather tan theorizing about process. Anyhow it seems highly probable that every *culture* recognizes trans-situational, enduring behavioral consistencies of the individual within its vernacular terminology, and it seems that both behavioral consistency within an individual and variability between individuals are *Universals* across all human populations (Child, 1968).

The definition of units of behavioural consistency is quite arbitrary, since individual behaviour in this direct observation sense has no inherent boundaries of time or space, as Palo Alto's communication theorists showed (Watzlawick, 1967). So the second, apparently narrower sense of *Personality* emerges now as a concept for investigation in which behavioural consistencies reflect *dispositions* that are not directly observable, but are in some sense *internal* to the individual. The *dispotition* is a potential for behaviour. The more elaborate is the model of internal psychological organization in which personality *dispositions* are embedded, the more an idea of *Personality* arises in the first sense: as a psychological process far from a strictly behavioural definition. *Dispositions* are organized in the individual. The experience of athropologists has provided us with an intuitive basis for viewing *Culture* like a symbolic organization rather than an assortment of unrelated pieces, and our clinical experience makes the assumption of psychological organization not only plausible, but also shaped by *Culture*.

There are Four Organizational Levels of Human Dispositions

Contemporary psychotherapies for personality disorders have shown that we cannot treat patients without the assumption that *personality dispositions* are organized in the individual and have got functional roles in that organization. It does not mean we have to give up the idea of personality as behavioural consistencies. Amplifying Levine's model (Levine, 1973, pp.4-10), I distinguish four *heuristic* levels, regardless its practical or theoretical usage:

1. *Observable behavioral consistencies* that distinguish one individual from another, that we can consider as 'personality traits' or 'diagnostic criteria' (for example, the DSM-IV criteria). These would be the material for empiricist anthropologists and ethnographists, behaviourist experimental researchers, most clinical psychiatry researchers and clinicians who make diagnosis.
2. *Personality dispositions* that underly observable behavioural consistencies. These are complexand have got motivational, affective and cognitive components. Every *disposition* may display a varied series of behavioural expressions. *Dispositions* would be the material for Ethnology, Cognitive Therapy, and first phases of Humanistic and Psychoanalytic therapies.
3. *Personality organization as a symbolic and dynamic individual structure* in which dispostions are embedded, where they contribute functionally. This would be a field for deep Psychoanalysis and psychoanalytical investigation.

Personality organization as a symbolic and dynamic estructure generated and embedded within Culture through one particular *culture*. This would be the field for Cultural and Philosophical Anthropology, Systemic Psychotherapy, some psychoanalytical theoretic developments of *Culture* (like Lacan's), and the deepest levels of Humanistic approaches to therapy.

Are there any Psychological Differences Between Human Populations?

Psychologists asssume that, despite cultural diversity, all human beings share determined mental traits. Anthropologists just occasionally accept the existence of psychological *Universals* - usually to question them. We already know that there is a wide variability in institutionalized behavior across human populations. The question now is whether there are actual differences in cognition, emotion and motivation, and their organization in personality, understood as properties of individuals rather than of their institutional environments (once we have purged the cultural bias of the observer), but conditioned by their cultural context. Social scientists attempting to establish the importance of a scientific perspective on human affairs usually reject the 'psychologization' of individuals. But it is clear that human beings exhibit more behavioral variation from one population to another than any other species, and it seems likely that some of these may be individual dispositions that are more than inmediate situational responses to enviromental pressures, as many cross-cultural investigations have shown. So it must be demonstrated that cultural traits and institutions have a direct effect on developmental process in the individual, rather than merely being associated with a behavioral transient disposition at one point in time under specific, inmediate, socio-economical circumstances. The fact is that a *culture* foreign from one's own cannot be completely acquired in adulthood, including in the term no only the most institutionalized customs but also the private patterns of thought and emotion. Personal contact across cultures can intensify awareness of differences in the ways in which cultural behaviour is personally experienced, as have shown travellers, anthropologists and inmigrants when telling their personal histories. Levine writes in regard to this (Levine, 1973, pp. 15-22):

'What the outsider experiences, then, is that not all the differences in individual response between his home and host groups are conscious, controllable, acquirable, and reversible. He can usually learn to behave in accordance with the host groups's explicit custormary rules and even empathize with their hopes and fears, but without acquiring the spontaneous feelings and beliefs that give these rules and motives deeper meanings and a culturally dinstinctive style of organization and integration. After he has learned all they can tell him and show him about how and why they behave as they do, there still seems to be much more left that differentiates his home group from them and that appears to be essential to how they think about themselves and organize their behavior but that they cannot easily express in words. He finds this is equally true of himself: there are aspects that he may not be able to conceptualize but is not free to give up or replace, and these aspects –however idiosyncratic their form- bear the stamp of his home group's culture.'

Table 5. Assumptions about cultural variation based on cross-cultural experience

1. Some culturally distinctive patterns of thought and feeling are not accessible to verbal formulation, neither voluntary control, but seem to influence the individual's decisions about regulating himself and adapting to his environment.

2. Such patterns are not easily reversed even when the individual is outside the *culture* that normally reinforces them. A change should require a "Learning III" process, in Bateson's terminology.

3. One can adapt himself to de demands of a new *culture* without eliminating these patterns, even though their behavioral manifestations are temporarily inhibited or restricted.

4. These patterns are normally acquired during the earliest life of the individual, and remain strongly fixed through early attachment processes that satisfy the family's need for "socialization" of that individual. Such patterns are (like the psychoanalitical transferential phenomena) unconscious, involuntary and persistent, and cannot be acquired by a foreign adult through conscious imitation.

5. These patterns represent dispositions of the person rather than symply of the enviromental situation or, to say it better: dispositions of the person fitted within the environmental symbolic structure that precedes that very person.

6. Given a long enough time and enough instituional change, the culturally distinctive behavior patterns of a population, including the private thoughts, emotions and personal preferences of its individual members, change, and the direction of that change bears some relation to alterations in the institutional environment. This is a historical change of social and/or cultural environment, reflected in cross-generational variation, but not a direct, feasible individual change. That is why sudden historical or social changes operate as traumatic events on individuals.

Based on Levine's work, I lists his assumptions about cultural variation in individual dispositions based on cross-cultural direct self-experience of ethnographic observers, adding some changes (see Table 5).

Theoretical Conceptions of the *Culture-Personality* Affair

There is not a systematic theory of its own about *Culture* and *Personality*. This matter has provided a fertile field for the extension of theories coming from a variety of disciplines like Sociology, Cultural Anthropology, Psychology, Psychoanalysis and others. Inspired by Levine's classification of the existing positions on the Culture-Personality affair, I propose six main classes (see table 2):

Positions against Culture-Personality Interaction
This has been the dominant position in the academic environment of sociology, economics, history and political science. These reject the basic assumptions on which the study of *Culture* and *Personality* is based on. The aforementioned Gustavo Bueno's criticism on the very idea of *Culture* is a good example of the philosophical background for this attitude. Adaptive responses of the individual are considered a rational or quasirational calculus of environmental probabilities for survival, and such considerations finally shape one's character. Therefore individual behavior reflects environmental contingencies calculated through application of the individual's capacities to perceive and logically process information about environmental demands, which are understood like ecological, institutional, organizational and ideological deterministic factors. Such perspective does not require to tackle with the psychology of the individual, apart from his capacity for adapting so as to maximize his rewards and minimize his risks. Aspects of individual behaviour are predictable from knowledge of the environmental context in which the individual plays a role, without reference to other characteristics of his own behavioral organization. Some anthropologist and sociobiologists go so far as to assert that there are no differences in personality across human groups, since personality traits have a normal distribution replicated in every human society. The very existence of individual differences in personality within each population would be the evidence for the falsity of the *Personality-Culture* affair. A more serious attack comes from social scientists who claim that knowing the way populations differ psychollogically is of little social significance, since motives and habits of individuals are primarily determined by powerful external forces, so it is negligible to measure individual characteristics independently. A less extreme form of this position admits that differences in personality and values can impede or facilitate the operation of supraindividual behavioral determinants in the short term, but that these are irrelevant in the long term. Such points of view are not necessarily oposed to comparative studies of personality, but these minimize the significance of personality factors.

Anti-personality Positions
Nowadays, the strongest theoretical challenge to the basic assumptions of the *Culture-Personality* affair are not coming from the large-scale perspective of social scientists mentioned before, but from the *symbolic interactionist* school of sociologists. They share the

ecological position, but concentrate on the individual's view of his inmediate social situation. They emphasize the normative social pressures that induce the individual to behave as he is observed to behave, and assert that the *Self* is generated from social interaction in daily life (Goffman, 1981): a pattern of social behavior that might be accounted for in terms of personality dispositions is better understood as reflecting situational pressures to which the individual is responding. The individual *Self* is therefore the key for examining the environment through the understanding of the individual's social behaviour, and what a culturologist would consider a personality disposition is now interpreted like a self-esteem-maintaining response to a situational constraint. Of course that anti-individual-personality thinkers (as they focuse on experiential effects and minimize the influcence of the individual's adaptive equipment) are strongly anti-psychoanalytical, close to those behaviorists of the social-learning school.

Psychological Reductionism

Psychological reductionism and psychological determinism consider consider individual psychological factors as independent causes that are enough for understanding cultural and social behaviors These have got a long history in social thought since the 19th Century. The major and more encompassing contemporary psychological reductionism of *Culture* is the Freudian School but it is of marginal interest today, except for some psychoanalytical circles. A first but naïve approach after Freud's was that of Géza Roheim during the 1950s, for whom the developmental patterns described by his master (the stages of psychosexual development, the *Oedipus Complex*, and the emergence of the three psychic instances: *Ego, Superego* and *It*) were *Psychological Universals* that determined interpersonal behaviour and social fantasies across all the *cultures*. Assuming that unconscious meanings found out among Western patients were applicable onto all cultural contexts, he analyzed myths, folk tales and beliefs of exotic peoples, without logical argument, neither method, nor historical or ethnological perspective. His, is not a serious attempt to explain cultural differences, as the findings are considered expressions of emotional preoccupations that are ubiquitous.

A more clarified view comes from those who saw Freud's wide-ranging attempts to uncover unconscious motives and residues of childhood experience as a possible basis for explaining the cultural differences described by ethnographers. *Culturalist* American Psychoanalysts like Erich Fromm, Erik Erikson and Abraham Kardiner were concerned with cultural matters without adhering a narrow psychological reductionism. A more empiricist approach to prove de psychoanalytical basis of cultural variations has been tried by David C.McClelland, a personality psychologist.

The Culturalist Reductionism

It results of the cultural relativist approach to *Personality*. Cultural relativists hold that understanding of a *culture* different from one's own requires seeing it from the indigenous point of view (that is saying there are only *Emics* perspectives). They reject the conceptual distinction between *Culture* and *Personality*. So there are hardly any *Universals* on which to base cross-cultural comparison, and the biological factors weigh less than cultural factors for the development of the individual. Despite the fact that they began their work theorizing from an Ego-psychoanalytical point of view, the *Boasian* anthropologists Ruth Benedict and Margareth Mead finally extended the relativist perspective onto the subject of *Personality*, demonstrating that psychologists had ethnocentrically presumed the universality of patterns of child rearing, sex-role behavior and mental disorder that were in fact variable from one culture to another (Harris, 1989). They stated that personality patterns not only varied across human populations, but were integral parts of persvasive, culturally dintinctive configurations where these fitted to get their meaning. Such meaning operates with regard to the other meanings fitted within the configuration. Therefore *Personality* became to the *Boasian* anthropologists another aspect of *Culture*, the mechanism for the emotional responses and cognitive capacities of the individual to be programmed in accordance with the general configuration of his particular *culture*. Patterns of behavior are manifested and carried by the individual, but are characteristically transmitted within a group from one generation to another generation through *Cultural Learning*. Therefore this formulation of the *Culture-Personality* affair leads to emphasize on child-rearing practices as primarily significant clues to the cultural values of a particular population. The transmission of *Culture* is, in Mead's view, a process of communication in which the child receives messages reflecting the dominant configuration of his *culture*, primarily during the infancy by his parents, who stablish communication by means of language or nonverbal implicit (culturally approved) reactions and reinforcements. The major criticism made against this position points that when *Culture* and *Personality* are assumed to be equivalent, there is no way of assessing the degree of adjustment between the individual and his cultural norms: it is assumed a good fit that may not exist, reducing *Personality* to a mere individual reflection of his *culture*, and personality development to the intergenerational transmission of that *culture*.

The Personality Mediation View

Evoking in some ways Karl Marx's thought, this position splits *Culture* into two parts, one of which is seen as made up of determinants of personality while the other one consists of expressions of personality. *Personality* is then a connective or mediator between both parts. Abraham Kardiner, a psychoanalyst, in collaboration with Ralph Linton, an anthropologist, first formulated this view. They criticized Mead's *configurationalist* approach as being too broad and vague. Instead, they put forth their own theory: the *Basic Personality Structure*. They believed that such structure could typify the members of each *culture*. Kardiner (1939) distinguished between *primary institutions* (those that produce the basic personality structure), and *secondary institutions* (those that are the product of basic personality itself). Examples of *primary institutions* are those things that are a product of group adaptation within an environment, like kinship, care of children, sexuality and subsistence. *Primary institutions* are shared by all members of society, so these constitute the *Basic Personality Structure* for such society. *Secondary institutions* emerge as individuals negotiate with the primary ones; these include religion, art, folklore, other expressive media that are influenced by, and satisfying to those aspects of personality shared by all members of society. From Kardiner's perspective, a change within a *primary institution* like subsistence will change the *Basic Personality Structure*, and then the *secondary institutions*. He also acknowledged that the diversity of personality types within a determined *culture* raised as social and political complexity of such society increased. It originated comparative studies since the 1950s that have found, for example, the influence of economic system on personality: farmers tend to make decisions in group, are distrustful and value hard work, while nomadic shepherds are more individualistic, trusting and laid-back.

In 1953, the anthropologist-psychologist team of John W.M. Whiting and Irvin L. Child published a similar theory (Levine, 1973, pp.56-57). They divide the environmental determinants of group personality into two parts: the *maintenance system*, which is the institutionalized ecology, economy and socio-political structure that function for the survival of the group within the external environment; and the *child training* or *socialization process*, which operates within the constraints set by the maintenance system, shaping personality in agreement with the adaptive needs of the group and often against the needs of individuals. The expressive aspects of *culture* are referred to as the *projective system*. Both theories remark that child-rearing practices operate under the constraints of the socioeconomic structure to form personalities in a society with common needs. This is subsequently reflected in the religious practices, art and folklore of the group. Psychological perspective, instead of the aforementioned reductionism, turns into one aspect, among others, within the *projective system (secondary institution)*. Cultural values (including the core religious and ethical ones) are managed to reconcile the childhood-derived unconscious goals with adult views on social reality; as both may be discrepant, values reduce the sense of incompatibility (cognitive dissonance) between them… At least while socio-economic crisis does not appear on the horizon.

Table 6. Six Culture-Personality theoretical approaches

Anti Culture-Personality affair	$C \longrightarrow P$
Anti-personality	$C \longrightarrow$ individualized
Psychological Reductionism	$P \longrightarrow C$
Culturalist Reductionism	$C = P$
Personality Mediation	$C_1 \longrightarrow P \longrightarrow C_2$
Dualism (Two Systems)	$P \longleftrightarrow C$

The Dualistic View

The 'two systems' view was formulated by Inkeles and Levinson in 1954, and Spiro (1961), based on ideas taken from Talcott Parsons. It represents *Personality* and sociocultural institutions as two systems interacting with each other. Psychological needs are satisfied by *Personality*. Socially valued performance in the roles that are institutionalized are satisfied by the sociocultural system. *Functional congruence* between the two systems is essential for the survival of society. So every society must ensure its congruence through socialization of the child. Parents are seen as much the mediators of stability as the facilitators of change, when novel institutional demands emerge, transforming them into personal characteristics of their children through socialization. There are institutionalized solutions for the unconscious conflicts of individuals, like religion, which is understood as a *projective system* for personality needs.

The Socialization Process

Concepts of Socialization

The socialization process is the transformation of a human individual from an infant organism into an adult who participates in society. There are three points of view of this process, corresponding roughly to the disciplinary orientations of Cultural Anthropology, Personality (Behaviroal) Psychology and Sociology (Levine, 1973, pp. 61-68):

Socialization as Enculturation

This is the viewpoint of anthropologists, most of whom still regard themselves as cultural relativists and cultural determinists. They prefer the term *enculturation* to *socialization* because the term *Culture* has got connotations not included in the concept of *society*. A basic problem of human life is the maintenance and continuity of patterns of *culture* through transmission from generation to generation. Parents belonging to a *culture* are disposed to similar educational practices that include nourishing, cleaning and taking care of babies and children. Such practices train children and vary considerably from one society to another, being probably the cause of many cross-cultural variabilities of adult personalities. The simpler form of this view shows *enculturation* as an automatic process of absorption in which the child acquires *culture* by simple exposure to it, without mentioning any specific mechanism but behavioral conditioning. One more complex viewpoint attempts to conceptualize cultural learning in terms of communication and information theory, for child rearing is seen as a process of communicating *culture* to the child encoded as implicit or explicit, verbal or nonverbal, messages. The most complex proposed enculturative process has been developed by Cognitive Anthropology, that is the ethnographic cross-cultural analysis of cognition. It covers learning, and the ways to mentally organize knowledge, perceptions and meanings. By means of cognitive science, Naomi Quinn and Claudia Straus (1994) suggest an approach that links the individual with his *culture*. They assume that every *culture* is a web of shared comprehensions as well as a changing product that implies the individuals to negotiate. According to Casson's Schemata Theory (1983), they postulate that mind constructs *schemata* in order to filter new experiences and re-construct past experiences, shaping memories and adapting them to present circumstances. A *schema* is developed when a set of related experiences forms a net of strong mental associations. *Schemas* generate simplified versions of experience in such a way that we tend to perceive and remember the modal or typical event instead of the unusual one, filling the gaps of lost information according to expectations created by stronger associations. People belonging to the same *culture* tend to share *schemas* because they have depended on the same mental stereotyped images. A baby learns that 'mother' goes together with 'food', and then constructs associations of images, words and emotions around maternity and food. Feelings are schematized too. Individual *schemas* come from individual experiences, as shared *schemas* are constructed from the common social experience.

Socialization as the Acquisition of Impulse Control

Behavioral psychologists and psycyhoanalists of the drive-theory persuasion think that humans are born with drives that are potentially dangerous to social life. They conceptualize the problem of socialization in terms of taming disruptive impulses and channeling them into socially useful forms. Freud outlined this concept of socialization in *Civilization and Its Discontents (1930)*, solving the conflict between the biological drives of individuals and the requisites of social life through identification with the father as the resolution of the *Oedipus complex*. More recent theories coming from Ego-psychoanalysis and behaviorism consider that the child's primary (innate) drives form the basis for his later social adjustment by acting as reinforcers for socially valued habits and for secondary (acquired) drives that reinforce the acquisition of a wide variety of positive social behavior patterns, including the internatilzation of models for complex social roles.

Socialization as Role Training

This viewpoint emphasizes the social purpose of socialization, that is the conformity of individuals to social norms and rules. The child is trained for participation in society, a participation that is understood in terms of'institutional goals' rather than on the individual's own terms. Unlike the Freudian, this sociological view stresses positive social prescriptions rather than proscriptions, overlooking any conflict between social needs and individualistic satisfaction. A simpler sociologicist version assumes that conformity is automatically achieved by the majority of individuals, who fill the institutionalized roles provided by the social structure antedating their very birth, through a process of recruitment and selection as though social structure was a personnel office of a firm. Only when it does not occur in deviant behaviour it is necessary to investigate the how and why.

One more complex form of this conceptualization relates to the Two-System position with regard to the *Personality-Culture* affair. It considers that the compatibility of early socialization with later role demands is far from unproblematic. Since conformity is not taken for granted, the adaptive accomplishment has to be explained in terms of complex mechanisms integrating individual behavior dispositions with the needs of the social structure. Given that *Personality* and social structure are separate systems with their respective requirements, drive reduction maintains *Personality* system, and role demands maintain the social system. Although these requirements do not necessarily take identical behavioral forms, some degree of compatibility must insure both the individual survival and the stability of society, allowing individuals sufficient satisfaction of their intrapsychic needs without neglecting role demands. The model of socialization emerging from these theoretical discussions is that the social system operates in two major indirect ways to socialize individuals: first, through family structure itself, which determines the nature of the child's earliest interpersonal experience, leaving a strong but simple normative residue, which in turn is affected by the wider social system it will be integrated within (this is what Talcott Parsons (1964) calls *primary socialization*). Second, through parental mediation when parents deliberately train their children for successful adaptation to the dinamic social order (this more specialized role training resembles Parsons's *secondary socialization*).

The emphasis on reinforcement and social function for role acquisition connects this viewpoint with the Darwinian model of adaptation, elluding symbolic internalization mechanisms.

1.2.4. EPIDEMIOLOGY OF PERSONALITY DISORDERS

S. González-Parra

Until recently, little attention has been paid to the epidemiology of personality disorders (PDs), if compared with other psychiatric disorders. Various reasons warrant its study. These are highly prevalent disorders – more than initially believed -, with decisive impact on the risk and prognosis of axis I disorders, causing severe economic and social problems. These patients use health services more intensively, have more depressive symptoms and score lower in functional disability scales (Hueston et al., 1999).

Studies find disparate rates because of methodological difficulties, for instance such basic issues as the definition of the disorders, the different measuring tools and the need of large populations – due to the low prevalence of certain PDs-. Nosology of PDs is fraught with conceptual problems, and diagnostic validity has been repeatedly questioned. Results change because of differences in international classification schemes and various measure instruments, which lack consistency. The interest on these disorders increased following the introduction of axis II in DSM III (APA, 1980), leading to a significant increase in their diagnosis (Loranger, 1990). The diagnostic threshold is lower in the DSM III than in the ICD-10 classification, and when the former is used, prevalence rates are higher (9% vs. 5%) (Samuels et al., 2002). Diagnosis is confounded when states and traits are mixed (Ferro et al., 1998), by their plastic evolution (Grilo & McGlashan, 1999), the overlapping of certain features with normality – particularly neuroticism (Austin & Deary, 2000) – or the high frequency of both axis I and axis II comorbidity. On the other hand, sociocultural factors exert enormous influence, as proved by higher rates of avoidant PD and paranoid PD in Europe than in USA (Torgersen et al., 2001).

According to Helgalson & Magnusson (1989), expectancy of development of a PD before the age of 81 is 5.2 percent. Incidence is difficult to measure because of the very nature of PDs – absence of a clear time of appearance, chronic course, and onset in childhood or adolescence-. This might explain why most psychiatric epidemiological research has been devoted to prevalence and comorbidity studies.

Among other factors, epidemiological data depend on the sample considered. In community samples, overall prevalence of PD stands at 10 to 13 percent (Lenzenweger et al., 1997; Weissman, 1993). Torgersen et al. (2001) report a prevalence rate of 13.4 percent in a community sample, with highest rates for avoidant PD (5%), paranoid PD (2.4%), and obsessive-compulsive PD (2.0%). Grant et al. (13), studying a large American sample, found a prevalence rate of 14.79 %, predominantly obsessive-compulsive PD (7.8%), paranoid PD (4.41%), antisocial PD (3.6%), schizoid PD (3.13%), avoidant PD (2.36%), histrionic PD(1.84%) and, dependent PD (0.49%).

Primary care studies reported by general practitioners identified a primary PD in 5-8% of patients in their practices; predominantly males and high frequenters of health services (Girolano, 1996). Usually these percentages increase when structured interviews are used, reaching prevalence rates as high as 12.7%; rates in women almost double those of males (15.8 vs. 9.8%). Most frequent diagnoses are schizoid PD (5.1%), anankastic PD (4.4%), and emotionally unstable PD, borderline subtype (3.8%) (El Rufaie et al., 2001).

Evidently, in psychiatric samples the prevalence of PD is much higher, ranging from 30 to 50 % in outpatient samples. Cluster B disorders are the commonest, cluster A being the less frequent (Fabrega et al., 1991). Among hospitalized patients, 15% have a PD as principal diagnosis for admission, and almost half of the remaining had comorbid PDs with significant impact on treatment response (Loranger, 1990). In samples of inpatients, borderline PD (BPD), schizotypal PD and histrionic PD predominate, whereas dependent PD and passive-aggressive PD are more prevalent in outpatient settings (Girolano, 1996).

Sociodemographic Correlations

Available data seem to reveal some trends related to different clinical and sociodemographic variables. Generally, risk factors for PDs include being black or Native American, young, with lower socioeconomic status (SES) and divorced, separated, widow or single (Grant et al., 2004).

Gender
Even though differences in prevalence between genders are scarce (more males in community samples), the status is different while considering specific categories (Maier et al., 1992). Grant et al. (2004), studying a large community sample, show greater prevalence of avoidant PD, dependent PD and paranoid PD in females, whereas antisocial PD was more frequent in males. Other authors have found male predominance in schizoid PD, narcissistic PD and antisocial PD (Zimmerman & Coryel, 1991).

Age
It has traditionally been assumed that there is a descending trend in the rate of PD with age, ascribed to a "spontaneous" tendency to improvement. The stability of the diagnosis is questioned, but it is unclear whether personality changes or a more adjusted functioning is learned. Some studies do not confirm this overall descending trend, but they do detect differences between PD categories in the second half of life. Rather than a drop in the number of diagnosed individuals, these findings suggest a cluster distribution change with age (Abrams & Horowitz, 1996). Thus, several studies describe a fall in the frequency of cluster B PDs with age, and an increase of cluster A and cluster C PDs (Torgersen et al., 2001). Furthermore, unspecified PD prevails in patients aged 50 or over (24). On the other hand, it has been argued than most PDs lessen in severity by middle age, with the exception of dependent PD, obsessive-compulsive PD and passive-aggressive PD (Loranger, 1996). Data suggest that impulsivity decreases with age, whereas obsessive and dependent behaviours persist or increase (Clarkin & Abrams, 1998).

Marital Status
Overall, individuals living alone, particularly single, predominate in cluster A and cluster C PDs. On the other hand, there is a positive prevalence correlation between stable relationships and schizotypal PD, narcissistic PD and dependent PD.

Education, Occupation and other Factors

Obsessive-compulsive PD correlates with higher educational level, as opposed to schizoid PD, schizotypal PD, antisocial PD, borderline PD and dependent PD, which are associated with lower educational levels (Mattia & Zimmerman, 2001). Overall, PD prevalence is higher in urban and low SES environments. Unemployment rates among patients range between 20 to 40%. Alcoholism, unemployment, and marital discord antecedents are more common in the PD group than in controls (Reich, 1988). Data show that all PD –with the exception of histrionic PD and obsessive-compulsive PD– worsen the functional level [(as assessed by GAF (Global Assessment of Functioning) scale]. Borderline PD is most disabling, and generates the highest rate of mental health visits (Jackson & Burguess, 2004).

Comorbidity

Axis I Comorbidity

PDs often present themselves associated with an axis I disease, complicating its treatment and prognosis, causing a more protracted course, worsening treatment compliance and increasing psychosocial risk (Reich & Vasile, 1993). It is estimated that 63.3% of PD have a comorbid axis I diagnosis (Mairer et al., 1995), mainly affective or anxiety disorders (Nakao et al., 1991). There is a closer link between avoidant PD and anxiety disorders, as well as between BPD and affective disorders (Maier et al., 1992). Comorbidity with eating disorders is well documented, particularly the association between bulimia nervosa and BPD, and the restrictive type of anorexia nervosa and avoidant PD (Díaz Marsa et al., 1995).

Axis II Comorbidity

In a community sample, there was a mean of 1.48 diagnoses per patient (Torgersen et al., 2001). Frequently, avoidant PD coexists with dependent PD and schizoid PD, and histrionic PD with passive-aggressive PD. Several studies, on the grounds of the high association rate between avoidant PD with schizoid PD, paranoid PD and dependent PD, suggest the existence of a mixed avoidant-dependent PD.

Suicide and Accidental Death

There is a relation between PD, accidental death and suicide. Up to 40% of suicide, victims fulfil PD diagnostic criteria, most often borderline PD (Sorderberg, 2001). Among individuals suffering a PD, there is also a link between suicide and male gender. Despite the extreme difficulty in quantifying its magnitude, the diagnosis of a PD seems to be associated to a reduced life expectancy.

Specific Epidemiological Data

Prevalence rates of PD found in relevant studies (Reich & Girolano, 1997; Moran, 1999; Törgersen et al., 2001; Grant et al., 2004) are presented in Table 7(Coid, 2003a).

Overall, cluster B PDs are the best studied, particularly antisocial PD and BPD (in this order). The reasons are apparent: those are the ones with greater legal-penitentiary and clinical impact, respectively. Data about other PDs are mainly derived from general studies.

Paranoid Personality Disorder (PPD)

The prevalence reported in the DSM-IV-TR (APA, 2000) ranges between 2-10% in outpatient samples and 10 to 30% in inpatients. There is no familial pattern and is more common in low SES groups, deaf people and minorities.

Table 7. PD prevalence rates (main studies)

PD	% population
Antisocial	0.6-3.0
Borderline	0.7-2.0
Narcissistic	0.4-0.8
Histrionic	2.1
Paranoid	0.7-2.4
Schizoid	0.4-1.7
Schizotypal	0.1-5.6
Avoidant	0.8-5.0
Dependent	1.0-1.7
Obsessive-compulsive	1.7-2.2
Other	4.4-13.0

Schizoid Personality Disorder (SPD)

Higher prevalence's are found in males (2:1). Several comorbidity studies have found an association with schizotypal PD, but it has been suggested that this category would better fit in developmental disorders – possibly in the autistic spectrum – than in PDs (Coid, 1999).

Schizotypal Personality Disorder (STPD)

Cluster A PDs are more frequently diagnosed among family members of schizophrenic patients, but a strong genetic link with schizophrenia has been solely found with schizotypal PD. In fact, ICD-10 includes schizotypal PD as a subtype of schizophrenia.

Histrionic Personality Disorder (HPD)

In mental health settings, prevalence is up to 10-15%. Even though pioneer studies suggested a female predominance, later studies do not back the initial findings. Prevalence seems not to be influence by race or educational levels. However, histrionic PD is significantly more frequent among separated and divorced than in married individuals. In women there seems to be an association with depression (17% of women with histrionic PD) or unexplained medical disease, and with substance abuse in males (Nestadt et al., 1990).

Borderline Personality Disorder (BPD)

This is the most common personality disorder in inpatients (14-20%) and hospital admissions (20-42%) (Geller, 1986). The prevalence of BPD in an outpatient setting is 10%. It is more common that individuals with this PD lack partner, are young (19-34 years), non-white, and live in urban and low SES communities (Swartz et al., 1990). It was assumed to be more frequent in females than in males (2:1), but several large studies have not confirmed this difference (Reich & Thompsom, 1987). There is also a significant relation between BPD and marital discord, physical disability, work-related conflicts, alcohol related difficulties and psychosexual problems. Longitudinal studies indicate that the disorder is more severe in the mid-20s, with a trend to improvement in the forth decade. These individuals use more frequently mental health services and have an increased suicide rate (9%) (Paris et al., 1989, Stone, 1990). BPD is the PD with a highest comorbidity rate. Ninety percent of subjects diagnosed with BPD have also a comorbid axis I diagnosis, compared to an estimated 50% for other PDs. The most frequent comorbid disorders are major depression, panic disorder, social phobia, simple (specific) phobia, posttraumatic stress disorder, substance-related disorders and eating disorders (Zanarini et al., 1998). The most common axis II comorbidities are with histrionic PD, antisocial/dissocial PD, schizotypal PD and dependent PD.

Narcissistic Personality Disorder (NPD)

It is more frequent in male and forensic samples, particularly associated with antisocial PD. In clinical populations, its prevalence may be as high as 2-16% (Zimmerman & Coryel, 1990).

Antisocial Personality Disorder (APD)

Numerous studies agree this disorder is tremendously overrepresented among prison inmates (as high as 75%), forensic psychiatric hospitals and drug addicts. In a psychiatric care setting, rates range between 3 to 30% (APA, 1994). It is more common in young adults (24-44), a period where subjects with APD have an increased mortality, symptoms diminishing by middle age (only 20% fulfils criteria by 45 years). It predominates among urban dwellers, with school failure, belonging to low SES groups, homeless and having family antecedents of APD. No racial differences have been found. Often, it is comorbid with alcohol abuse/dependence (85.6%), drug abuse/dependence (34.6%) and depression (25%) (Swanson et al., 1994).

Male predominance is obvious (between 2:1 and 7:1) (Zimmerman & Coryel, 1990). Several authors have raised the question about its less frequent diagnosis in women because of the emphasis in aggressive aspects and in behavior disorders in childhood and adolescence, precisely one of the main diagnostic criteria for this disorder.

Avoidant Personality Disorder (AvPD)

Prevalence among psychiatric outpatients reaches 10% (Zimmerman & Coryel, 1990). It is more common in singles, those who live alone or with their parents and lack friends. Studies to date do not show gender differences. In clinical samples a high comorbidity with dependent PD and with phobias – particularly, social phobia- is found. It shares several features with the latter and boundaries between them are questioned (Turner et al., 1993).

Dependent Personality Disorder (DPD)

An increased comorbidity with other PD – i.e. BPD- has been reported, but several authors point out that these data are explained by a lack of clear boundaries in axis II categories. Aetiology is related to the influence of early social factor, and certain forensic samples relate it to neuropsychiatric factors (Coid, 1999).

Obsessive-compulsive Personality Disorder (OCPD)

It is more common in white, high educational level, married and employed males. An increased comorbidity with anxiety disorders has been found.

Conclusion

PDs have a chronic course, are diagnosed in a significant proportion of the population (10-13%) and involve a substantial social, familial and occupational burden, consuming health and judicial resources. Epidemiology can help us knowing them better, enabling us approaching their etiology and building a conceptual framework to organise directed health policies, as well as progressing in prevention and intervention strategies. In fact, it has already been demonstrated that interventions during childhood and adolescence are effective and efficient (Coid, 2003).

Data hint that PDs are overrepresented in certain population subgroups and this information can be useful in the investigation of determinants and consequences of these disorders, as well as the needs of these persons.

Many issues remain to be elucidated, such as a risk factor classification and a construct validation, external validation criteria (psychological tests, behavioural indicators, and biological markers or treatment response), genetic factors predisposing to certain PDs, or comorbidity.

On the other hand, understanding the natural history of these disorders will help us delineating protective and risk factors, comorbidity models, diagnostic validity, its predictive value on prognosis of disease –psychiatric or non-psychiatric – and patterns of use of health resources.

Most studies in this field come from Western countries. The scarce work done in developing countries (Levav et al., 1989) indicates that their PD prevalence rates may be significantly lower. Solving methodological problems will permit us understand the specific influence of sociocultural factor in preventing these disorders or improving their course.

1.2.5. SPECIFIED PERSONALITY DISORDERS: BRIEF CLINICAL PICTURE

M. Caballero González and H. Blasco-Fontecilla

Introduction

We would like to stress that this chapter is not intended to give a comprehensive view of personality disorders (PDs) as several books are devoted to this topic. The main objective is to give a clear and succint clinical view of PDs in the context of suicide behavior. Due to limitations on space, we will focus only in the PDs of the current international classifications.

The DSM IV-TR classifies PDs into three different clusters, namely cluster A, cluster B, and cluster C PDs. It must be stress that this clustering has not been consistently validated, and has several limitations. Paranoid PD, schizoid PD, and schizotypal PD are classified in cluster A, subjects being characterized by eccentric behaviors. Antisocial PD, borderline PD, histrionic PD, and narcissistic PD are the PDs grouped in cluster B. They are mainly characterized by instable mood, and dramatic or erratic behavior. Evitative PD, dependent PD, and obsessive-compulsive PD are cluster C PDs, being anxiety or fear their core characteristic. This clustering system is not used in the ICD-10 classification. Though the clinical profile of PD described in this classification is very similar to that of DSM-IV-TR, the major differences are that in the former the schizotypal PD is considered a subtype of schizophrenia, while in the DSM classification is considered a PD. Moreover, narcissistic PD is not described in the ICD-10 classification. Finally, the DSM-IV-TR equivalent of Borderline PD is the ICD-10 emotionally unstable PD, which includes an impulsive type and a borderline type.

Paranoid Personality Disorder (PPD)

Paranoid states are firstly mentioned in the Hippocratic Corpus. The Greek term paranoia means "a mind beside itself". The term resurfaces in the 18th century, being used to referring to several different disorders. In 1918, Kretschmer described a "sensitive personality", involving excessive suspiciousness and exaggerated reactions to setbacks. Birnhaum described paranoid subjects as full of overvalued ideas with high emotional burden (Millon, 1996).

The three classical core characteristics of PPD are suspiciousness, feeling of being "chased", and grandiosity. According to Akhtar, there is a wide dissociation between the image presented to the outside world, as suspicious, touchy, argumentative, stubborn, distrust, concerned about exploitation or treason by others, hostile and with a tendency to counterattack at minimal provocation, grandiose, moralist, etc., and self-image, they feel fearful, shy, doubtful, and vulnerable to erotomania (Akhtar, 1990; Dowson & Grounds, 1995). They are unable to grasp surrounding reality as a whole, and emotionally cold and rigid minded. A fear of losing independence and of intimate relationships to avoid betrayal is also frequently found, and jealousy may be marked; furthermore, they usually avoid groups of people, unless they feel in a dominant position (Dowson & Grounds, 1995).

They are usually reluctant to disclose personal information, and show an extreme concern about confidentiality and personal data (Dowson & Grounds, 1995). This is important, as the information given, particularly in stressful situations – e.g. after a suicide attempt- may be conscious or unconsciously biased. Moreover, under stress they may experience transient "psychosis-like" phenomena (Dowson & Grounds, 1995). Criticism is difficult to accept, and they fear losing control –they may have an irrational fear of taking medications or submit to authority- (Dowson & Grounds, 1995), thus psychiatric treatment being very complicated. PPD may be a predisposing factor for homicide. Stone (1998) points out that many fanatics, including political terrorists, have a paranoid personality structure. Crimes committed by paranoid politicians and religious fanatics are countless.

The most common defence mechanisms are projection, fantasy and blame (Colby, 1977).

Schizoid Personality Disorder (SPD)

There is a substantial relationship between schizoid personality and schizophrenia (Dowson & Grounds, 1995). Kretschmer first proposed that schizophrenia and schizoid personality are two stages of the same disease. At present, this theory is not fully accepted, and the antecedent of a schizoid personality is far from established in all schizophrenic patients.

The key feature is the inability to experience the pleasant aspects of life (emotional immunity), leading to great difficulties in establishing social relationships. Indeed, Ribot coined the term "anhedonia" to refer to a syndrome featuring decreased capacity to feel pleasure. Reich (1933) also stressed their core characteristic: the lack of psychic contact with the others. They are not antisocial, but asocial (Millon, 1998), because they do not need nor wish contact with other people – and this is the main difference with avoidant PD, where the subjects, although socially impaired, want to have social contacts-. They have few close friends, if any. They are also emotionally reserved – or emotionally immune-, thus not responding to feelings expressed by others. They are lifeless, and their speech is poor and concise. They usually lack energy and vitality. At the same time, they seem pleased and satisfied with their lives and are happy about keeping out social ambitions and competitiveness they see in others.

They can rarely experience intimate emotions, that they feel particularly uncomfortable. In the rare occasions they reach intimacy with a close family member, they can feel at loss without them, but also absorbed while with them (Gunderson, 1995). Thus, they may look for relationships giving them a sense of safety, but independence at the same time. Rarely, if overwhelmed by social circumstances, they may suffer acute psychotic disorders (Robinson 1996; Millon, 1998).

They have low interest in sexual relationships, which are usually cool, lived as a contract obligation, and strongly intellectualized (Coderch, 1987). Males rarely marry, and women may choose dominant husbands wishing emotional distance (Robinson, 1996). People find them boring, uninteresting and lacking a sense of humour (Dowson & Grounds, 1995).

They prefer isolated activities. They look for isolated and non-competitive jobs that others would find difficult to tolerate. When allowed by their intellectual gift, they devote to disciplines like mathematics, philosophy or basic research. Rarely, they are able to develop creative ideas. Their intellectual activity and fantastic world becomes their shelter and replaces their emotional carencies. When pressed by social circumstances, they withdraw and take refuge in themselves. If this is not possible, it might be lived as stressful. It could be hypothesized as a precipitant of suicide behavior.

Cloninger (1986, 1993) said that these subjects are characterized by little reward dependency, low harm-avoidance, and scarce novelty seeking.

As they are unmoved by emotions, there are few reasons to build up complex intrapsychic defences. Kernberg (1967) suggested that dissociation is the main defence mechanism of the schizoid person. Other authros point at intellectualization and schizoid fantasy or split as the most frequent defence mechanisms.

Schyzotypal Personality Disorder

In 1906, Meyer argued that schizophrenia could present without delusions, hallucinations or deterioration. Zilboorg (1941) called these patients as "ambulatory schizophrenics". Rappaport (1945) identified a subset of patients which he labelled as "preschizophrenics" characterized by a trend to isolation, obsessive-phobic ideation and psycotic episodes under stress. Schafer (1948) distinguished between schizoid character, and schizophrenic character. The latter is much alike to what we now call schizotypal personality disorder. The term schizotypal was coined by Rado in 1950, referring to an entity closely related to the concept of schizophrenia, suggesting a probable heritable predisposition.

Whether this disorder should be considered a personality disorder or not is still under debate. The revised version of the fourth edition of the Diagnostic and Statistical Manual of Mental Disorders (DSM-IV-TR) considers it is a personality disorder, but the last version of the ICD-10 places it with schizophrenic disorders (Dickey et al., 2005). On the other hand, some authorities stress the difficulty in differentiating schizoid and schizotypal personality disorders, and find data suggesting that both should be included in a common diagnostic category (Shedler, Western, 2004), and that they are genetically related to schizophrenia (Dowson and Grounds, 1995).

These subjects are the most bizarre among all PDs. They are characterized by disturbance of thought and social communication processes, eccentricity, peculiarity, socially inadequate mannerisms, and are also perceived as bizarre, odd or ostentatious (Dowson and Grounds, 1995).

Similarly to schizoid subjects, they lack interest on social relationships. They do not engage in intimate relationships attributable to conscious restriction based on the fear of being rejected. They live in their own world, usually full of fantasies, fears and unreal relationships. They feel themselves socially alienated and rejected from the surrounding world, which experience as strange to them. (Dowson and Grounds, 1995; Millon, 1996).

There is a significant inability to organize thoughts or a disorganized way of processing information. They are not capable to differentiate significant from peripheral events. Nevertheless, cognitive ability is not severely impaired, and only the interpersonal sphere is usually disrupted. They tend to misinterpret human interactions, and everybody else's thoughts, feelings and actions are perceived idiosyncratically. They typically have magic thoughts, corporal illusions, rare beliefs (i.e. superstition, telepathy, etc.), suspicions, and a mix of reality and fantasy. Their inner world is a chaotic mix of childhood memories, perceptions and feelings, posing them at risk in the management of stressful life events. An expected consequence is the erratic educational and occupational histories they have given their intellectual abilities. (Dowson & Grounds, 1995; Millon, 1996).

The main defence mechanism is self-annihilation. Magic beliefs and ritual behaviors can be used to neutralize hypothetical unconscious perversions.

Antisocial Personality Disorder

Clinical Origins

Pinel (1809) was the first to suggest that repeated, aimless antisocial behavior might be a mental disorder. This led to the term "mania sans délire" and was the precursor of Prichard's congenital deficiency of the moral sense or "moral insanity" (1835) (Dowson and Grounds, 1995).

The term "psychopathic" first appeared in the mid-19th century German literature to mean "psychologically damaged". Kraepelin, Moebius and Schneider used this term to refer to what we currently consider a PD.

Cleckley (1941) set the basis of psychopathy as "an impaired learning ability with relative unresponsiveness to social reinforcement, so that these individuals do no react with appropriate affect to situations that would normally produce an emotional response. Although there is awareness of social values, these do not influence motivation, resulting in irresponsibility, unreliability, poor judgement and relative inability to profit from experience" (Dowson & Grounds, 1995).

Several authors (i.e. Morey, Hare, Sanislow) have postulated that antisocial subjects share some characteristics with narcissistic individuals (Kernberg, 1984). Blasco-Fontecilla (2006, 2007) suggests that the main difference between Narcissistic PD and APD is that the subjects who are diagnosed with the former PD may have a higher intelligence and a better impulse control. Therefore, it is easier that crime of the former remains uncovered, and narcissist person's behaviour focuses in daily living activities not so easily labelled as antisocial.

Another controversial issue is that of the use of APD and psychopathy as synonymous. By using both terms as synonymous it hampers comparison between studies, is an obstacle for research and produces confusion in the clinical arena. Moreover, ICD-10 chooses the term dissocial for the definition of this disorder. In spite of the term antisocial PD being used as synonym of psychopathy, sociopathy, and psychopathic personality (Moran & Hagell, 2001), they are similar but not equivalent terms (Blasco-Fontecilla, 2006; 2007; Livesley et al., 1994). Lykken (1995) postulated that sociopathy and psychopathy is the two extremes of a continuous spectrum, depending on the heritable background or social learning. Blasco-Fontecilla (2006; 2007) suggest that according to recent literature, antisocial PD could be used as a wide concept related to the description of antisocial behaviour executed by some people. The psychopathy would be a aub-category included in APD, and would describe a subset of the most highly aggressive and emotionally cold individuals (fitting into the description by Cleckey). He suggests that psychopathy would be more related to crime and perhaps has stronger genetic influence (although this is not established). The sub-category of psychopathy might fit into the subgroup of extremely cold children displaying various antisocial behaviours despite apparent good educational quality of their parents (Wootton et al., 1997). Nowadays, we have initial evidence that psycopathy scores in early adolescence predict adult psychopathy, in other words, that there is a relative stability of psychopathy from adolescence into adulthood (Lynam et al., 2007).

Indeed, several authors have postulated a clear distinction between at least two types of antisocial subjects (see table 8). Karpman (1948) differentiated between primary psychopaths – they closely resemble those subjects identified by Cleckley's criteria- from secondary psychopaths, characterized by the presence of other disorders, mainly anxiety. Hare et al. (1991) found two different dimensions in psychopaths: factor 1 (F1), closely linked to personality traits such as cruelty, egoism and remorseless manipulation of others, and factor 2 (F2), more related to a description of behaviour with greater resemblance to the DSM description of antisocial PD (Loeber et al., 2003). Thus, a low anxiety level and the inability to be genuinely depressed may be characteristic of the primary psychopath (Blasco-Fontecilla, 2006; 2007), and be related to "a relative lack of effect of social constraints and punishments for selfish and impulsive acts" (Dowson & Grounds, 1995). The outcome and response to treatment is often very different compared to those with secondary or symptomatic psychopathy (Blackburn, 1988). Thus, the inability to feel anxiety, and to become genuinely depressed may be a poor prognosis factor for antisocial subjects, as it would make them impermeable to current available treatments, leading to a disturbing question, that is, what to do with them (Blasco-Fontecilla, 2006; 2007).

Clinical Picture

APD may be the best-studied PD. Diagnostic criteria according to current classifications arise from longitudinal studies carried out by Robins (1966). Its diagnosis is at present one of the most reliable among PDs (Mellsop et al., 1982). In fact, it is one of the few diagnostic categories which has been in every DSM edition and the only validated PD (Paris, 1997). One of the main differences between APD and other PDs is that its diagnosis relies on behavioural criteria (amenable to observation) rather than characterological criteria (Coid, 1999). Present international classifications almost exclusively describe behaviours, paying little attention to phenomenology or mental functioning. This results in a syndrome describing a criminal lifestyle, with more dubious relation with a PD.

Cloninger (1987) defined a set of first-order characteristics as high novelty-seeking, low harm-avoidance, low dependency on reward as well as a set of second-order traits (impulsiveness-aggression, oppositional, and opportunistic behaviour).

They are characterized by a chronic and generalized antisocial style that begins before adulthood. Alcohol and drug abuse is common. They cheat, lie or manipulate for their own benefit or pleasure and are remorseless. They can make self-injury gestures, and express somatic complaints. They are impulsive, irresponsible, and show dysphoria and low tolerance to boring. They have to dominate in the relationships. They are incapable of learning from experience. They do not care about their own safety or the others, which leads to risky behaviour. Irresponsibility is evident at work and in spending, because they maintain debts, leave jobs without anticipating consequences, etc. In light of psychoanalytic theory, they would be driven by the pleasure principle, with a malignant ego ideal and an undeveloped superego.

Table 8. Different nomenclatures to the same problem: diagnostic heterogenity in antisocial subjects (Blasco-Fontecilla, 2007)

Author	Group of antisocial subjects characterized by lack of the social emotions (love, guilt, shame, empathy, and remorse)	Group characterized by observable antisocial behaviors
Karpman (1941)	Idiopatic psychopath	Symptomatic psychopath
McCord (1983)	Primary psychopath	Secondary psychopath
Lykken (1995)	Psychopath	Sociopath
Mealey (1995)	Primary sociopath	Secondary sociopath
Arias et al (1996)	"Real" psychopath	"Symptomatic" psychopath
Hart & Hare (1997)	Factor 1	Factor 2

Since cheating and manipulation are essential features of APD, gathering information of other sources can be particularly helpful. Moreover, the information reported in an assessment might be biased.

Borderline Personality Disorder (BPD)

Clinical Origins

This disorder has recently been included into the modern psychiatric nosology (DSM III, in 1980, and ICD-10 in 1992). Its conceptualization is considered the main contribution to PDs after Schneider. Its roots are in psychoanalysis. Initially was understood as an intermediate stage between neurosis and psychosis.

In 1925, Reich spoke for the first time about impulsive character standing out from those previously delineated. Alexander described a series of patients carrying an irrational way of life. In 1938, Stern considered a "borderline neurosis group" of patients between neurotic and psychotic categories resistant to psychotherapy. Kernberg´s (1967) description of the "borderline personality organization" focused the disorder on their characteristics of mental functioning, such as a poor capacity to tolerate anxiety or control impulses, together with "identity diffusion", "splitting", and with a high rate of psychopathological correlates (Dowson & Grounds, 1995). Gunderson's (1981) concept of BPD included intense mood changes, impulsivity, manipulative suicide attempts, transient loss of reality, high socialization, and disturbed close relationships (Dowson & Grounds, 1995).

It was included in the DSM III (1980) and it is preserved in the later editions despite wide criticism to its nomenclature as it breaks the classic psychiatric tradition of denominating the disorders referring to the basic characteristic of the disorder. Firstly rejected by the ICD-10 (1992), it was finally included as the *emotionally unstable personality disorder*, with two subtypes: borderline and impulsive.

Clinical Picture

It is one of the most controversial PDs. This confusion may be partly be explained in the fact that it is a PD whose roots are in different conceptualizations. It has been suggested that it belongs to the spectrum of schizophrenic disorders, impulsive disorders (Zanarini), trauma, affective disorders (Akiskal), a type of personality structure organization (Kernberg), or a specific form of personality change (Gunderson, DSM and ICD).

There is an important debate about its core feature. Some authors think it is impulsiveness while others emphasize the importance of affective, self-image and interpersonal relationship instability. They show unpredictable and frequent mood swings probably due to a marked degree of reactivity to environmental events, and instability in every area of personality functioning. They are very dependent on the close ones, fear being abandoned, and may make frantic efforts to avoid real or imaginary neglect (Dowson & Grounds, 1995). Complaints of chronic feelings of emptiness are frequents. Under stressful conditions, they may experience brief psychotic episodes, with a clear dissociative taste. Interpersonal relationships are characterized by conflict and manipulation.

It is the PD with the closest relationship to suicidal behaviour. Self-destructive and suicide behavior are very common. They may be precipitated by stressful life events and have diverse purposes like attracting attention, expressing anger or relaxing (Linehan, 1993). Moreover, subjects diagnosed with BPD have a very high comorbidity rate with both axis I and axis II disorders.

Identity disturbance, a concept coined by Otto Kernberg is frequently found in these subjects. It is manifested as sudden changes in every area of personality, self-image or sexual identity, so that they can be promiscuous. Matched with the typical swings between *idealization* and *devaluation* of the others, it explains why they usually have distorted interpersonal relationships.

Histrionic Personality Disorder (HPD)

The Greek term *hysteria*, which means uterus, was used by Hippocrates to explain certain symptoms and behaviors in women. The term *histrio, -onis* (actor in latin) was used to refer to the mimetic behavior of actors in classical Rome. In the first half of 20th century, several authors established some of the basic features of hysterical personality (i.e. being emotionally and love demanding, being easily influenced, etc.). Furthermore, Wilhelm Reich and Henry Ey attempted to distinguish HPD from other manifestations of hysteria.

Traditionally associated to female gender, this might reflect a prejudiced tendency of clinicians to ascribe HPD to women. Indeed, nowadays the trend is to use the term histrionic PD instead of hysterical disorder, mainly due to the pejorative social and professional connotations historically linked with the word *hysteria* .

Kernberg (1967) outlined features that may help to differentiating between histrionic PD from other disorders, like emotional liability, dependent and exhibitionistic needs, pseudohypersexuality, sexual inhibition, masochism, and competitiveness (Dowson & Grounds, 1995). Cloninger (1987) defines HPD by novelty-seeking, low harm-avoidance and high dependency on reward, and as second-order features, emotional vulnerability and narcissism.

Basically, they look for attention in an exaggerate and dramatic way. They are sexually seducing, capricious, and do not correctly differentiate between attraction and intimacy. This pattern of inappropriate sexually and seductive behavior may be part of a general pattern in which they find difficult to relate to the preferred sex in a non-sexual way (Livesley & Schroeder, 1991). Sexual relationships range between promiscuity through normality to unresponsiveness (Dowson & Grounds, 1995).

Emotions and interpersonal relationships are characterized by shallowness, selfishness, being suggestible, and a tendency to boring (Millon & Davis, 2001). They express emotions in a demanding way. They consider themselves sociable, friendly and nice. Initially enthusiastic for every new activity, soon after, they do not persist and there is a rapid decline in performance. They tend to view relationships as having a greater level of intimacy than is actually the case (Poll, 1991). They usually engage in emotionally dependent relationships, and romantic fantasy is typical.

They rate high in novelty seeking and may be creative, but at the same time are inconstant, momentary enthusiastic, and become easily bored. They are unlikely to be good at logical analysis thinking. They can be seen in a very distressed state, sometimes leading to hospital admission, but this rapidly improves. The day after, sometimes it is difficult to reconcile the serene subject found by the clinician with the emotionally fraught patient described few hours before. (Dowson & Grounds, 1995).

They can have personality traits typical of other PDs like emotional dependence, narcissism, and impulsive-aggressive features (Cloninger, 1987). Thus, a high comorbidity rate with BPD and other PDs is common.

They have angry tantrums or manipulative dramatic despair with rapid recovery, aimed at influencing the feelings or behaviours of others (Dowson & Grounds, 1995). Thus, they can suicide behaviors – particularly, low lethality overdoses- directed to punish partners or family members.

Narcissistic Personality Disorder (NPD)

This term originated in the Greek myth of Narcissus, who fell in love with his own image mirrored in the water, and became death. Kohut (1968) introduced the term "narcissistic personality disorder" to describe disturbances in several areas including grandiosity and pronounced angry reactions. The Narcissistic PD was included in DSM classification since its third edition (DSM-III) (APA, 1980). However, it is not accepted in ICD-10, on the ground that its clinical identity is not unequivocally established. (Dowson & Grounds, 1995).

The main features have been described as "a pervasive pattern of grandiosity (in fantasy or behaviour), lack of empathy, and hypersensitivity to the evaluation of others" (American Psychiatric Associations, 1987). Ronningstam & Gunderson (1990) tried to systematically describe NPD, and proposed nine criteria for its diagnosis:

1. Sense of superiority: they usually have an unrealistic view of themselves. They consider themselves as superior to others, follow very hierarchical relationships, and special favours, rights or privileges are expected. However, they have a very fragile self-esteem, and hypersensitivity to criticism.

2. Sense of exclusivity: the thought of being unique, leading to a sense of not being understood.
3. Exaggeration of ones capacities: although they use to have high performance and achievement, they tend to exaggerate abilities and achievements in an unrealistic manner.
4. Pretentiousness: they tend to act in an exhibitionist way.
5. Grandiose fantasies of success, power, beauty, fortune and ideal love.
6. Self-focused conduct and a tendency to be self-referential: concern about oneself, associated with marked indifference towards others' opinions and reactions.
7. Need of attention and admiration.
8. Shallow and arrogant behavior.
9. They tend to legitimate their exploitative and despotic behavior based on their great personal achievements.

An important issue is distinguishing observable behaviors, on which frequently relies the clinical description of the disorder, from underlying ones, which tend to remain concealed. In this respect, Akhtar (1989) proposes that, although they show grandiosity and interpersonal exploitation, they internally feel themselves as envious, doubtful, unable of love, prone to chronic boring, careless and not paying attention to what is happening in his surroundings, among others. They are often incapable of maintaining durable interpersonal relationships.

Avoidant Personality Disorder (AvPD)

The term "avoidant personality" was introduced by Millon (1969). It was firstly used in the third edition of the DSM system of classification. In the ICD-10 is labelled as "anxious personality disorder".

These individuals suffer excessive and generalized anxiety in social situations and intimate relationships. They do want social relationships but feel themselves incapable of promoting them. It has been argumented that the lack of social engagement in schizoid PD and avoidant PD is dependent on different aetiological roots. In the case of avoidant PD, low self-esteem and self-consciousness are based on the social impairment, but they desire relationships; on the other hand, schizoid subjects are indifferent to social relationships (Dowson & Grounds, 1995). Koldobsky (1995) label them as "supplicants" in relationships, they beg being socially accepted. They fear disapproval, critic and rejection, and are worried about being ridiculed by others. Finally, they usually restrict their life to family members.

It is not rare that they turn to alcohol and illicit drugs to cover up their miseries. Generally, they are chronically dissatisfied with their own life. Suicide behavior may happen in situations where they can loose control, suffering episodes of outrage and anger.

The main defence mechanism is fantasy. Millon and Davis (1996) made a perfect description of the inner psychic experience of these subjects: "As they are unable to overtly express their feelings, they accumulate them and use to turn them to a world of fantasy and imagination. The need of affect and intimacy of the avoidant individual may sublimate in artistic activities of great sensitivity".

Dependent Personality Disorder (DPD)

Several psychoanalytical formulations (Abraham, Fenichel, Bowlby) contributed to the link between dependent and passive-aggressive behaviors into the category of passive-dependent personality found in the first edition of DSM in 1952. The passive-dependent personality was defined as a subtype of passive-aggressive personality. In 1987, in the DSM III-R was used the term "dependent PD", which is valid until present day (DSM IV-TR, ICD-10) (Dowson & Grounds, 1995; Millon, 1996), to name those individuals who have a pronounced need of affect and social approval.

As stated by Millon (1980) "the centre of gravity lies in other, not in them". They live according to the wishes of others and their needs are subordinated to them. Their fear of being abandoned is constant and they are always trying to please and avoid everything which could upset the one from whom they depend. They allow other to take control on their lives, basically due to their lack of self-confidence. They usually denigrate themselves and have important difficulties at work, because they have problems to function autonomously. (Dowson & Grounds, 1995).

Intimate relationships are usually dysfunctional due to the pathological dependency on the other, and they can be exploitated. As stated by Oldham & Morris (1996), the partner gets fed-up hearing "tell me that you love me, that you won't leave me, and one day he can't longer endure it and goes away". As soon as a couple relationships finishes, they suddenly and arbitrarily look for another who care and support them.

Cloninger (1987) defined the passive-dependent personality in terms of low novelty-seeking, high harm-avoidance, and dependency on reward, with second-order traits being meticulousness, rigidity and passive-avoiding attitude. Their main defence mechanism is introjection.

Obsessive-Compulsive Personality Disorder (OCPD)

Sigmund Freud (1908) described certain individuals with the so-called anal character as "orderly, parsimonious and obstinate...". Abraham (1921) gave a full view of the disorder that lead to Kahn's descriptions (1928) of the "anankastic person" (Dowson & Grounds, 1995). Unlike DSM IV TR, ICD-10 classification has preserved the term anankastic. This may have the advantage of avoiding the implicit association and nosological confusion with obsessive-compulsive disorder (OCD). This is most important, as recent studies have demonstrated that not all OCD patients have a OCPD.

Perfectionism is the core characteristic of these subjects. They are also rigid-minded, stubborn, dogmatic, moralistic, preoccupied with symmetry and unimportant details, humourless, indecisive, and do not tolerate ambiguity in social relationships; moreover, they have strong difficulties in throwing away useless objects (Dowson & Grounds, 1995). As these authors stressed, some of the obsessional traits, if moderate, can be viewed as "positive descriptions such as dependable, precise, punctual, having high standards, persistent, stable and determined", and indeed, they usually focus intensively at work, having difficulties "to delegating task and responsibilities".

Other typical traits are lack of adaptability to new situations, attachment to routine, lack of expression of affection. As stressed by Dowson & Grounds (1995), "Although they appear unemotional, this may hide resentment, anger and, perhaps, aggressive fantasies".

Cloninger (1987) characterizes them as having low novelty-seeking, high harm-avoidance and low dependency of reward, and the second-order traits of rigidity, alienation and modesty, derived of their concern about keeping order, respecting rules and having everything organized.

1.2.6. PRECURSORS OF PERSONALITY DISORDERS

C. Pinto

Introduction

The complex interplay between biology and environment makes the precursor factors for the development and maintenance of personality disorders (PD) difficult to understand. Genetic studies show our biological predisposition to a range of traits, but it is also well established how genes influence the environment we choose to interact with, therefore predisposing us to a variety of experiences. Genes also mediate the way in which we respond to our circumstances (Goodyer, 2006).

The International Classification of Diseases, 10TH edition (ICD-10) (WHO, 2006) makes an explicit differentiation between the concepts of "personality change" and "personality disorders", despite of including all of them in the same block (F60-F69 Disorders of adult personality and behaviour). Their main difference is that personality disorders are developmental conditions, which appear in childhood or adolescence and continue into adulthood, while personality change is acquired, following severe brain disease or insult (e.g. encephalitis, head injury, etc), severe trauma or stress, or serious mental illness. Personality disorders are classified according to clusters of traits that correspond to its predominant behavioural manifestations (WHO, 2006). Personality disorders are sometimes comorbid with some Axis I diagnoses and if a personality condition precedes or follows a psychiatric diagnosis, both should be diagnosed.

In the present chapter, we will start with a brief historical overview on ideas about personality development, and we will review both biological and environmental factors playing a part, and their interactions. Due to limitations of space, we will focus only in one of the most frequently studied environmental influences in personality: attachment. Attachment patterns have an impact on biological systems (e.g. neuroendocrine regulatory system), and on the development of the neurocognitive cytoarquitecture and neurotransmitter systems of the individual. We will finish the chapter by briefly reviewing precursors of specific types of personality disorders, the most widely studied until now being the antisocial and the borderline PD.

Historial Overview

Hippocrates in the Fifth Century B.C. already suggested a biological basis to personality and PD. It was thought that the dominance of one of the four body humours -black and yellow bile, blood and phlegm- would confer the individual vulnerability to certain mental and physical conditions. In the Nineteenth Century, the study of the skull shape (phrenology) took preponderance and in the Twentieth Century, the theories of Kretschmer and Sheldon sought the relationship between body build and personality (Moore & Farmer, 1984).

However, in the early part of the twentieth century, other approaches were starting to emerge, and the aetiology of both healthy and pathological psychological development was mostly attributed to environment. Psychodynamic theories focused in early attachments to the carer, as it was evident that a history of rejection, coercive or over-protective parenting and abuse led to personality difficulties. Learning theory was used to explain the development of normal personality and personality disorder, the hypothesis for the last being that genetically predetermined traits were exacerbated by faulty learning (Casey, 1998).

In recent decades, it has become accepted that a small number of dimensions can describe the wide variability of human normal and abnormal personality, and that they reflect operations of specific brain systems (e.g. neurocognitive, neuroendocrine systems). Currently, there are a number of studies that have tried to find genetic basis for personality traits, mainly for novelty/sensation seeking behaviour, fear/anxiety, affiliate behaviour, and aggressiveness. However, we need to remember that these genetic based dispositions can be altered by environmental factors (Tobeña, 2003).

Attachment Disorganisation and Personality Disorders

Attachment theory was influenced by ethology and described how evolutionarily determined behaviours in the infant, such as clinging, following and seeking attention from a safe familiar adult, elicit corresponding caregiving responses from the attachment figure. The infant is initially dependent on the caregiver's ability to provide containment and regulation (Clarke et al., 2002) and it is postulated that the experience of repeated interactions of the child with the caregiver become incorporated into mental representations or 'inner working models' that guide expectations and behaviours.

Bolwby (1973) described two types of interactions between the caregiver and the child that have a direct impact on attachment: the speed and intensity to which mother responds to the child's distress (the arousal-relaxation cycle) and the number of interactions that the caregiver initiates (the positive interaction cycle). Repeated successful completion of both cycles helps the infant to develop trust and become attached to her/his caregiver.

Infants who receive consistent, sensitive and reassuring responses from their primary caregivers are likely to develop 'secure' inner working models that make them feel safe and confident; their positive social experience will have biological developmental consequences, enabling them to better regulate their homeostatic arousal, their feelings and behaviour. A distressed infant gets highly aroused when he perceives a potential threat in his environment. This response is mediated by the sympathetic system of the autonomic nervous system. Noradrenaline gets released, which increases heart rate and blood pressure, and the mother restores homeostasis by soothing the infant. Thus, the early parent-child relationship serves as the foundation for the emergence of self-regulation skills and the mother is the primary affect regulator. The successful outcome of secure attachment is the development of the basic machinery to self-regulate affects later in life (Fonagy et al., 2002).

Infants with worse care giving levels are likely to develop patterns of attachment that are described as 'insecure'. Insecure attachment (ambivalent, avoidant) generates anxiety and a mix of feelings towards the attachment figure: love and dependency combined with fear of rejection, abandonment or harm. Further observations led to an additional attachment category (disorganized), in which the infants' strategies for managing their attachment needs appear to collapse under stress, leading to contradictory behaviours (Main & Fonagy, 1986). Disorganised attachment is relatively common, occurring in about 14% of children in non-clinical populations, rising to about 24% in disadvantaged groups and up to 80% in severely neglected or abused groups (Van Ijzendoon et al., 1999). Although there is some evidence that the presence of polymorphism of the DRD4 gene may be implicated in disorganised attachment (Green & Goldwyn, 2002), various factors point to its environmental basis; most notably, it is relationship specific, at least in infancy (a child may be disorganised with one parent but not with the other), and it is strongly predicted by environmental factors such as neglect, abuse and parental unresolved states of mind in relation to attachment-related loss or trauma. Studies have consistently found that this category in infancy is the one most associated with later psychopathology. It is known that some of the same factors that predispose to disorganized attachment (early childhood adversity, especially neglect), are risk factors for the development of PD. Insecure attachment prevents the development of a proper affect regulatory capacity. Following the example of a distressed infant, an insecurely attached one will not be able to balance sympathetic hyperarousal in response to threat, and this can lead to a prolonged fight/flight state, or state of 'freezing' if the situation is perceived to be beyond her/his control. (Sarkar & Adshead, 2006)

Recent studies showing that the rearing environment of a child has a direct effect on the development of brain structures and pathways involved in affect regulation have identified the right hemisphere as playing a key role in the social and biological functions of the attachment system in the infant (Wang, 1997). Secure attachments will lead to healthy right hemispheric maturation during the critical period (first 2–3 years of life) but experiences of abuse, neglect or inconsistent caring will lead to impaired development of neural pathways that subserve emotional behaviors. Therefore, impaired emotional regulation is likely to persist through life.

Sarkar and Adshead (2006), in a recent review have brought together developmental and neurobiological research, and conclude that the concept of personality disorder is best understood as disorganization of the capacity for affect regulation, mediated by early attachments as described above. People who have experienced insecure attachment are at risk of developing dysregulated affective systems. It is well established that people with personality disorders have difficulty in keeping relationships that require good affect regulation and tend to experience disorganized relationships. Their inability to regulate negative affects lead them to frequently respond with anger. They overuse the flight-fight response to cope with stress, which is frequently perceived everywhere, making them feel unsafe and distrust others. People with personality disorders tend to present with external locus of control: their negative feelings are somebody else's fault that need an external solution. These responses are immature, as it is a developmental task that is resolved in children at the age of 5 years.

Precursors of Specific PDS

As highlighted above, it is the antisocial and the borderline personality disorder that have been studied in more detail. A significant association between schizophrenia and paranoid personality disorders has been described (Kendler et al., 1985), but the most clear-cut finding from family studies is the association between schizophrenia and schizoid personality disorder (Kendler et al., 1984). This is further supported by findings of brain similarities in magnetic resonance imaging (MRI) and in deficits in attention and information processing. In terms of the histrionic personality disorder, twin studies have shown a modest effect for hysterical traits, but this has not been replicated so hereditary aspects are thought to be unlikely. Hereditary factors may be etiologically relevant in the anankastic personality disorder, and shyness is a long-lasting constitutional trait, probably linked with avoidant personality disorder. (Casey, 1998)

Dissocial Personality Disorder

The criteria for dissocial personality disorder in ICD-10 are similar to those for antisocial personality disorder in DSM-IV. However, in DSM-IV, evidence of conduct disorder with onset before age 15 years is required for the diagnosis. (APA, 1994)

New-onset antisocial behavior in adulthood is rare (10%) and most antisocial adults have long histories of behaviour problems reaching back to childhood. However, 60% of children showing antisocial behavior do not develop antisocial personality disorder in adulthood (Goodyer, 2006).

Moffitt's (1993) developmental taxonomy tries to explain this apparent paradox by differentiating two distinct subgroups within the antisocial young people. The first and less prevalent group begins in early childhood, is more frequent in males and has associated several risk factors such as inadequate parenting (e.g. inconsistent discipline, abuse, rejection) and/or socioeconomic deprivation. Neurodevelopment difficulties are common and reduced levels of arousal, including reduced plasma cortisol levels have been described. These findings suggest a role for executive (prefrontal) and temporo-limbic (amygdale) dysfunction (Dolan, 2004). In summary, childhood onset processes seem to arise from neurocognitive deficits, emotional dysfunctions and language problems (particularly pragmatics and social discourse) (Goodyer, 2006). The children in this group rapidly display negative emotions when frustrated, have poor impulse control, hyperactivity, and lower IQ. This leads to poorer outcomes in life, such as increased exclusions and drop-out from school, poor work record, peer problems, teenage pregnancy and marital instability (Hill, 1984). The second group has the onset of the antisocial behaviours during adolescence, not associated with the previous group's early risk factors but more a product of the tensions of adolescence and growing up, wanting to conform with a peer group, etc. It has better outcomes as persistence in antisocial activities is not expected once young people grow up and gain rights and responsibilities.

The main postulates of this model have been supported (mainly the poor long-term prognosis for early-onset disruptive behaviours), but studies have also shown that a small proportion with marked early disruptiveness go on to show good adaptation in adulthood; and there is little knowledge at this stage to explain what protective factors play a part on this (Rutter et al., 2006). What is known is that children from a criminogenic environment who did not later become delinquent were, at the age of 10, less daring, more neurotic and shy and spent less leisure time with their fathers (Farrington et al., 1990). This finding would also point towards a genetic contribution to antisocial personality disorder, via the genetic markers already found for some personality dimensions/factors outlined above. Adoption and cross-fostering studies confirm the genetic contribution to antisocial personality disorder, stating that environment may play a role, but only if there is a pre-existing genetic predisposition. Apart from genetics, other likely biological contributors are temperamental factors and child psychiatric conditions such ADHD (only if comorbid with conduct disorder).

Both ICD-10 & DSM-IV include the concepts of psychopathic and sociopathic personality disorders under dissocial and antisocial personality disorders respectively. However, it is important to emphasize that the dissocial/antisocial personality disorder criteria focus on antisocial behaviors and the concept of psychopathy on personality traits.

Frick (1998) coined the term "callous-unemotional traits", and they appear in the breeding ground of a unique temperamental style called low behavioral inhibition. These children have low fear and they do not respond to the type of socialization (gentle, non-power, assertive discipline) that leads to conscience development in more fearful children. The style used by parents to socialize their child has less impact on the development of conduct problems in children with callous-unemotional traits, suggesting that genetic or neurodevelopment factors make a more significant contribution in children who are callous (Dolan, 2004).

Emotionally Unstable Personality Disorder (Impulsive and Borderline)

Many theories of the origins of borderline personality disorder (BPD) have proposed a central role for adverse and traumatic experiences in childhood. Childhood trauma (e.g. abuse, neglect) is extremely common among borderline patients: up to 87% have suffered childhood trauma of some sort, 40–71% have been sexually abused and 25–71% have been physically abused (Perry & Herman, 1993). Other studies report percentages as high as 90% in terms of memories of past experiences of neglect and sexual abuse by a male non-caregiver and/or inconsistent treatment by a female caregiver (Zanarini et al., 1997). Their difficulties in modulating emotion also appear to be linked with early trauma, which makes these patients unable to think about their own thoughts and feelings, as well as about those of others. They are preoccupied with their disturbed early relationships yet unable to give a coherent account of them, which, in combination with defective affect regulation, produces the typical impulsivity of individuals with BPD. The lack of a sense of self is a core feature of the psychopathology of BPD. Splitting is often very marked in borderline patients, and its link with sexual abuse has been confirmed in recent research. (Winston, 2000)

Other factors identified also to be of etiological significance are parental mental illness, drug abuse, marital discord and witnessing parental violence (Casey, 1998). The combination of maternal inconsistency and high maternal over involvement assessed in adolescence was also associated with the emergence of BPD. Inconsistent mother-child interactions are likely to inhibit the child's capacity to read the states of mind of the parent, and hence limit his ability to think of other's behaviors in mental state terms. This may be the reason why they report more dissociative experiences (Hill, 1984).

Despite of having increasing evidence of trauma during childhood being relevant in the etiology of BPD, many cases have no history of abuse, and so there is probably a continuum of those who have a strong genetic basis to develop BPD and those in whom traumatic upbringing is causal, with most cases having a mixture of both elements. Some biological studies show decreased rapid eye movement latency among subjects with this disorder similar to the pattern observed in unipolar depression, but there is more evidence that early insults to the brain such as birth injury, damage through infection or trauma during childhood, ADHD, epilepsy and other neurological conditions can contribute to BPD, particularly in men (Casey, 1998).

Conclusion

The study of the multiple factors that play a part in the genesis of personality disorders is a fascinating area that has developed in the last decades. Future research will focus on genetic mechanisms, as well as on these genes´ interactions with their environment. As in many of the psychiatric conditions, understanding the interplay between nature and nurture, both of them varying in their contribution and continuously changing each other, will be of vital importance in identifying at risk populations for the development of these complex disorders.

1.2.7. DIAGNOSTIC TOOLS FOR PERSONALITY DISORDERS

J. J. Rodríguez-Solano and C. Franco-Porras

Introduction

In the last two decades, it has been a great proliferation of measure instruments designed for the evaluation of maladaptative personality traits, personality dimensions or Personality Disorders (PDs). Probably this owes two main factors: firstly, in 1980, the American Psychiatric Association (APA) recognized the importance of PD, created and independent axis and defined the PD following the criteria of the DSM-III. Secondly, new research on personality and psychopathology shows the intrinsic relation between these two factors (Clark & Harrison, 2001). Moreover, there is a low reliability of the diagnosis achieved by the clinical impression during the no structured interview (Zimmerman, 1994). Due to the great and growing interest on the correct diagnosis of the PD, several measured instruments have been developed. The principal aim of these instruments is to improve diagnostic reliability. The development of these diagnostic tools for PDs has allowed a more precise use of this category for research on PDs (Cheng et al., 1997). The personality's diagnostic instruments have some difficulties:

- Measured instruments do not give "gold standard" criteria to confirm the diagnosis. Therefore, they do not solve the problem of the validity of the diagnosis on PDs.
- Despite the good reliability between observers during a common interview, the test-retest reliability decreases when time between both evaluations increases (Zimmerman, 1994).
- Diagnostic concordance is poor when different measured instruments are used (Perry, 1992).

- Difference between trait and state is not clear yet. Personality is a persistent trait more than a characteristic state (Loranger et al., 1991). The analysis of the PDs should evaluate longitudinal patterns more than short and transversal evaluations.
- Evaluation of personality characteristics in the course of a mayor, chronic and recurrent psychiatric disorder might be clearly affected.
- Many personality traits are egosintonic for patients. There for, patients will not be able to evaluate and give appropriate information about their personality traits. In other cases, the patient will delivery tries to hide them. Information given by a significant other is necessary to increase reliability.

Not only some of these problems are due to the evaluation instruments used, but also the intrinsic nature of PDs. Current classifications may contribute to their complexity. There are many instruments to evaluate personality. In this chapter, we review the self-report questionnaires and the structured interviews. These two are the most used tests in research and clinic for the evaluation of PDs. Both types of instruments can be classified in those based on personality traits and those based on diagnostic criteria. Those tools based on diagnostic criteria -self-report questionnaires and interviews semi-structured- have two main problems. One problem is their moderate-low convergent and other the low discriminate validity. Moderate-low convergent validity may be due to the nucleus of PDs´ nature. On this matter, it is necessary much more research to clarify the current concept of PDs. In addition, its low discriminate validity might be due to the high co-morbidity between several PDs. In conclusion, research on PDs is hazardous. Researchers use different evaluation instruments and they identify different groups with PDs. These PDs might be different depending on the evaluation tool used. Thus, it is difficult to replicate the results despite the different groups receive the same diagnostic label (Clark & Harrison, 2001). Clark et al. (1997) affirm that the main problem is the concept of PDs more than the lack of suitable DSM-III diagnostic criteria or the evaluation techniques. The handicap of the instruments based on personality traits is the application for clinical purposes due to the high prevalence of the medical categorical model used in clinic.

Self-report Questionnaires

Self-report questionnaires are the most utilized instruments in research for the evaluation of PD. The main reason for this is its efficiency. They are quick and easy to apply in comparison to diagnostic interviews. However, they lack reliability and validity, especially for the evaluation of categorical diagnosis (Clark & Harrison, 2001). On the other hand, their advantage is a better-standardized evaluation because they eradicate the differences between interviewers.

Self-report Questionnaires Based on Personality Traits
The main problem of current international classifications of PDs is the poor reliability and validity of their diagnostic categories. Thus, many authors propound the evaluation of personality traits-dimension of personality more than categorical diagnosis (Clark & Harrison, 2001). Moreover, international diagnostic categories are not more than

desadaptative personality traits grouped together. The problem of these self-report questionnaires is their difficulty for clinical application because clinicians are more familiar with diagnostic categories.

Some of these self-report questionnaires based on personality traits were designed for the evaluation of normal personality characteristics and afterwards they were used for PDs. On the other hand, others are focused designed for the study of PDs. Some of these questionnaires evaluate a unique personality trait, but others study multiple personality features in order to have a global assessment of the pathological traits of the person (Clark & Harrison, 2001).

Dimensional Assessment of Personality Pathology-Basic Questionnaire, DAPP-BQ

This test was developed by Livesley et al. (1989). The authors try to identify the prototypic characteristics of DSM-III-R diagnostics. This test defines 79 personality traits. Those traits were evaluated for specialist clinics and analyzed in patients and control population. The test has 290 items grouped in 18 factorial scales. This questionnaire has very good intern consistency and has been proved to have good convergence with other self-report questionnaires based on personality traits.

Schedule of Nonadaptive and Adaptive Personality, SNAP

This questionnaire has been developed by Clark (1993) and it is built with DSM personality disorders criteria and other diagnostic sources. This test also adds axis I categories that share characteristics with axis II. Later, those criteria were under a factorial analysis and the results were 12 dimensional scales based on traits and 3 temperamental scales of major order. The questionnaire consists in 375 self-report true-false items. It has been demonstrated to be a stable test and with intern consistency (Clark & Harrison, 2001).

NEO Personality Inventory-Revised, NEO-PI-R

This test was developed by Costa & McCrae (1992). The standard questionnaire is a concise measure of the five major domains of personality, "the Big Five": Neuroticism (N), Extroversion (E), Openness to experience (O), Agreeableness (A) and Conscientiousness (C). It is a well-validated instrument. It is the most useful test for a detailed assessment of normal adult personality. It has been demonstrated a good correlation with DSM system when applied on PDs (Costa & Widiger, 1994). Each version contains 240 items and each item is rated on a 5-point scale. The test is completed in about 30-45 minutes.

Temperament-Character Inventory, TCI

This questionnaire was developed by Cloninger et al., (1994) and it is based on author's neurobiological personality model (Cloninger et al., 1993). Following this model, personality consists in two dimensions, temperament and character. The temperament would delimit the type of disorder and it is evaluated with four scales: Novelty Seeking (NS), Avoidance of Harm (AH), Reward Dependence (RD), and Persistency (P). Character would determine the presence or not of a personality disorder. This item is evaluated with three measured character domain scales: Self-Directedness (SD), Cooperativeness (CO), and Self-Transcendence (ST). Temperament would be linked to a neurobiological system based on genetic determination and will keep stable along life. Character would be determined by social learning during interaction with the environment. The questionnaire consists of 240 true/ false questions. The psychometric characteristics of this test have been evaluated. It has been concluded temperament and character have an appropriate intern consistency, apart from persistence factor that has a low-moderate Alfa coefficient. A good convergent validity has been shown in comparison with MCMI-II (Bayon et al., 1996).

Eysenck Personality Questionnaire Revised, EPQ-R.

This test is the revised version of Eysenck Personality Questionnaire (EPQ) (Eysenck & Eysenck, 1975). The questionnaire consists of 100 items and evaluates three dimensions: Psychoticism (P), Neuroticism (N) y Extraversion (E). Moreover, the test includes a Lie scale (L) that might be interpreted as social desirability.

The Karolinska Scales of Personality, KSP

The Karolinska Scales of Personality (KSP) is a self-questionnaire designed by Schalling & Edman (1993) and based on theories of biologically based personality dimensions. Its purpose is to assess stable personality traits correlated with biologically relevant disposition associated with psychopathological vulnerability. The test consists of 135 items that are organized in 15 different scales, and these last are divides in four groups: extroversion, lack of assertiveness, anxiety and aggressiveness.

Self-report Questionnaires Based on Diagnostic Criteria

Many of the available questionnaires are designed for diagnostic purposes following DSM criteria, including passive-aggressive and depressive personality disorders that are included on DSM-IV-TR. Self-report questionnaires have a good sensibility but low specificity that is the reason for their high rate of false positive results. Due to this fact, Loranger (1992) considers that the only purpose of these tests is as screening instruments, but they are not useful for PDs diagnosis.

Millon Clinical Multiaxial Inventory-III, MCMI-III

Millon Clinical Multiaxial Inventory (MCMI-III) (Millon et al. 1994) is the last version of the questionnaire Millon-Illinois Self Report Inventory (MI-SRI) and it is adapted to DSM-IV criteria. Originally, the MI-SRI was developed by Millon and Disenhaus (1972). The authors have adapted the questionnaire following the evolution and changes of different DSM criteria and therefore the test have received different changes along these years, as MCMI and MCMI-II due to DSM-III and DSM-III-R changes respectively (Millon 1977, 1987). The test is based on Millon´s personality theories (Millon, 1967 y 1969). The purpose of the test is to measure, in psychiatric population, the relation between cognitive, interpersonal and intrapsychics factors. It is a 20-30 minute test that consists of 175 true/ false questions. The test has 24 clinical scales divided in 4 sections: clinical patterns of personality, severe personality disorders, clinical syndromes and severe syndromes. In the first two scales, it includes all DSM-III-R and DSM-IV PDs, including self-destructive disorder, the passive-aggressive and the depressive personality disorder. In the section of clinical syndromes it covers all most prevalent axis I disorders. The test pretends the results and interpretations of the questionnaire will follow DSM multiaxial criteria. It also has three correction scales -

disclosure, desirability and debasement- that help to detect careless or confused information gave by the patients.

Minnesota Multiphasic Personality Inventory, MMPI-2

Minnesota Multiphasic Personality Inventory (MMPI-2) was created by Butcher & Megargee (1989). It consists of 567 true/ false items divided in 10 subscales: Hypocondriasis (Hs), Hysteria (Hy), Depression (D), Psychopathic deviate (Pd), Masculinity-feminity (Mf), Paranoia (P), Psychasthenia (Ps), Schizophrenia (Sc), Hypomania (Ma) and Social introversion (Si). It takes around 60-90 minutes to be completed. This is a diagnostic instrument that evaluates not only personality but psychopathology from a dimensional point of view. MMPI-2 scales are not equivalent to DSM diagnostic criteria. MMPI-2 scales refer to personality traits but DSM´s refer to symptoms (Youssef et al., 2004). Morey et al. (1985) designed a new group of scales for this questionnaire that allowed to representing the 11 DSM-III PDs.

Personality Disorder Questionnaire-IV, PDQ-IV

This test was developed by Hyler (1994). It is the adapted version of the original Personality Disorder Questionnaire (PDQ) to DSM-IV version. It is a 85-question, true-false questionnaire. It takes 20-30 minutes to be completed. It encloses two validity scales to evaluate possible patient's distortion on their answers. The authors found that the test has a high sensitivity buy low specificity. All experts recommend this test as a screening questionnaire due its brevity and high proportion of false positives.

OMNI and OMNI-IV

OMNI and OMNI-IV are two personality inventories developed by Loranger (2001). OMNI evaluates normal and pathological characteristics of personality. OMNI-IV is an abbreviate version of the first one that only includes the measure evaluation of personality disorders for DSM-IV. Both inventories have validity scales. OMNI-IV consists of 210 items. Psychometric characteristics on intern congruence, reliability and validity are good as seen in author's studies.

Diagnostic Interviews

Diagnostic Interviews Based on Personality Traits

Vast majority of interviews based on personality traits evaluate a unique diagnostic category. There are two exceptions Tridimensional Interview of Personality Style (TIPS) by Cloninger (1987) and Personality Assessment Schedule (PAS) by Tyrer & Alexander (1988). Both questionnaires cover different personality traits. Clark & Harrison (2001) point out that each of these interviews follow a personality model that partially covers DSM criteria. Interviews based on personality traits meticulous examine the disorder for which they are designed. This is the main disparity between interviews based on personality traits and interviews based on diagnostic criteria.

Tridimensional Interview of Personality Style, TIPS

This interview was designed by Cloninger (1987) in order to make a systematic diagnosis of different aspect of personality. The theoretical base for this interview has been mentioned along this chapter. The instrument includes questions that yield the characteristic traits of each of the three temperament dimensions – novelty seeking, avoidance of harm, dependence on reward- and all of its six possible combinations. The answers are scored in a seven points scale. For one subject, each trait is evaluated twice, the year before and in the middle of adolescence in order to evaluate the evolution of personality during development. PDs are defined following nine groups of traits.

Personality Assessment Schedule, PAS

Personality Assessment Schedule (PAS) is the last version (Tyrer & Alexander, 1988) of the semi-structured interview designed by Tyrer & Alexander (1979). It is a standardised interview in which the interviewee is asked for information related to 24 personality characteristics. Ratings for each trait are made on a nine-point scale from 0-8. The interview is completed in about 60 minutes. These traits were grouped in 6 PDs categories that correspond to ICD-9 categories: explosive, asthenic, paranoid-aggressive, histrionic, anancastic and schizoid. There is also an adapted interview for DSM-III. Authors recommend to pass the interview to the subject and to a significant other to confirm the information gave by the subject and there select the most truly one in case of discrepancy.

There is a quick version of PAS (Merson et al., 1994). It only takes about ten minutes to be completed and allows a fast screening of PD following ICD-10 criteria. It has been found a moderate concordance between both versions (Van Horn et al., 2000). Inter-rater reliability is good and due to it´s a global interview that yields personality dysfunction from trait-dimension perspective, nowadays, this interview is taking special relevance in US (Clark & Harrison, 2001).

Diagnostic Interview for Borderlines Revised, DIB-R

Diagnostic Interview for Borderlines Revised (DIB-R) was developed by Zanarini et al. (1989). They review the original version of DIB designed by Gunderson et al. (1981). The main purpose is evaluating the concept about borderline personality disorder given by Gunderson that was the basic influence for DSM criteria. Despite the superposition between DIB-R and DSM is not perfect, Clark & Harrison (2001) consider this overlapping moderate/high moderate enough to evaluate borderline personality disorder. The interview takes around 60 minutes to be completed. It consists of 182 items that evaluate the following four main areas, impulsive pattern, affect, psychosis and interpersonal relationships. The original interview included another area, social adaptation. The psychometric characteristics of DIB have been widening evaluated. It has been shown its inter-rater reliability (Frances et al. 1984) and its discriminate validity with other diagnosis of axis I (Kolb J. and Gunderson, J.G., 1980). But, on the other hand, it does not have good discriminate validity with other axis II diagnosis (Soloff and Ulrich, 1981). In a study, the same authors (Zanarini et al. 1989) have proved that the psychometric characteristics of DIB-R are superior to DIB.

Diagnostic Interview for Narcissism, DIN

Diagnostic Interview for Narcissism (DIN) developed by Gunderson et al. (1990) evaluates 33 narcissisms aspects all along through 105 questions. These questions points in five fields: grandiosity, interpersonal relations, reactivity, affect and mood states, and moral and social opinions. The interview takes about 45-50 minutes. The interview was developed after a wide review of literature, based on several theories and after a systematic examination of narcissistic patients. The interview has a good overlap with DSM criteria. The questionnaire has good reliability between interviewers and intern consistency according to its authors.

Psychopathy Check List-Revised, PCL-R

Psychopathy Check List-Revised (PCL-R) was designed by Hare (1991) following the concept of psychopathy of Cleckey (1941). First, the author elaborated Pychopathy Checklist (PCL) and later on the PCL-R. This last version evaluates 18 items that are clustered in two different dimension: factor 1 (F1), based on personality traits –glibness/superficial charm, grandiose sense of self-worth, pathological lying, conning/manipulative, lack of remorse or guilt, shallow affect, callous/lack of empathy, failure to accept responsibility for own actions– that positively correlates with narcissistic and histrionic PDs following DSM criteria. Factor 2 (F2) includes traits —need for stimulation/proneness to boredom, parasitic lifestyle, weak behavioural, controls, early behavioral problems, lack of realistic, long-term goals, impulsivity, irresponsibility, juvenile delinquency, revocation of conditional release— that positively correlates DSM criteria for antisocial personality disorder. The scores are given by the clinical interview and the available information from the subject. The interview has adequate psychometric characteristics according to its authors.

Diagnostic Interview for Depressive Personality, DIDP

The interview was developed by Phillips et al. (1990). It is designed for the diagnosis of depressive personality traits, that are stable and persists in the subject all through his life. The interview pretends to distinguish from major depression disorder and disthymia

Semistructured Interviews Based on Diagnostic Criteria

The advantage of the semi-structured interviews is that they increase diagnosis reliability compared with clinical impression. On the other hand, this reliability is lower than the reliability showed in questionnaires. Reliability depends not only in the content of the interview but also on the study's design and the training and quality of the interviewer (Clark & Harrison, 2001). Semi-structured interviews are more specific so they have less false positive results. Also, they better might clear up the questions and avoid subject's comprehension difficulties. Interview's reliability test-retest is still low. Zimmerman (1994) found that the test-retest reliability for IPDE had an average kappa value of 0.46 for any PD. Thus, the diagnosis of any personality disorder is unstable in weeks using any kind of diagnostic tool (Clark & Harrison, 2001). It seems that the low reliability found is due to arbitrary cutting points when doing categorical diagnosis, thus giving a measure error (Heumann & Morey, 1990). Another two handicaps are: firstly, they need a trained professional to interview and secondly, time to complete the test is longer.

Some of these interviews as IPDE (Loranger et al., 1994) and SCID-II (First et al., 1997) have a self-screening questionnaire with a true/false pattern. Meanwhile, the self-screening tool of SIDP-IV (Pool et al., 1995) is a brief interview done by the clinician. These questionnaires have a high sensitivity and low specificity. They offer a global view of the presence of a PD in the person to whom the test is applied. If the score is below a cut point it is assumed that there is no PD but if the score is above that limit, the complete interview should be used. These questionnaires are indicated for the screening of those people who are in very low probability to have a PD. The identification of positive cases with these tests is not useful because the test has many false positive cases (Guthrie & Mobley, 1994; Lenzenweger et al., 1997). The best indication of these instruments would be to rule out a PD when a complete evaluation of the whole population could not be done (Clark & Harrison, 2001).

Structured Interview for DSM Personality-IV, SIDP-IV

It was developed by Pfohl et al. (1995) and designed according to DSM-IV and CIE-10. The interview has different versions for DSM-III-R (SIDP-R) and DSM-III (SIDP) respectively (Pfhol et al. 1989, Pfohl et al. 1982). It is a semi-structured interview. It is organized by topics of interest or PDs. Organization by topics of interest allows a more fluid and natural interview. Organization by diagnosis allows choosing between groups of diagnosis without using the entire interview. Inter-rater reliability is improved by an intensity score that goes from zero a three and interviews are able to formulate additional questions and use external informers if they consider necessary. The interview gives two kinds of measures: one categorical and other dimensional in intensity. It takes about to 2-2,5 hours to complete the test.

Structured Clinical Interview for DSM-IV Axis II Personality Disorder, SCID-II

Structured Clinical Interview for DSM-IV Axis II Personality Disorder (SCID-II) is the last version for DSM-IV and is designed by First et al. (1997). The version for DSM-III-R was done by Spitzer et al. (1987). SCID-II has 119 items and they go through all of the PDs criteria of DSM-IV. It also includes those proposed for additional studies. It is organized by diagnostic criteria so it may explore each PD individually. This organization has received negative comments due to its astron effect (Widiger y Frances 1987). When a subject has pointed positively to some diagnostic criteria of a PD, the likehood to find a positive score on the following criteria for that same PD is increased. The interview starts with an introductory general question and then they evaluate PD with a variable number of questions for each one. Author suggests to asking about all the questions for clear up criteria, also considering the information reported by a significant other in order to contrast information. An intensity scale of 4 points is used to its evaluation and categorical and dimensional data are obtained. The test takes about 30-90 minutes to be completed and this characteristic is one of the advantages of the test. Thus, when the subject does not meet the criteria for one PD, the test allows skipping that disorder and evaluates the next. In addition, the test has a Personality Questionnaire (SCID-II PQ) that consists in 119 true/false questions that allow identifying the criteria of PDs that are going to be evaluated deeper during the interview, meanwhile negative PDs are omitted. The psychometric characteristics of this interview are correct (Clark & Harrison 2001).

The Diagnostic Interview for DSM-IV Personality Disorders, DIPD-IV

The diagnostic Interview for DSM-IV Personality Disorders (DIPD-IV) was designed by Zanarini et al. (1996) and it is the review version for DSM-IV. The original test is the DIPD formulated for DSM-III-R (Zanarini et al. 1987). DIPD-IV is a semi-structured interview that evaluates the answers given by participants to questions for each diagnostic criterion using a 3 points scale. It requires about 90 minutes to be completed. This interview elicits clear-up questions according to the clinical judgment of the outside reader, and allows to ruling out other Axis I diagnosis. At the Collaborative Longitudinal Personality Disorders Study (CLPS) it has been found that this interview has good reliability (Zanarini et al., 2000).

Personality Disorder Interview-IV, PDI-IV

Personality Disorder Interview-IV (PDI-IV) is a semi-structured interview elaborated by Widiger et al. (1995) to the evaluation of DSM-IV personality disorders. A long interview takes around two hours to be completed. It goes through all PD diagnostic criteria and elicits clear up questions of the answers given by subjects. It gives a categorical and dimensional score because of the sum of each criterion's scores. It is organized for topics and PDs. The authors show acceptable psychometric data.

International Personality Disorder Examination, IPDE

International Personality Disorder Examination (IPDE) is a semi-structured interview developed by Loranger et al. (1991, 1994) in a join program with the World Health Organization (WHO) and the American Alcohol Drug Abuse and Mental Health Administration (ADAMHA) for the study of PDs following ICD-10 and DSM-IV diagnostic criteria. It is the result of the modification of the Personality Disorder Examination (PDE) by Loranger (1988). It was designed in two different blocks, one for evaluation of PD following DSM-IV (WHO, 1995) and the other one for ICD-10 (WHO, 1996).

IPDE tries to create a stable point between a spontaneous and natural clinic interview and the standardized model of diagnostic tools. Questions are organized in topics, divided in 6 parts: work, self, interpersonal relationship, affect, reality and impulse control. The interview has open questions, so the interviewer can adapt the questions to the specific context of the interview. IPDE also includes the additional information given by a significant other. This last information will score if this information is more trustworthy than the one given by the patient. IPDE is design for adults older than 18 years old, but can be used for people over 15 years old. Personality refers to an individual's usual characteristic that requires a minimal duration of five years (in adolescents only 3 years), and at least one criteria should be present before 25 years old. If the all the criteria for PD were meet after that age, it is considered as a "late onset" of the PD. It also includes manifestation during the current year (past 12 months). If the criteria were met in the past, but no during last year it is considered that the diagnostic criteria were "in the past".

IPDE allows categorical and dimensional diagnostics for PD giving researchers more reliable information. The interview takes about 60 to 90 minutes to be completed depending on interviewer's experience. One advantage of the interview is the computerized correction systems attached to the tool. It has versions in different languages. DSM-IV's module has 99 questions and ICD-10 has 67. Even more, each module has an abbreviate formulation, the IPDE-SQ (International Personality Disorder Examination, Screening Questionnaire). This questionnaire consists of 59 true/false questions for ICD-10 and 77 true/false questions for DSM-IV. These questionnaires allow to screening out those subjects who have no a PD, allowing a faster complete interview. The authors point out that the interview has good and appropriate psychometric characteristics (Loranger et al., 1994).

IPDE-SQ for DSM-IV is a tool that has been used for research in this book. By using a higher cutting point for the diagnosis of PDs, thus decreasing the number of false positive, the authors hope to be able to diagnosing PD (see later).

Conclusion

In this chapter we have review the updated tools and diagnostic instruments for the evaluation and diagnosis of PDs. Most of them have been designed following the current international classification's criteria. Most of them are easy to apply but require some training from the clinician. The reliability of the diagnosis depends on each tool. The clinician has a great battery of instruments to apply depending on patient ´s characteristics and the study.

SUICIDE BEHAVIOR

1.3.1. INTRODUCTION

M. M. Pérez-Rodríguez

Suicide is a significant public health issue. It is among the top 10 causes of death in every country, and one of the three leading causes of death in the 15 to 35-year age group. In the year 2000, approximately one million people died of suicide. This represents a global mortality rate of 16 per 100,000 or one death every 40 seconds (World Health Organization, 2006). The highest annual rates are in Eastern Europe, with more than 10 countries with more than 30 suicides per 100,000 individuals. The lowest rates are found in most Latin American and Muslim countries, fewer than 6.5 per 100,000 (World Health Organization, 2005). In the United States, in 2003, suicide accounted for 31,484 deaths: 86.3 per day or 10.8 per 100,000 per year (Center for Disease Control, 2006). In the National Comorbidity Survey, a nationally representative survey carried out in the US from 1990 to 1992 in a sample of 5,877 subjects aged 15-54, the reported lifetime prevalence of suicide attempts was 4.6% (Kessler et al., 1999).

The burden of suicide can be estimated in terms of DALYs (disability-adjusted life years). According to this indicator, in 1998 suicide was responsible for 1.8% of the total burden of disease worldwide, varying between 2.3% in high-income countries and 1.7% in low-income countries. This is equal to the burden due to wars and homicide, roughly twice the burden of diabetes, and equal to the burden of birth asphyxia and trauma. (World Health Organization, 2000). Suicidal behavior is prevalent in psychiatric emergency services. It has been estimated that suicide behavior is present in at least one third of psychiatric emergency room patients (Dhossche, 2000).

Suicidal behavior arises from different motivations. Those subjects who harm themselves to consciously manipulate others would be at one end of the spectrum, while those individuals who really want to die would be at the other end. The assessment and management of these two populations should be different; however this is not usually the case in real-life clinical conditions (Gold Jr., 1987).

Individuals with mental disorders have increased risk of suicide (approximately 10 times higher than the general population) (Harris & Barraclough, 1997). It has been estimated that more than 90% of individuals who commit suicide suffer a mental disorder, mainly affective disorders (30-90%), substance abuse (19-60%) and schizophrenia (2-14%) (Arseneault et al., 2004; Beskow et al., 1990). Patients with major depression have a suicide rate of 10-15%, three times higher than the general population. It has been estimated that depressive patients commit 80% of completed suicides. Actually, the most effective way to prevent suicide is to properly diagnose and treat mental disease (US Public Health Service, 1999).

The first conceptualizations of suicide –highly influenced by psychoanalytic theories-regarded suicide as the result of a depressive, self-blaming process derived from initially homicidal ideas. Later on, suicide has been considered an irrational act directed towards another individual in order to deliver him/her the hostile message "see what you made me lose" (Sullivan, 1992). Nowadays, suicide is considered a complex, multi-factorial phenomenon that ranges from transient suicide ideation to completed suicide (Mann et al., 1999) and is the result of a dynamic interaction among the patient's personality, his/her affective state, and the social environment, among other factors (Gold Jr., 1987).

Predicting which patients will commit suicide is extremely difficult (Allgulander & Fisher 1990). Suicide risk assessment is currently based on clinical variables (Motto et al., 1985). The presence of suicide ideation is the best predictor of attempted suicide, which is the best predictor of another suicide attempt or completed suicide (Lecubrier, 2001). It is estimated that approximately 1 out of 10 suicide attempters finally commit suicide (Suominen, 2004), and around 20-30% of suicide completers have prior suicide attempts. This highlights the need to identify other risk factors for suicide attempts and completed suicides in order to improve prevention (Mann et al., 1999). One important question that remains unanswered is whether suicide attempts and completed suicides may represent two separate –albeit overlapping- populations.

The attempts to predict suicide risk based on biological markers have been scarce and mainly related to serotonergic parameters (Asberg et al., 1973; Samuelsson et al., 2006). Some of these biological markers have yielded better results than other methods based on clinical factors (Samulesson et al., 2006).

Finally, several studies support the theory that the impulsivity and lethality of a suicide attempt are inversely correlated (Baca-García et al., 2001). Elliot et al. (1996) found that medically severe suicide attempts were more frequently associated with unipolar depression and affective disorders secondary to drug abuse, while non-severe attempts were associated with bipolar depression and borderline personality disorder.

Brief Historical Review

Contextualization is essential when approaching any complex human behavior such as suicide. In ancient Greece, suicide was considered a disgraceful act. Life was considered a gift bestowed by the Gods, and life and death were subjected to the will of the Gods. However, important schools of thought such as the Stoics, the Cynics and the Epicureans developed a slightly more accepting attitude towards suicide (Retterstol, 1998).

Under Roman Law, attempted suicide became a punishable offence due to its financial consequences. The suicide of a slave meant a substantial financial loss for the master, and the suicide of a soldier weakened the army. However, heroic sacrificial suicide was highly praised.

Suicide was considered wrong and unworthy by Jewish law, although exceptions were found, primarily if suicide would help to avoid disgrace through captivity or torture. The Old Testament describes several examples of suicide. In the New Testament there is a famous suicide: Judas Iscariot hanged himself after betraying Christ. During the early Christian period acts of martyrdom were common. Changes came during the fourth century, and the Church developed an extremely antagonistic attitude to suicide. Nevertheless, these attitudes did not prevent suicide from taking place. For example, 5,000 Albigenses of southern France committed mass suicide while being persecuted as heretics in 1218 (Retterstol, 1998).

The *Renaissance* brought modifications in the perception of suicide. In the 17th century, suicide became a recurrent topic in British literature, and was presented as an answer to guilt or lovelessness. Shakespeare included suicide in several of his works. Robert Burton (1577-1640), in his book *Anatomy of melancholy*, provided the first psychiatric interpretation of suicide, describing it as the expression of severe depression.

During the 18th century, most suicides were attributed to mental illness. Against the opposition of the Church, there was increasing social pressure for the legalization of suicide. The philosopher David Hume (1711-1776) in his "Essay on Suicide" (1783) maintained that an individual must have the right to decide about his own death if pain, illness, shame or poverty make life unbearable (Retterstol, 1998). The most representative book about suicide written in this century was *Young Werther's Sufferings* (1774), by Johann Wolfgang von Goethe (1749-1832). This book illustrates the influence of sociocultural factors on suicide, since its romantic view of suicide triggered whole suicide epidemics.

The first studies on suicide from social, medical and epidemiological standpoints were carried out in the 19th century (Morselli [1852-1929]; Durkheim [1858-1917]). During the XXth century, the *westernalization* phenomenon seems to be associated with an increase in suicide behaviors. The great migrations that have been taking place may also influence suicidal behaviors. The influence of mass media on suicidal behavior may be important, particularly in children and adolescents. Regarding legislation, attempting suicide was a punishable offence in Britain until 1961 and in Ireland until 1993 (Retterstol, 1998).

Regarding other religions outside the Western sphere, monotheist religions generally regard suicide as a sin against God. Among them, Islam probably represents the most condemning attitude towards suicide. The Buddhist attitude towards suicide is generally negative, while Hinduism has a much more tolerant position. In countries like Japan (where religion is based on Shintoism and Buddhism) suicide has been a part of the national culture and traditions.

1.3.2. METHODS OF SUICIDE

M. Leira-San Martin

Suicide is a significant public health issue: the WHO estimates that suicide accounts for almost 2% of the deaths in the world (WHO, 2000). The epidemiological data vary from country to country, and several explanations have been considered for national and regional variations in suicidality rates: genetic and biological factors, psychopathological conditions and cultural and sociodemographical issues are some of the matters more thoroughly investigated to explain this variability across different geographical areas.

About the suicide phenomenon, Psychiatry has recently focussed research on clinical and genes issues, trying to determine whether specific phenotypes could be identified as prone to develop suicide behaviour. This kind of research tries to lead the clinicians and health authorities to preventive activities, in order to make morbidity and mortality associated to suicide decrease.

Some researchers have emphasized that from the perspective of suicide prevention, research into the methods of suicide seems to be particularly promising, as it has been shown repeatedly that restricting access to the prevailing method of suicide in a country will decrease suicide rates (Diekstra & Gulbinat, 1993; Gunnell & Frankel, 1994; Lewis et al., 1997) and that the lethality of the method used significantly correlated with the degree of intention to die (Beck et al., 1975; Beautrais, 2004; Rapelli & Botega, 2005). The study of the different methods of suicide has been a matter of interest for forensic science researchers and epidemiologists, besides mental health professionals.

Individuals in different countries choose different suicide methods (Farmer & Rohde, 1980). The availability of the method appears to strongly influence the method selection (Stone, 1999; Snyder, 1994; Ojima et al., 2004). An important question is whether restriction of the tools for suicide can reduce suicide rates: Gunnel et al. (2000) observed a decrease in suicide rates after detoxification of domestic gas, which is reduction in its carbon monoxide and lethality. Lester & Abe (1989) reported that requiring prescriptions for sedatives and hypnotics in Japan led to a decrease in their use for suicide, but did not lead to an increase in the use of other methods. On the other hand, Wintemute et al. (1999) conducted a cohort study and concluded that the purchase of a handgun is a substantial risk factor for suicide. Despite these findings, not all the investigations carried out about restricting the access to lethal substances/tools show the same positive effects in reducing the incidence of suicide behavior (Lester & Leenars, 1993; Rosengart et al., 2005).

In this chapter, we will try to reflect the relevance of the study of the methods of suicide, and its implications for clinical and preventive interventions in suicide treatment.

Classification

Methods of suicide can be classified with regard to diverse criteria:

- *Potential lethality of the method:* we could generally describe high lethality methods (i.e. use of firearms, hanging, jumping from high places) and low lethality methods (i.e. self-poisoning) considering the potential severity of the medical consequences of their use. Some of these methods can be more or less lethal according to the way they are used and to environmental circumstances. This means that lethality depends not only on the method itself, but also on the individual's intention to die. Individuals who choose high lethality methods tend to show more severe suicide intent, and severity of the attempt and lethality strongly correlate when the individual has accurate information of the medical consequences of the method chosen (Kumart et al., 2006). However, occasionally, people with less severe intent (low intention to die) may carry out highly lethal attempts (especially when they lack of information about the potential lethality of the method chosen, or when they commit highly impulsive attempts). Lethality of episodes involving firearms has been shown in study (Shenassa et al., 2003) to be 2.6 times higher than for suffocation and 8.0 times higher than for jumping/crash suicides.

- *Mechanism for inducing death:* methods of suicide have suffered from little variations through the years, despite technical advances that introduce slight differences in methodology. There are mainly three mechanisms for inducing death by suicide (Corbella, 2005).

  a) *Asphyxia*. People tend to choose a fast method, based in making breathing unable. This can be obtained by two ways: sudden and persistent constriction of the airway (hanging) or drowning into water (submersion) and obstructing the air exchange between blood and lungs.

  b) *Heavy trauma*. The individual uses a highly strong power to cause lethal lesions. There are three possible ways:
     - The energy emerges from the individual itself: this is the case of jumping from heights, when the distance to the ground is used to get enough acceleration to generate high energy in the impact.
     - An external source of energy is used. This is the case of car-crash suicides or railway suicides.
     - An external object with specific power to generate damage. This is the case of firearms or cutting/sharp objects.

  c) *Self-poisoning*. The individual uses the intense chemical changes induced by a substance to die. Nowadays, substances used for this purpose are predominantly medications, domestic products (caustics or gas) and pesticides in rural areas.

  d) *Other methods*. These methods are less frequent and specific from some geographical areas, as could be self-immolation (burning oneself), suicides using explosives or some ritual procedures (as Hara-kiri). A particular situation called "double suicide" is not exceptional, especially when the individual has made previous failed attempts. This is the case of people who uses two different methods at the same time, trying to raise the level of lethality of the attempt.

- *Determined vs non-determined methods:* determined (high-threshold) methods are those that involve more violent and painful procedures. From this perspective, it is supposed that an individual must cross a suffering threshold to choose this kind of method for suicide, which implies a "point of no return", and tend to be related to more severe attempts. In western countries, it is a well-known phenomenon that men more often choose determined methods (shooting, jumping from a high place), while women usually prefer low-threshold methods, where the chance of intervention by others and rescue is greater (for example, poisoning) (Bille-Brahe & Jesseng, 1994; Wiedemann & Weyerer, 1983).

The association between choosing a violent method of suicide and severe mental illness has been recognized.(Pounder, 1985; Cooper & Milroy, 1994) Violent methods, assessed with a higher level of lifetime aggression and a higher level of impulsivity, are often associated with lifetime substance abuse or dependence and psychotic disorders (Dumais et al., 2005).

- *The ICD 10 Classification:* In chapter XX of its annexe, the ICD 10 classification of mental and behavioural disorders considers a number of different methods of self-harm under the concept of `suicide and intentionally self-inflicted lesions.´ No stratification or further analysis is performed about different methods considered.

Suicide Attempters and Suicide Completers

It is widely accepted that the strongest predictor for committing suicide is the presence of a prior suicide attempt. Moreover, it is said that the risk of suicide is regarded as 50-fold for suicide attempters, compared with that of the general population (Suokas & Lonqvist, 2001). For every completed suicide, at least 10 times as many people make a non-fatal suicide attempt or deliberately harm themselves, often seriously enough to require some kind of medical assistance (Diekstra & Gulbinat, 1993)

Despite these data, most survivors of a suicide attempt remain still alive 5 years after the self-harm episode (Beautrais, 2003). Although lethality and suicidal intent are strongly correlated (Rapelli & Botega, 2005; Haw et al., 2003) when survivors of near-fatal self-harm were interviewed, `only´ two-thirds had suicidal thoughts during the preceding weeks (Douglas et al., 2004). The different rates of severity of the attempt, the motivation and reasons that underlie the attempt, the lethality of the method chosen and the medical consequences of the attempt are nuclear issues that lead to many researchers to consider that suicide attempters and suicide completers represent different populations, with different clinical profiles.

Suicide attempters may show many different motivations for self-harm, apart from the wish to die: these comprise demanding help from others, escaping from painful thoughts, relieving tension and others. Frequently, suicide attempt is preceded by interpersonal conflicts, especially in Western countries (Bancroft et al., 1976; Simon et al., 2001). All these reasons can explain the tendency of suicide attempters to choose a method of lower potential lethality than suicide completers, requiring fast availability and little planification/ preparatives for the execution of the suicidal act. The most frequently chosen methods in this group of patients are overdosing/self-poisoning, and cutting with sharp instruments (Nada-Raja et al., 2004). Self-poisoning in developed countries is estimated to explain approximately 3.0 suicides per 100,000 annually (from a total of 14.9 suicides per 100,000) (Baca-García et al., 2002). Self-poisoning has a low fatality rate (estimated between 1.2% and 11.4%) (Stone, 1999). Psychotropic medications accounted for more than 80% of cases of self-poisoning in an Australian study (Buckley et al., 1995). In rural areas, domestic toxic products (as pesticides) may be more frequently used than psychotropics because of availability, being these substances more lethal but with little premeditation and scarce knowledge about treatment options or lethality of the poison chosen (Eddlestone et al., 2006; Rapelli & Botega, 2005).

A recent Brazilian study (Rapelli & Botega, 2005) which analyzed clinical profiles of serious suicide attempters admitted to a university hospital in the city of Sao Paulo came to support the idea that, according to the severity of the intent (measured by the SIS score) and the lethality of the attempt (using the Likert Scale), three different groups of patients could be identified: a first group of patients characterized by self-poisoning with medication and low suicidal intent (mostly female), involved in highly impulsive and ambivalent suicide attempts; a second group of people (mostly males) who ingested pesticides and presented both moderate degrees of lethality and suicidal intent; and a third group of patients (predominantly males) who used more violent methods (firearms, hanging, cutting, being run over) and could be considered as `aborted´ suicides, showing the highest severity an lethality scores of all patients.

With respect to suicide completers, there is an interesting study carried out in Japan (Nishimura et al., 1999) that examined the changes in choice of method and the lethality score between the last attempted suicide (LAS) and completed suicide (CS) in 416 suicide victims in Kobe City. They found that suicidal victims tend to choose the same method as that of LAS at the time of CS. When they changed the method selected, they used a more lethal method to complete suicide. Among all methods, injury to themselves by sharp instruments was the most common method of LAS, while hanging was the most common method of CS. Interestingly, this study didn't show any significant differences in mean lethality scores by sex, although some preferences in the method selected could be described (more males chose hanging for CS, while more women chose drowning for CS).

Biological Issues

Genetics

Tryptophan hydroxylase (TPH) is the rate-limiting enzyme in the biosynthesis of serotonin (5-HT). The TPH gene was among the first candidate genes for association studies of suicidality. Two different TPH isoforms have been identified: TPH 1 (responsible for peripheral serotonin generation) and TPH 2 (considered as the brain-specific enzyme). A significant association of the TPH1 A779C polymorphism with a history of violent suicide attempts has emerged from several studies (Nielsen et al., 1994; Nielsen et al., 1998; Roy et al., 2001). However, contradictory results have been reported in a subsequent study (Mann et al., 1997). Owing to the discrepancy of the results together with the diagnostic heterogeneity with either committed suicide as clear-cut act or a history of suicidal attempts, the impact of the TPH1 gene on suicidal behaviour remains still ambiguous (Bondy et al., 2006). TPH2 gene seems to be a better candidate, but investigations in polymorphisms of this gene are relatively scarce, and no association with lethality or method of suicide has been yet reported, to our knowledge.

The serotonin transporters (5-HTT) gene has a common polymorphism, which results in either an S- (short) or L- (long) allele. The relation between the S-allele and violent suicide methods was underlined in a study by Courtet et al. (2003, 2004). In a study carried out by our group, Baca-García et al. (2002) found that S-allele females were overrepresented among non-lethal female suicide attempters. In contrast to these positive findings, a variety of studies did not observe an association of the 5-HTTLPR with suicidality, neither in post-mortem studies (Mann et al., 2000) nor in studies investigating DNA of suicide attempters (Rujescu et al., 2001; Geijer et al., 2000).

There is considerable evidence that the density of the 5-HT2A receptor is upregulated in parietal cortical regions of depressed suicide victims (Mann, 2003). A recent systematic review and meta-analysis of suicide association studies, enrolling suicide attempt or completion but not ideation, found no association with the 5-HT2A T102C variants (Anguelova et al., 2003).

The data with the MAO A gene, which was repeatedly and consistently associated with impulsive-aggressive personality traits, do not propose a direct relation to suicidal behaviour, but it might orient an act towards violence in subjects with other suicide risk factors (Courtet et al., 2005).

Concerning cathecol-o-methyltransferase (COMT) gene, it has been shown across different ethnic groups that schizophrenic patients with the Met allele had a higher propensity for violence (Kotler et al., 1999; Koen et al., 2004) but no convincing results are found showing an association between catecholamine-synthesizing and – metabolising enzymes or dopaminergic receptors and suicide.

Neurochemistry

Post-mortem brain analyses have given interesting data on the serotonergic, noradrenergic and dopaminergic neurotransmitter systems and the cellular morphology of suicide victims. Serotonergic abnormalities, which are related in a variety of psychopathological dimensions such as anxiety, depressed mood, impulsivity and aggression, are the focus of many investigations. In a seminal study, Asberg et al. (1976) suggested that a low cerebrospinal fluid (CSF) 5-HIAA concentration could be related to the incidence of violent suicidal acts. Other investigators have come to replicate these results, suggesting that low level of serotonin metabolites in CSF correlate with a history of highly lethal suicide attempts (Mann & Malone, 1997; Placidi et al., 2001; Sher et al., 2006). It has been reported that the more lethal the suicide attempt, the lower the CSF 5-HIAA and the more blunted the prolactin response to fenfluramine (Mann et al., 1995; 1997; Malone et al., 1996). The implication of other paths of neurotransmission in lethality of the suicidal behavior is more controversial, and results of research involving noradrenergic and dopaminergic systems are scarce.

Seasonality

In general, suicide frequencies peak in spring and early summer and are low in autumn and winter months (Massing & Argenmeyer, 1985). The recent growing research about the role of neurotransmitters in psychiatric disorders and in violent behaviour has deliberately improved the perspectives of biological explanations in seasonality of suicide (Preti & Miotto, 1998). On the other hand, sociological arguments help to explain that a higher level of social activity in spring and summer months leads to higher social tensions and thus to the seasonal peak in the second quarter of the year.

Anyway, seasonal patterns of suicide have been largely observed through different studies showing particular findings:

- The replication of suicide seasonalities in the Southern Hemisphere has shown similar, but inverse patterns compared with the Northern Hemisphere (Flisher et al., 1997).
- Apart from unimodal patterns also bimodal patterns have been found in some instances (for example in women's suicides (Yip et al., 2000).

- Divergences between urban and rural contexts have been largely confirmed, suicide seasonality being more pronounced in rural contexts (Micciolo et al., 1991).
- The amplitudes of suicide seasonality have obviously decreased in the recent decades (Yip et al., 2003).
- Recently, differences of suicide seasonality by suicide methods have regained some attention, and seasonality appears to be related particularly to violent suicide methods (Maes et al., 1993; Hakko et al., 1998).

Ajdacic-Gross et al. (2003) et al. carried out a study about seasonality in suicide and suicide methods in Switzerland: in their sample, hanging and firearms were the most common methods in completed suicides between 1969 and 1994, predominantly in males. Suicides due to hanging depicted unequivocal seasonal patterns, the highest frequencies found in April-June and the lowest in November-December. Drowning suicides also showed a distinct seasonality, but with particularities: the peak shifted to May, June and July. Jumping from high places also showed a seasonal fluctuation, while suicides due to firearms and cutting (both denoted as the most violent methods besides hanging) did not show any seasonality in general. Drowning and jumping from high places were mostly chosen by females in this sample.

Among violent suicides, hanging appears to exhibit seasonal patterns most clearly, while seasonality in suicide by drowning may be related to what sociologists have called opportunities (increasing its frequency in the swimming season). Availability of suicidal means without seasonal interferences is characteristic for suicides due to poisoning.

Another study shows seasonal variations in suicide in Lithuanian population, with hanging being the only method showing significant seasonal peaks (higher frequency in summer) and seasonal amplitude decreasing over time (Kalediene et al., 2006).

Psychopathological Correlates

Substance Use Disorders

The suicide rates are significantly higher among alcohol abusers (Rossow, 1996). In a recent study in Slovenia (Bilban & Skibin, 2005) it was found that only 25.4% of their sample (n=508) were sober by the time of committing suicide. Men were intoxicated in 45.3% of the suicide cases, while women in only 18.3%, differences being statistically significant. Suicide by firearms was almost exclusive of men (94.5%). Furthermore, only men suicide by electricity, jumping in front of vehicles, by fire and hanging. Women, on the other hand, frequently used drowning and jumping from heights. Alcohol may play a role in suicide by making easier for an inhibited individual to commit a violent act.

Overdosing is the most frequent method of suicide in drug dependent individuals, though it may be difficult to differentiate accidental from suicidal overdoses in fatal cases.

Schizophrenia

Individuals with schizophrenia are at a high risk for suicidal behavior. 10-13% of individuals with schizophrenia commit suicide, and 20-40% attempt suicide (Drake et al., 1984). In a sample of schizophrenic and schizoaffective individuals (Harvaky-Friedman et al.,

1999), 52% of those who had attempted suicide made moderate to extreme lethality attempts. For the most severe attempts, suicidal behavior included overdosing (42%), slitting one's wrists (16%), jumping (8%) or hanging (6%). Suicide attempts were serious, and compared with other groups without schizophrenia, the rate of suicide attempts by overdose was relatively low, and the rate of more lethal methods was higher. Risk is consistently highest during the early phases of the illness, with two thirds of suicides occurring during the first 5 years after diagnosis (Harris & Barraclough, 1997).

Affective Disorders

Major depression is the psychiatric disorder most frequently associated with suicide (Henriksson et al., 1993). Melancholia at baseline is associated with more serious past suicide attempts and with the probability of future attempts. A higher level of cognitive impairment in this group has been suggested as an explanation (diminishing cognitive flexibility and influencing decision-making) (Grunebaum et al., 2004).

In a sample of bipolar patients, Michaelis et al. (2003) could find two different profiles of suicide attempters: bipolar patients who made and survived a single suicide attempt (with high seriousness of suicidal intent, resembling "failed completers") who showed mixed states less frequently by the time of the attempt, and bipolar patients who made multiple suicide attempts. They found no other clinical differences between the two groups, thus leading us to consider not only clinical or diagnostic issues to evaluate risk of suicidality.

An Italian study (Raja & Azzoni, 2004) comparing lethality among unipolar and bipolar patients (n=80) found bipolar cases to be over-represented in the high lethality risk group. They found no association between lethality and the intensity of anxiety/depressive symptoms. As in general population, men used more violent methods.

Borderline Personality Disorder

Suicide attempts by patients with Borderline Personality Disorder (BPD) are widely characterized as "communicative gestures" or "ambivalent" attempts, yet 10% die by suicide, making BPD one of the most lethal of psychiatric disorders (Gunderson & Ridolfi, 2001). Suicidal ideation and attempt behaviour precede completion by years, becoming a chronic and habitual response to adverse life events for these patients. Impulsivity, aggression and affective instability are prominent personality traits related to temperament in BPD. These personality traits have been associated with high-frequency, low-lethality suicide attempts independent of diagnostic context. However, the relationship of these traits to medical lethality and suicide completion in BPD remains ill-defined (Soloff et al., 2000).

In a study about high-lethality status in patients with BPD, the authors conclude that a lethal outcome depends on the synergy of multiple risk factors not directly related with diagnosis, as could be older age, socioeconomical poorer status, comorbid depression or antisocial personality disorder and longer history of treatment (Soloff et al., 2005).

Geographic and Cross-cultural Differences

In Europe, Goldney (2002) reviewed suicide from the global perspective, and showed high rates in the Baltic States and countries of the Russian Federation, and low rates in some

Mediterranean countries. Throughout the last decade of the 20th Century, Lithuania had the highest suicide rates in Europe among both men and women aged 25-64 years. A recent study (Tamosiunas et al., 2006) describes the trends in suicide deaths in urban population in Lithuania by gender, dates and suicide method over the period 1984-2003. The frequency of death by suicide among males was 48% higher in 1994-2003 than in 1984-1993. The corresponding increase among females was 28%. The most common methods of suicide among men were hanging, strangulation and suffocation (87.4% among all suicide deaths). The proportions of hanging, strangulation and suffocation in males increased by 6.9%, compared to a 24.2% increase in deaths from handgun, rifle and shotgun firearm discharges and a 216.7% increase in deaths from poisoning with solvents, gases, pesticides and vapours. Among females, the most common methods of suicide were hanging, strangulation and suffocation (68.3% of all suicide deaths). The proportion of hanging deaths among females increased during the time period examined, whereas the proportion of poisonings with solid or liquid substances decreased. With regards to the Balcans, a paper (Bosnar et al., 2004) which analysed the influence of the war period (1991-1995) in suicidality rates and methods compared to pre-war and post-war periods showed that mortality rates from suicide raised during the war period, with a peak in the use of firearms for committing suicide, while hanging was the most frequently used method all through the pre-, post- and war periods. Levels of alcohol intoxication were significantly higher in suicide victims during the war period with respect to the other periods.

Cyprus has the lowest suicide mortality in Europe, though this could be partially due to underreporting. In this population, most favoured means by males were poisoning (by solids or liquids), firearms and hanging. In females, they were jumping from high places, poisoning (by solids or liquids) and hanging (Zacharakis et al., 2004). In Southern Italy (Pavia et al., 2005), hanging/suffocation (44.1%) and jumping from high places (23.2%) were also the most frequently used methods of suicide, showing lower global suicidality rates compared with national trends.

In rural areas, some particular issues with regard to methods of suicide can be seen. In a Scottish study (Stark et al., 2006) carried out with a farming population, deaths using firearms were overrepresented (29% of farming deaths compared with 3.6% in the general male population). Firearms availability among this population seems a reliable explanation for these figures. In other rural settings, the difficulty in the access to firearms make other more available methods (i.e. pesticides) the most commonly employed for committing suicide (Eddleston et al., 2006; Kumar et al., 2006).

An interesting comparative study (Ojima et al., 2004) has focused on different methods of suicide in Japanese vs The United States populations, taking into account different races all along the USA and clarifying differences between genders and age groups. The rates in Japan were higher than in the United States in most of the age groups for both genders. The rates for males were about three times higher than females within Japan, and about four times higher within the United States. The top two methods in Japan were hanging (70.4% for males and 60.0% for females) and jumping from a high place. Gases were the third among males, and drowning was the third among females. The most common method was firearms among both genders in the United States. The second most common method was hanging among males and drugs among females, and the third was drugs among males and hanging among females. For each race in the United States, the three most common were the same between both genders for Whites, Blacks, Hispanics and male Natives. For Asians, the most common method was hanging, at about half between both genders, and the second was firearms. The authors explain the higher rates of suicide in Japan using cultural explanations, since that Japanese tend to think that an individual has the right to die (conceiving suicide as a "normal" behaviour) and have less religious considerations regarding suicide. The use of firearms in US in a higher proportion compared with Japan may be a question of availability. It is remarkable that Asian population in the US tended to use similar methods to Japanese (hanging, jumping from high places) rather than to Americans. Nevertheless, younger Asian population used firearms for suicide in a higher proportion than the older ones.

There is a recently increasing interest in knowing the impact of the media in suicide behaviours. In developed societies, where there is a widespread access to information in different ways (newspapers, television and the internet) people can get information about suicide through different sources. Non-scientific media have put into the light some recent ways of cluster or "agreed" suicides, characteristically in adolescent and younger populations, who use the internet to communicate each other. We need more time and scientific analysis to determine if this kind of behaviour may be emerging in developed countries. A recent study (Yip et al., 2006) analysing the impact of the suicide of a celebrity in Hong Kong showed that there was a significant increase in suicides following the celebrity death, many of the victims dying by jumping (in a similar way to the celebrity). The death of this pop singer resulted in extensive and often dramatic media coverage.

Table 9. Leading causes of death for the total population in 2003: United States

Rank	Cause of death	Number of deaths	Percent of total deaths
1	Diseases of heart	685,089	28.0
2	Malignant neoplasms	556,902	22.7
3	Cerebrovascular diseases	157,689	6.4
4	Chronic lower respiratory diseases	126,382	5.2
5	Accidents (unintentional)	109,227	4.5
6	Diabetes melitus	74,219	3.0
7	Influenza and pneumonia	65,163	2.7
8	Alzheimer's disease	63,457	2.6
9	Nephritis, nephrotic synd, nephrosis	42,453	1.7
10	Septicemia	34,069	1.4
11	Intentional self –harm (suicide)	31,484	1.3
12	Chronic liver disease and cirrhosis	27,503	1.1
13	Essential hypertension	21,940	0.9
14	Parkinson's disease	17,997	0.7
15	Assault (homicide)	17,732	0.7

Data from U.S. Department of Health And Human Services, 2006.

1.3.3. EPIDEMIOLOGY

L. Jimenez-Treviño

Introduction

Suicide is one of the leading death causes in the world, especially among young people. Suicide represented 1.4% of deaths around the world in year 2001. This indicates that more people are dying from suicide than in all of the several armed conflicts around the world and, in many places, about the same or more than those dying from traffic accidents. According to WHO estimates, in the year 2020, approximately 1.5 million people will die from suicide, and 10 to 20 times more people will attempt suicide worldwide (WHO, 2000). These figures represent one death every 20 seconds and one attempt every 1-2 seconds, on average. In year 1998, self-inflicted injuries represented 1.8% of the global burden of disease and are expected to increase to 2.4% in 2020 (Bertolote & Fleischmann, 2002). Suicide was the 11th leading cause of death in the U.S. in 2003 (NCHS, 2003).

Global Suicide Rates

The highest rates for both men and women are found in Europe, specially in countries from the former Soviet Union such as Latvia, Russia, Ukraine or Estonia, with rates over 50 suicides per 100,000 population. There is a second group of countries with suicide rates between 20/100,000 and 30/100,000 including the Scandinavian countries, island countries such as Japan or Cuba and the rural China (Table 10). On the other side, the lowest suicide rates (between 0/100,000 and 1/100,000) are found in countries that follow Islamic tradition such as Egypt, Iran, Jordan or Syria and Hispanic American countries such as Peru, Honduras, Dominican Republic or Guatemala.

Suicide by Gender and Age

Rates of suicide are not distributed equally throughout the general population. One important demographic marker of suicide risk is age. Suicide deaths represent a particular public health problem in young and elderly people. In all countries, suicide is now one of the three leading causes of death among people aged 15-34 years (WHO, 2000). Until recently, suicide was predominating among the elderly, but now suicide figures are higher in younger people in both absolute and relative terms, in a third of all countries. Also, the age group in which most suicides are currently completed is 35-44 years for both men and women (Bertolote & Fleischmann, 2002).

Table 10. Age-adjusted suicide rates by country/100,000 people/year

Country	Year	Suicide rate per 100,000 population	
		Male	Female
America			
Argentina	1996	9.9	3.0
Brasil	1995	6.6	1.8
Canada	2001	18.7	5.2
Colombia	1994	5.5	1.5
Cuba	1996	24.5	12.0
Mexico	1995	5.4	1.0
Paraguay	1994	3.4	1.2
U.S.A.	2001	17.6	4.1
Uruguay	1990	16.6	4.2
Venezuela	1994	8.3	1.9
Europe			
Austria	2003	27.1	9.3
Belgium	1997	31.2	11.4
Denmark	2000	20.2	7.2
Estonia	2002	47.7	9.8
Finland	2003	31.9	9.8
France	2001	26.6	9.1
Germany	2001	20.4	7.0
Italy	2001	11.1	3.3
Lithuania	2003	74.3	13.9
Norway	2002	16.1	5.8
Portugal	2002	18.9	4.9
Russia	2002	69.3	11.9
Spain	2002	12.6	3.9
Sweden	2001	18.9	8.1
Ukraine	2002	46.7	8.4
United Kingdom	2002	10.8	3.1
Rest of the world			
Australia	2001	20.1	5.3
China (rural)	1999	20.4	24.7
China (urban)	1999	6.7	6.6
India	1998	12.2	9.1
Iran	1991	0.3	0.1
Israel	2000	9.9	2.7
Japan	2002	35.2	12.8
New Zeland	2000	19.8	4.2
Republic of Korea	2002	24.7	11.2
Singapore	2002	11.4	7.6
Syria	1985	0.2	0.0
Thailand	2002	12.0	3.8
Zimbabwe	1990	10.6	5.2

Data from WHO, 2007.

There is a clear tendency for suicide rates to increase with age (see Table 11). Higher rates of suicide in elderly people are more relevant in the most highly developed countries due to population ageing. In fact, most countries from Europe and North America have suicide rates over 30/100.000/year in the >75 age group. Although suicide rates are generally higher among older people, the absolute number of cases recorded is actually higher among those under 45 years of age than among those over 45 years, given demographic distributions (NCHS, 2003).

Males are four times more likely to die by suicide than females on average. The ratio of the suicide rate among males to that among females ranges from 1.0:1 to 10.4:1. The predominance of suicide in males is constant in every country and age group with the exception of rural areas of China. This ratio seems to be influenced, in part, by the cultural context. Generally speaking, the difference between the sexes in terms of suicide rates is narrower in Asian countries than elsewhere in the world (ratios vary from 3:1 in Europe and 4,1:1 in America to 1,3:1 in Asia). The often large differences in rates between countries and by sex show how important it is for each country to monitor its epidemiological trends to determine the population groups at greatest risk for suicide (NCHS, 2003). In relative terms, suicide was the 8th leading cause of death for males, and 19th leading cause of death for females in year 2000 (Krug et al., 2002).

Table 11. Suicide rates/100,000 people/year by gender and age group

Age Group	Male	Female
5-14 years	1.5	0.14
15-24 years	22.0	4.9
25-34 years	30.1	6.3
35-44 years	37.5	7.7
45-54 years	43.6	9.6
55-64 years	42.1	10.6
65-74 years	41.0	12.1
75 + years	50.0	15.8

Data from WHO, 2006.

Sociodemographic Factors

Culture, religion, race and ethnicity are also important factors in the epidemiology of suicide. Within countries, the prevalence of suicide among Caucasians is approximately twice that observed in other races, although an increasing rate among African Americans has recently been reported in the United States (Miniño et al., 2002). This pattern of higher prevalence among Caucasians has also been reported in South Africa and Zimbabwe (Moscicki, 1985). Exceptions to the generally higher rate among Caucasians are found in the former Soviet republics of Armenia, Azerbaijan and Georgia (Lester, 1998). Belonging to the same ethnic group seems to be associated with similar suicide rates, as in the interesting example of Estonia, Finland and Hungary, all of which have very high rates, even though Hungary is geographically quite distant from Estonia and Finland. Conversely, different ethnic groups – even if they live in the same place – may have very dissimilar rates of suicide. In Singapore, for instance, ethnic Chinese and Indians have much higher rates than ethnic Malays (Wasserman et al., 1998). Suicide rates are frequently higher in indigenous groups, for example in some indigenous groups in Australia (Yin, 1998), China (Province of Taiwan) (Hunter, 1991) and North America (Cheng & Hsu, 1992).

A comparison of suicide rates according to the prevalent religious predomination in countries reflects a remarkable difference between countries of Islam, where committing suicide is most strictly forbidden, and countries of any other prevailing religion. In Muslim countries the total suicide rate is close to zero (0.0-0.3 per 100,000 population), while in Hindu and Christian countries the total suicide rate is around 10 per 100,000 (9.1-12.6 per 100,000 population), and in Buddhist countries the total suicide rate is distinctly higher at 17.9 per 100,000 population. Highest suicide rates are found among atheist countries (Bertolote & Fleischmann, 2002).

Higher levels of social and national cohesion reduce suicide rates. Suicide levels are highest among the retired, unemployed, divorced, the childless, urbanites, empty nesters, and other people who live alone. Suicide rates also rise during times of economic uncertainty (although poverty is not a direct cause). Epidemiological studies generally show a relationship between suicide or suicidal behaviors and socio-economic disadvantage, including limited educational achievement, homelessness, unemployment, economic dependence and contact with the police or justice system (García Resa et al., 2002).

Suicide Methods

The method used to commit suicide varies and is greatly influenced by availability, perceived effectiveness and final bodily state.

In the United States, guns are used in approximately two-thirds of all suicides (NIMR, 2000) while in other parts of the world, hanging is more common (see Figure 1). In China, intoxication by pesticides is the most common method (Yip, 2001).

In the past two decades, in some countries such as Australia, there has been a remarkable increase in hanging as a suicide method, especially among younger people, accompanied by a corresponding decrease in the use of firearms (De Leo et al., 1999).

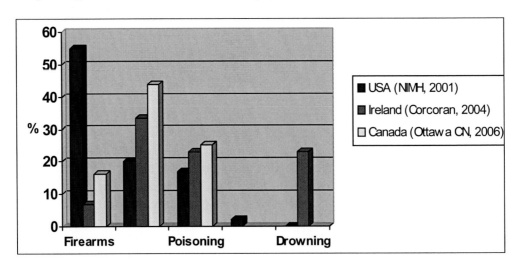

Figure 1. Methods of suicide in different countries.

In general, elderly people tend to adopt methods involving less physical strength, such as drowning or jumping from heights; this has been recorded particularly in Hong Kong SAR, China, and Singapore (Yip et al., 1998). Nearly in every country, women tend to adopt non-violent methods (for example, psychotropic overdose) both in fatal and in non-fatal suicide attempts (Schmidtke et al., 1996).

Apart from age and sex, the choice of method in suicide may be influenced by other factors such as traditions (the traditional practice of self disembowelment with a sword – *hara kiri* - continues to occur in Japan) or imitation, especially among young people and in relation to the death of a celebrity (Schmidtke & Haffner, 1998), or due to heavy media coverage of an specific method of suicide (for example, the epidemic Internet-connected suicide pacts in Japan during year 2005 with more than 100 victims).

Suicide Trends

Despite the advances in psychiatric treatments and suicide prevention, suicide rates have experimented a slight to moderate increase in the last 50 years (see Figure 2). Suicide rates have increased by 60% worldwide. There has been an increase of approximately 49% for suicide rates in males and 33% for suicide rates in females between 1950 and 1995.

Suicide rates in the U.S. can best be characterized as mostly stable over time. Since 1990, rates have ranged between 12.4 and 10.7 per 100,000. Suicide rates have been mostly stable also in Europe (table 4), with a moderate decrease in countries such as Denmark and United Kingdom where suicide prevention programs have been implemented.

Suicide rates among young people have increased in the last 50 years to such an extent that the age distribution of cases of suicide has been inverted, a phenomenon that appears to exist in all continents and is not correlated to levels of industrialization or wealth. While in year 1950, most of suicides were committed by people over 45 years old, in year 2000 most of suicides were committed by people under 45 year old, being now the group at highest risk of suicide in a third of countries, in both developed and developing countries (Bertolote & Fleischmann, 2002).

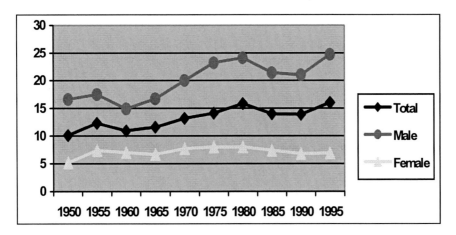

Figure 2. Evolution of global suicide rates by gender 1950-1995.

Table 12. Evolution of suicide rates in Europe (per 100,000 population/year)

	Year 1955	Year 1970	Year 1985	Year 1999/00
Austria	23.4	24.2	27.7	19.6
Belgium	13.6	16.5	23.1	19.8
Denmark	23.3	21.5	27.9	14.4
Finland	20.0	21.3	24.6	22.5
France	15.9	15.4	22.5	17.5
Greece	3.8	3.2	4.0	3.6
Ireland	2.3	1.8	7.8	11.3
Italy	6.6	5.8	8.3	7.1
Norway	7.5	8.4	14.1	13.1
Poland	5.7	11.2	13.3	15.1
Portugal	9.2	7.5	9.7	5.1
Spain	5.4	4.2	6.5	8.1
Switzerland	21.6	18.6	25.0	18.1
United Kingdom	10.7	7.9	9.0	7.5

Suicide Attempts

Suicide attempts also represent a major public health problem due to their incidence (between 8 and 25 times more frequent than completed suicide), morbidity (438.00 people visited the emergency department for self-inflicted injury in 2003 in the U.S. and Europe reports about 700,000 suicide attempts per year) and mortality (10% of the suicide attempters will finally commit suicide and 1%-2% will commit suicide in the first year folllowing the attempt). Suicide risk in suicide attempters is 100 times higher than in general population (Hawton & Fagg, 1988). Opposite to completed suicide, more women than men report a history of attempted suicide, with a gender ratio of 3:1 (Weissman et al., 1999).

Available figures show (both relative to their population size and in absolute numbers) that nonfatal suicidal behaviour is more prevalent among younger people than among older people. The ratio of fatal to non-fatal suicidal behaviour in those over the age of 65 years is usually estimated to be of the order of 1:2–3, while in young people under 25 years the ratio may reach 1:100–200 (McIntosh, 1994; McIntire & Angle, 1981).

Generally, the methods used for suicide attempts are most often methods of low lethality, specially self-poisoning with psychotropics (Figure 3).

Relatively few countries have reliable data on nonfatal suicidal behaviour, the main reason lying in the difficulty of collecting information. The European Region of WHO has been conducting one of the largest collaborative projects in the field of suicidological research for the last 15 years, the WHO/EURO Multi-Centre Study on suicidal Behaviour (Schmidtke et al., 2004). Data has been collected in up to 45 European cities and has provided a wealth of knowledge on the epidemiology, demography, clinical aspects, associated factorsand methods employed in a vast number of cases of suicide attempts (Table 13 shows data from this study).

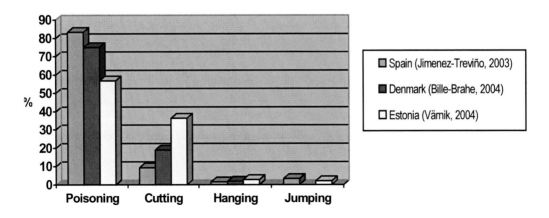

Figure 3. Methods of suicide attempts in different countries.

Table 13. Suicide Attempts/100.000 people/year

Country	Year	Male	Female
Austria	1998	136	153
Denmark	1999	108	151
Finland	1997	378	294
France	1997	277	558
Germany	1999	91	116
Italy	1997	80	79
Netherlands	1992	78	134
Spain	1991	20	62
United Kingdom	1999	287	428
Sweden	1998	82	181
Switzerland	1998	74	145

Data from WHO-EURO, 2004.

1.3.4. RISK FACTORS

A. Ceverino Dominguez, E. Baca-García,
M. M. Pérez-Rodriguez, C. Díaz-Sastre and H. Blasco-Fontecilla

Introduction

There is not a single reason to explain why some people try to kill themselves. Suicide is a complex phenomenom that ranges between suicidal ideation to completed suicide. It is influenced by psychosocial, sociodemographic, biological, genetic, and psychiatric factors. Blumenthal (1986) stressed 5 areas of vulnerability to suicide (psychosocial factors, biological factors, personality, psychiatric disorders, and familial/genetic factors). Similarly, other authors considered four areas: live events, psychiatric disorders, biological factors, and familial factors.

Psychosocial Factors

Adam (1990) considered that both *macrosocial* (i.e. civil state) and *microsocial factors* (related to specific vulnerable areas of an individual, like particular live events) could influence in suicidal behavior as predisposing or precipitants factors.

Age

In the Western industrialized countries, a high correlation is found between age and risk of suicide (Geijo & Franco, 1997; López García et al, 1993) in both men and women (Ros Montalbán, 1997; La Vecchia et al., 1994). Suicide behavior is very uncommon before puberty –no suicides are found before the age of 5, and children become familiarized with death between 6 to 14 years old-, but it increases in adolescents and young adults, being the highest risk in people aged 65 or older, particularly men older than 75 years old (Geijo & Franco, 1997; López-García et al., 1993). Garrison (1989) found a rate of 3% in primary school, 11% in Highschool, and 15-18% in superior academic levels. Klerman et al. (1987) found an increase of 150% of deaths by suicide between 1960 to 1980, mainly due to people aged between 18 to 30 years old. However, previous data from the U.S. and Holland demonstrates that high rate of suicide was also found at the beginning of XX century (López García et al, 1993). Suicide attempts are more frequent among women aged between 15 to 24, and men aged between 25 to 34 (Schmidtke et al., 1996). To sum up, although the risk of completed suicide is higher with age, the relative importance of suicide is higher in young populations, and suicide attempts are more frequent among young women (López García et al., 1993; Ros Montalbán, 1997).

The sharp increase in those aged 55 or over may have to do with some factors like fear to death, disease or pain, retiring, death of partner, medical illness, alcohol, impotence, dependence, and loneliness, among others. Frierson (1991) analysed the characteristics of 95 suicide attempts in a population aged 60 to 90 years old, and stressed that, they were more frequently men, with medical illness, living alone, antecedents of mental disorders, used more lethal methods, and were not impulsive.

Gender and Sexual Orientation

A constant finding in suicide research is that of women attempting suicide more than men, while men have higher rates of completed suicides in different cultures and societies (Alexander & Peterson, 2001; Allebeck et al, 1988; Diekstra, 1993; Giner et al., 1974; La Vecchia et al., 1994; Lester, 1969; López García et al., 1993; Pirkola et al., 1999; Rich et al, 1988; Schmidtke et al., 1996). Men complete suicide 2 to 4 times more frequently than women, while the same applies for women with regard to attempting suicide (Abramowitz et al, 1982; Earsl, 1989; Geijo & Franco, 1997; Lejoyeux et al., 1994; Mann et al, 2000; Mirón et al, 1997; Sáiz & Montejo, 1976; Vallejo Ruiloba, 1998; Chinchilla Moreno, 1997). It is calculated that in the U.S. a women attempts suicide every 78 seconds, and every 90 minutes a woman dies by suicide.

This gender difference was not always the same. In the U.S., the ratio of suicide men/women between 1930 to 1971 was 2,5:1, increasing to since 1971 to the current ratio 4:1 reached in the nineties (4,4:1 in 1996) (AFSP, 1998). Some cultural exceptions are found (i.e. women in China or those Americans of Chinese origin but older than 45 have comparable rates of suicide than men). In the U.S. this ratio is higher in those aged 85 or over (14:1) but the higher increase is found in those aged between 15 to 24 (the current ratio is 5,9:1, compared to the 0,7:1 ratio found at the beginning of the 20th century).

With regard to *lethality* of the methods, some differences exist between men and women and this may explain the differences previously reported. Women usually try to suicide by non-lethal methods – i.e. drug overdose- (Rich et al, 1988), and they try to avoid damaging the body, particularly the head, while men tend to use violent methods (Lester, 1969) – i.e. weapons, hanging-. However, in a recent report in the U.S., the most commonly used method of suicide was weapons (approximately 60% of suicides) in both males and females (Sleet et al, 1998). Some of the given reasons to explain these differences are social (women do have less experience with weapons), availability, psychological (women prefer non-painful methods), and type of suicide attempt. Other plausible explanations are that women have a higher serotonin activity (Mann, 1988) or artefactual findings, hormonal, genes, etc. (Leal & Crespo, 1999).

On the other hand, homosexuals do have 2 to 7 times a greater risk of suicide than general population. There is a great controversy in the U.S. with the study by Gibson (1986) who reported that suicide among homosexual people accounted for 30% of annual deaths in the youth, and that this is the principal cause of death among gays, lesbian, bisexuals and transsexuals. Some of the reasons given to explain this are identity disturbance, hostile environments, isolation, alcoholism, antecedents of family violence, HIV, etc. (López García et al, 1993). However, other authors point out that the majority of studies lack reliability. Moreover, the real rate of homosexuality is difficult to calculate, as some people are reticent to give such information (Moscicki, 1997).

Race

In the U.S., more than 70% of completed suicides are of white people, and the highest rates of suicide are found among white people aged 85 or over. Mann (1995) said that among the 30.906 reported suicides in the U.S., 24.724 were men and 22.448 of white race. However, black men have a higher risk than white women do. Oquendo et al. (2000) also found that white men were the ones with the highest rate of completed suicide, while men from Puerto Rico (the ones with the greater prevalence of depression in this study) and Mexico seemed to be relatively protected of suicide when depression was taken into account. They concluded that Hispanic people in the U.S. had a lower risk of suicide, and suggested that this may be explained by sociocultural differences, something similar to the *familism* (close family ties, religious support, etc.) reported by Hope & Martin (1986).

On the other hand, some ethnic minorities, like Native American Indians or Eskimos have high rates of suicide, and in the last decades, an increase of the risk of suicide is found among young black people in the U.S., but not in comparable Hispanic youth populations (López García et al, 1993).

Different authors try to explain these differences by socioeconomic factors and life styles. Neeleman et al. (1996) carried out a study in Camberwell, a London district where several different ethnic groups live altogether. They found that differences on suicide can be explained by differences in the rate of people being jobless.

Urban/Rural Area

A greater rate of suicide is found in the urban media (Giner & Leal, 1982; Gutierrez García, 1998; Lejoeux et al., 1994), although the lethality of methods is lower (López García et al, 1993). The last authors stressed that the rate of death people with not a clear cause are much more elevated in the urban media, suggesting that suicide may be one of the possible explanations.

Social Class, Job Situation, Profession

It is difficult to correctly assess the influence of *social class* in suicide due to confounding factors. In 1971, Lester found a positive relationship between completed suicide and quality of life, and a negative relationship between the quality of life and suicide attempts (López García et al, 1993). Similarly, Tejedor & Sarró (1997) reported a higher frequency of completed suicide in upper classes, and a higher rate of suicide attempts among the lower classes. Other authors have also found that among suicide attempters, people with lower incomes predominate (Hawton et al., 1999).

Regarding the *job situation*, there is a statistical association between unemployment and suicide behavior. People unemployed are at a greater risk of suicide behavior when compared to general population (Hawton et al., 1999; Chastang et al, 1998; Schmidtke et al., 1996). The longer the period of unemployment, the greater the risk (López García et al., 1993; Morton, 1993; Platt, 1986). Chastang et al. (1999) reported that the risk of suicide in men after a year of being unemployed was two to 5 times greater, and similar results were found in women. Paradoxically, high rates of suicide are found in countries with the lowest rates of unemployment – i.e. Switzerland- (López García et al, 1993), and unemployment *per se* is not considered a vital precipitant of suicide (Adam, 1990). In a study carried out in unemployed suicide attempters, Shapiro et al. (1984) found that only 4% considered that unemployment was directly related to their suicide attempt (Shapiro et al., 1984). Several confounding factors can influence the relationship between suicide behavior and unemployment, like economic crisis or mental disorders (Chastang et al., 1999; López García et al., 1993). The results of the different studies carried out in the last decades are contradictory, so that not a clear conclusion can be drawn with regard to the influence of unemployment in suicide behavior (Adam, 1990; Velamoor & Cernovsky, 1990; Pritchard, 1990; Lester & Yang, 1991).

Another issue is that of women joining into the labour market, which has been related to an increase in the rates of suicide in women (Diekstra, 1990; Lester & Yang, 1991). Moreover, job instability is more associated with suicidal behavior in men than women due to the social importance of work on them (Chastang et al., 1999).

Regarding the different professions, some authors have claimed that doctors, particularly women, might have an increased risk of suicide (López García et al, 1993). De la Cruz et al. (1988) reviewed this topic in deep. They concluded that among doctors, only women have an increased risk of suicidal behavior when compared to general population, that interns of psychiatry had similar rates to the general population and other interns, and finally, that psychiatrist, surgeons and dentists, among others, have an increased risk of suicide behavior. Some authors do consider that this data cannot be taken into account due to confounding factors. Thus, Holmes & Rich (1990) said that the rate of suicide among men doctors in the U.S. is greater than the rate of the general population, but similar to the rate of white men older than 25 years old, group of people were the majority of doctors are included. However, they also said that the rate of women doctors was very similar to the one of men, and thus, greater than expected for white women aged 25 or over. In a recent study focused on the prevalence of suicide behavior among mental health workers it was concluded that there are no differences among the different professional categories, but as a group, the mental health workers have an increased life prevalence of suicide behavior than the general population (Ramberg & Wasserman, 2000). Lawyers and pharmacist are also reported to have an increased risk of suicide (Holmes & Rich, 1990). On the other hand, politicians and people related to religion were at a lowest risk. In the U.S., the marines have an increased risk of suicide but this could be due to their lower age and poor social nets.

Civil Status

Durkheim (1982) stressed the protective role of the family. López-García et al (1993) said that the risk was the double in singles when compared to married people. Other studies confirm this result, independently of gender and age. Suicide is more frequent in those divorced or widowed (Geijo & Franco, 1997; López García et al., 1993; Seguí Montesinos, 1989). Those who are married and have children are the less likely to suicide (Lejoyeux et al., 1994). López-García et al. (1993) thought that the risk for women was greater if widowed, while in men both separation and divorce posed them to a greater risk of suicide. The risk of suicide is particularly high – especially in men- in the first year after the death of their partner (López García et al, 1993).

It must be taken into account that others influence this variable, like gender or age. Thus, while marriage is usually considered a protective factor of suicide, in the youth might be a stressor. Thus, those who are married and attempt suicide are usually young adults or old depressed women, being conjugal problems common precipitants of suicide behavior (López García et al, 1993).

Religion

Durkheim (1982) said that religion was a protective factor of suicide. Some authors are of the opinion that the loss of religious values is the reason for the increase of suicide rates observed between 1960 to 1980 (López García et al., 1993). Catholics are reported to have a lower rate of suicide than Jews, and those a lower rate than Protestants (Geijo & Franco, 1997). Stack (1992) also found a lower rate of suicide among Catholics, but this may be influenced by a lower notification among Catholics due to the stigma associated to suicide. Stack (1992) said that what really protect against suicide was the existence of religious thoughts.

Social Isolation and Emigration

It has been postulated as the variable that mediates the relationship between other psychosocial factors and suicidal behavior (Giner & Leal, 1982; López García et al., 1993). Several retrospective studies demonstrate the strong link between social isolation and completed suicide (Lejoyeux et al., 1994). The presence of children at care is a protective factor, particularly in women (Hoyer & Lund, 1993; Axelsson & Lagerkvist-Briggs, 1992; Hoyer & Lund, 1993; Malone et al., 1993). Moreover, the presence of an extended family is also protective. Some authors (Hoppe & Martin, 1986) tried to explain the lower rates of suicide among the U.S. residents coming from Mexico are due to *familism*.

Emigration, due to their inner social isolation and uprooting, is associated with an increased risk of suicide (Geijo & Franco, 1997; Chandrasena et al., 1991; Ferrada et al., 1995), but the risk is lower when all the family members emigrate (López García et al, 1993). This back the theory of social integration by Durkheim (1982).

Stress and Recent Life Events (RLE)

There is an elevated incidence of stressful recent life events in the previous months of a suicide or suicide attempt (Adam, 1990; Yufit & Bongar, 1992). Adam (1990) found that they were 4 times more frequent in suicide attempters than in the control group. Men suicide attempters seem to have more RLE than women (Heikkinen et al., 1992). RLE have also been related to suicide ideation (Garrison et al., 1991). It is generally accepted that the stress needed to precipitate a suicide attempt is the sum of cumulative RLE. What is not really know is the mechanism through which RLE may exert its action (Yufit & Bongar, 1992).

Family discord and job problems are reported as risk factor for suicide both in men and women (Heikkinen et al., 1994). With regard to age, the most important RLE in young people are interpersonal conflicts, personal loses, economic problems, separation and legal conflicts. In old people, medical problems, social isolation and retirement are reported as precipitants of suicide behavior (Frierson, 1991).

One of the most pernicious RLE is that of sexual abuse in the infancy. They younger the children when abused, the more suicide attempts will have when adult (Boudewyn & Liem, 1995). Physical abuse has been related to suicidal ideation in both male and female adolescents (Straus & Kantor, 1994). In a study, those adolescent who completed suicide had a frequency of childhood abuse 6 times greater than non-abused children (Deykin et al., 1985).

Social and Economic Crisis

The risk of suicide is greater during economic crises (López García et al, 1993). During times of economic stability, the contrary also applies (Wasserman, 1992). Other studies have found a negative correlation between suicide and economic and industrial activity (Goto et al, 1994).

Social and values crisis are also related to suicide, but some confounding factors may have something to do. Social disorganization leads to individual disorganization, the latter making more difficult people to overcome critical situations (Uña Suárez, 1985). The peak of youth suicides in the U.S. was in 1910, at the same time of a great cultural and political disorganization (Diekstra, 1990; Diekstra & Garnefski, 1995).

War, Military Service and Political Regime

Suicide rates are lower during Wars – i.e. both World Wars and the Spanish Civil War- including both neutral and non-neutral countries (López García et al., 1993; Somasundaram & Rajadurai, 1995). This might be due to an increased social cohesion during war (Durkheim,

1982), to the well-known decrease of suicide when homicide rates increase and *vice versa* (Uña Suárez, 1985), or just to confounding factors as the decrease of unemployment rate during War (Lester & Yang, 1991). Moreover, Vietam War veterans have also an increased suicidal risk. This might be explained by the high rates of post-traumatic-stress-disorder (Bullman et al., 1991; Hendin & Haas, 1991).

Some authors are of the opinion that in peaceful time *military service* should note be considered a stressful life event (López García et al, 1993). Those who attempt suicide during military service have conflicts before and during the military service, and it is frequently found a history of familial suicide behavior, and personal history of psychiatric disorders and violence.

Currently, it is not probable that a specific political regime may influence the rate of suicide. Indeed, no differences are found between countries under different political systems while huge differences on suicide's rates are found in *a priori* culturally similar countries. This is the case of Hungary, a country with a well-known burden of suicide, independently of political regimens. However, a sharp increase of both suicide and homicide rates was detected in the "new-born" countries formed after the falling of the Soviet Union in 1991 (Lester, 1998). A curiosity is that in the U.S. in the period from 1940 to 1972 was detected that the rate of suicide and accidents was lower during the years of presidential elections (López García et al, 1993).

Prisons and Hospitals

Going to *jail* is a stressful life event that may precipitate suicidal behavior. This might be secondary to the inner characteristics of the new situation and with the high rate of mental disorders – particularly personality disorders- among prisoners (Bonner, 1992). It is calculated that suicide is three times more frequent in prisoners than in the general population (Geijo & Franco, 1997). In the U.S., suicide is the first cause of death among prisoners, and the rate is 9 times that of the general population. The risk is particularly high in the first 24 hours. The profile is of a young white man without partner who is at first time at jail and with antecedents of drug or alcohol use problems (Geijo & Franco, 1997).

With regard to *hospitals*, suicides can be precipitated by the diagnosis of a poor prognosis disease, terminal phase of a chronic disease, etc. (López García et al, 1993; Hackett & Stern, 1994; Tejedor & Sarró, 1997), and Central Nervous System (CNS) diseases – i.e. Huntington disease, epilepsy or multiple sclerosis- and HIV (Cote et al., 1992; Henderson & Ord, 1997; Lipe et al., 1993; Schoenfeld et al., 1984; Stenager et al. 1992). Mirón et al. (1997) stressed the role of physical suffering, more even than psychopathology. The risk of suicide of neurological patients is nearly twice that of the general population, and the risk is particularly high in the first 5 years after the diagnosis of the disease (Stenager et al., 1992). The risk of suicide in those diagnosed of Huntington disease is 4 to 8 times the one of the general population (Lipe et al., 1993; Schoenfeld et al., 1984), particularly if depressed and without dementia (Kraus, 1975). Nearly half of the patients diagnosed of multiple sclerosis have depression during the course of the disease and 28% attempt suicide (Stenager et al., 1992). Regarding epilepsy, the risk of suicide is particularly high in those with temporal epilepsy, who have 25 times more risk than the general population (Méndez & Doss, 1992).

Another factor to be taken into account is that being discharged is another risk factor of suicide (López García et al, 1993). Litman (1992) said that 0,2-0,5% of the discharged patients completed suicide during the year following the hospitalization.

Epidemic Suicide

Mimetic suicides or suicides by imitation are particularly common in the youth (Schmidtke & Hafner, 1988). One of the first documented cases is that of the influence of the novel *Young Werther's Sufferings* (1774), by Johann Wolfgang von Goethe (1749-1832), whose romantic view of suicide triggered whole suicide epidemics. A behavior can be contagious if there is a motivation to do so, it is known how to do it, and it has been previously observed (Prieto-Cuellar & López-Sánchez, 1995).

Some studies back the idea that mass media might precipitate epidemic suicides (Gould, 1990). Young populations are particularly at risk (Phillips et al., 1992). In an experimental study by Phillips et al. (1992), suicides that take place in the tube were deliberately miss-reported, leading to a significant decrease of suicide by this method. Hawton et al. (2000) also reported an increase of the rate of suicides in Scotland and Wales following the death of Diana, particularly in women of the same age range, particularly in the week following the funeral. However, other studies do not find such a relationship, and confounding variables may mediate the impact of the media on suicide behavior (López García et al, 1993).

Biological Factors

Monoamines

The relationship between a deficit in serotonergic function and suicide behavior is backed by studies on 5-Hydroxyindoleacetic acid (5-HIAA) in cerebrospinal fluid, a blunted prolactin response to fenfluramine, platelet studies, post-mortem studies, and neuroimagen studies (Turecki, 2005).

In the post-mortem studies a decrease of prefrontal pre-synaptic serotonin transporters, particularly in ventral areas, an increase in the pre-synaptic union to $5-HT_{1A}$ receptors in the rafe nuclei, and possibly an up regulating in $5-HT_{1A}$ and $5-HT_2$ post-synaptic receptors. This suggests that a reduction of the level of serotonin in this brain area is implicated in the brain circuits that regulate impulsive and violent behaviors, leading those subjects with "low" serotonin levels to behave impulsively or aggressively when faced to stressful life events (i.e. suicidal behaviors) (Turecki, 2005).

Hormones

Suicide behavior may be influenced by the menstrual cycle. In a study of our group, the suicide rate during the menstrual period was higher than expected (Baca-García et al., 2003), and a low brain serotonin level was hypothesized as the factor mediating this relationship, independently of psychiatric diagnosis. Low oestrogen levels during the menses might be associated with a decrease on brain serotonin activity, leading to an increase on the risk of suicide behaviors (Baca-García et al., 2003).

Moreover, a low level of dehydroepiandrosterone (DHEA) in veterans with PTSD has also been related to suicide attempts (Butterfield et al., 2005).

It is calculated that more than 70 to 80% of suicides take place in the context of a depressive disorder, where an activation of the hypothalamic-pituitary-adrenal axis is found. In a recent study, Pfennig et al. (2005) observed that suicide behavior was associated with a blunted response of corticoids in the combined dexamethasone-CRH test. The lower hormone levels were observed among those with a more recent suicide attempt. They concluded that suicide behavior might dysregulate (HPA) axis in depressed individuals. However, this study has been severely criticised by its methodology (Young & Coryell, 2005).

Obesity and Lipids

No clear findings are found in this area. In a recent study, Magnusson et al. (2006) reported a strong association between the Body Mass Index (BMI) and suicide in a cohort of more than a million of men who were followed up to 31 years. They report an inverse relationship between BMI and suicide: for every increase of 5 kilograms/m^2 of BMI the risk of suicide decreased a 15% (IC95%:9-21). Their results were not a consequence of the presence of any mental disorder, suggesting that those factors related to BMI might be causally linked to suicide. They suggest that BMI might be a marker of another factor relevant to understanding the aetiology of suicide. They reminded that BMI is closely associated with insulin resistance, which in turn is associated with cholesterol level, triptophan metabolism, and brain serotonin levels.

In the early nineties, several articles were published claiming a plausible link between pharmacological treatments aimed to lower blood cholesterol and an increased risk of violent deaths and suicide in men. Since, other authors have reported similar results. However, some other authors did not find such a relationship and pointed to the poor methodological strategies previously used (Zhang et al., 2005). These authors have documented in a general population sample in the U.S. a significant association between low levels of HDL-C and a higher prevalence of suicide attempts in young women.

Genes

The main candidate genes in suicide behavior are serotonin genes that can be classified in three groups:

1. Genes involved in the synthesis of serotonin: three polymorphism of the tryptophan hydroxylase 1 (TPH1) – it is involved in the biosynthesis of peripheral and pineal serotonin- have been intensively studied (A218C, C779A, and A-6526G), and with regard to TPH 2 – which is involved in the biosynthesis of brain serotonin-, results are not conclusive due to the scarcity of studies.

    In a meta-analysis (Li & He, 2006) of 34 studies – with a total of 3.922 cases and 6.700 controls- a strong association has been found between A218C and A779C polymorphisms and suicide behavior. Bellivier et al. (2004) found that in Caucasian race, the A218C polymorphism was "dose-dependently" related to suicide behavior.

2. The serotonin transporters gene promoter (5-HTTLPR) - where a "large" (L) allele or "short" (S) allele can be found- and intron 2 (VNTR) polymorphisms – which includes 9, 10 or 12 copies of an element of 17 pb-.

    In a meta-analysis of 25 studies focused on the 5-HTTLPR (Lin & Tsai, 2004) it was concluded that there was no association between this polymorphism and suicide behavior, even when only considering Caucasian subjects. However, they also reported that the "s" allele was positively associated with violent suicides when compared to non-violent suicides.

    López de Lara et al. (2006) found a significant association between completed suicide and the presence of at least one copy of the allele 10 in the locus locus STin2.

3. Genes implicated in the catabolism of serotonin (Monoaminoxidase/MAO). As reported by Courtet et al. (2005), the genes of the MAO-A seem to be related to the use of violent methods in suicidal behaviors.

Functional Neuroimaging

To sum up, the majority of studies have found that there is a dysfunction on serotonin neurotransmission and in the fronto-tempral processes in the individuals with suicide behavior. In the reviewed carried out by Audenaert et al. (2005) are summarized the main findings at the moment, namely a hypometabolism of fronto-temporal cortical areas associated with the degree of suicide intention, a reduction in the index of binding of the serotonin transporters in frontal and medial areas of impulsive violent individuals, and an increase of the index measuring the binding to 5-HT2A receptor in impulsive-aggressive suicidal subjects.

Mental Disorders

With regard to the topic of clinical markers of suicide risk, to avoid repeating information, we refer readers to the chapter entitled "personality disorders and suicide: the role of comorbidity" (chapter 2.7), where a review of the role of each mental disorder and its relationship with personality disorders and suicide is carried out.

1.3.5. GENES-ENVIRONMENT INTERACTION IN SUICIDE

D. Sáiz-González

Introduction

Human Genome Project. Genome and Proteinome

In the 50th anniversary of the DNA double helix description by Watson and Crick, genetics received an unsuspected relevance, especially with the definition of the structure of all human genes in the Humane Genome Project (HGP). The process could be carried out with the development of hibridation in situ techniques, restriction enzymes and the polymerase chain reaction as well as the technological development. The complete description of human DNA chain in the HGP, mean the end of the pre-existing biological premise that consider that the number of genes of a species increases when its complexity grows (Lander, 1996). Not only the total number of genes described was disappointing (30,000 compared with 26,000 of the fly of mustard), but also the species-specific genes were not enough to satisfy established theories. However, some of the most relevant findings of this project, emphasize the preferred distribution of genetic material in exons (DNA that codifies proteins), which would indicate a crucial regulating role of these elements (duplication, retrotransposition, elements of repetition). Nevertheless, the most important conclusion was that genes that codify proteins are qualitatively different from those from other species. More complex structures, dominions and duplications were found to increase the potential combinations of genes and proteins. Therefore, the complexity and diversity of the human being could be explained. Nevertheless, the variability of the DNA intraspecies is only 0.1% and the most frequent mechanism is the Single Nucleotide Polymorphism (SNP), also influenced by environmental factors. Some authors compare the biological impact of the HGP with the anatomy of Vesalio description in the 19th century, like key source of knowledge in the future development of medical sciences (Collins et al., 2003). Different applications of the HGP have been distinguished in different aspects as Biology -that studies structural definition (SNP), protein isolation and influence of environmental factors, as well as give universal access to this information-, and Public Health – that have clinical applications, treatment and definition of risk factors and prevention-. In addition to this, the HGP should protect this information about individual genome, and impulse its use for the improvement of the quality of global life. This new vision of genetics means the transition between the classic, Mendelian genetics to a new multifactor and polygenic model of disease (Mckusik, 2001).

Environment. New Concept of Psychiatry Genetics

The new word envirome borne in this context, meaning the various environmental influences that acts on the genome and express in the proteinome. It includes the structure and functions of the environmental agents (conditions and processes) that acts throughout the individual life like stress factors, prenatal agents, etc. The pathology is determined by the influence of some environmental factors in a genetically susceptible individual. The classification and simplification of these factors is very controversial. In fact, the methodology of these studies is being deeply investigated nowadays.

Genetics -Environment Interaction

The Interaction between genetics and environment was studied in psychiatry in order to elucidate the relation between combinations of genes, environmental factors and the conduct. The learning process has been considered, like able to change the genetic expression and to modify patterns of neuronal connectivity. The new theories of development reject the genetic determinism and defend the plasticity as an influence of the nurture on the individual. This explains the epigenetics evolution and the changes that define the biological diversity. These theories end in the predominant theory of neurodevelopment in schizophrenia that includes the interaction nature-nurture through the life of the individual, and explains the different results that an environmental factor could produce in the same genome, according to the moment that it occurs (Rose, 2001). The microarray techniques deeply improved this investigation, measuring the genetic expression. It has been possible to relate schizophrenia to low expression of G-protein signalling 4 (RGS4) (Mirnics et al., 2001; Brzustowicz et al., 2000). Neurodevelopmental diseases like schizophrenia would include an alteration in neural transmission with the alteration of some proteins linked with synapses transmission. According to this theory, the protein expression determines disease's episodes. The current tendency is to consider that some genes regulate the expression of a characteristic, in which different environmental factors take part. These environmental factors establish the protein expression and therefore they model the gene response to different stimulating factors. The disappointing results obtained in the first investigations seem to be related with these old thinking "one gene, one disease". Fitting this to the most complex reality of a genetic model, with a dense genes network and multiple environmental factors that interact influencing the development of the brain and their functions, collected data that are more hopeful. Hariri et al. (2002) following this new vision obtains different response in Functional Magnet Nuclear Resonance (fMNR) of 5HT transporter polymorphisms in amygdale before a stressful stimulus.

Genome and Environment Interaction in Suicide Behaviour

The interaction between nature and nurture is expressed like vulnerability to stress in susceptible individuals with genetic risk for the pathological state. This relation has been studied in different pathologies with positive results (Tienari, 1991; Kendler et al., 1995).

This revolutionary concept looks for not one gene correlation with one disease, but for the genetics expression activation systems. The non-share environmental factors in individuals with the same genetic information could help in the determination of the relevance of these variables that seem to be the key of the biodiversity. In psychiatric illness, the environmental contributions as well as the epigenetic factors are essential.

The studies that investigate genes and environment interactions are full by doubts about viability and have some detractors (Eaves, 2006). However, according to some authors (Moffitt et al., 2005; Caspi & Moffit, 2006), there is scientifically strong evidence about this relation and steps to drive the investigation in order to describe more genes implicated.

There are only a few studies towards suicide and environment-genome interaction. Caspi published in 2003 a revolutionary paper, which changed the psychiatric genetics. The investigation focuses the modulation of a functional polymorphism of the transporter gene (SLC6A4) of serotonin (5HT), in the individual vulnerability to suffer for depression and suicide in relation with long life stress (Caspi et al., 2003).

The positive relation between adverse stressors during the life, and depression and suicide risk is well known for the individuals with biological predisposition (following the stress-diathesis model). However, other individuals with the same adverse events never became depressed. In order to explain this question, the genetics of behaviour point to disease susceptibility in relation with individuals in high genetic risk. Caspi et al. studied the implication of a functional polymorphism in the promoter region of 5HTT gene, in the genetics mediation for the susceptibility for depression and suicide in relation with life adverse events (Caspi et al., 2003). Both serotonin and its transporter had been deeply studied, with good and known results in the investigation of depression and suicide (Lin & Tsai, 2004). Two alleles were distinguished in the promoter region of the gene (located in 17q11.2). One is the short allele named "s" with low efficacy in transmission, and other one long "l". The short allele is related with depression only when the serotoninergic stress response is considered. In animal models, "s" mice showed exaggerated fear response and higher levels of corticotrope hormone than "l" mice, only if the stress factor is present. In a different study with rhesus monkeys, there was a lower level of CFR serotonin levels in "s" monkeys with stressful stimulus, comparing with the others (Caspi et al., 2003). Neurofunction works in humans conclude in a higher amygdale activity in fear response to a stress stimulus in the individuals with the "s" allele when comparing with all the other individuals (Hariri et al., 2002).

Caspi et al. reclutated 1037 children and evaluated them (until 3 years old), every 2 years to 26th. The 17% was "ss" genotype, 51% was heterocigotes and the other 31% was ll. They measured the stress events until 21 to 26 years old in the individuals (with a form in which they classified 14 events), and the total number of adverse events were similar in the three groups. The depressive episodes were measured with structured interviews. The 17% of the sample suffered some depressive episode during the last year, according with the standard prevalence for gender and age. The suicide attempts and ideation was present in 3% of the individuals. The stress events were significance for the development of a depressive episode and suicide conduct in the individuals with the "s" allele (s/s and s/l). This risk does not exist in "ll" individuals, despite the stress conditions. Similar results were obtained for new diagnosis of depression, the worse evolution of the depression, the information given by other individual different from the proband about the episode, and childhood abuse and adult depression. In order to confirm that the environmental factor is not the result of other gene interaction that predispose for the stress events, the sample was also analyzed according to cause-effect sequence (Caspi et al., 2003).

This work has been replicated in various papers referring only to depression but there is no mention of suicide attempt or ideation. Most of the papers replicate Caspi´s conclusions about depression and 5HTTPR relation, mediated by stress adversity (Eley et al., 2004; Grabe et al., 2005; Kaufman et al., 2004; Kendler et al., 2005; Whilhelm et al., 2006; Taylor et al., at press). However, some authors obtained partial accordance with these results (Surtees et al., 2006) (association between depression and environment but not implication of the polymorphism), and one could not replicate it at all (Gillespie et al., 2005). These negative results could be attributed to the mix of s/s and s/l groups because only s/s group turned to be significant, the use of a dependent value with restricted range instead of a more continuous value to measured depressive symptoms, and the use of standardized measures to determine the early environment stress (Taylor et al., at press).

Regardless these conclusions need to be replicated in suicide, the results would be important in prevention, treatment and management of patients, and it could be useful in the way to find endophenotypes in suicide and depression.

The most prevalent genetics variants would be the most resistant ones following the evolution scale. The present vision of the pathology considering the interactions between genetics and environment could clear the aetiology of many diseases and helps in the clinical practice (Caspi et al., 2003).

The environment aggressions are very important in their interaction with genetics not only during adult life, but also during the childhood. Caspi measured the influence of children maltreatment and suicide. However, there are some other factors, like perinatal (intrautero, during birth or just after the birth) with relevance. Other severe mental illness like schizophrenia has been related with obstetric and neonatal complications (Jones et al., 1998), especially the low weight at birth and malnutrition in adult chronic diseases.

These circumstances could affect the fetal body structure and physiologic and metabolic pathways. Some works related mental disorders, like antisocial personality disorder or affective disorders with malnutrition in child during the last half of pregnancy (Brown et al., 1995). A significant number of obstetric, neonatal and maternal complications have been reported in suicide investigation among adolescents, when comparing with control group (Salk et al., 1985). This relation is due to stress vulnerability mediated by adverse factors in early life although other works obtained antagonised results (Neugebauer & Reuss, 1996).

A recent paper by Mitterdorfer-Rutz *et al. (2004)*, evidence the suicide risk in the future individual, depending on environmental intrauterine factors. In a cohort of 713,370 individuals, suicide attempt and consumption in young adults was studied, in relation with some early perinatal conditions and parents characteristics (including psychosocial items). In the pregnancy complications was included the pathology of pregnancy like hypertension, the birth itself like cesarea and the registration of weight and tall. The maternal items measured were age, academic level (socio-economic status) and number of children. A multivariante analysis of data could conclude that the low weight at birth as well as adolescent mother was related with increased risk of suicide in the future young adult. Other factors related with suicide behavior were being four children or more and low academic level in the mother. However, family aggregation of suicide was the most relevant variable for suicide in the future individual (Oquendo & Baca-García, 2004).

This work could open a new line in the investigation of environmental factors, focus on perinatal circumstances, parent's characteristics, and educational style, and although the difference between genes and environment interactions should be clarified. All these relevant factors could be related with psychopathology in mother: a depressed mother could not take care of herself and this result in low weight at birth in offspring, could not maintain a work or prepare herself to work life, etc. (Oquendo & Baca-García, 2004). The authors admitted in this paper the probable relation between psychopathology in mother and suicide aggregation in family, and fetal growth and adverse factors in mother. Some other variables like low socio-economic status, early pregnancy risk, and fetal malnutrition, could be related with psychopathology in mother. The presence of mental illness in the mother multiplicates the risk of mental disorder on child, including suicide (Mitterdorfer-Rutz et al., 2004). Substance abuse and use of drugs in mother during the pregnancy as well as pregnancy care could stop the normal growing in child, especially the development of central nervous system.

The influence of stress during pregnancy could mediate some epigenetic changes that produce activation/deactivation of genes, and disturbance in protein expression. In addition to this, some works in mice observed that an adverse genotype is as risky as and adverse uterus environment, for the development of anxiety in the future offspring (Lesch et al., 1996).

In conclusion, these perinatal factors could be central in future investigation of gene-environment studies in suicide. In fact, recent investigations replicates partially these results but, only for the depression symptoms and not for the suicidal behaviour. For example, studies referring depressive symptoms during pregnancy associated depression in child and s/s genotype. Other publications consider season of birth discrepancy as risk factor for suicide in relation with 5-HTTLPR (Courtet et al., 2006). Season of births variations has been considered important in different mental disorders, and could be a confounding variable when investigating in genetics ignoring environmental factors (Chotai et al., 2003). Suicide attempts are more serious among the individuals born from February to April, especially between men and only in s/s allele (Courtet et al., 2006).

In a pilot study, our investigation group found an association between suicide behavior and the polymorphism of the serotonin transporter promoter area mediated by low hormone states (during menses and menopause). In this preliminary study, "l" females were overrepresented in the group of suicidal fertile female attempters, as well as suicidal postmenopausal attempters (Baca-García et al., 2003). We hypothesized that there was a relation between sexual hormones, the genotype and suicide conduct in women and this relation could be mediated by hormone regulation of the gene. Opposite to estradiol, progesterone did not show any significant differences (Mann Whitney U=895.5, p=0.21). These analysis are preliminary but internally consistent. Patients with "s" allele and "l" show increased risk of suicide in follicular phase, especially in "l" women. The "l" group was more vulnerable to suicide in low-estrogens phases.

Genes-hormone interaction needs further investigation in order to clarify their relation, and some aspects of suicide genetics.

1.3.6. MODELS OF SUICIDE BEHAVIOR

E. Baca-García and M. Mercedes Pérez-Rodriguez

Several nomenclatures and classifications for suicide behavior have been used during the last 150 years. The cornerstone of suicide behavior is the self-destruction, the act against the self existence. In addition, two concepts are part of the core of this behavior: intentionality and lethality. Most of the nomenclatures, classifications and derived models of suicidal behavior combine the following concepts: self-destruction, intentionality and lethality. In fact, the two most widely used suicide behavior nomenclatures (OMS, 1976; O'Carroll et al., 1996) (see Table 14) combine these concepts (implicitly of explicitly). For a recent update we remit the interested reader to the review by Silverman (2006).

Table 14. Suicide-related behavior according to O'Carroll et al. (1996)

Terms for suicide-related behaviors			Intent to die from suicide	Instru-mental thinking	Outcome		
					No injury	Nonfatal injury	Death
Suicide-related behavior	Instrumental behavior	Instrumental suicide-related behavior					
		Without injuries	No	Yes	X		
		With injuries	No	Yes		X	
		With fatal outcome	No	Yes			X
	Suicidal acts	Suicide attempt					
		Without injuries	Yes	+/-	X		
		With injuries	Yes	+/-		X	
		Completed suicide	Yes	+/-			X

Despite the dynamic postulates that consider suicide as a personal and non-generalizable behavior, several models have arisen that aim to understand suicidal behavior. Some of these models have clinical utility; moreover, some of them have interest from the preventive and public health points of view.

We will focus on several models (Plutchik & van Praag, 1989; Plutchik et al., 1989; Fawcett et al., 1996; Mann, 1998; Mann et al., 1999) from the last twenty years that combine clinical, sociodemographic and biological suicide risk factors. One relevant difficulty in predicting suicide is that most suicide risk factors, when used as screening tests, have low specificity (Cohen, 1986). Mann et al. (2006) have suggested that "this problem might be reduced if risk factors could be used in combinations such that each additional risk factor introduces significant new risk information and updates risk estimates". Rihmer et al. (2002) have classified hierarchically the relevant factors for suicide behavior. They consider three levels of prediction: primary (psychiatric), secondary (psychosocial) and tertiary (demographic). The primary factors correspond to clinical risk factors for suicide. They are well known and have low predictive utility (Mann, 2005; Mann et al., 2006). The research on biological factors has been focused on the aminergic system, cholesterol and hormonal factors. Biological research is still far away from achieving clinical utility (Mann et al., 2006). For these reasons, all these models should be considered tentative. Some authors have attempted to quantify the influence of biological factors on suicide risk. Mann et al. (2006) explored the predictive potential of two biological markers (5-hydroxyindoleacetic acid in cerebrospinal fluid, CSF 5-HIAA, and the dexamethasone suppression test, DST) through meta-analyses of prospective biological studies. They obtained odds ratios for prediction of suicide of 4.48 and 4.65 respectively. The prediction model that required both DST and CSF 5-HIAA tests to be positive resulted in a sensitivity of 37.5%, a specificity of 88%, and had a positive predictive value of 23%. The prediction model that required either DST or CSF 5-HIAA tests to be positive resulted in a sensitivity of 87.5%, a specificity of 28%, and had a positive predictive value of 10%. Samuelsson et al (2006) reported that, in hospitalized male psychiatric patients with high suicide risk, CSF 5-HIAA may be a better predictor of early suicide after attempted suicide than the Beck Suicide Intent Scale (SIS) or the Beck Hopelessness Scale (BHS).

Suicidal behavior is the result of several risk factors that force the person to cross the "antisuicidal barrier". The existence of a threshold ("antisuicidal barrier") for suicide behavior is a constant in all the models and supports other elements of the models, the gathering or stress factor. These elements implicate a third term: predisposition for suicide behavior. Mann's group (Mann, 1998; Mann et al., 1999; Mann, 2005; Mann et al., 2006) - following Monroe & Simons (1991) stress-diathesis model- has done a major contribution to suicidiology systematizing these elements and incorporating all the clinical and biological knowledge on suicide behavior. In addition, suicide behaviors systematized on this way offers the opportunity to develop some strategies to prevent and treat suicide behavior (Mann, 2005).

- Stress factors: psychiatric conditions (depression, alcohol use, drug use), psychosocial crises (interpersonal loses), noradrenergic system, HPA axis.
- Diathesis factors: genetics, childhood abuse, drug abuse, personality disorder, serotoninergic system, protective factors (religion).

Aggressiveness and impulsivity are two traits that are part of the predisposition factors (diathesis) that drive the person toward the suicidal behavior (Turecki, 2005). These forces reflect Meninger's postulates on suicide behavior. Therefore, impulsive persons with several predisposing factors react to different stress factors with aggressive behavior against themselves.

The role of aggressiveness and impulsivity in the models has been criticized (Muller-Oerlinghausen, 2004). This criticism is important because aggressiveness and impulsivity are the cornerstone for integrating psychological and biological forces in suicide behavior. The main argument against the role of aggressiveness and impulsivity in the models is that suicidal behavior, impulsivity and aggressiveness are not well-defined behaviors and they are so complex that it is not plausible to explain them with simple biological correlates.

In summary, stress-diathesis models are useful because they help to understand and possibly prevent suicidal behavior. However, we still need a better definition of suicidal behavior in order to improve diagnosis and research. In addition, impulsivity and aggressiveness need to be redefined to reflect more closely the biological aspects of suicide behavior.

PART II: PERSONALITY DISORDERS AND SUICIDE: RESEARCH AND CLINICS

"The potencial for committed suicide items from life-long personality characteristics as well as from somewhat predictable triggers"
(Leonard, 1972)

INTRODUCTION AND OVERVIEW

H. Blasco-Fontecilla

2.1.1. INTRODUCTION

Every suicide researcher tries to answer the question of whether or not life is worth living, as previously made Albert Camus in *Le Mythe de Sisyphe*. An important question to tackle is why the majority of patients with major depressive disorder – the major psychopathological risk factor for suicide behavior- do not ever try to suicide. It is my opinion that the role of personality is vital in differentiating among patients with an axis I disorder, particularly depression, who do not try to kill themselves and others who do so. Birtchnell (1981) said, "a person who has made a suicide attempt represents a certain type of individual who resorts to this form of behavior under stress". Suicide is a very complex phenomenon resulting of the interaction of environmental factors on the personality of the subject (Vinoda, 1966). Depressive patients who make suicide attempts show higher hostility, tendency to acting-out, orality, irritability, drugs misuse and legal problems (Paykel & Dienelt, 1979; Weissmann et al., 1973). A high level of personal disturbance and interpersonal difficulties has been found in subjects with strong suicidal thoughts (Mehryar et al., 1977).

This introductory chapter will focus firstly on giving an overview of the influence of personality and personality disorders (PDs) on suicide behavior, and secondly on explaining the methodology of our research, which is necessary to read some of the subsequent chapters.

2.1.2. OVERVIEW

Research on both PDs and suicide has each separately been hampered by conceptual and methodological problems so that the study of their interaction is difficult. One of the main problems is that suicide completers and suicide attempters correspond to two separate but overlapping populations (Frances et al., 1986). Furthermore, the presence of a suicide attempt is the major risk factor for suicide. The relative risk for suicide in a sample of suicide attempters was about 40 times higher than expected in the general population (Milos et al., 2003).

Suicide Behavior

Suicide attempters (SA) are usually women, young, diagnosed as "neurotic" or with a PD, their attempts are more impulsive and by using non-lethal methods; on the other hand, *suicide completers* are usually older men diagnosed with an axis I disorder – particularly depression, alcoholism or both-, suicide taking place in a private setting and by using lethal methods (Clayton, 1985). Moreover, it is also possible to find different sub-populations among SA. Thus, Stanley et al. (2001) found that SA who self-mutilate were a particularly disturbed and possibly at greater risk for completed suicide for several reasons: they experience more feelings of depression and hopelessness, are more aggressive, display more affective instability, underestimate the lethality of their suicidal behavior, and think of suicide for longer and more frequents periods of time. Overstone & Kreitman (1974) classified SA in *repeaters* and *non-repeaters*. The former were mainly psychopaths, drug addicts, alcoholics, subjects who have long histories of instability and chronic personal and social disorganization and unresponsive to psychiatric treatment. Lester et al. (1989) compared *un-socialized SA* with *depressed SA*. The former group made less severe suicide attempts and had more prior suicide attempts, and what is more important, they obtained similar depression inventory scores when compared to the depressed SA. The depressed SA appeared to have a negative self-image only when depressed, while the un-socialized SA appeared to be losers and their self-image seemed to be continuous and realistic. They might attempt suicide impulsively in response to problems because of their poor problem-solving skills and disability to think abstractly.

SA who eventually suicide can be distinguished from those who will not by having made a previous attempts likely to be fatal, being unemployed, living alone, being male, and having communicated the suicidal intent (Tuckman & Youngman, 1963; Ettlinger, 1964; Pallis et al., 1982). Interestingly, while in 10% of *suicide completers* no mental disorder is diagnosed, Ernst et al. (2004) found out that this was due to inability of psychological autopsy method to detect underlying psychiatric disorders. They stressed that the majority of these suicide subjects with no psychopathological condition diagnosed may had either an axis I disorder and/or a PD, as in their 16 subjects sample the majority of subjects were eventually diagnosed with a PD or pathological gambling. These subjects were more alike to suicide individuals meeting criteria for an axis I disorder than to living normal controls in measures of psychopathology other than axis I disorders. They also reminded that axis I conditions other than the usually considered, e.g. pathological gambling, may be present in these apparently mentally "normal" individuals. Brent et al. (1993) found similar results in adolescents. Isometsa et al. (1995) found in a random sample of 229 subjects who committed suicide that the prevalence of PDs among subjects aged 20 to 34 was 43% -or 56% when undetermined cases were included-, a rate similar to that reported by Lesage et al. (1994) and Rich et al. (1992).

The number of previous *suicidal attempts* is the strongest clinical predictor of future *suicidal behavior* and *suicide* in all psychiatric populations (Paris et al., 1989; Apter et al., 1991; Suominen et al., 2004). It is often estimated that around 10 to 15% of SA will eventually suicide, but there is an outstanding lack of studies in the era of modern psychiatric treatment (Suominen et al., 2004). These authors found in their 37-year follow-up study that 13% of a 100 SA self-poisoning sample eventually completed suicide, being this outcome more frequent in men. Two-thirds of the suicides occurred at least 15 years after the initial suicide attempt. When undetermined, and undetermined plus accidental deaths were included as possible suicides, the proportion of suicides raised up to 16% and 19% respectively. The authors concluded that the presence of history of a suicide attempt by self-poisoning appeared to be a high risk factor to completing suicide throughout the entire adult lifetime. *Completed suicide* is more likely in males using violent, non-overdose methods (Rihmer et al., 1995). There is some evidence that patients using violent non-overdose methods resemble those who suicide (Murase et al., 2003).

SA diagnosed with PDs have the highest level of repetition (Pompili et al., 2004). Frances et al. (1986) summarized the different possible ways of understanding the relationship between *PDs* and *suicide*: (1) Suicide could be an inherent component of certain PDs. In fact, DSM-III included suicide behaviors as a diagnostic criteria in both borderline PD and histrionic PD; (2) PDs may predispose to suicide behavior (3) or to axis I disorders, which in turn would independently increase the risk of suicide; (4) PD might execute its suicidal influence through axis I disorders -taking into account the majority of patients with major depression do not have suicide behaviors, the presence of a comorbid PD may explain this-; (5) a combination of different personality traits that cut across the traditional categorical classifications might better predict suicidal behavior – the authors suggested the combination of impulsivity and decisiveness-, so the study of these personality traits could be more important in predicting suicide than the traditional categories we frequently use; (6) axis I disorders that are associated with suicide may predispose to an augmented prevalence of axis II disorders, which may then independently contribute to increased risk of suicide, and finally (7) the association between PDs and suicide could be accidental. Nowadays, this last hypothesis cannot be defended as it has been demonstrated that the rate of PDs – controlling for axis I disorders- among suicidal patients is higher than expected. The prevalence of PDs among SA using different nosological and diagnostic classifications is around two thirds (Crumley, 1979; Friedman et al., 1983; Casey, 1989; Gomez et al., 1992). Moreover, increasing information is available with regard to the relationship between specified PD and suicide. However and in spite of these authors recommending the study of the relationship between the different diagnostic criteria of borderline PD and suicide, few studies have been carried out at present.

Mental Disorders and Suicide Behavior

Mental disorders are essential predictors of suicide (Balon, 1987). They are considered a *necessary* but not *sufficient* cause for suicide (Davis & Schrueder, 1990; Cheng et al., 1997). While the majority of suicides are among subjects diagnosed with a mental disorder, the vast majority of them do not kill themselves (Davis & Schrueder, 1990). A mental disorder is found in 90% to 100% of those who suicide (Cheng, 1995; Lecubrier, 2001). Robins et al. (1959) found a psychiatric disorder in 94% of their sample of suicides. The same applies to suicide attempts. Thus, Beautrais et al. (1996) studied a 302 series of consecutive suicide attempts finding out 90.1% were diagnosed with at least one mental disorder at the time of the attempt. Lester (2001) stated that "the major psychological factors found to be associated with and predictive of suicidal behavior are depression (especially hopelessness), and psychological disturbance, labelled variously as neuroticism, anxiety or emotional instability".

Traditionally both *depressive disorders* and *substance use disorders* –particularly *alcoholism*- have been quoted as the leading mental disorders associated to suicide in Western and non-Western societies and the theoretical benefit of lowering number of suicide attempts by 80% if depression was eliminated (Beautrais et al., 1996; Cheng, 1995; Henriksson et al., 1993). Severe depression and alcoholism are frequently comorbid among suicidal patients and the risk of suicide is greatest when comorbidity is present (Cheng, 1995). Indeed, the conceptualization of suicidality is embedded in the context of depression and the applicability of the risk factors found in depressive patients to suicidal behavior in the context of PD is unknown (Gerson & Stanley, 2002). In traditional conceptualizations developed from suicidality seen as secondary to major depression, suicidal behavior is usually understood as a response to a deep sense of despair desire for death where the suicidal act may worsen the depressive state. However, there are good reasons not to assume the presumption that suicidal behavior is simply an epiphenomenon of a primary affective disorder. Bronisch (1996b) has convincingly argued that suicide remains a phenomenon on its own right, independent of depression. Thus, suicidal behavior can be found in states apart from guilt or depression (Ronninstam & Maltsberger, 1998). Suicidality in subjects diagnosed with *borderline PD* seems to function as a regulator of emotional state, to be transient in nature and not to result in a deepening of a depressed mood – in fact, subjects often feel better because the act can serve to give them back a sense of emotional balance- (Gerson & Stanley, 2002). Maltsberger (1994) also differentiated patients with acute suicidal depression from those with chronic suicidal personalities.

Personality Disorders and Suicide Behavior

More recently, however, while some clinicians may underestimate the potential for suicide attempts in patients with a PD, the diagnosis of a PD, particularly *borderline PD, antisocial PD, narcissistic PD* and *depressive PD*, has begun to be considered to carry the most serious suicide risk at a level comparable at least to that of *major depression* (Bronisch, 1996; Gerson & Stanley, 2002; Lambert, 2003). Philip (1970) found that 50% of their sample of one hundred SA was diagnosed with a *character disorder*. Foster et al. (1999) found in their psychological autopsy study that PD, particularly antisocial PD, avoidant PD, and dependent PD, after controlling for axis I diagnosis, continued being independent risk factors for suicide. Cheng et al. (1997) stressed that the diagnosis of a PD is associated with an increased risk of substance abuse, a life-long perception of alienation, and difficulties in creating and maintaining supportive social networks, which may underlie several of the risk factors for suicide. Some authors have begun to consider that *personality assessment* should be more carefully evaluated when assessing suicide risk. Eyman & Eyman (1992) maintained that although traditionally personality evaluation was not very useful for suicide risk assessment, it was useful in identifying vital personality traits that may protect or hinder a subject when responding to major life stress and emotional crises, which ultimately might determine suicide risk.

A diagnosis of a PD is found in 9% to 28% of *suicides* and "follows depression, schizophrenia, and alcoholism in order of importance as major risk factor" (Soloff et al., 1994). The role of PD as a risk factor for attempted suicide is even greater, with rates up to 77% (see below). However, the relationship between *suicidal behavior* and *personality disorders* has only been studied in dept in the last two decades (Links et al., 2003). It is difficult to know whether the presence of a PD is an independent factor predicting suicide, as it is frequently comorbid with other psychiatric diagnoses, and impulsivity, aggressiveness, mood instability and undesirable life events are likely to be associated with suicide in this group (Davis & Schrueder, 1990).

The prevalence of PD in the general population has been estimated at 6 to 13% (Maier et al., 1992; Weissman, 1993). In primary care, the diagnosis of a PD is the principal diagnosis in 5% to 8% of patients, while 40% to 50% of psychiatric inpatients have a PD (Casey, 1989). Up to 77% of *SA* (Casey, 1989; Ferreira de Castro et al., 1998; Gomez et al., 1992; Suominen et al., 1996), and between one to two-thirds of individuals who suicide are diagnosed with at least one PD (Cheng et al., 1997; Foster et al., 1999; Henriksson et al., 1993; Lesage et al., 1994), mainly in the cluster B (Barraclough et al., 1974; Bronisch, 1996; Henriksson et al., 1993; Marttunen et al., 1991), but rates around two-third of suicides have been reported when using more specific structure or semi-structured interviews to assess the presence of PD (Cheng et al., 1997; Lesage et al., 1994). Moreover, in an 18-year follow up study of 7921 patients was found that, in males, the diagnosis of a PD was the third most common psychiatric diagnosis associated to suicide (Baxter & Appleby, 1999). In one autopsy psychological study with a ramdom sample of 229 victims, about one-fith (19%) received a cluster B diagnosis (Isometsa et al., 1996), greater than the estimated prevalence of about 5% in the general population (Samuels et al., 1994).

Reversely, a history of suicidal behavior is found in 55% to 70% of subjects diagnosed with a PD (Casey, 1989; Clarkin et al., 1984; Gomez et al., 1992). Moreover, Harris & Barraclough (1998) concluded in their meta-analysis that the suicide risk among individuals diagnosed with a PD is seven times higher than expected and among the ones treated for attempted suicide 38 times the expected value. SA diagnosed with a PD have the highest level of recurrence (Casey, 1992). Indeed, some authors have suggested that patients primarily diagnosed with a PD should be considered at a high risk of suicide - similar to the one of major affective disorders- and that high suicidality should not always be regarded as etiologically linked to major depression (Ahrens & Haugh, 1996). Maris et al. (2000) estimated that the suicide rate among subjects with a diagnosis of borderline PD ranged between 3 to 9%, similar to the rate of patients with schizophrenia.

Several authors have reported rates of around 50% of PD in *parasuicide* (Ovenstone, 1973; Pierce, 1977). Although *parasuicidal acts* are not the same that *suicide attempts*, they are also associated to an increased risk of suicide. Diekstra (1993) found that 10% to 14% of people who make parasuicides eventually suicide. Södeber (2001) found a rate of PD of 78% - particularly borderline PD- among parasuicidal patients. He also stressed that although the presence of an axis I disorder was very frequent, the vast majority of subjects had a comorbid axis II disorder. Moreover, 20% of the group diagnosed with a PD had no concurrent axis I diagnosis. He finally suggested that more than half of the cases the PD might be left undiscovered in clinical practice.

Very often, clinicians find suicidal or parasuicidal behavior in PD to be an expression of temper tantrums or rage attacks after frustration. Suicide behavior may be useful to expressing rage against others and against the self in an impulsive way, which is quite typical of women diagnosed of borderline PD or histrionic PD and in men diagnosed with narcissistic PD, malignant narcissism and antisocial PD; moreover, it may be a coldly prepared act of revenge or defeat of other that would express the triumph over the others and would be typical of narcissistic individuals (Kernberg, 2001).

Some specific PDs have been more consistently associated with suicide behavior and greater mortality than others (Allebeck & Allgulander, 1990a). The majority of studies have focused on *borderline PD (BPD)* and *antisocial PD (APD)*, which have been consistently associated to suicide attempts and suicide (Ahrens & Haug, 1996). A history of multiple or severe suicide attempts is more common in patients diagnosed with PD, particularly BPD (Kjellsber et al., 1991; Kullgren, 1988; Paris, 1990). In a psychological autopsy study with a case-control design among young men (18 to 35 years) it was found that an axis II diagnosis was made in 57.3% of suicide victims while only 25.3% of control group had a personality disorder (odds ratio=4.0, 95% confidence interval=2.0-7.9). Antisocial and especially borderline PD were prominent, specially taking into account that seven out of the eleven suicide victims diagnosed with antisocial PD also had borderline PD (Lesage et al., 1994). Cheng et al. (1997) found that among three different non-westerns ethnic groups, the most prevalent category among suicidal subjects were *emotionally unstable PD* –including impulsive (F60.30) and borderline (F60.31)-, *anankastic* (F60.5) and *anxious* (F60.6) types, in order of importance. There is an outstanding lack of data about the potential influence of other PDs apart from APD and BPD on suicide behavior (Isometsa et al., 1996).

Several associated factors to the diagnosis of PDs like the presence of comorbid mood disorders or substance disorders, childhood sexual abuse, degree of impulsive or antisocial trends and, a history of irregular psychiatric care discharges can increase the risk of suicide (Lambert, 2003). Comorbidity with an axis I disorder – mainly depressive syndromes and substance use disorders or both- in suicide completers diagnosed with a PD seem to be the rule (Isometsa & Henriksson et al., 1996), posing these subjects to a maximum risk (Foster et al., 1999; Maris et al., 2000).Yen et al. (2003) found that the presence of a BPD, the diagnosis and course of a drug use disorder, and major depression prospectively predicted suicide attempts; the combination of this three factors seem to be a particularly high-risk combination (Lambert, 2003). In a sample of 229 random subjects using the psychological autopsy method was found that suicide among individuals diagnosed with a cluster B PD was more likely associated with previous non-fatal suicide attempts and psychoactive substance use disorders but less with physical disorders, whereas subjects diagnosed with a cluster C PD were found to be similar to other suicide victims with no PD. Few suicide victims were diagnosed with a cluster A PD (Isometsa et al., 1996). Henriksson et al. (1993), found that among suicides an axis I diagnosis was nearly always found (93%), mainly depressive disorders or a depressive syndrome and alcohol dependence/abuse. An axis II diagnosis was made in 31%, being the diagnosis of PD not otherwise specified the most prevalent. The diagnosis of PD was the main diagnosis in 9% of all suicides and in nearly a third among those diagnosed with a PD. *Childhood abuse*, particularly when prolonged or in cases of incest, has been associated to both BPD and major depression, being the odds of a sexually abused victim attempting suicide 10 times greater than the one of a non-abused patient (Soloff et al., 2002).

Table 15. Suicide risk factors in subjects with personality disorders
(taken from Lambert, 2003)

1. Comorbidity with major mood disorders, addiction and some anxiety disorders.
2. History of childhood sexual abuse, especially incest and prolonged abuse.
3. Antisocial and impulsive traits.
4. Younger age compared to general population at risk for suicide.
5. Inadequate psychiatric treatment of personality disorders and comorbid disorders.
6. Reduction in psychiatric care, including recent irregular discharges.

Another interesting topic is that among SA not diagnosed with a PD a reduction of the risk of suicide soon after the suicide attempt is found, while in subjects diagnosed with a PD, no such a "cathartic" outcome is found. These subjects go on presenting despair and suicidal ideation. This may partly explain the tendency of subjects with PDs to engage in repetitive suicidal attempts (Gomez et al., 1992). However, subjects diagnosed with BPD can use parasuicidal behavior - more than genuine suicide attempts- to stabilize their mood.

Finally, we are not of the same opinion of Links et al. (2003) who think that "for a meaningful discussion of the suicide risk associated with personality disorders, one must by definition focus on youth in late adolescence and early adulthood" as we think that the role of personality and PD, although of great importance in the youth, is also vital to explain the complex phenomenon of suicide in all age populations. Unfortunately, the majority of studies in the area have been carried out only in young populations.

2.1.3. OUR RESEARCH

We would like to stress that, as Isometsa et al. (1996) pointed out, "the almost nonexistent data concerning suicide among subjects other than those with borderline and antisocial personality disorder". This was the major reason for us to carry out this research.

Some of the following chapters are based in the PhD entitled "Personality disorders and suicide" carried out by Dr. Blasco-Fontecilla and directed by Dr. Baca-García and Professor Dr. Sáiz-Ruiz. All the chapters based on the research of our group will be quoted (*). The following methodology is applicable to all of them.

Sample and Procedure

446 *suicide attempters* (SA) were recruited at two general Hospitals in Madrid (Spain) between January 1999 to January 2002, covering a catchment's area of around 900,000 people. Both hospitals provide free medical coverage. External funding was available for the first 235 consecutive assessments by a research psychiatrist available for on-call patient recruitment. The following non-consecutive assessments were made by residents in psychiatry with specific training to assess suicide attempts. As assessment conditions where slightly different, we feared to find some differences. However, no significant differences were found with regard to neither socio-demography nor categorical diagnosis of specific PD.

After hearing a complete description of the study, subjects provided written informed consent. As our group has reported previously (Diaz et al., 2003), approximately 84% of SA consent to take part in our studies. Refusing SA did not significantly differ in demographics from consenting SA. As some of the SA had more than one suicide attempt, only the first recorded suicide attempt was analysed. As recommended by the US National Institute of Mental Health, a suicide attempt was defined as a self-destructive behavior with the intention of ending one's life, independent of the resulting damage (O'Carroll et al., 1996). To some analysis, SA were divided in four age groups (18 to 35 years, 36 to 50 years, 51 to 65 years and older than 66 years).

A *healthy control group* -blood donors with no previous axis I or II diagnosis, no previous suicidal behavior and no first degree familial antecedents of mental illness- (n= 515), and a *psychiatric control group* - psychiatric inpatients whose reason to be in the Hospital was not a suicide attempt- (n= 86) were used for some analysis.

Scales

The diagnosis of PD was made by using the DSM-IV version of the *International Personality Disorder Questionnaire-Screening Questionnaire* (IPDE-SQ). The DSM-IV version, in contrast to the ICD-10 one, allows making the diagnosis of narcissistic PD, and schyzotipal PD. The *IPDE-SQ* is a short and efficient screening questionnaire (Egan et al., 2002). These authors reminded that it is not recommended to make personality diagnosis, basically due to the lack of specificity and high rate of false positives typical of screening questionnaires. In order to increasing specificity, two strategies could have been carried out: firstly, by using the full *International Personality Disorders Examination* (IPDE), which is a semi-structured interview designed to make diagnosis of both ICD-10 and DSM-IV PD (Ei-Rufaie et al., 2002); secondly, and this is the one we used, by using an adjusted cut-off to diagnose PD. We included one or two additional criteria besides those suggested by the IPDE authors to adjust the rates of PDs in our sample of controls to the rates of PDs in the general population (Cooke & Hart, 2004). We included one more criterion to diagnose paranoid (i.e. 5 out of 7 criteria instead of the 4 criteria scheduled by IPDE authors), schizoid, histrionic, dependent and avoidant PDs, and two more criteria for the remaining PDs. Pérez-Urdániz et al. (2005) considered six items of each PD to diagnose them. Ekselius et al. (1994, 1995) also used and adjusted cut-off point to diagnosing PD using the SCID-screening questionnaire. They added one more criterion to the ones specified by the authors of the SCID-screening questionnaire. They found a good concordance between the results of the adjusted cut-off screening questionnaire, the full interview and diagnosis made by clinicians.

Following recommendations by DSM-IV (*American Psychiatric Association*, 1996), psychosocial and environmental problems in the last two years and in the last month preceding a suicide attempt were recorded. We used the proposed classification by DSM-IV. Psychosocial and environmental adversities were openly asked, not inducing answers (contextual method). Later on, they were coded in accordance with the Social adjustment scale (Holmes & Rahe, 1967), which has previously been used in the research of suicide (Rich et al., 1991). We used the standardized and adapted Spanish version by González de Rivera & Morera (1983). This is a 43 items scale, every item value being from 0 to 100 vital changes unit (VCU). Two indexes are obtained: an index of vital events (IVE) and a social readjustment index (SRI) –which is the sum of all the values of all the items-. Items were grouped altogether following the most simple way, based on the previously done by Rich et al. (1991) and Heikkinen et al. (1997). Furthermore, *St. Paul Ramsay Life experience scale* was used in order to code all RLE in the month preceding suicide attempts. They were coded in a severity scale ranging from one to seven, being the eight used when no information was available.

Limitations

The major limitation of our study is that, as said before, the IPDE-SQ is not recommended to make diagnosis of PDs, basically due to the lack of specificity and high rate of false positives typical of screening questionnaires (Egan et al., 2003). We rejected using the full *International Personality Disorders Examination* (IPDE) based on logistics and ethical problems derived of the long time scheduled for a full interview. As said before, other authors have used a similar strategy to our with similar results (Ekselius et al., 1994; Pérez-Urdániz et al., 2005). Furthermore, results reported by Dirks (1998) back our work. They found a rate of 56.6% of PDs in their sample of parasuicidal subjects assessed in the emergency room. Although we found a relatively higher rate of PDs in our sample (74.2%), this might be due to the different instrument and systems of classification used, and to differences in the populations studied (they studied parasuide and we studied suicide attempts). Furthermore, our rate of PDs in our inpatient control group (48.8 %) is similar to those reported by others (Molinari et al., 1994; Ross et al., 2003).

CLUSTER B PERSONALITY DISORDERS AND SUICIDE BEHAVIOR

H. Blasco-Fontecilla

Cluster B PDs are characterized by impulsivity, affective instability, personal rejection and intolerance to frustration, among others (Blaszynski & Steel, 1998). There is an emphasis on the study of the relationship between Cluster B or DSM-IV Dramatic PD cluster, particularly borderline PD and suicide behavior that appears to have been intuitively correct (Reich, 1998). Subjects diagnosed with a cluster B PD who self-mutilate are more anxious, depressed, and impulsive, tend to have suffered more abuse, and are often unaware of the lethality of their attempts, than patients with cluster B PDs who do not self-mutilate (Stanley et al., 2001).

2.2.1. NARCISSISTIC PERSONALITY DISORDER (NPD)

"Pathological narcissism" is characterized by structural deformities including pathological grandiose self, unintegrated object relations, inconsistent superego functioning, and impaired affect regulation (Ronningstam & Maltsberger, 1998). Narcissistic personality disorder (NPD) is characterized by extreme grandiosity, lack of empathy for others, and extreme self-involvement, among others. Covert narcissistic features are inferiority, insecurity, vulnerability, shame, and envy (Akhart, 1989; Gabbard, 1989). The concept of narcissism as an internal regulation system of self-esteem, which is subject to constant challenges and changes in order to keep the subject in a stable, but dynamic balance, is widely accepted (Geiser & Lieberz, 2000). Curiously, it seems that the so-call personality dimension of narcissism is the one with the highest genetic heritability (Livesley et al., 1993).

NPD is uncommon in both community samples and clinical settings (Links et al., 2003). They probably make up less than 1% of outpatient samples and the vast majority of information regarding these subjects is based on theoretical formulations and clinical experience, rather than on empirical evidence (Links & Stockwell, 2002). The question of whether NPD is a coherent, stable construct distinct from other PD remains controversial

(Ronningstam et al., 1995; Gunderson et al., 1990). Several studies have found similarities between NPD and the remaining cluster B PDs (Morey, 1988b; Ronningstam et al., 1995), and the passive-aggressive personality (Livesley & Jackson, 1986), which questions the validity of this construct. As said before, narcissistic and antisocial subjects share some characteristics (Kernberg, 1984). Whether they should be separated disorders or not is still an open question (Gunderson & Ronningstam, 2001). These authors indicate that the main difference is that narcissistic subjects have more grandiosity than antisocial individuals do. I (Blasco-Fontecilla, 2006, 2007) have suggested that the main difference between Narcissistic PD and Antisocial PD is that the subjects diagnosed with NPD may have a higher intelligence and a better impulse control than those diagnosed with APD; moreover, those subjects diagnosed with NPD do fit well with the clinical picture of psychopaths as described by Cleckey or the more recent description of factor 1 (F1) of psychopathy, closely linked to personality traits such as cruelty, egoism and remorseless manipulation of others, etc. reported by Hare et al. (1991).

Few data are available regarding the risk of suicide in subjects with NPD (Pompili et al., 2004). According to the psychological autopsy method, it is an infrequent diagnosis in suicides (Links et al., 2003). However, Kernberg (1984) postulated that NPD or narcissistic personality traits could make an individual vulnerable to suicidal behavior. The risk for suicide attempts in subjects with NPD may be high due to their fragile self-esteem (Perry, 1990), which can be raised through suicidal behavior (Ronningstam & Maltsberger, 1998). Apter et al. (1993) carried out a post-mortem study in 43 consecutive suicides among Israeli males aged 18 to 21 years during compulsory military service and found out that the most common axis II diagnosis were schizoid PD (37.2%) and NPD (23.3%). Moreover, in a 15-year follow-up of inpatients was found that the presence of narcissistic traits or NPD was associated with a higher probability to dying by suicide when compared with patients with no NPD or narcissistic traits (14% vs 5%, $P < 0.02$) (Stone, 1989). Narcissistic traits in BPD are also associated with an increased risk of suicide (Stone, 1989).

Although suicide attempts often take place when the narcissistic subject is depressed, and indeed they have an increased risk for suicide when they have a comorbid depression (Maltsberger, 1997), suicidal behavior in these subjects is not merely an expression of a depressed state (Ronningstam & Maltsberger, 1998). Ego-syntonic suicidal tendencies in narcissistic patients without depressive syndromes can emerge in emotional crises or with the underlying fantasy that suicide reflects triumph over death (Kernberg, 1992). Narcissism might contribute to suicide through narcissistic rage secondary to a narcissistic injury, real or perceived, like a sudden drop in social position (Kernberg, 1984). Ronningstam & Maltsberger (1998) suggested several meanings of the suicidal act, including an effort to raise their fragile self-esteem through a sense of mastery over death; a vengeful act against a narcissistic trauma; an attempt to defend themselves against imagined narcissistic threats – "death before dishonour"; a desire to destroy or attack an unsatisfactory self; and finally, the false belief of indestructibility. Other authors think they try to kill themselves because of their easily broken self-esteem and in response to perceived narcissistic injury (Perry, 1990). Those who kill themselves while apparently enjoying life, being successful and happy individuals can be labelled with the so-called "Richard Corey suicide", which is a fictional character from the poem by Edwin Arlington Robinson (Ronningstam & Maltsberger, 1998). Suicidal behavior would be the result of narcissistic rage, not depression, in response to sudden, catastrophic disintegration driven by overwhelming shame and envy (Kavka, 1976).

Moreover, suicidal behavior in narcissistic subjects may provide an escape from painful feelings while expressing rage and retaliation with a sense of active mastery (Rothstein, 1980), and provides means to assert power and triumph over the therapist (Kernberg, 1984).

Ronningstam & Maltsberger (1998) analysed three cases of suicide attempt in NPD subjects. They found the following characteristics in them: 1) Their incapacity to protect the body, that is, the failure of self-protecting functions; 2) the incapacity to identify and respond adaptively to painful life events; 3) intense rage reactions in response to defeats; 4) the incapacity for empathy; 5) the more hidden characteriological vulnerability characterized by hypersensitivity to other's reactions, deep feelings of inferiority and fear of rejection. They concluded that subjects with a combination of affect dysregulation, grandiosity, and narcissistic vulnerability may attempt suicide in response to interpersonal difficulties. Suicidal behavior may be an effort to protect the self from a narcissistic injury while maintaining a sense of invulnerability and mastery (Ronningstam & Maltsberger, 1998). Apter et al. (1993) said that the young soldiers retrospectively diagnosed with a NPD and that seemed to be capable of handling service-related stress may have been at risk due to their perfectionist and isolative personality traits. In so far as suicidal episodes can be unpredictable in them, suicide risk assessment is of major importance (Links et al., 2003).

2.2.2. BORDERLINE PERSONALITY DISORDER (BPD)

Introduction

Borderline personality disorder (BPD) is considered a stable disorder, of long duration, multifactorial and that can be traced to adolescence or early childhood (Zlotnick et al., 2003). This disorder has a waxing and waning course, as they may or may not meet criteria for the disorder, depending on what is going on in their lives (Grilo et al., 2000). Most of them no longer meet full criteria for the disorder by age 40, being the possible mechanisms behind remission maturation – e.g. impulsivity decrease with age, a process that could reflect biological maturation-, social learning, and the avoidance of conflict intimacy (Paris, 2002c). 76-80% of subjects diagnosed with BPD are women (Widiger & Weissman, 1991).

It is generally accepted that patients with BPD improve over time (Paris, 2002c). If survival is efficiently managed during youth, suicidality decreases, among others (Kjellander et al., 1988). However, there is a subgroup of patients characterized by enduring impulsivity, comorbid personality pathology, poor pre-morbid functioning and suicidal ideation or behavior that will not fare well (Sansone et al., 2002). Moreover, parasuicide behaviors are resistant to change (Antikainen et al., 1995). Sansone et al. (2002) found that self-harm behavior remained relatively sustained through the 50s. Indeed, suicidal behavior could be considered a poor prognostic factor of BPD.

Suicide Attempts in BPD

Suicidal behavior is a multi-determined phenomenon and a common complication in patients with BPD (Trull et al., 2003; Brodsky et al., 1997). Some authors think that subjects with BPD are at the same level of suicide risk than patients diagnosed with major depressive disorder (MDD) (Lambert, 2003) or at a higher risk (Yen et al., 2003). Patients with BPD attempt suicide for the first time earlier in life than depressed patients (Soloff et al., 1994). The close relationship between suicidal behavior and BPD is not only due to self-destructive behavior being a criterion in DSM-IV (Links et al., 2003) but also to the remaining criteria, such as impulsivity, aggressiveness and affective instability, contributing to a pattern of disturbed relationships with others and difficulties meeting the challenges of life (Mehlum et al., 1994). In fact, BPD is the only PD, which includes suicidal behavior as a criterion (Bronisch, 1996). Patients diagnosed with BPD frequently engage in self-destructive behavior but not all BPD patients, however, display suicidal behavior (Mehlum et al., 1994). Suicidality is usually central to the borderline construct, is the most important issue for treatment, and the most frequent source of conflict and anguish for clinicians and relatives (Gunderson & Ridolfi, 2001). Suicidal behavior can be seen as a way of communicating distress (Paris, 2002) or an expression of narcissistic crisis (Wasserman & Cullberg, 1989).

Friedman et al. (1983) found that among 76 adolescent inpatients, those diagnosed with both BPD and MDD made more numerous and more serious suicide attempts than those with depression with any other axis II diagnosis or with depression alone. Women with BPD and comorbid depressive personality traits who show few active coping strategies and few reassuring thoughts are more likely to engage in suicidal behavior (Rietkijk et al., 2001). The identification of which criteria –excluding self-injury- of BPD are associated with suicidal behavior could lead to the development of more specific therapeutic interventions. Brodsky et al. (1997) found that impulsivity was the only criterion of BPD associated with suicide attempts once depression and substance abuse were controlled. They stated that the single trait of impulsivity, rather than global severity of BPD, was the real factor associated to suicidal behavior, including suicide attempts. The presence of history of childhood abuse was also associated with a higher prevalence of suicide attempts. Yen et al. (2004) found that suicidal behaviors were predicted in order of significance by affective instability, identity disturbance and impulsivity, while suicidal attempts only were predicted by affective instability. As Brodksky said, the presence of history of childhood sexual abuse also predicted suicide attempts but curiously not suicide behaviors. Thus, they concluded that affective instability was the BPD criterion most strongly associated to both suicide behaviors and suicide attempts suggesting reactive mood shifts related to affective instability could be more decisive for suicidal behaviors than negative mood *per se*.

A history of suicidal behavior is found in 60% to 78% of individuals with BPD (Gunderson, 1984; Shearer et al., 1988; Zanarini et al., 1990). Crumley (1979) found a high incidence of BPD in subjects aged 15 to 24 years who engage in suicidal behavior. Gunderson (1984) found that among inpatients with BPD, 75% had made at least one previous suicide gesture. Fyer et al. (1988) found an 81% rate of suicidal behavior in adult inpatients with BPD. To summarize, approximately 70% of borderline patients engage in self-injurious behaviors and nearly one in 10 will eventually suicide (Frances et al., 1986; Paris et al., 1987; Kullgren 1988; Paris, 2002a; Gerson & Stanley, 2002). Thus, in a 27-year follow-up of 64 borderline patients was found that the leading cause of death among the 18.2% that had died of all causes was suicide with a 10.3%. Moreover, this rate may be higher as not always was possible to locate all the subjects. The mean age of the subjects with BPD who suicide was 37.3 +/- 10.3 (Paris & Zweig-Frank, 2001). Other studies have reported rates of suicide from 3 to 9% (Isometsa E et al., 1996).

Given the strong association between suicidal behavior and BPD, several hypotheses have been postulated. BPD patients: 1) may be more predisposed for Axis I disorders, which in turn, increase suicidal risk; 2) may face more frequently undesirable life events as a consequence of their irrational and impulsive behavior; 3) may have more interpersonal difficulties and problems in psychosocial adjustment; and 4) may have fewer coping resources to adapt to stressful life events (Kaplan & Sadock, 1998). Fyer et al. (1988) found that suicide gestures were associated with BPD alone while serious suicide attempts could be related to the presence of comorbidity in BPD patients. Curiously, most completions occur late in the course of illness, in their thirties, often after a series of failed treatments and in a state of withdrawal and hopelessness, while few among patients in their early 20s complete suicide, when attempts are very common (Paris, 2002a). Moreover, hospitalization can lead to regressive complications (Gunderson, 2001) and there is no evidence that therapy actually prevents completion (Paris, 2002c).

(Completed) Suicide and BPD

The majority of subjects with BPD who eventually suicide are female, after multiple attempts and in their thirties –suicide attempts peaked in the twenties- (Paris, 2002). However, the risk of suicide is higher in males than females (Kjellsber et al., 1991). It has been estimated that 10% of suicide attempters (SA) diagnosed with BPD will eventually suicide (Fyer et al., 1988). Retrospective studies have found rates between 9% to 33% of suicides (Kullgren et al., 1986; Runeson, 1989; Runeson et al., 1991). Longitudinal studies report rates of suicide ranging from 3% to 9% (McGlashan, 1986; Stone et al., 1987). The rate of 9% is about 400 times the rate of suicide in the general population in the US (US census bureau, 1995). Paris (2002a) concluded, after reviewing several articles and finding striking convergent results, that one in ten patients with BPD would complete suicide, what is similar to the rate found in patients with MDD (Guze & Robins, 1970) and schizophrenia (Wilkinson, 1982). In selected high-risk samples, such as young people, BPD is diagnosed up to 33% of suicides (Runeson, 1989). The longer is the follow-up, the higher are the rates of suicide: Akiskal et al. (1985) reported a 4% rate during a 6-36 month follow-up, Pope et al. (1983) found a 7.4% rate on a 4-7-year follow-up and finally, Stone et al. (1987) found a 9.5% rate on 15-20-year follow-up.

Several authors have tried to find out what are the differences between BPD patients who go on showing suicidal behavior and eventually suicide compared to those who do not. Kjelsberg et al. (1991) carried out a case-control study comparing 21 subjects diagnosed of BPD who suicide to 21 matched inpatients with BPD. They found several variables significantly associated with suicide: childhood losses, previous serious suicidal attempts, lack of therapist contact, non-comorbid anxiety neurosis, hospitalization for more than a week, and discharge for violating treatment contract. They thought the single most important factor was childhood losses. They considered suicide as an expression of narcissistic crisis owing to the actualization of primary object loss (Wasserman & Cullberg, 1989). Soloff et al. (1994) summarized the putative risk factors for attempted suicide or suicide in BPD patients: 1) comorbidity with affective disorder and/or alcohol/substance abuse; 2) repeated attempts; 3) severity of BPD; 4) hostility, impulsivity, aggressiveness and antisocial traits. However, they found that the borderline patients at the highest risk for suicidal behavior were older, had histories of impulsivity, antisocial PD, depressive mood and prior suicide attempts, but not comorbid affective disorder, alcoholism, substance abuse or severity of illness. They also said that patients with both borderline PD and antisocial PD reported higher seriousness of attempt but their attempts were indeed of lower lethality. Moreover, borderline patients with comorbid antisocial PD had less frequently major depression.

Documented risk factors for suicide are comorbid antisocial PD (Shearer et al., 1988; Stone, 1989; Runeson & Beskow, 1991) alcoholism (Kernberg, 1993), past attempts (Soloff et al., 1994), higher education (Paris et al., 1989), prior hospitalization within the past five years (Stone et al., 1987), lack of employment, and early loss (Mehlun et al., 1994). Paris (2002) said that the ones who suicide tend to be older men who suicide in their first attempt and do not usually seek treatment, whereas SA who repeat tend to be younger women who readily seek treatment. Comorbidity with axis I disorders, mainly affective disorders (McGlashan, 1987) and substance use disorders (Rich & Runeson, 1992) or both (Lesage et al., 1994; Friedman et al., 1983; Fyer et al., 1988; Stone, 1990) significantly increase the risk of suicide in them. Paris et al. (1989) did not found that comorbidity with an affective disorder was a risk factor, suggesting this could be due to BPD patients having no necessarily melancholia or depression being different in those patients. Kullgren (1988) found that patients who eventually suicide showed more frequently antisocial behavior and a poorer impulse control, abused more drugs, and lacked the capacity to engage in meaningful relationships. Kjelsberg et al. (1991) said that the lack of contact with a therapist of the suicidal group could be an indicator of the lack of this capacity. They suggested that BPD patients with earlier serious suicide attempt or lack of therapist contact or discharge for violating the contract were at the highest risk for suicide. On the other hand, anxiety and a stable relationship with their therapists may have a protecting role in them. Allebeck et al. (1988) also found that the lack of friends was predictive of suicide in a cohort of 50465 young men conscripts. Paffenbarger & Asnes (1966) found that early loss or absence of the father was predictive of suicide for men but not for women. Allebeck et al. (1988) found that, independently of whether the missing parent was the father or the mother, children grown up with only one parent had an increased suicide rate. The number of previous suicides attempts is also predictive of suicide (Paris et al., 1989; Kjelsberg et al., 1991; Kullgren, 1988), and the strongest predictor of suicide and future suicidal behavior in all psychiatric populations including BPD (Paris et al., 1989; Mehlum et al., 1994; Brodsky et al., 1997). Paris et al. (1989) said that higher education was a risk factor for suicide but Kjelsberg et al. (1991) failed to confirm these data. The former authors supported the relationship between high education and suicide "by the crushed expectations of educated persons with severe psychopathology".

Biology of Suicide in Subjects with BPD

Biological research in BPD is focused in serotonin metabolism and cholesterol. Atmaca et al. (2002) found evidence that low serum cholesterol and leptin levels were associated with several dimensions of BPD – impulsivity, aggressiveness and suicidality- but not with the presence and severity of depression. However, they did not control for economic status and other psychosocial factors, and also the size of the sample was small. Moreover, borderline patients have low levels of cerebral spinal fluid 5-hydroxyindoleacetic acid, the main metabolite of serotonin (5-HT) and a reduced prolactin response to fenfluramine challenge, an indicator of serotonin regulation (Harwitz & Ravizza, 2000). Both markers are related to suicidal –particularly violent suicidal- behavior and impulsivity, such as that typical of BPD (Soloff et al., 1994). Several of the symptoms of BPD, and particularly affective instability, suicidal behaviors, and impulsive aggression are related to serotonergic dysfunction (Hansenne et al., 2002). These authors found blunted prolactine responses to flesinoxan – a potent and selective 5-HT$_{1A}$ agonist- among BPD individuals with a past history of non-violent impulsive suicide attempts as compared to BPD subjects without such a history, which is consistent with the inverse relationship between central 5-HT dysfunction and impulsivity, aggressiveness and suicidal behavior (Cocarro et al., 1989; New et al., 1997). Unfortunately, they did not assess irritability and impulsivity, and therefore, correlations with prolactine were not calculated.

Role of Abuse in BPD

In this chapter I will focus on the relationship of abuse in subjects with BPD who have suicidal behaviors. Readers interested in this area will find interesting the articles by Brodsky & Stanley (2001) and Molinari (2000).

Early childhood experiences of sexual and physical abuse and parental neglect are risk factors for both the diagnosis of PD (Roy et al., 2001; Bierer et al., 2003) and suicidal behavior in adulthood (Brodsky & Stanley, 2001). In an outpatient sample of 182 subjects with PDs was found that 78% met criteria for some kind of childhood trauma and that sexual and physical abuse were significant predictors of paranoid PD and antisocial PD, while emotional abuse was a predictor of BPD; that is, physical and sexual abuse were antecedent traumatic occurrences in disorders with externally directed psychopathology – paranoid PD and antisocial PD-, whereas emotional abuse was associated with a disorder characterized by affective instability and impulse dysregulation (BPD)- (Bierer et al., 2003). Moreover, they found that history of suicide attempts was predicted by emotional abuse. Van der Kolk et al. (1991) also found that childhood sexual/physical abuse and neglect were associated with self-mutilation and suicide attempts in patients with a PD.

Several studies have reported higher rates of suicidal behavior (Briere & Runtz, 1986; Stepakoff, 1998) as well as higher levels of affect dysregulation (van der Kolk et al., 1996) in subjects who suffered sexual abuse compared to non-abused individuals, but these studies failed to include possible confounding variables, such as the diagnosis of BPD. Zlotnick et al. (2001) found that, in patients with major depression, the relationship between childhood sexual abuse experiences and adult affect dysregulation or suicide attempts were determined more by the influence of BPD and post-stress syndrome (PTSD), than by sexual abuse *per se*. In other words, childhood sexual abuse may predispose to BPD or PTSD, which in turn would pose to those individuals to a higher risk of suicidal behavior.

Recurrent self-destructive behavior, including non-suicidal and suicidal behaviors, is a hallmark characteristic of subjects diagnosed with BPD (Brodsky & Stanley, 2001). Several authors have suggested an etiologic role for childhood abuse in the development of BPD, particularly self-destructiveness. Childhood abuse has been associated with an increased incidence of suicidal ideation and self-harm behaviors, independent of diagnosis (Soloff et al., 2002). Brodsky et al. (1997) found that subjects with BPD that reported a history of physical or sexual abuse in childhood were more likely to have made a suicide attempt than those who did not report such an abuse history. Moreover, abuse was also associated with the number of previous suicide attempts after controlling for MDD and substance abuse. This is consistent with the previous reported relationship between childhood abuse and self-damaging behaviors and suicide attempts (Briere & Runtz, 1990; Dubois et al., 1997; van der Kolk et al., 1991; Wagner & Linehan, 1994). Wagner & Linehan (1994) also said that subjects diagnosed with BPD who report childhood sexual abuse are more likely to make more lethal suicide attempts. Stone (1992) found that among adolescents who suicide, patients diagnosed with BPD were more likely to have experienced parental humiliation and parental brutality in their past.

Brodsky et al. (1997) hypothesized that there could be an aetiological relationship between childhood abuse and impulsivity as both factors were associated to suicidality in borderline patients. Impulsivity and aggressiveness may be personality traits secondary to early childhood experiences of trauma and loss, or alternatively, mainly inherited traits that underlie both childhood abuse as well as adult trait impulsivity, or finally, they may be inherited traits that are worsened by environmental experiences of abuse (Brodsky & Stanley, 2001). Silk et al. (1995) found in a sample of 55 borderline inpatients that overall severity of reported sexual abuse was significantly associated with severity of borderline psychopathology. Soloff et al. (2002) found that in patients with BPD, the history of childhood sexual abuse increased tenfold the risk of suicidal behavior compared with subjects without such a background. They also found that the number of suicide attempts was predicted –even independently- by a history of sexual abuse, by the level of hopelessness and, by the severity of BPD. Moreover, the severity of sexual abuse was associated with a trend toward greater hopelessness, with antisocial traits and with severity of comorbid depression. They hypothesized all these factors could mediate the influence of childhood sexual abuse to developing BPD. They also found in their prospective study that the presence and severity of childhood sexual abuse, but not physical abuse, predicted adult suicidal behavior independent of other known risk factors. Moreover, given the presence of sexual abuse, the likelihood of adult suicidal behavior in BPD was increased by severity of BPD, hopelessness, or comorbid major depressive disorder or antisocial traits. Contrary to expectations, they found no association between occurrence, severity, or duration of sexual abuse and severity of BPD psychopathology. They concluded that childhood sexual abuse might contribute to the development of BPD but was neither necessary nor sufficient to explain the full picture of BPD. Finally, a childhood history of sexual abuse and an adult history of being a victim of violence are associated with repeated hospitalizations for borderline patients (Zanarini et al., 2001).

Management of Suicide Behavior in BPD

Several topics are of interest from a clinician point of view. Firstly, clinicians should take into account the enduring nature of suicidal ideation and suicide behavior in BPD, in contrast to SA diagnosed with other mental disorders, where the suicidal ideation and behavior are more linked to affective states. Suicidal inclination in subjects with BPD is characteriollogically anchored and not episodic (Mehlum et al., 1994). Moreover, it is a poor prognosis predictor, as patients with BPD who do not engage in suicidal behavior have a global mental health comparable to non-BPD patients (Mehlum et al., 1994). These authors also suggested that SA diagnosed with a BPD could be considered more prototypical "borderlines" because they retained more frequently the diagnosis at follow-up. Indeed, suicidal or self-damaging behavior has been postulated as the core feature of BPD (Nurnberg et al., 1991).

Secondly, clinicians usually consider some of the suicide attempts of individuals with BPD to be `manipulative´ or not to have the same risk of suicide than those made by, for example, subjects with major depression. The study carried out with severe SA by Dingman & McGlashan (1988) lends statistical credibility to such impressions but it may lead clinicians to underestimate the seriousness of suicide attempts by subjects with BPD (Kiellander et al., 1998). Indeed, several authors have stated that `manipulative´ attempts, usually considered less serious, continue to be associated with an alarmingly high suicide rate (Paris et al., 1989; Stone, 1990; Mehlum, 1994). This could have to do with the proneness of patients with BPD to engage in self-injurious behavior, used as a way of lowering their anxiety. Self-injurious behavior has also been related to an increase in the risk for suicide (Linehan, 1993; Stanley et al., 2001). Stanley et al. (2001) found that the higher risk for suicide in subjects who engaged in self-injurious behavior was due to their high level of depression, hopelessness, impulsivity and finally, because they misperceive and underestimate the lethality of their behaviors. Women with BPD report different reasons to engage in non-suicidal behavior – to generate feelings, distract themselves and express anger- and suicidal behavior – because they think their life is troublesome to others- (Brown et al., 2002). Dingman & McGlashan (1988) found that although a history of serious intent places a subject at high risk for future suicide, this risk is lessened in patients, particularly females, with a history and symptoms suggesting BPD.

Thirdly, it seems important to differentiate between acute and chronic suicidality. The former is usually managed in an acute inpatient unit, while the same management might be inappropriate or even counterproductive in the latter (Paris, 2004). Chronic suicidality in BPD patients has at least three functions for the patients: to dealing with painful affects or to escape inner suffering, to communicating distress and to establishing a sense of control (Paris, 2004).

Finally, clinicians should be aware of the increasing suicidal risk of BPD patients with comorbid affective or substance abuse disorders when assessing suicide potential (Fyer et al., 1988).

2.2.3. ANTISOCIAL PERSONALITY DISORDER (APD)

The literature on personality-related suicide risk has highly been focused on BPD. Literature on APD and suicide is relatively scarce. At least two subtypes of individuals who attempt suicide have been postulated: depressed/withdrawn and irritable/aggressive (Apter et al., 1991). These authors found that sadness did not correlate with suicidal behavior in violent male patients, suggesting that although major depression is an important risk factor for suicidal behavior, the increasing risk of suicidal behaviors among patients with externalizing disorders –including APD- may be secondary to impulsivity and anger (Verona et al., 2004).

Cleckey (1976) maintained that psychopaths were relatively immune to suicide. However, the growing incidence of suicidal behavior in prison and jail settings may indicate this could not be true (Haycock, 1991; McKee, 1998). Rydelius (1988) found in an 18 year follow-up of 1056 boys and girls admitted to a compulsory probationary school for antisocial behavior that the percentage of deaths was higher than expected, being suicide the most frequent cause of death. Moreover, several authors have found APD or criminal behavior to be a predictor of subsequent suicide attempts (Buglass & Horton, 1974; Morgan et al., 1976). A relationship between APD and suicidal behavior has been postulated (Verona et al., 2001). Indeed, the diagnosis of APD is associated with an increased death rate (Black et al., 1996), particularly with violent deaths (homicide and suicide) (Martin et al., 1985). Men with APD are up to 12 times more likely to attempt suicide than those without APD (Mulder et al., 1994; Martens, 2000). Beautrais et al. (1996) found that the risk for a serious suicide attempt was 3.7 times higher among subjects with APD. Thee risk was particularly high for men under 30 years, who were 9 times more likely to have a suicide attempt than those without an APD. Moreover, there is also a relationship between criminality and suicidal behavior both in young and adult people (Verona et al., 2001). Widom (1978) did not use clinical diagnoses but reported a suicide attempt rate of 28.6% in a sample of "non-institutionalized psychopaths".

The diagnosis of APD does not include past suicidal behavior as a criterion but it was suggested to be included in the DSM-III (Garvey & Spoden, 1980). It has also been proposed that suicidal behavior may be included as a DSM-IV diagnostic feature of APD to give a more complete and precise picture of this PD (Martens, 2001). However, it raises the question whether it would be useful to consider as a criterion a symptom –suicidality- that is relatively common in psychiatric disorders (Dilling, 2001). Allebeck et al. (1988) found that early indicators of APD - deviant behavior and a lack of friends- were strongly predictive of suicide.

The rate of suicide attempts in subjects diagnosed with APD range between 11% to 42% (Robins, 1966; Maddocks, 1970; Woodruff et al., 1971), but up to 72% of patients with APD may attempt suicide (Garvey & Spoden, 1980). Their suicide attempts are usually considered non-serious, with no real intention to die, secondary to interpersonal loss or problems and in order to manipulate others or to act out their frustration (Garvey & Spoden, 1980; Frances et al., 1988; Frances et al., 1996). This lack of seriousness may suggest that they have no real intention of killing themselves and they use suicide attempts to manipulate others, to act out their frustration or to have a secondary gain (e.g. hospital admission) (Pompili et al., 2004). In a military hospital setting, suicidal behavior may be regarded as an alternative channel to alleviating distress (Sayar et al., 2001). Frances A et al. (1996) hypothesized that the 5% rate of suicide found in subjects with APD might be explained by the presence of a concurrent affective disorder, substance abuse or other PD.

These rates of suicide attempts contrast to those of suicides. Suicide rates reported among patients with APD vary considerably as most studies use no operationalized criteria (Bronisch, 1996). Moreover, there is a great comorbidity between APD and BPD. Robins (1974) found a rate of 11% of suicide attempts and a rate of suicide similar to that found in psychiatrically normal controls. However, other authors have estimated that 5-6% of subjects diagnosed with APD or psychopathy eventually die by suicide (Helgason, 1964; Maddocks, 1970; Miles, 1977). Rich et al. (1988) reported a 3% rate of APD among both female and male suicide victims in their psychological autopsy study, which in any case, is lower than the 8% found in BPD in long-term follow-up studies (Bronisch, 1996). The traditional assumption derived from Cleckey and other classical authors that antisocial individuals could be so self-centred to actually try to kill themselves could be inconsistent with current findings (Lambert, 2003). Indeed, in a case-control study of 302 suicide attempters, the diagnosis of APD was the third most important etiological factor only behind mood disorders and non-affective psychosis (Beautrais et al., 1996). This might be explained by the differences between the two personality factors found in psychopaths by Hare & Hart. As said before, APD and psychopathy may be two different concepts, although somewhat related (see chapter 1.2.5). Taking into account the differences between the two concepts, Verona et al. (2001) found in a sample of 313 male residents of a Florida security prison, that suicidal history was substantially related to APD and to the antisocial deviance factor of the PCL-R (F2), but not to the affective-interpersonal factor (F1) of psychopathy, which measure the emotional deficit of some psychopaths (Links et al., 2003). The correlation between overall APD symptoms and PCL-R F2 scores was .83 (Verona et al., 2001). These results "indicate that it is the antisocial and impulsive features of psychopathy, and not the personality or interpersonal features that are associated with higher suicide risk". Regarding the relationship between suicidal behavior and PCL-R F2, after controlling for the negative emotionality (NEM) and Constraint (CON) factors of the MPQ, the relationship between PCL-R F2 and suicide was eliminated, which provides persuasive evidence that impulsive antisocial behavior and suicidal behavior in this population are associated expressions of a common dispositional vulnerability (Verona et al., 2001).

Suicide and violence have been connected in diverse theories (Stalennheim, 2001) such as Freud's psychoanalysis, who considered suicide an aggressive act (Sullivan Everstime & Everstime, 1992). Personality traits associated with suicidal behavior have also been associated with violence towards others (Stalenheim, 2001). Moreover, Plutchik et al. (1989) proposed a two-stage model of countervailing forces where suicide and violence represent the expression of the same underlying aggressive impulse, and the presence or absence of different factors would determine whether the aggression is expressed or not, and toward whom would be directed. Moreover, it seems that among re-incident criminal violent subjects, those who attempt suicide are a far more disturbed group than non-attempters, suicidal behavior indicating per se a very severe personality disturbance in criminal offenders (Stalenheim, 2001). Apter et al. (1991) suggested that management of suicide risk should be different in highly violent patients. Thus, the theory of a common predisposition to both externally and self-directed harm seems particularly applicable in this violent population (Stalenheim, 2001).

Finally, in the same way subjects with BPD tends to improve with time, some level of improvement by late middle age can also be found in some subjects diagnosed with APD (Black et al., 1995; 1997).

2.2.4. HISTRIONIC/HYSTERICAL PERSONALITY DISORDER (HPD)

The concept of HPD arose out of the clinical observation that women who had conversion symptoms tended to have certain personality characteristics in common (Kendell, 1983). Although it is usually associated to female gender, no differential risk was observed for gender in an American study (Grant et al., 2004). These authors found that the odd of HPD was elevated in the lowest-income groups, and widowed/separated/divorced.

Several references have been made to the liability of histrionic personalities to threaten suicide (Kendell, 1983). Hysterical personality traits have been related to suicide attempts in both men and women (Pretorius et al., 1994). Suicide attempts are frequent in people with HPD or histrionic personality traits, as a way of emotional blackmail, coercion to the ones who take care of them, or to attract attention (Rubio Larrosa, 2004). When the diagnosis of BPD was not coined, the diagnosis of HPD predominated among women who repeated suicide attempts (Kendell, 1983). Most suicide attempts arise out of disturbed relationships between close relatives or sexual partners. Due to their demanding, egocentric behavior and dependence, their interpersonal relationships are characteristically stormy and fragile (Kendell, 1983). They are also prone to fluctuations in mood in response to stress and use drugs (Kendell, 1983). Moreover, Angst et al. (1990) found a relationship between histrionic personality traits and brief recurrent depression in women but not in men – thay they tried to explain by the small number of men included in the study-. Subjects with the diagnosis of HPD have greater emotional instability, than subjects with other PDs and neurotic diagnoses (Slavney & Rich, 1980). Self-ratings of mood instability and hysterical personality traits have also been positively correlated in men (Ravins & Slavney, 1979). Finally, but most important of all, their suicide attempts are *par excellence* a manipulative act. Although some suicide attempts by subjects with HPD take place in "a mood, albeit short-lived, of genuine despair", usually it is clear from the circumstances that its main purpose was to coerce someone else into behaving in a way more similar to the patient's liking (Kendell, 1983).

Although their suicide attempts, mainly recurrent overdoses, are non-fatal in nature, it is not uncommon for those with histrionic personalities to die by suicide in the end. Like most other cluster B PDs, they tend to mature slowly, but even so, some fail to adapt to situations where their ability to obtain attention and affection and to manipulate is not any more useful, becoming increasingly more lonely, prone to bouts of depression and sometimes get addicted to alcohol; the final overdose takes place in this setting (Kendell, 1983).

CLUSTER A PERSONALITY DISORDERS
AND SUICIDE BEHAVIOR

H. Blasco-Fontecilla

From a conceptual point of view, Cluster A PDs are usually considered to be closely related to psychotic syndromes, particularly schizophrenia. Indeed, schyzotipal PD is considered a subtype of schizophrenia in the ICD-10 classification (WHO, 1993). Rubio Larrosa et al. (2002) carried out a study comparing the clinical profile of cluster A PDs and BPD. They found that the presence of suicide ideation, history of suicide attempts, and history of self-harm were more frequent in subjects with BPD than in those diagnosed with a cluster A PD, concluding that BPD was a more severe disorder. In a sample of 123 consecutive *suicide attempters (SA)*, the diagnosis of a cluster A PD was the less frequent among PDs. Similarly, in a psychological autopsy study, the diagnosis of cluster A PDs was very rare in suicide completers (Isometsa et al., 1996).

2.3.1. PARANOID PERSONALITY DISORDER (PPD)

Paranoid PD is more frequent in women, low-income groups, with lower education level and among widowed/divorced/separated in the community (Grant et al., 2004). However, paranoid inpatients are more frequently males (Fulton & Winokur, 1993).

It is traditionally accepted that subjects diagnosed with paranoid PD do not usually try to attempt suicide. They project aggressiveness outwardly. Their rigid minded style may lead them to behave aggressively when defending their ideas, but this aggressiveness is externally directed. However, suicide behaviors and suicides with ritual characteristics have been described in fanatic situations (Rubio Larrosa, 2004). Moreover, Maj-Liz et al. (1999) found in their sample of 123 consecutive SA that paranoid PD (n = 8), borderline PD (n= 33), and avoidant PD (n= 22) were the most frequent PD diagnosed in cluster A, cluster B, and cluster C, respectively. This is very similar to what Foster et al. (1997; 1999) found in a sample of suicides. Hawton et al. (2003) found that 45.9% of suicide attempters were diagnosed with a

PD at follow-up, and paranoid PD was the third most prevalent, following anxious PD and anankastic PD.

2.3.2. Schizoid Personality Disorder

The construct of schizoid PD seems solid as inter-correlations with other PDs are at a satisfactory low level (Livesley & Jackson, 1986). The odd of schizoid PD is greater among Americans with a low education level, within a low-income group, and widowed/separated/divorced (Grant et al., 2004).

Schizoid subjects are usually considered to have a low frequency of suicidal behaviors. They might be at risk of suicidal ideation when feeling desperate or with anhedonia (Rubio Larrosa, 2004). Their personality profile – i.e. introversion, lack of social relationships, difficulty to communicate their feelings- makes really difficult to detect their potential suicidal tendencies. In a sample of 43 completed suicides among Israeli adolescent males during compulsory military service, both narcissistic and schizoid personality traits were frequent. Furthermore, schizoid personality was the most prevalent (37.2%) axis II diagnosis, while narcissistic personality was the second most prevalent (23.3%). BPD was only diagnosed in 4.7% of this sample (Apter et al., 1993). 53.5% had also a diagnosis of major depressive disorder. Although this study has the common limitations of psychological post-mortem suicide studies, the authors hypothesized that previously unreported difficulties at home and school, and the need to minimize or overcome them may have been particularly strong in narcissistically vulnerable subjects with unrealistically high self-expectations. Moreover, it must be taken into account that this study was based in a very narrow and particular population, so that, their results are difficult to generalize to other populations.

2.3.3. Shizotypal Personality Disorder (STPD)

The category of `Schizotypal personality disorder´ was first introduced in the DSM-III (American Psychiatric Association, 1980) to describe patients, usually relatives of schizophrenics, who exhibited cognitive, affective, and interpersonal disturbances similar to, although milder than those that characterize schizophrenia (Gunderson et al., 1983). While in the ICD-10 classification is considered as a type of schizophrenia (WHO, 1993), it is considered a PD in the DSM system of classification (APA, 1987; 1994; 2002). It is calculated that 25% of the subjects diagnosed with STPD will eventually develop clear-cut schizophrenia, and will have a higher risk of suicidal behaviors (Rubio Larrosa, 2004). Prominent negative symptoms counter the emergence of suicidality in patients with schizophrenia spectrum disorders, where STPD is classified, suggesting that the deficit syndrome defines a group of at relatively low risk for suicide (Fenton & McGlashan, 1997). These authors also found that two positive symptoms, suspiciousness and delusions, and in general, paranoid schizophrenia, are associated with an increased risk of suicidal behavior.

In a sample of 76 consecutive patients, ten (13.2%) met DSM-III criteria for STPD. They not only were more likely to receive an axis I diagnosis but also to have a history of *attempted suicide* (60% of them, compared to the 18% of the non-SPD patients) (Bornstein et al., 1988).

Dingman & McGlashan (1988) found that although a history of serious attempt places a subject at a higher risk for future suicide, this risk is lessened in patients with an axis II diagnosis of schizotypal PD compared with patients with any axis I diagnosis except schizophreniform psychosis.

Chapter 2.4.

CLUSTER C PERSONALITY DISORDERS AND SUICIDE BEHAVIOR

H. Blasco-Fontecilla

Although empirical evidence shows that between 55% to 70% of subjects who attempt suicide meet diagnostic criteria for a PD (Clarkin et al., 1984; Casey, 1989), most of the studies have focused on BPD (Soloff et al., 2000) and APD (Frances et al., 1988). The prevalence rates of cluster C PDs in the general population are between 5 to 10% (Chioqueta & Stiles, 2004). Obviously, the prevalence in psychiatric outpatient samples is substantially higher. Torgersen (1988) reported a 55% for avoidant PD, a 47% for dependent PD, and a 20% for obsessive-compulsive PD in a sample of 298 outpatients.

Compared to Cluster B PDs, subjects diagnosed with a Cluster C PD are usually considered to have a lower risk for suicide behaviors (Rubio Larrosa, 2004). In a study of suicide completers in Finland it was found that individuals diagnosed with Cluster C PDs have not an increased risk of suicide when compared to controls, while those with a cluster B PD had so (Isometsa et al., 1996). However, they also found that cluster C PDs made up 10% of all suicides in the random sample, which was more than the estimated prevalence of 2-4% in the general population (Samuels et al., 1994). In 96% of cases, they were associated either with depressive syndromes (74%) or with psychoactive substance use disorders (30%). When they controlled for axis I disorders, no significant differences between suicide completers with or without cluster C PDs were found. Brent et al. (1994) reported similar results in a sample of adolescent suicide completers.

Dirks (1998) reminded that specific PDs may increase or decrease the risk of repetitive suicidal behavior. Indeed, in a recent work of our team, we found that, in our sample of SA, the diagnosis of a cluster C PD may indeed protect against suicide behavior in subjects diagnosed with drug dependence or adaptative disorder (Blasco Fontecilla et al., 2002). However, we also found that a comorbid diagnosis of a cluster C PD in patients diagnosed with a depressive disorder was associated to more severe suicide attempts. Some authors have found that cluster A and C PDs are risk factors for suicide. Fosters et al. (1999) identified all clusters of PDs as risk factors for suicide, but after adjustment for axis I disorders only cluster A and cluster C PDs remained significant risk factors. Moreover, in an interesting case-control psychological autopsy study was found that the diagnosis of cluster C was the only one that was associated with an increased odds ratio of suicide in men (Schneider et al., 2005). The same applied for cluster B PDs in women. In a study made to assess suicide risk in psychiatric outpatients with specific cluster C PDs, 87 outpatients meeting diagnostic criteria for a PD and 53 psychiatric outpatients meeting criteria for an axis I disorder – patients with a lifetime history of psychotic disorder, alcohol and, drug addiction were not included- were compared (Chioqueta & Styles, 2004). The authors found that dependent PD, but not avoidant PD or obsessive-compulsive PDs, as well as Clusters A and Cluster B PDs were significantly related to suicide attempts. This association remained significant after controlling for both a lifetime depressive disorder and severity of depression for the cluster A and the cluster B PDs, but not for dependent PD. The results underline the importance of assessing suicide risk in patients with cluster A and cluster B PDs, while the assessment of suicide risk in patients with cluster C PDs seems to be less important as long as assessment of a comorbid depressive disorder is appropriately conducted. However, Hawton et al. (2003) found, similarly to Dirks (1998), in their sample of SA more cases of anxious PD than previous reports. They thought that their relatively low frequency of emotionally unstable PD was due to the exclusion of individuals with repetitive minor self-injury based on the recognition that they differ from "real" SA. Furthermore, in a study of adolescent suicide completers it was found that Cluster A, Cluster B, and Cluster C PDs, and DSM-IV Appendix B PDs during adolescence were all associated with elevated risk for suicidal ideation or behavior during early adulthood after co-occurring psychiatric disorders and suicidality during adolescence were controlled statistically. They concluded that the increase in risk was not accounted for by co-occurring Axis I disorders or suicidality during adolescence (Johnson et al., 1999).

2.4.1. AVOIDANT (ANXIOUS) PERSONALITY DISORDER (AVPD)

Avoidant personality disorder is more frequent in women. It has been positively associated to a lower education level, to be widowed/divorced/separated or never-married, and negatively to living in a metropolitan area (Grant et al., 2004). A prevalence of 5.2% in the general population has been reported (Klein et al., 1995). Cooke & Hart (2004) gave prevalences in a range between 0.5% to 5%.

Millon (1997) said that subjects diagnosed with AVPD had an increased risk for suicide ideation and suicide behaviors. In a study made to identify consecutive patients admitted to inpatient care at a somatic or psychiatric ward after a parasuicide behavior, avoidant PD was diagnosed in 6%, compared to the 55% of BPD diagnosis found (Soderberg, 2001). The identification of parasuicidal patients was based on the definition used in the WHO/EURO multicentre study on *parasuicide*. Chioqueta & Stiles (2004) found a rate of 18% of suicide attempts in subjects diagnosed with AVPD in an outpatient sample. Moreover, 66% of subjects diagnosed with AVPD had a comorbid diagnosis of lifetime depressive disorder. They concluded that AVPD was not significantly associated with suicide attempts. They argued that, the reluctance in taking personal risk typical of subjects with AVPD may render them less vulnerable to suicide attempts. However, AVPD has been found to be the most prevalent PD in at least two studies of SA (Dirks, 1998; Hawton et al., 2003). This may have to do with the exclusion of subjects with repetitive minor self-injury based on the recognition that as a group they differ from SA (Hawton et al., 2003). Hawton et al. (2003) found that 90.1% of their sample of SA were initially diagnosed with at least one Axis I disorder, particularly an affective disorder, while 45.9% of the subjects were diagnosed of at least one PD at follow-up, especially *anxious PD,* anankastic PD, and paranoid PD. Similarly, Maj-Liz et al. (1999) reported that 99% and 56% of their sample of 123 consecutive SA had an axis I and an axis II diagnosis, respectively. In the cluster C group (n = 23), AVPD was predominant. In a case-control study, the diagnosis of AVPD was the second most prevalent diagnosis among suicides (9.7%) – only after the diagnosis of emotionally unstable PD-, compared to a 5.3% of anxious individuals in the control group (Cheng et al., 1997). Furthermore, Foster et al. (1997; 1999) found AVPD to be among the most frequent PDs – alongside with borderline/emotionally unstable PD and paranoid PDs- in a sample of suicides. Finally, in an interesting study of *extended suicide attempts,* a sample of nine female were evaluated (Meszaros & Fischer-Danzinger, 2000). The most frequent axis I diagnosis was severe depression with psychotic symptoms. After stabilization, the most prevalent PD was avoidant (5 out of 9).

2.4.2. OBSESSIVE-COMPULSIVE/ANANKASTIC PD (OCPD)

The diagnosis of obsessive-compulsive PD is associated with a higher education and white race (Grant et al., 2004). It has been reported a prevalence of 9.3% in the general population (Black et al., 1993). However, Cooke & Hart (2004) reported a lower prevalence, in a range from 1.7% to 2.2%.

Chioqueta & Stiles (2004) found a rate of 14% of suicide attempts in subjects diagnosed with OCPD in an outpatient sample. Moreover, 75% of subjects diagnosed with OCPD had a comorbid diagnosis of lifetime depressive disorder. Finally, they found that OCPD was not significantly associated with suicide attempts. Dirks (1998) found that the diagnosis of *anankastic PD* decreased the risk of reports of previous *parasuicide.* However, Hawton et al. (2003) reported that, OCPD was the second most frequent PD in a sample of SA. Moreover, it has been related to severe suicide attempts (Rubio Larrosa, 2004). This may be related to the higher rates of perfectionism found in subjects diagnosed with OCPD, which is associated with an increased risk of suicidal behavior (Masson et al., 2003). In a case-control study of suicides, no significant differences in the rate of anankastic diagnosis was found (6.2% vs. 6.5%) (Cheng et al., 1997). Moreover, Dirks (1998) found that anankastic PD was associated to a lower risk of repeated parasuicide after some other risk factors were taken into account.

It might be concluded that although there is an outstanding lack of information with regard to the role of OCPD and suicide attempts, it seems that OCPD is not related, in general, to an elevated risk of suicide attempts. Chioqueta & Stiles (2004) said that, a possible explanation was that it may be difficult to patients with OCPD to attempt suicide considering their extreme attention to procedures, details, and rules. However, the same personality risks may pose these subjects to an increased risk of severe suicide attempts and completed suicide.

2.4.3. DEPENDENT PERSONALITY DISORDER (DPD)

A prevalence of 10.3% of dependent PD has been reported in the general population (Drake et al., 1988). Cooke & Hart (2004) found a lower prevalence (1.0% to 1.7%).

A close relationship between dependence and depression and between dependence and suicidal inclination has been found (Birtchnell, 1996). Chioqueta & Stiles (2004) found that 90% of subjects diagnosed with dependent PD had a comorbid diagnosis of lifetime depressive disorder. They also found in their outpatient sample that, among cluster C PDs, those diagnosed with dependent PD had the highest percentage of suicide attempts (35%) compared to avoidant PD (18%) and to OCPD, but it was lower than the 43% found in cluster A PDs, and particularly, the 61% found in cluster B PDs (Chioqueta & Stiles, 2004). However, it must be taken into account that the number of subjects diagnosed with a cluster A or a cluster B PD was very low (n= 14, and n= 13, respectively). Their results suggest that DPD, but neither OCPD nor AVPD were significantly related to suicide attempts. However, this association was no longer significant after controlling for lifetime depressive disorder, while both cluster A and cluster B PDs remained significantly associated with suicide attempts even after controlling for both lifetime depressive disorder and severity of depression, thus suggesting that the risk of suicide attempts in patients with cluster A PDs and cluster B PDs is independent of comorbid lifetime depressive disorder. The authors suggested that it may be difficult for subjects diagnosed with dependent PD to attempt suicide due to "their submissive and passive tendencies". Moreover, suicide attempts in subjects with DPD may be a way of self-humiliation and to make their caregivers to draw attention on them (Rubio Larrosa, 2004).

Chapter 2.5.

SUICIDAL PERSONALITY

H. Blasco-Fontecilla

In the seventies it was postulated the existence of a *suicidal character*. Subjects with this diagnosis would be characterized by egosyntonic self-destructiveness and suicidal behaviors would be "chronic elements of general interpersonal transactions rather than the results of the breakdown of normal ego defences in response to unconscious conflicts" (Schwartz et al., 1974). However, the belief in a specific *suicidal personality* was abandoned several years ago (Casey, 1989). Indeed, Philip (1970) concluded that there was no unique *suicidal personality,* and that there was little ground to support the notion of a *suicidal personality,* but recognized that poorly integrated personalities were frequent among suicide attempters (SA).

More recently, Mehlum et al. (1994) pointed out that the concept of borderline PD as "the suicidal personality disorder" may be justified, as individuals with this diagnosed are characterized by affect dysregulation, impulsiveness, aggressiveness, disturbed relationships and difficulties in coping with life events, among others, making them chronically suicidal. Moreover, it has been suggested that there is no one suicidal personality, but several (Engstrom et al., 1996; Stalenheim, 2001). The *temperamental vulnerability hypothesis* suggests that some personality traits may make someonelse susceptible to different types of psychopathology, including suicide behavior (Stalenheim, 2001). Indeed, Engstrom et al. (1996) said that there might be several different profiles or types among SA, and that this personality heterogeneity might also explain why some different personality dimensions have been associated with suicidality. They tried to classify a sample of 215 SA by using cluster analysis and found six mutually exclusive clusters of individuals with different temperament profiles. Two of them, *cluster 1* and *5*, were close to `normality´ and no personality pathology correlates were found. The other four clusters showed different personality profiles that make subjects more vulnerable to suicide attempts. In their study, *cluster 3* was the most disturbed subgroup. It was characterized by high Psychoticism, low Socialization, high Anxiety, high Aggressiveness, high Suspicion and high Impulsivity. They are the group with special needs for social support. *Cluster 2* was described as the `neurotic and introverted´ subgroup and characterized by scoring high in all Anxiety variables and in Detachment, and low in Socialization, showing paranoid and schizoid traits. *Cluster 4* was characterized by scoring high on Conformity, Psychoticism and Impulsiveness. Finally, *Cluster 6* people scored high on the scales describing different forms of Anxiety, Suspicion, Guilt, and low in Socialization. Stalenheim (2001) found that the temperament profile of their 61 male forensic psychiatric population sample was very similar to one of the subgroups (cluster 3) described by Angstrom. These subjects were characterized by scoring very low in Socialization and high in Anxiety, Impulsiveness and Aggressiveness. These studies can be criticized by their difficultness to be applied by clinicians.

Finally, at least two suicidal types have been identified in past research: an irritable/aggressive subtype, and a depressed/withdrawn subtype; high rates of violent and antisocial behavior are characteristic of the former – which is characterized by reduced serotonergic functioning and would entail greater impulsivity and more hostile negative affect (anger, rage)-, and the latter is characterized by depressive symptoms (Verona et al., 2001). People with the temperamental disposition of the antisocial PD have a heightened risk for hostile and aggressive behaviors toward self or others, particularly under conditions of accumulating stress (Verona, Patrick, & Lang, 2001).

DIMENSIONS OF PERSONALITY AND SUICIDE*

D. Braquehais Conessa

2.6.1. INTRODUCTION

Personality can be defined, in accordance with biological, cognitive and/ or behavioral paradigms, as "the dynamic organization of the psycho-biological systems that modulate the adaptation to the experience" (Szerman, 2004). Within the personality realm, it is precise to distinguish the *temperament,* which has a biogenetic foundation, to the *character,* acquired as much by the own experience as by the influence of socio-cultural means (Millon & Davis, 1998).

Hippocrates (460-377 BC) was the first one in relating the conduct of a subject to an alteration in its organism, when defending its theory of the four *humours* related to the four elements. Galen (131-203 AC) elaborated the Hippocratic thought and gave the systematic form to that typology of the temperament. Although the doctrine of the four humours was accepted during a long period of time, there were also voices against it. Thus, Gall (1758-1828), founder of the phrenology, related the characteristics of the personality to certain dimensions of the brain (Laín-Entralgo, 1978; Ateneo, 2004).

In the 20th century, Kretschmer (1888-1964) and Sheldon (1899-1977) are the earliest exponents of a constitutional approach. They associated some body types with certain personality traits and mental diseases. Different psychopathologists, like Kraepelin (1913), Schneider (1950) and Khan (1931), have also described the different types of personality. They have speculated about their possible association with some mental diseases (Schneider, 1980; Martos-Rubio, 2000; Millon, 1998).

On the other hand, Jung (1921) described four primary ways of experiencing the world: two rational functions (thinking and feeling), and two perceptive functions (sensation and intuition). In any person, the degree of introversion/ extroversion of one function can be quite different to that of another function, thus showing one type of personality or another (Millon, 1998).

The term `*dimension of the personality*` was firstly used by Paulov (1935), when raising the existence of some basic properties of the nervous system which were able to explain the individual differences in animals and human beings (Martos-Rubio, 2000). The term dimension can also be conceived as a statistical variable. Individual differences are then related to the degree in which the variable is present. Different models of personality have appeared in the last forty years as a result of the factorial analysis of the different tests used to investigate personality. Thus, by using a factorial analysis strategy, a three dimensional model of personality (*extroversion, neuroticism and psychoticism*) was postulated by Eysenck (Eysenck, 1997; Mc Hugh & Slavney, 2001; Evenden, 1999). Gray proposed that the dimension introversion-extroversion was indeed a dimension of susceptibility to the punishment and that neuroticism was in direct relation with the degree of sensitivity to the stimuli (Gray, 1981). Zuckerman talked about *sensation-seeking* among other personality traits (Zuckerman et al., 1993). Cloninger tried to integrate all these findings in one model. In his personality concept, four temperamental traits (*novelty seeking, harm avoidance, reward dependence* and *persistence*) and three character dimensions are included (Cloninger, 1987; Cloninger, 1993). Since then, many other factorial models have appeared and the generalization of the findings obtained in the multiple studies on personality has become more difficult. The diagnostic manuals of mental disorders, like the DSM-IV, try to group the characteristics of personality in different diagnostic profiles in order to simplify not only clinical activity but also psychiatric investigation (APA, 1995).

It is also essential to differentiate two terms concerning personality features: state and trait. The term trait alludes to the stable individual characteristics that can predispose an individual to endure certain disorders, whereas the term state refers to the circumstances that can unleash the disorder in individuals with predisposition to go through certain mental diseases (Yehuda et al., 1988; Mann & Arango, 1992; Fawcett et al., 1997).

2.6.2. THE ROLE OF PERSONALITY DISORDERS IN SUICIDE

Definition of Suicide

In 1976 the WHO (Gracia-Marco et al., 2004) divided the theoretical groups that were speculating about the suicidal behavior in: a) theorists for whom the ideas, the threats, the attempts of suicide and the complete suicides are expressions of the desire to die; b) those which distinguish between patients who give themselves death and those who want to be hurt, but not to die; c) clinicians and researchers who consider the diverse motivations of those who try to commit suicide; d) theorists for whom every attempt of suicide must be considered independently.

Due to these differences, the International Association for the Prevention of the Suicide (IASP) (Sarró & Nogué, 1992) has recently underlined the need to develop a definition of the suicidal behavior that could be applied to all the studies dedicated at investigating the risk and protective factors of suicidal conduct. Anyhow, at present it is accepted that suicide attempts and completed suicide must be studied separately (Klerman, 1987; Moscicki, 1995; Angst et al., 1999; Kessler et al., 1999). However, some clinical profiles of suicide attempts and completions can overlap, especially in the so-called nearly lethal suicide attempts (Hawton, 2001; Simon et al., 2001). It is necessary to emphasize that for one completed suicide there are nearly ten suicide attempts (Geijo & Franco, 1997; Mann, 2004). In fact, the presence of a previous suicide attempt represents a key risk factor to repetition and to completed suicide (Sarró & Nogué, 1992; Wintemute et al., 1999; Seguí-Montesinos, 1989; Cheng, 1995).

Personality Disorders and Suicide

Suicidal behavior is a complex phenomenon in which biological, clinical and psychosocial factors are involved. Diverse epidemiological studies carried out in adults show that at least 90 % of the suicidal subjects endure a mental disorder, mainly depression, alcoholism and schizophrenia (Geijo & Franco, 1997; Healy et al., 1999; Lejojeux et al., 1994; Leibenluft et al., 1994; Maris, 2002; Moscicki, 1997; Mann, 2002; Pirkola et al., 1999). Mann et al. (1993, 1998, 1999a, 1999b), have proposed a stress-diathesis model in which the risk for suicidal acts is determined not merely by a psychiatric illness (the stressor) but also by a diathesis. The diathesis for suicidal conduct includes a combination of factors such as sex, religion, familial and genetic components, childhood experiences, psychosocial support system, availability of highly lethal suicide methods and various other factors (Mann, 2002).

Although PDs are often comorbid with severe psychiatric diagnoses, they also appear to confer an independent risk for suicide. It is believed that 40 % of the patients who attempt suicide fulfil criteria of PDs, especially of cluster B PDs (Beautrais et al., 1996; Mann et al., 1990). In fact, it is estimated that the risk of suicide in them is even 7 times higher than in general population (Beautrais et al., 1996; López-García et al., 1993), especially in patients with a diagnosis of borderline personality disorder (BPD) or antisocial personality disorder (APD) (Beautrais et al., 1996; Mann, 2002; Maris, 2002).

Duberstein & Conwell (1997) reviewed case-based and cohort studies on completed suicide in individuals with PDs and found that about 30%–40% of suicides occur in individuals with PDs, with increased risk conferred by the presence of BPD, APD, and possibly avoidant PD and schizoid PD diagnoses. Lesage et al. (1994), when comparing 75 young men who died by suicide to a demographically matched group of men in the community, underlined that it was the prevalence of BPD what was significantly increased among those who died by suicide (28.0% versus 4.0%). Hawton et al. (1993) compared 62 individuals who died by suicide or possible suicide to 124 matched control subjects and found that an increased risk of death was associated with the presence of a PD. In some other studies, Hawton and colleagues highlight that some cluster B personality traits, in addition to other factors, were related to completed suicides in young people (Hawton et al., 1988, 1997, 1999).

In a random sample of all persons who died by suicide in Finland within a 1-year period, Isometsa et al. (1996) also found that 29% of the subjects (N=67) had an axis II disorder, principally cluster B personality disorders. All individuals with a personality disorder also had at least one axis I diagnosis, which in 95% of the patients included a depressive syndrome, a substance use disorder, or both. In many cases, those with personality disorders had gone through one or more stressful life events, particularly the week before suicide (Heikkinen et al., 1997).

Suicide attempts may also be more likely to occur in individuals with PDs and, conversely, among individuals who attempt suicide, PDs are commonly observed.

Ahrens and Haug (1996), in a case-control study of 226 patients with a PD who were admitted to a psychiatric hospital, stated that patients with a PD - including, but not limited to

BPD- were more likely than other hospitalized patients to have had a suicide attempt immediately before admission, with persistent clinically relevant suicidal behavior within the first 24 hours after admission (39% versus 24%).

Soloff *et al.* (1994), in an initial study in 84 patients with a diagnosis of BPD (72,6 % of them with a history of suicide attempts with an average of 3,39 attempts *per* patient), observed that the suicidal conduct was significantly related to psychopathic traits of personality, previous suicide attempts, prior impulsive actions and depressive mood but not comorbid mood disorder or substance use disorders. Later on, the same group of investigation (Soloff et al., 2000), when comparing 32 patients with BPD, 77 depressed patients and 49 with BPD and depression, found that the characteristics of the attempts of suicide were similar in these three groups, although the patients who fulfilled both conditions (BPD and depression) had a more intense history of suicidal conduct, related to a higher degree of hopelessness, impulsivity and/or aggression.

Mann *et al.* (1999b) studied a group of 347 consecutive patients who were admitted to a university psychiatric hospital, and found that comorbid BPD was more common among the 184 patients who had attempted suicide than among those with no prior suicide attempts. The authors also found that the measures of impulsiveness and aggressiveness were higher in the group of patients with history of attempts of suicide opposite to those who never tried to commit suicide.

In a study of 114 consecutive suicide attempters (SA) referred to a general hospital in Helsinki, SA diagnosed with major depression without comorbid alcohol dependence had higher suicide intent and lower impulsiveness than SA with non-depressive alcohol dependence (Suominen et al., 1997). Precisely, Brodsky *et al.* (1997) analyzed data for 214 inpatients with a diagnosis of BPD and found that impulsivity was the only characteristic associated with a higher number of suicide attempts.

Regarding APD, De Moore & Robertson (1999), in a retrospective study of patients who tried to commit suicide by using violent methods, observed that choosing firearms was related to male gender, alcohol abuse, previous legal problems and BPD or APD diagnoses. Casey *et al.* (1989), when following 60 patients with history of suicide attempts, found that a diagnosis of PD was found in over 65% of the cases and was mainly of the explosive type. It was significantly more common in men than women were and the dimension measuring sociopathy was equivocally linked to male gender. There were no other associations between gender and the other dimensions measured. Using a categorical approach to personality, suicide intent was not significantly different between the categories of personality; there was no correlation between dimensional or categorical measures of personality and suicide intent when the severity of depression was controlled. By itself personality did not contribute significantly in determining variance in intent but it did interact significantly with age. Roy *et al.* (1990), after analyzing the results of 298 alcoholics, found that 19 % (n=57) had tried to commit suicide and that this group showed a major incidence of APD together with a more impulsive pattern of alcohol abuse.

Comorbid mood disorders are common among SA with PDs. Van Gastel *et al.* (1997), in a study of 338 depressed psychiatric inpatients, found significantly more suicide attempts and more suicidal ideation among those depressed inpatients with a comorbid PD than among depressed inpatients without a PD. Corbitt *et al.* (1996) found that the 30 patients with major depressive disorder and comorbid BPD were just as likely to have made a highly lethal suicide attempt as the 72 patients with major depressive disorder alone. However, those with comorbid BPD were more likely to have a history of multiple serious suicide attempts, and past suicidal behavior was better predicted by the number of personality disorder symptoms than by the number of depressive symptoms. Oquendo *et al.* (2004b) have carried out a two-years prospective study in patients who had endured a Major Depressive Episode in the context of a Unipolar Depression or Bipolar Disorder. They underline the importance of valuing the degree of pessimism and the factor impulsiveness-aggressiveness (specially related to cluster B personality disorders) as some key risk factors for attempted suicide in this group of patients.

According to Cornelius *et al.* (1995) depressed alcoholic patients differ from depressed non alcoholic patients in two depressive symptoms (higher risk for suicide and low self-esteem), as well as in the presence of greater impulsivity, functional impairment, and abnormal personal and social history markers. Koller *et al.* (2002), when studying the results obtained by 182 patients with alcohol dependence, found that patients with history of more violent suicide attempts showed higher scores in aggressiveness and impulsiveness than the healthy control group.

Oquendo *et al.* (2003) also studied 156 patients with a diagnosis of depression and observed that the comorbidity with the post-traumatic stress disorder (PTSD) (especially in women), increased the possibility of attempting suicide, independently of the presence of substance abuse disorders, cluster B personality traits and/or a history of childhood abuse. Kotler *et al.* (2001) also found, in a group of 46 patients with a diagnosis of PTSD compared with 42 patients without it and with 50 healthy controls, that the impulsiveness was the most important risk factor for attempted suicide in patients affected by PTSD.

In conclusion, individuals with PDs, and particularly those with a BPD or APD, have an increased risk for suicide and for suicide attempts. These risks appear to be further amplified by the presence of comorbid disorders.

2.6.3. PERSONALITY TRAITS, PSYCHIATRIC SYMPTOMS AND SUICIDE

Personality Traits and Suicide

Some personality traits or certain psychiatric symptoms may play a role in increasing risk for suicidal acts. The personality characteristics that have frequently been related to a greater risk for suicide are: problematic coping strategies, inability to support stable interpersonal relationships, neuroticism, external *locus* of control, hostility, irritability, low self-esteem, despair, intense feelings of fault and/ or of shame following minimal mistakes, cognitive rigid style and perfectionism (Chance et al., 1996; Beautrais e a, 1999; Josepho & Plutchnik, 1994).

Stravinski and Boyer (2001) collected data from 19,724 persons who returned the Quebec Health Survey and tested whether there was an association between loneliness and suicidal thoughts or behaviors in the general population. A significant correlation was found between experiencing suicidal ideation or attempting suicide and living unaccompanied, having no friends or feeling alone, with psychological distress being the strongest correlate of suicidal ideation. Of those individuals who were severely distressed and very lonely, 25% reported serious suicidal ideation or actions. Overall, thoughts of suicide were reported by 3.1% of the population, and 0.9% had attempted suicide.

According to Eysenck's model, suicidal ideation has been related to neuroticism and/ or psychoticism (Irfani et al., 1978), suicide attempts to high neuroticism and low extroversion (Benjaminsen et al., 1990) and completed suicide to high neuroticism, high perseverance and depressive pessimism (Duberstein et al., 1994).

When completed suicides are analyzed retrospectively, some personality traits seem to have played an important role in committing suicide. Conner et al. (2001) reviewed the literature on psychological vulnerabilities to completed suicide and found that suicide was consistently associated with five constructs - impulsivity/aggression, depression, hopelessness, anxiety, and self-consciousness/social disengagement-. Psychological vulnerabilities likely influence suicide risk independently, by exacerbating other psychiatric or social risk factors in individual patients.

On the other hand, Josepho and Plutchik (1994) investigated the relationship between interpersonal problems, coping styles, and suicide attempts in 71 adult psychiatric inpatients. Patients who were hospitalized after a suicide attempt had more interpersonal problems and, after controlling for the effect of interpersonal problems, the investigators found that greater suppression, less minimization, and less replacement were significantly related to increased suicide risk scores.

Kaslow et al. (1998) conducted an empirical study of the psychodynamics of suicide among 52 patients hospitalised for a suicide attempt and 47 psychiatrically hospitalised control subjects with no history of suicidal behaviors. Overall, 49% of the subjects had depression, 25% had substance use disorders, and 63% had a cluster B PD. Individuals who had attempted suicide were significantly more likely to report childhood loss combined with adulthood loss, had more impairment in their object relations and viewed relationships in a more negative manner, showing lower levels of individuation and separation. However, Schotte et al. (1990), analysed the stability of interpersonal problem-solving skills in a short-term, longitudinal study of hospitalized suicide ideators (N = 36). They found marked changes in depressive symptoms, state anxiety, hopelessness, and suicide intent over time, and these improvements were associated with improvements in interpersonal problem-solving skills. That is the reason why they argued that interpersonal problem-solving deficits may be a concomitant, rather than a cause, of depression, hopelessness, and suicide intent.

Maser et al. (2002) examined the correlations between suicide and clinical and personality factors in 955 depressed patients who were followed over 14 years. During that time, 3.8% died by suicide, and 12.6% attempted suicide. Suicide within 12 months of intake to the study was strongly associated with the clinical situation. Beyond one year after intake, suicide was associated with temperamental factors, including high levels of impulsivity and shyness. Those SA and those who died by suicide shared core characteristics, including previous attempts, impulsivity, substance abuse, and psychic turmoil within a cycling/mixed bipolar disorder.

Beautrais et al. (1999) studied, in a case-control study in young people, the contribution of a series of measures of personality and/or cognitive style to serious suicide attempt risk. They found that individuals making suicide attempts had elevated odds of hopelessness, neuroticism, introversion, low self-esteem, impulsiveness, and external locus of control. When allowance was made for intercorrelations between these measures, hopelessness, neuroticism, and external locus of control remained significant risk factors for serious suicide attempt; self-esteem, extraversion, and impulsiveness were not significantly associated with suicide attempt risk. Non-significant findings were explained by the presence of substantial correlations between these measures and measures of hopelessness, neuroticism, and external locus of control.

Recently, Mann (2004) has raised the importance of identifying which factors facilitate the *externalization* of the conducts (related to the extroversion of Eysenck) and which propitiate the *internalization* (more according to the dimension *introversion* of Eysenck). Individuals with greater impulsivity and aggressiveness, specially APD and other conduct disorders would tend to externalise the problems, whereas persons with anxious - depressive disorders would have a tendency to internalise the problems, being both the pessimism and the despair the main triggers for attempting suicide in that group of patients. In accordance with Beck's model, when a patient deals with certain difficulties he or she has may activate the same cognitive schemes that led him to attempt suicide in the past.

Specific Psychiatric Symptoms and Suicide

Some psychiatric symptoms as hopelessness, anxiety, command hallucinations, impulsiveness or aggressiveness have been consistently associated with an increased risk of suicide, independent of diagnosis. It should be noted that anxiety, hopelessness and impulsiveness-aggressiveness can also be considered not merely "state" symptoms but also stable personality "traits".

Fawcett *et al.* (1997) proposed a four hypothetical pathways-model leading to suicide in clinical depression: (1) an acute pathway involving severe anxiety/agitation associated with high brain corticotrophin-releasing factor (CRF or CRH) levels, (2) trait baseline and reactivity hopelessness, (3) severe anhedonia, and (4) trait impulsiveness associated with low brain serotonin turnover and low total cholesterol as a possible peripheral correlate. The authors believed that anhedonia severity is a risk factor and trait, and they also consider that baseline hopelessness and sensitivity are traits related to chronic suicide risk. They also presented data suggesting the relation between reduced serotonin turnover and violent suicide.

Anyhow, some studies show a significant relationship between *anxiety* and suicide (Apter et al., 1989; Arranz-Marti et al., 2004; Korn et al., 1997; Stein et al., 1998), whereas others deny it (Placidi et al., 2000). However, although the relationship between anxiety and suicide attempts is still unclear and specific measures of anxiety have not been found to be predictive of suicide (Brown et al., 2000), severe anxiety does seem to increase suicide risk at least in some subgroups of patients and it should be taken into account in the assessment of suicidal behavior.

Hopelessness has also been consistently identified as a main factor associated with an increased risk of suicide (Conner et al., 2001). Young *et al.* (1996) hypothesized that a patient's hopelessness is comprised of a baseline level of hopelessness when not depressed (trait hopelessness) and an increment in hopelessness related to the severity of depression at the time and the person's rate of increase in hopelessness as a function of severity of depression (sensitivity or state hopelessness). After analyzing the longitudinal data of 316 patients, they found that baseline hopelessness predicted a future suicide attempt, while sensitivity and hopelessness when depressed did not.

Beck *et al.* (1995) followed 207 patients who were hospitalized for suicidal ideation but who had not made a recent suicide attempt and tried to identify predictors of later suicide. After a follow-up period of 5-10 years, 14 individuals (6.9%) had died by suicide. A score of 10 or more on the Hopelessness Scale correctly identified 91% of the eventual suicides. Taken in conjunction with previous studies showing the relationship between hopelessness and suicidal intent, those findings indicated the importance of degree of hopelessness as an indicator of long-term suicidal risk in hospitalized depressed patients.

In a subsequent study that included an expanded sample of 6,891 psychiatric outpatients seen between 1975 and 1995 and followed for up to 20 years, and used survival analysis to identify factors associated with increased risk for suicide (Brown *et al.*, 2000) hopelessness was identified as one of the main risk factor for suicide, with patients who scored above 8 on the Beck Hopelessness Scale being at four times greater risk for suicide in a given year than those with lower scores.

Wetzel (1976) studied 154 SA, threateners, and psychiatric controls, and 94 subjects were retested one month later. Both hopelessness and depression were significantly greater in suicidal subjects. Depression and hopelessness were also sensitive to changes in suicide risk during the one-month follow-up. Anyhow, in all analyses, hopelessness correlated more highly with suicide intent than did depression.

Fawcett *et al.* (1987) in a prospective study in patients with major depressive disorder found that hopelessness, loss of pleasure or interest, and mood cycling during the index episode differentiated the suicide group. Diagnostic subcategories, suicidal ideation at entry to the study, suicide attempts during current or past episodes, and medical severity of prior attempts did not differentiate the suicide group.

Hopelessness is also more outstanding in individuals who have reported previous suicide attempts, compared to individuals without such a history. For example, Hall & Platt (1999) in a study of 100 patients who made a severe suicide attempt suggested that severe anxiety, panic attacks, a depressed mood, a diagnosis of major affective disorder, recent loss of an interpersonal relationship, recent abuse of alcohol or illicit substances coupled with feelings of hopelessness, helplessness, worthlessness, global or partial insomnia, anhedonia, inability to maintain a job, and the recent onset of impulsive behavior were excellent predictors of suicidal behavior.

Cohen *et al.* (1994) also found greater levels of hopelessness in the 43 suicide attempters among 184 individuals with a first admission for psychosis.

Malone *et al.* (2000) in a group of 84 patients with major depression, found that the depressed patients who had not attempted suicide expressed more feelings of responsibility toward family, more fear of social disapproval, more moral objections to suicide, greater survival and coping skills, and a greater fear of suicide than the depressed patients who had attempted suicide. Scores for hopelessness, subjective depression, and suicidal ideation were significantly higher for the SA. Reasons for living correlated inversely with the combined score on these measures, considered an indicator of "clinical suicidality". Neither objective severity of depression nor quantity of recent life events differed between the two groups.

Across diagnostic groups, hopelessness appears to relate to the seriousness of suicidal ideation and intent, independent of diagnosis (Fowler et al., 1986; Harkavy et al., 1999; Lesage et al., 1994; Minkoff et al., 1973; Stanley et al., 2001). For instance, Weisman et al.(1979), when comparing a sample of drug abusing (N = 86) and nonabusing individuals (N= 298) suicide attempters, found that drug abuse status was not a significant contributor to the severity of suicidal intent. However, it was found that hopelessness accounted for a significant proportion of the variance of intent.

Soloff *et al.* (2000) assessed the relationship of hopelessness to suicide attempts in inpatients with major depressive disorder (N=77) as well as in inpatients with borderline personality disorder alone (N=32) or in combination with major depressive disorder (N=49). Across groups, increased hopelessness was associated with an increased number of suicide attempts as well as an increase in the lethal intent associated with attempts.

Factors such as *impulsivity, hostility* and *aggressiveness* may also act individually or together to increase suicide risk. It can be accepted that the concept of impulsivity covers a wide range of "actions that are poorly conceived, prematurely expressed, unduly risky, or inappropriate to the situation and that often result in undesirable outcomes" (Moeller et al., 2001). On the other hand, ''aggression'' is a heterogeneous construct, and it is likely that subgroups of individuals with particular types of aggression are at higher risk for suicide. Conner et al. (2003) argued that a subtype of aggression, the so-called reactive aggression (Barratt, 1994; Barratt et al., 1997; Coccaro et al., 1989; Dodge et al., 1987; Kavoussi et al., 1997; Poulin et al., 2000; Vitiello et al., 1997), underlies the link with suicide and this type of aggression has also been related to impulsive actions. Conner hypothesized that partner–relationship disruptions amplify risk for suicide in the near term among reactive aggressive individuals, particularly those with psychiatric disorders. As for hostility, it is possible to define it as a miscellany of anger and grief associated with indignation, scorn and resentment that is frequently directed to insult or destroy some objects and that usually involves verbal or motive responses (Buss & Durke, 1957). Some authors go so far as even to raise the existence of a continuum between anger, hostility and aggression.

It should be remembered that Maser et al. (2002), when following 529 patients with affective illness for up to 14 years, revealed that, beyond 12 months, higher levels of impulsivity and low assertiveness were the best prospective predictors of completed suicide. Mann et al. (1999), in a study of 347 consecutive patients admitted to a university psychiatric hospital, found that rates of lifetime aggression and impulsivity were greater in the 184 patients who had attempted suicide than in those without a history of suicide attempts and aggression.

This relationship is independent of the diagnosis. For example, Brodsky *et al.* 2001), in a study of 136 depressed adult inpatients, found that individuals with at least one prior suicide attempt had significantly higher scores on measures of impulsivity and aggression than individuals without reported suicide attempts. Corruble *et al.* (1999), in a study with 50 depressed inpatients, observed that impulsivity was higher in the patients with suicide attempts and that the scores obtained were lower after the hospitalization. The same group of investigation, in another study with 127 depressed patients (Conner, 2004), have found that only the dimensions cognitive impulsivity and lack of planning are responsible for increasing the risk of suicide attempt (Conner, 2004). Oquendo *et al.* (2000), in an investigation with 44 patients with a DSM-III-R diagnosis of bipolar disorder, discovered that SA were more likely to have more lifetime aggression than nonattempters, although lifetime rates of impulsivity were not increased among those with a prior suicide attempt. Placidi *et al.* (2000) analysed data for 272 inpatients with at least one major depressive episode and found significant increases in measures of aggression and impulsivity in those with a history of suicide attempts, compared to those without suicide attempts. Suominen *et al.* (1997), in a sample of 114 consecutive SA found that SA with major depression without comorbid alcohol dependence had higher suicide intent and lower impulsiveness than attempters with non-depressive alcohol dependence. Suicide attempts differ between subjects with major depression, alcoholism or both disorders in terms of impulsiveness and suicide intent. Spivak *et al.* (2003), in an open trial with 44 patients in treatment with clozapine or haloperidol for 6 months, observed that clozapine notably reduced the risk of suicide thanks to the reduction of the impulsivity.

It is clear that the study of the role that impulsiveness and aggressiveness play in suicide attempts has recently impelled many studies of investigation in different mental diseases and psycho-social conditions related to suicidal acts (Angst & Clayton, 1986; Beautris et al., 1996; Brodsky et al., 2001; Conner et al., 2003; Koller et al., 2002; Mann et al., 1999; Maser et al., 2002; Placidi et al., 2000; Plutchnik et al., 1989; Roy et al., 1990; Soloff et al., 1994, 2000; Stanley et al., 2001). All of them discover that impulsivity and aggressiveness confer a risk for suicide attempts, generally independent of diagnosis.

On the other hand, it should be remarked that when studying the relationship between suicide and impulsivity we can consider impulsivity as a *state* (impulsive act) rather than a *trait* (stable characteristic of the personality). It has been generally accepted that suicide attempts are more impulsive while completed suicides are more planned (Klerman, 1987). Conner (2004) points out that, up to the moment, there have been three ways of defining a suicide attempt as not planned: a) some authors determine that a suicide attempt is impulsive (or not planned) if the period of time between suicidal ideation and suicidal act is inferior than: five minutes (Hawton, 2001; Suominen et al., 1997; Williams et al., 1980), twenty minutes (Dorpat & Ripley, 1967), two hours (Li et al., 2003) or twenty-four hours (Brent, 1987); b) others use two questions of the Beck's Suicide Intent Scale (SIS) (Beck & Kovacs, 1979): 1) active preparation of the attempt; and, 2) degree of premeditation (Baca-García et al., 2001; Brown et al., 1991; Suominen et al., 1997) and, c) other authors (Soloff et al., 2000) have chosen the so-called *planning* factor of the SIS. This factor has been obtained after the factorial analysis of the responses obtained in eight questions of the SIS (1,2,3,5,6,7,8 and 15), with a high internal consistency as well as a high grade of agreement between examiners (Díaz et al., 2003; Mieczkowiski et al., 1993).

The factors more clearly related, up to the moment, to the degree of planning of the attempt have been: severity of the depression (Brown et al., 1991; Li et al., 2003; Simon et al., 2001; Soloff et al., 2000; Williams et al., 1980), hopelessness (Brent, 1987; Brent et al., 1991; Simon et al., 2001; Soloff ct al., 2000; and lethality (Baca-García et al., 2001; Mann & Malone, 1997; Mann et al., 1989). Gender and age have not been yet significantly associated with planned suicide attempts (Alexander & Peterson, 2001; Earls, 1989; Giner et al., 1974; Mann et al., 2000; Weissman et al., 1999).

2.6.4. OUR RESEARCH

Our group of investigation, conducted by Dr. Baca-García (2001), studied all the suicide attempters (SA) who attended our general hospital 24 hours after the suicide attempt, and signed the consent form, finding an inverse relationship between impulsivity of the attempt and lethality. In a subsequent investigation (Diaz et al., 2003), after conducting an exploratory analysis of the SIS, we compared two large samples of suicide attempters from a general hospital and found two clear and different factors: expected lethality and planning. In both samples, male gender and depression tended to be associated with higher scores in both subscales (small to medium effect sizes). Hospitalization was associated with higher scores in both SIS subscales (medium to large effects) suggesting that these subscales were reasonably good predictors of suicide attempt severity (see chapter 2.1.3 for further information with regard to methodology of our research). Please, do take into account that the suicide attempters sample size may vary as it is an ongoing research and we go on recruiting patients.

In a recent study of our group (Braquehais, 2006), not published in press, our group of investigation has accepted the challenge of investigating in depth the relation between impulsivity, aggressiveness, suicide attempts and lethality. We studied 332 suicide attempters attended in a general hospital in Madrid in the first twenty-four hours after the attempt and compared them with 495 healthy controls. We used, between others, the Barrat Impulsivity Scale (BIS-11) (Barrat, 1994), the Brown-Goodwin Lifetime aggression Questionnaire (Brown et al., 1979), the *Suicide Intent Scale* de Beck (Beck & Kovacs, 1979) and the *Lethality Rating Scale* (Beck et al., 1974). The most important findings we obtained were: 1) Impulsivity and aggressiveness were both higher in suicide attempters than in the control group. When comparing these results with the findings obtained by Mann *et al.* (1999) in a similar study conducted in New York city, we found no differences in impulsivity in the two groups but aggressiveness was higher in both groups in New York city compared with the scores obtained in Madrid; 2) impulsivity and aggressiveness were higher in suicide attempters who fulfilled diagnosis criteria for Axis II personality disorders (specially cluster B personality disorders) compared with suicide attempters without such diagnosis; 3) there were no differences in impulsivity and aggressiveness between suicide attempters with an Axis I diagnosis and those who did not have it, except for the cases with substance abuse disorder; 4) a positive correlation was observed between objective lethality and the degree of planning of the attempt, between the expected lethality and the objective lethality as well as between the expected lethality and the degree of planning of the attempt; 5) finally, we did not find any relationship between aggressiveness and objective lethality not either between expected lethality and aggressiveness.

2.6.5. CONCLUSION

It is clear that more studies are needed to clarify the complex interactions between personality and suicide. Suicide and suicidal behaviors cause severe personal, social and economic consequences. The probability of suicidal behavior also depends on a diathesis that includes hopelessness, increased lifetime impulsivity and some other personality traits (Mann, 2002). The management of suicidal behavior involves an assessment of risk, the treatment of the primary associated psychiatric disorder, paying special attention to some specific personality traits and states and also reducing the access to highly lethal methods for committing suicide.

Chapter 2.7.

PERSONALITY DISORDERS AND SUICIDE: THE ROLE OF COMORBIDITY*

H. Blasco-Fontecilla, A. Ceverino-Dominguez, E. Baca-García and J. Sáiz-Ruiz

2.7.1. INTRODUCTION

Comorbidity between mental illness and personality disorders (PDs) is probably the most important risk factor for suicide and characterizes an important subgroup of suicide attempters (SA) who are at particularly high risk of repeated suicidal behavior (Cheng 1995, Foster et al., 1999; Hawton et al., 2003). The impact of comorbidity on the risk of suicidal behavior may be attributable to specific personality characteristics, such as impulsivity and aggression. In two different studies, nearly 50% of patients who attempted suicide had both Axis I and Axis II diagnosis (Suominen et al., 1996; Hawton et al., 2003). Hawton et al. (2003) did not find any sociodemographic differences between the group of patients with and without comorbid Axis I and Axis II diagnosis. However, several differences in psychological characteristics were found. The group with a comorbid diagnosis had more persistent depression and suicidal ideas, hopelessness, aggression, impulsivity, low self-esteem and a greater frequency of previous suicide attempts. The number of associated disorders linearly increases the probability of attempting suicide. It is also the only significant predictor of lethality (Lecubrier, 2001).

A patient who is diagnosed with an Axis I or II diagnosis has an elevated likelihood of presenting a comorbid diagnosis (Lecubrier, 2001). Subjects diagnosed with depression or psychosis who suicide have usually a comorbid diagnosis, mainly a substance use disorder (SUD) and/or a PD (Elliot et al., 1996). The combination of a PD plus a mood disorder and substance abuse is frequently found in subjects who suicide (Allebeck et al., 1991; Duffy & Kreitman, 1993). The combination of a borderline personality disorder (BPD) and affective disorder is particularly lethal (Frances A et al., 1986; Friedman et al., 1983). The majority of SA with PDs are usually diagnosed with a comorbid diagnosis (Suominen et al., 1996). Among subjects with PDs, comorbidity with other mental disorders, particularly depression and SUD is the rule (Cheng et al., 1997; Mattunen et al., 1991; Runeson & Beskow, 1991). In one psychological autopsy study was found that the estimated risk of suicide in those with Axis I-Axis II comorbidity was over 6 times greater than the corresponding risk in those with a diagnosis of an Axis I disorder alone (Foster et al., 1999). Nearly all SA with a PD had also a comorbid depressive disorder – particularly depressive disorder not otherwise specified-, and/or a SUD in the study carried out by Suominen et al. (2000). Cheng et al. (1997) reported similar results in a case-control study of suicides. Furthermore, they found that the odds ratio of suicide for the comorbid diagnosis of depression and emotionally unstable PD was 18 times the one for depression. Houston et al. (2001) found in their sample of 27 suicides aged 15-24 that 55.5% were diagnosed with a depressive disorder, PD were present in 29.6%, personality trait accentuation in 55.6%, and co-morbidity of psychiatric disorders and PDs in a third of cases. They concluded that the process leading to suicide in young people was usually long term and with untreated depression in the context of a PD or personality traits accentuation, that would make them vulnerable to engage in interpersonal difficulties, leading to suicide behavior.

The high risk of early mortality associated to suicide in patients with PD is particularly related to comorbidity with depression (Pope et al., 1983; Cheng et al., 1997), particularly major depressive disorder (MDD). Henriksson et al. (1993) found that 93% of suicide victims had at least one Axis I diagnosis. Only 12% have no other comorbidities. Isometsa et al. (1996) found in their psychological autopsy study of 229 ramdom suicides that all the suicide victims diagnosed with a PD had also at least one Axis I diagnosis, mainly depressive syndromes (73%), psychoactive SUD (61%) or both (39%). They also found no evidence of impulsive suicides without an Axis I diagnosis. 67 subjects met DSM-III-R criteria for PDs (cluster B= 43, cluster C= 23 and cluster A=1). They compared subjects diagnosed with a PD with a sex and age-matched suicide victims group without a PD. The presence of depression did not differentiate those with or without a PD. However, the presence of a depressive disorder not otherwise specified –but not the overall prevalence of depressive syndromes- was significantly higher in the suicide victims with a cluster B PD. Moreover, suicides among subjects with a cluster B PD was more commonly associated with previous nonfatal suicide attempts and psychoactive SUD.

Borderline PD (BPD) is often comorbid with Axis I disorders, especially with mood disorders, SUD, and anxiety disorders (Trull et al., 2003). Multiple Axis I comorbidity is highly indicative of BPD diagnosis (Zanarini et al., 1998). *Emotionally unstable PD* is one of the most frequent PDs associated with suicide behaviors. Other studies also support the great comorbidity between BPD, affective and/or SUD in subjects who suicide and indeed, comorbidity might be the rule rather than the exception (Lesage et al., 1994; McGlashan 1987). It seems that Axis I diagnosis might be necessary (Isometsa et al., 1996) but not sufficient to explain suicidal behavior in patients with BPD (Fyer et al., 1988; Soloff et al. 1994).

Friedman et al. (1983) found in their retrospective study with 53 young inpatients treated for depression that among the 36 patients with a combination of BPD and depression, 33 had made one or more suicide attempts. Clements et al. (1985) suggested several hypotheses based on a more descriptive study. Their study was based in the internal reviews of all death in the Department of Psychiatry at the University of Rochester Medical Center. They found that among 15 deaths, 9 were attributed to suicide. In seven of them, severe PD –particularly BPD- and MDD was found. What is more striking is that eight of the nine patients denied suicidal ideation prior to discharge, that in seven cases the staff perceived a lessening in patient's depression but, in no case did the staff perception match the subject's subjective feelings. They suggested that a therapeutic relationship that fails to provide stability and accentuates change might increase the suicide risk in patients with both BPD and MDD and, that the standard treatments for these patients (20 years ago) – e.g. stressing independence and maturation- could be counterproductive. They also reminded that patients with BPD are particularly vulnerable to job and family live events. In four cases, suicide happened close to hospital discharge, a well-known stressor for these patients. Finally, they found that indirect markers in suicide risk assessment – like patient's self-reported hopelessness and lack of improvement or the dynamics of the therapeutic relationship- may be better suicide risk identifiers than direct markers – such as the therapist's perceptions of patient's psychosocial functioning, external appearance or response to questions about suicide ideation-.

2.7.2. REVIEW

Mood/affective Disorders

Traditionally, mood disorders and, particularly, *major depressive disorder (MDD),* are the principal risk factors for suicidal behavior. However, the majority of depressive subjects do not attempt suicide, and the difference between those who try to kill themselves and those who do not, is an important question of great clinical interest (Pendse et al., 1999). The lifetime risk of suicide of subjects with mood disorders is 15% (Boardman & Healy, 2001), but ranges from 6% (Inskip et al., 1998) to 19% (Goodwin & Jamison, 1990). As Boardman & Healy (2001) prevented, if these percentages are applied to all people suffering of mood disorders, the rate of suicide would be several times higher, suggesting that the relatively high rates of suicide may be due to the fact that subjects with affective disorders who are at a higher risk for suicide are more likely to be referred to secondary care than those without an affective disorder (Brown et al., 1985). The generally accepted idea that suicidal behavior in subjects diagnosed with a mood disorder could be associated with either number of affective episodes or severity has not been demonstrated (Sher et al., 2001). Moreover, the role of psychotic symptoms in suicidal behavior in people diagnosed with a mood disorder is not clear (Coryell & Tsuang, 1982; Maris et al., 2000). However, some authors have found an increased risk of suicide when psychotic symptoms are present in depressed subjects (Roose et al., 1983; Wolfersdorf M et al., 1987). Beck (1986) has suggested that, in people with affective disorders, cognitive dysfunctions – particularly hopelessness- are strong predictors of suicidal behavior. Comorbidity with substance abuse and PDs is the most frequently associated to suicide behaviors among depressed patients (Corbitt et al., 1996; Cheng et al., 1997).

Differences in personality influence the rate at which particular individuals experience negative affective states and also may influence how these affective states are experienced (Gruzca et al., 2003). It could be hypothesized that comorbidity with PDs –particularly, cluster B- or certain personality traits is of great importance in this area. The prevalence of PDs is high among patients with depressive disorders (Nemeroff et al., 2000), particularly dysthymia (Spalletta et al., 1996). In epidemiological surveys using DSM-III criteria, comorbidity between PDs and mood disorders vary from 10% to 13% (Weissman, 1993). Kraepelin (1921) was the first author to postulate that affective states arose from enduring personality characteristics and depressive, irritable, manic and cyclothymic personalities were considered the temperamental basei of the full-blown types of the illness (Henry et al., 1999). Benjamin (1996) said that specified PDs characterized by self-blame and self-attack (dependent, avoidant, obsessive-compulsive, histrionic, borderline, narcissistic, and passive-aggressive) are likely to show "comorbid" depression.

Certain personality types measured by the Temperament and Character Inventory (TCI) can be associated with mood disorders and suicide behavior (Cloninger et al., 1998). These authors found that cyclothymic and melancholic character were both associated with an increased risk for depression, but only the latter was linked to an increased risk of suicide attempts. Moreover, schizotypal personality was also associated with an increased risk for depression and suicide attempts. Furthermore, subjects with PDs characterized by both *low Cooperativeness* and *low Self-directedness* are at increased risk of both attempted and completed suicide.

Major Depressive Disorder (MDD)

Traditionally, MDD has been considered the diagnosis more closely associated to suicide. Malone et al. (1995) suggested that the presence of MDD could be *necessary* but insufficient to explain suicidal behavior in patients with MDD but without BPD. However, suicidal behavior may not to be related to *severity* of depression (Cornelius et al., 1995; Malone et al., 1995). Depressed SA do not have more severe depression than non-attempters in terms of either severity of depression or number of episodes (Malone et al., 1995). However, the presence of a *sensitive personality* has been associated to suicide among severe depressed males (Bradvik & Berglund, 2001). What remains unclear is whether *melancholic* patients are at a higher risk than non-melancholic patients. This has to due with the different opinions regarding what depression should be considered (Hansen et al., 2003). *Psychotic depression* is considered a subtype of MDD with delusions and/or hallucinations (APA, 1994). Serreti et al. (1999) studied the differences between psychotic and non-psychotic depression. They found that psychotic depression was more frequently associated with cluster A PDs, particularly paranoid PD, and a higher presence of cluster B PDs – mainly histrionic PD- was diagnosed among non-delusional depression. They could not replicate the findings of a higher risk of suicide attempts reported by Johnson et al. (1991) or suicides found by Roose et al. (1983) for psychotic depression.

Although several studies have documented that the presence of a PD in both major and non-major depression is a risk factor for suicide (Corbitt et al., 1996; Isometsa & Henriksson et al., 1996) not all the authors are of the same opinion (Brieger et al., 2002). Moreover, although it is traditionally assumed that comorbid PDs affect negatively on the course of unipolar MDD, there is a lack of good empirical data to support this asseveration (Brieger et al., 2002). It could be hypothesized that the diagnosis of "only" one comorbid PD could not be enough to make this asseveration true, being necessary at least the diagnosis of two or more PDs. It would also be interesting to know whether or not comorbidity with cluster C could provide with a protective effect (Blasco Fontecilla, 2002). Indeed, Brieger et al. (2001) found that the presence of a comorbid cluster C PD in patients with major depression did not affect the course of depression.

Fava et al. (1996) have reported that patients with early-onset MDD have a significantly higher prevalence of PDs. Henriksson et al. (1993) found that MDD was associated with a diagnosis of a PD in 31% of suicides. Hansen et al. (2003) found that non-melancholic MDD was associated to a higher prevalence of a more vulnerable personality style or comorbid PD, increasing suicide risk. In another study, patients with MDD and a comorbid diagnosis of any cluster A or B PD reported more suicide attempts than patients with a cluster C PD (Brieger et al., 2002). Depressed patients with comorbid BPD showed more suicidal behaviors (Rothschild & Zimmerman, 2002). Corbitt et al. (1996) studied the relationship between PDs and suicidal behavior in a sample of 102 psychiatric inpatients with MDD, using standardized structured interviews. They found no differences between SA and non-attempters in the number of cluster A`s or cluster C`s criteria met, but the presence and severity – expressed by the number of criteria the patients met- of cluster B, and particularly BPD, were positively correlated with the number and lethality of previous suicide attempts. Reich (1998) suggested that the route to suicidal behavior can either be reached by personality factors or by high levels of depressive symptoms.

Yen et al. (2003) recently made the first study to prospectively examine course of Axis I diagnosis as a risk factor for suicide attempts in the context of a PD sample. They found in their 2-years follow-up with 621 participants that among those who attempted suicide (9.3%), the majority met criteria for BPD (77.6%). Conversely, 20.5% of subjects with a BPD made a suicide attempts during the follow-up. They found no statistical significant differences in MDD between attempters and non-attempters, suggesting that a recent diagnosis of MDD did not appear to distinguish those who are likely to make a suicide attempt in subjects with a PD. Finally, when patients diagnosed with a MDD have a comorbid cluster C PD, they usually have no more comorbid PDs, while those patients with MDD who have a comorbid cluster B or A PD have more probabilities to be diagnosed with another PD (Brieger et al., 2002).

The link between BPD and affective disorders, particularly MDD, is controversial (Rogers et al., 1995). BPD is frequently comorbid with MDD (Joyce et al., 2003). Comorbidity between them may be explained by MDD being secondary to BPD (Kernberg, 1967), BPD being a *forme fruste* of affective disorders (Akiskal, 1981), or both disorders to sharing similar risk factors (Gunderson & Elliot, 1985). Currently, the majority of authors are of the opinion that they are two different disorders (Soloff et al., 1991; de la Fuente et al., 2001). Gunderson & Phillips (1991) concluded that the two disorders may coexist but are not etiologically related disorders. Furthermore, Cluster B PDs have been considered to lower the threshold for suicidal behaviors, and MDD could trigger suicidal behaviors (Oquendo et al., 1997).

Subjects with a diagnosis of BPD and comorbid MDD have a higher risk of suicide behavior than patients affected only by MDD (Malone et al., 1995). What it is still not clear is whether comorbidity between BPD and MDD increases or not the patient's risk for suicide attempts beyond the effect of each of these disorders independently. Generally, retrospective studies have found that co-occurring BPD/MDD is more closely associated to suicide behaviors than patients with a simple diagnosis of MDD (Corbitt et al., 1996; Kelly et al., 2000). Subjects with a diagnosis of BPD and comorbid major depression are associated to a higher risk of suicide behavior than patients affected only by major depression (Malone et al., 1995). Moreover, suicidality is also associated to cluster B personality traits even if the patients did not fully meet diagnostic criteria (Corbitt et al., 1996). In a prospective study, Mehlum et al. (1994) found no significant differences in rates of mood disorders in patients with different PDs. Moreover, the diagnosis of BPD continued to be associated with suicidality 2 to 5 years later. However, in a study with BPD patients, depressed mood, but not comorbid affective disorder, was found to be associated with a history of suicidal behavior (Soloff et al., 1994). Similarly, severity of depressed mood may be a better predictor of suicide behavior than the MDD diagnosis in subjects diagnosed with a PD (Yen et al., 2003). Thus, further studies are needed to state whether or not MDD remains a significant risk factor in BPD patients.

Probably, the best study carried out in this area is the one of Soloff et al. (2000). They compared 81 inpatients with BPD, 49 patients with BPD and comorbid Major Depressive Episode (MDE), and 77 inpatients with a MDE alone. Patients with both disorders had the greater number of suicide attempts and the highest level of objective planning. Impulsivity and hopelessness predicted lethality in all three groups. Moreover, hopelessness predicted objective planning in the group with both diagnoses. They found that suicidal behaviors were more frequent is the sample of patients with BPD – particularly with comorbid MDE but also without MDE- compared with the sample of individuals with MDE with no comorbidity. The number of lifetime attempts was predicted by the presence of BPD diagnosis and comorbidity, level of hopelessness and history of aggression. No differences were found in lethality as rated by the Suicide Intent Scales but the global sample of patients with BPD showed a greater lifetime level of medically lethal suicidal behaviors compared with the sample of individuals diagnosed with MDE without comorbidity. They concluded that patients with comorbidity had a higher risk for suicidal behavior, and that suicidal behavior in inpatients with BPD should not be considered "less serious" than the one of inpatients with MDE.

Regarding completed suicide usually is accepted that concomitant major affective disorder increases the risk of suicide in BPD –and *vice versa*- as SUD does (Frances A et al., 1986). BPD patients with a comorbid diagnosis of MDD have been found to have the highest suicide histories (Cheng et al., 1997) and to be at a higher risk of eventual suicide (McGlashan, 1986). A recent prospective study found both BPD and MDD were unique significant risk factors for suicide (Brown et al., 2000). However, several other authors have fail to find any differences in prevalence rates of affective disorder between BPD patients who suicide and non-suicidal BPD patients (Kullgren, 1988; Paris et al., 1989). Hampton (1997) stated that the completion of suicide in BPD subjects was often not related to a comorbid mood disorder (Mehlun et al., 1994) and to the degree of suicidal ideation (Sabo et al., 1995). Moreover, Kjelsberg et al. (1991) found that BPD patients who committed suicide did not show more depressive symptoms than the control group, what is contrary to suicide in psychiatric patients in general and could suggest that the mechanisms leading to suicide in BPD patients are different from those of psychiatric patients in general. Finally, Heikikinen et al. (1997) found that, the type of PD and comorbid Axis I disorder were not relevant, while the presence of multiple stressful life events was an important factor.

Depressive Syndrome

Isometsa & Henriksson et al. (1996) found in their psychological autopsy study that the depressive syndrome preceding suicide often was milder than MDD. Suominen et al. (2000) also found that comorbid *depressive disorder not otherwise specified* but not comorbid MDD was frequently associated in SA with a cluster B PD. In addition, Ahrens & Haugh (1996) found out that the main differences between the individuals with a primary PD that were suicidal –compared to the non-suicidal personality disorder individuals- were that they had more frequent suicide attempts, were more often childless or separated from their spouse and finally, had a more sturdily expressed depressive syndrome. However, only 3% of patients with PDs had a comorbid Axis I affective disorder, what made them hypothesize that suicidality in individuals with PDs is not due to major affective disorders. Moreover, as Schwartz et al. noted, "Existential despair needs to be differentiated from depressive illness...". It is our opinion that there is a tendency among clinicians and researchers to diagnose every manifestation of acute depressive feelings as major depressive episodes. We agree with Kernberg, who thinks there is an overdiagnosis of MDD in patients who attempt suicide. He says that "in severe personality disorders in which characterologically based suicidal behavior coincides with the presence of multiple neurotic symptoms, including a characterological depression, depressive reaction, or neurotic depression" (Kernberg, 2001). Finally, little information is available regarding the relationship between a disorder and a subthreshold disorder (Lecubrier, 2001) and about the relationship of these subthreshold disorders and suicide behavior.

Recurrent Brief Depression

Angst et al. (1990) proposed a subtype of mood disorder - *brief recurrent depression (RBD)-,* with the same diagnostic criteria of MDD but duration is less than two weeks, with a monthly frequency and over a period of at least one year. Currently, it is a well-defined clinical disorder that meets the symptomatic criteria for a depressive episode, but last less than 2 weeks – typically 2-3 days-, take place about once a month, and do not occur solely in relation to menstrual cycle (WHO, 1992; Pezawas et al., 2003).

BRD is associated with an increased risk of suicidal behavior. Montgomery et al. (1983) documented the relationship between the diagnosis BRD and attempted suicide. What still is not clear is whether the risk of a suicide attempt is even higher than the one of subjects with MDD. Patients diagnosed with BRD had a higher incidence of attempted suicide when compared to patients with MDD (Angst et al., 1990). These authors also found a relationship between histrionic personality traits and BRD in women but not in men, but this might have to do with the small number of men included in the study. In an ulterior work they found the reverse, that is, that suicide attempts were less frequent in subjects diagnosed with BRD than in MDD (Angst & Hochstrasser, 1994). Some other authors reported that the risk for suicide attempts is higher in patients diagnosed with RBD in a primary care setting (Maier et al., 1994; Weiller et al., 1994). Finally, the co-occurrence of MDD and RBD (the so-called *combined depression)* is associated with rates of suicide attempts higher than those of either single RBD or MDD (Montgomery et al., 1989; Angst & Hochstrasser, 1994).

Bipolar Disorder

Comorbidity between PDs and bipolar disorder ranges from the 4%-12% repoerted in the studies made in the eighties (Gaviria et al., 1982; Boyd et al., 1984), to the higher rates (50-58%) found in more recent studies (Koenisbert et al., 1985; O´Connell et al., 1991; Peselow et al., 1995). These differences might be due to the different methodologies used to assessing PDs (Üçok et al., 1988). These authors, by using the Structured Clinical Interview for DSM-III-R Personality Disorders (SCID-II), compared 90 bipolar outpatients to 58 control subjects. They found that all the clusters of PDs were significantly more frequent in the group of patients with bipolar disorder, particularly cluster B and C PDs. They also found that the most frequent concurrent PD were, in order, histrionic PD, obsessive-compulsive PD, paranoid PD and BPD. Furthermore, suicide attempts were significantly more prevalent in the group of bipolar outpatients. Unfortunately, they did not analyze the influence of comorbid PD in bipolar patients regarding suicide behavior. Henry et al. (1999) found that, among 72 bipolar I patients sample, a depressive temperament – compared to a hypertimic temperament- was associated with a high history of suicide attempts.

Substance Use Disorders (SUD)

Some subjects diagnosed with a PD are substance abusers and *vice versa*. Substance abuse is one DMS-III criteria for both BPD and antisocial PD (Frances A et al., 1986). Indeed, in previous follow-up studies it has been found a surprisingly low rate of MDD or substance abuse when BPD improves in later-middle age (Paris & Zweig-Frank, 2001).

There is a high comorbidity between BPD and SUD (van den Bosch et al., 2001). A comorbid diagnosis of substance abuse in patients diagnosed with BPD increases suicidal behavior (Runeson & Beskow, 1991; Soloff et al., 1994). In a seven-year follow-up of patients with BPD, patients who had a comorbid substance abuse showed more self-mutilating and suicidal behavior than patients without this comorbidity (Links et al., 1995). These patients also perceived themselves to be at higher risk of suicide than did the patients without comorbidity, subjects with substance abuse but without BPD, and patients with BPD alone. Furthermore, in a study of 64 female borderline patients with and without a comorbid substance abuse disorder it was found that the patients in the group with comorbidity were four times more likely to have attempted suicide than the BPD-non-comorbid group. Unfortunately, the authors did not study the temporal relationship between suicide attempts and substance abuse, so it was impossible to be conclusive about the nature of the suicide attempts – which could be the result of substance abuse lowering the threshold to engage in suicide attempts or reflect non-intentional overdoses- (Van den Bosch et al., 2001).

On the other hand, patients with alcohol and/or drug use disorders often have comorbid PDs (Bourgeois et al., 1999; van den Bosch et al., 2001). Addictive disorders, which are associated with aggression and impulsivity, are related to suicidal behavior (Bergman & Brismar, 1994). *Heroin* users have higher rates of mortality than peers matched for gender and age (Hulse et al., 1999). The suicide standardised mortality ratio (SMR) for heroin users has been estimated to be 14 times that of matched peers (Harris & Barraclough, 1997). Despite much is known of risks for attempted and completed suicide in the general population and the high rates of them among heroin users, this topic has received little research attention. The rate of attempted suicide among heroin users range from 17% to 47%, being depression and relationship break-ups the most commonly cited reasons for attempting suicide (Darke et al., 2004). Rounsaville et al. (1982) found that among 533 treated opiate addicts, 54% met DSM III criteria of antisocial PD. This PD was the most prevalent Axis II diagnosis among SA. In a descriptive study, Mills et al. (2004) found that, in a cohort of 210 young Australians aged between 18 and 24 and diagnosed of *heroin dependence*, the prevalence of antisocial PD and BPD was of 75% and 51%, respectively. Moreover, a 17% had attempted suicide the previous year and 32% had a lifetime history of attempted suicide. Darke et al. (2004) found in their 615 heroin users that a recent history of suicide attempt was related to current MDD, current suicidal ideation, a diagnosis of post-traumatic-stress syndrome (PTSD) and a diagnosis of BPD. Similarly to Darke & Ross (2001), they also found that a diagnosis of antisocial PD was not significantly associated with recent suicide attempt history.

Regarding *alcohol*, it has been calculated that 15-20% of female's suicide attempts and 30-40% of male's suicide attempts are made by alcohol abusers or alcohol-dependent subjects (Rygnestadt et al., 1992). Lejoyeux et al. (2000) found that the rate of *alcohol dependence* among suicidal patients was 23%, while Suominen et al. (1997) found a 41%. It is calculated that about 7-8% of alcohol-dependent subjects suicide (Inskip et al., 1998). Roy & Linnoila (1996) calculated that 21% of suicides were alcoholics and reversely, that 18% of alcoholics subsequently suicide. Beck & Steer (1989) said that alcoholism was the strongest single predictor of suicide in a sample of SA. There are several risk factors for suicide among alcoholics, like being divorced or widowed, having recently lost a close relationship, being depressed or actively drinking, and having made a previous suicide attempt (Roy, 1992). Henriksson et al. (1993) found that *alcohol dependence* was associated with a diagnosis of PD in 36% of suicide victims. The rate of suicide for male alcoholics is 75 times greater than expected for the general male population (Kessel, 1960). Some authors have found that alcohol dependence is especially frequent among multiple SA examined in the emergency room. Reynolds & Eaton (1986) compared 99 multiple SA to first attempters and found that a history of alcohol or drug dependence was more frequent. Lejoyeux et al. (2000) found that alcohol dependent subjects examined in the emergency room (ER), when compared to nondependent individuals, showed more frequently antisocial PD. However, attempted suicide was as frequent in alcohol-dependent patients as in non-dependent patients. Koller et al. (2002) found in their sample of 182 detoxified alcohol-dependent subjects that they scored higher in different measures of impulsivity or aggressiveness, thus suggesting that impulsive and aggressive personality traits might be important factors in the pathogenesis of suicide attempts in alcoholics. However, they found no interaction between increased impulsive-aggressive behavior and concurrent BPD or APD.

Regarding the relationship of suicide and *benzodiazepine (BZD) use or abuse* in a non-multi-substance use context, few studies have been done. Garvey & Tollefson reported, when comparing a small sample of 5 BZD misusers to a non-misuser group of 66 patients, a higher percentage of SA in the misuser group. However, these authors did not investigate the independent factors associated with suicidal behavior. Lekka et al. (2002) compared fifty-five high dose regular BZD users to 55 psychiatric controls, matched for demographic characteristics and psychiatric diagnoses (control A), and to 55 psychiatric controls, matched only for demographic characteristics (control B) and found that, the only independent factor associated to a history of suicide attempt was the presence of comorbid BPD.

Finally, *smoking* is also related to increased rates of suicide (Davey et al., 1992; Hemenway et al., 1993; Tanskanen et al., 1998). Mann et al. (1999) found that the association between smoking and suicidal acts was independent of any association of psychiatric illness with smoking.

Anxiety Disorders

Some follow-up studies have reported that neurotic patients have increased mortality due to suicide (Noyes, 1991). However, these studies have methodological flaws and lack diagnostic validity as in some of them the potential influence of confounding variables, like depressive neuroses, PDs or comorbid alcohol dependence, was not taken into consideration (Miles, 1977).

Traditionally, anxiety disorders *per se* have been considered mild risk factors for suicide behavior. A study with 129 hospitalizations after a suicide attempt reported that *anxiety disorders* were associated with the attempts (OR CI 95% 1.3-7.4%), but this association was conditioned by comorbidity with affective disorders, substance abuse and antisocial PD. However, comorbidity with Axis II diagnoses may amplify the influence of anxiety disorders on suicide behavior. In a study carried out by our group, 110 (34.8%) out of our sample of 318 SA were at least diagnosed with one anxiety disorder, being *generalized anxiety disorder* the most prevalent diagnosis among anxiety disorders (Blasco-Fontecilla, 2002). Comorbidity with any Axis II disorder was the rule. The most frequent comorbid PD were BPD (25.6%), evitative PD (22.2%), and paranoid PD (15.5%). This is consistent with the data of Henriksson et al. (1993), who found that anxiety disorders were associated with a diagnosis of PD in half of suicide victims. Moreover, BPD is often comorbid with Axis I disorders, especially with mood disorders, SUC – or both- and anxiety disorders (Trull et al., 2003).

Panic Disorder

There is a great controversy regarding the relationship between *panic disorder* and suicidal behavior. The reported rates of suicide attempts in patients with panic disorder range dramatically, from 2% to 42% (Weissman et al., 1989; Noyes et al., 1991; Friedman et al., 1992; Lupine et al., 1993). While some authors consider that panic disorder is associated with a high risk of suicide attempts (Ikebana et al., 2004), several prospective studies have found no such a statistical significant association (Brown et al., 2000; Warshaw et al., 2000; Yen et al., 2003). Furthermore, in a reanalysis of the Epidemiologic Catchment's Area (ECA) study panic disorder was not associated with an increased risk of suicide attempt after controlling for comorbid disorders (Horning & McNally, 1995). Warshaw et al. (2000) concluded that panic disorder *per se*, without other risk factors, was not a predictor of suicide. Iketani et al. (2004) said that previous studies failed to assess comorbidity with PDs. It could be suggested that this striking discrepancies are due to the fact that the majority of authors didn't take into account the role of comorbid PD. Friedman et al. (1992) found a 2% suicide behavior rate in pure *panic disorder* patients that increased up to 25% in *panic disorder* patients with comorbid BPD. Warshaw et al. (2000) also found that panic disorder was a predictor of suicide in the concurrence with BPD (or any other PD), history of suicide behavior, eating disorders, recurrent depressive disorder, MDD, or substance or alcohol abuse. Having a partner or children were protective factors. The authors also recommended inquiring about these risk factors in clinical settings in order to perform a quick (but careful) screening that would classify panic disorder patients into two different risk groups, those with low suicide behavior risk (those without comorbidity) and those with high suicide behavior risk (those with comorbidity).

Other authors have focused on the differences between *early-onset panic attack* and *late-onset panic attack*. It has been suggested that a high genetic load may be involved in early-onset panic attack (Battaglia et al., 1995). This disorder might be a special type of panic disorder with a different biological basis (Segui et al., 1999). Goodwin & Hamilton (2002) found that *early-onset fearful* – that is, with a cognitive fear component of madness or dying-*panic attack* (prior to age 20) was associated with a higher likelihood of substance abuse and major affective disorders, antisocial PD and suicidal ideation and suicide attempt, among others. Half of these individuals had suicidal ideation and 20% had made a suicide attempt. These rates were 3-14-fold higher than those among subjects with other types of panic attacks. Iketani et al. (2004) found that the early-onset panic disorder group had statistically significant higher prevalence of serious suicide attempts than the late-onset group and that all the attempts happened after onset of panic disorder. Moreover, in their study, all the subjects who made serious suicidal attempts had comorbid PDs. Both Cluster A and B were over-represented in the early-onset group and when using logistic regression analyses, a statistically significant association between suicide attempts with comorbid cluster B, particularly BPD and histrionic PD, was found.

Placidi et al. (2000) point out the shortage of studies on the relationship among aggressiveness, impulsivity and anxiety symptoms. In their study of patients with *major depression*, they found that the relationship of aggressiveness and impulsivity to a history of suicide attempts was independent of the presence of symptoms of anxiety or *panic disorder*. The relationship among aggressiveness and *panic attacks* has received very little attention, even though in clinical cases it is well documented that aggressiveness and suicide ideation may occur during the attack, as pointed out by Korn et al. (1997). They found high rates of suicide ideation, suicidal and aggressive behavior, and a high risk of suicide or violent behavior during the *panic attack* in patients with *pure panic disorder*. They also found that the rates of homicide and suicide ideation and of aggressions and private property destruction –but not of suicide behavior- were higher in panic disorder patients with comorbid major depression. They found a high correlation among the psychometric measures of impulsivity, self- and hetero-aggressiveness, suicide and violent behavior risk associated to the *panic attack*, and suggested that those individuals with chronic impulsive and aggressive behaviors (i.e. those with BPD) were more likely to experience moments of control loss during the panic attacks. This hypothesis supports the findings of Fava (1990) who reported that, in patients diagnosed with *major depression* and comorbid *panic disorder*, those who had trouble regulating aggressiveness and impulsive behavior were the ones at the highest risk of suicide ideation and suicidal or aggressive behavior.

Goodwin & Hamilton (2003) hypothesized that there is a relationship between *antisocial personality disorder* (APD) and anxiety disorders and stressed the little available data on this area. Tomasson & Vaglum (2000) reported very high rates (61%) of anxiety disorders in a sample of patients with APD and alcohol use disorders - 43% of them were diagnosed with panic/agoraphobia-. Goodwin & Hamilton (2003) also found that 53.3% of adults diagnosed with APD also met criteria for an anxiety disorder during their lifetime. Some other authors have reported an association between APD and obsessive-compulsive disorder (Hollander et al., 1996; Kolada et al., 1994). Goodwin & Hamilton (2003) suggest that some antisocial behavior develops as a way of coping with anxiety among subjects lacking the emotional resources to solve problems and manage frustration in more effective ways. They suggest that, contrary to previous data suggesting that anxiety comorbidity may decrease the risk of suicidal behavior –based on the idea that fear is protective against suicide behavior (Placidi et al., 2000)-, anxiety may increase vulnerability to suicidal behavior among adults with APD. They found that, after controlling for depression, alcohol, and substance abuse, the presence of a comorbid anxiety disorder in individuals with APD increased the likelihood of suicidal behavior. Moreover, they also found that in the absence of anxiety disorders, the likelihood of major depression was lower in individuals with APD, suggesting that severe anxiety may play a fundamental role in mediating the relationship between APD and depression. This is consistent with the differentiation between subjects with APD and subjects with psychopathy (Frick & Ellis, 1999; Goodwin & Hamilton, 2003). When subjects with APD do not feel anxiety, it is most probable to them to be diagnosed as pure or primary psychopaths – those diagnosed by the F1 dimension described by Hart & Hare (1997)-. If they are not able to become genuinely depressed, they wouldn't be at a higher risk of suicide behavior, in contrast with the remaining antisocial subjects – those who feel anxiety and can sometimes be genuinely depressed- (Blasco Fontecilla, 2006; 2007).

Dissociative Disorders

Studies addressing the relationship among *dissociative disorders* and suicide are also quite scarce, despite the fact that – thanks to the diagnosis of *multiple personality disorder*-these disorders have been very popular in the U.S., inspiring movies like "Primal Fear". Ross & Norton (1989) stress how hard it is to diagnose multiple personality. Indeed, they are usually comorbid with other mental disorders, but not a dissociative disorder. They explain that two of the most common first manifestations of the disorder are suicide ideation and suicide behavior. In a clinical series of 236 patients, they found that 72% of patients attempted suicide at least once, and 2.1% accomplished suicide. These data are consistent with those of Putnam et al. (1986), who estimated the rate of suicide attempt as first psychiatric manifestation of the disorder at about 70%. In their sample of 100 patients, they frequently found depressive and dissociative symptoms and a history of psychiatric traumas in the childhood, mainly childhood abuse. Childhood abuse – physical, psychological or sexual, or childhood neglect- has been associated with *dissociative disorders* -mainly *multiple personality disorder* (Boor, 1982; Coons et al., 1988; Darves-Bornoz et al., 1996)-, *conversive disorders, somatization disorders, PTSD, BPD, depression*, sexual promiscuity, school failure (Paoluci et al., 2001), and *bulimia nervosa* (Matsunaga et al., 1999). Kaplan et al. (1995) studied suicide behavior in ambulatory psychiatric patients and found that abuse (both in the childhood and the adulthood) was related to earlier suicide behaviors and higher number of suicide attempts. Among individuals with history of sexual abuse, those who had suicide behaviors were the ones with higher levels of depression, somatization and dissociation. This may be used as a way to identify the patients with the highest suicide behavior `potential´ in order to prevent suicide behaviors. In a sample of 51 sexually abused women, Anderson et al. (1993) found that 88.2% had a dissociative disorder, 54.9% had multiple personality, and they had high rates of other diagnoses such as BPD, substance abuse and depression and a high rate of suicide behaviors. Fetkewicz et al. (2000) reported that suicide attempts were more frequent in *multiple personality disorder* patients after being diagnosed with the disorder.

Yargic et al. (1998) performed an interesting study in Istambul. They compared 20 patients with *multiple personality disorder* with groups of 20 patients with other diagnoses – schizophrenia, panic disorder and complex partial epilepsy- using two scales, the Dissociative Disorders Interview Schedule (DDIS) and the Dissociative Experiences Scale (DES). They found that those patients diagnosed with a multiple personality disorder not only had received many other diagnoses but also had a higher suicide attempt rate than the other groups. Kaplan et al. (1998) associated dissociative symptomathology with aggressive behaviors and, more specifically, with suicide behavior, but not with homicides. Finally, some studies have reported that SA have higher levels of pain endurance than other individuals. This might be explained as a result of dissociation mechanisms inherent to the development of suicide tendencies, related to insensitivity to pain and indifference to their own bodies (Orbach et al., 1996; 1994).

Rechlin et al. (1997) also reported that *pseudo-crises* were frequently associated with depressive symptoms, impulsivity disorders –*bulimia nervosa, substance abuse, antisocial* and *borderline personality disorder*- and self-destructive and suicidal behaviors, suggesting that patients with pseudo-crises may have an important misbalance in affection and impulse control.

Post-traumatic Stress Disorder (PTSD)

Zlotnick et al. (2003) found that a comorbid diagnosis of *PTSD* in BPD women did not significantly increase the degree of borderline pathology and psychiatric morbidity, but did significantly increase the probability of hospitalization, general dysfunction, impulsiveness and suicide proneness. Moreover, Yen et al. (2003) found that PTSD is not a significant predictor of suicide attempts after controlling for BPD.

Eating Disorders (ED)

The risk of suicide of eating disorders (ED) is comparable with that of other severe mental disorders (Harris & Barraclough, 1997). In women diagnosed with ED the prevalence of suicide attempts is significantly elevated in community samples (Favaro & Santonastaso, 1997; Corcos et al., 2002). Viesselman & Roig (1985) reported that of 46-60% of inpatients diagnosed with an ED had suicidal ideation, 20% had made a suicide attempt - 40% of them were potentially lethal-. Favaro & Santonastaso (1997) said that 29% of their patients showed suicidal ideation. Youseff et al. (2004) found that 23.7% of their sample diagnosed with an ED attempted suicide. Similarly, Milos et al. (2004) found that 26% of patients with an ED had a history of suicide attempt. This rate is four times higher than the lifetime prevalence found in general female populations in Western countries (Weissman et al., 1999).

In general, the risk for suicide or attempted suicide is considered higher in bulimic than in anorexic patients. Those with a *purging type* have a higher rate of history of suicide attempts (Milos et al., 2004; Youssef et al., 2004). Youseff et al. (2004) found that the rate of suicide attempts among women with Bulimia Nervosa (BN) was of 28.6%, higher than the 21.4% found in patients with *Anorexia Nervosa* (AN). Herzog et al. (1992) found a history of suicide attempts in 10% of restricting anorexics, 22% of bulimic anorexics and 13% of normal weight bulimics. Favaro & Santonastaso (1997) found that SA were older, with a longer duration of illness, and weighted less if they had AN. These findings may confirm the hypothesis that purging behaviors are associated with disturbed impulse control (Lacey & Evans, 1986; Fahy & Eisler, 1986) and that *impulsivity* is an important antecedent of suicide attempts (Mann et al., 1999). Moreover, patients with repeated suicide attempt history were only found in the group of purging ED (Milos et al., 2004). Furthermore, individuals with history of attempted suicide (HAS) were significantly more frequently diagnosed with any-Axis I disorder – particularly, affective disorders- and with a Cluster B PD than patients with no HAS. This finding supports the hypothesis of a relationship between suicide attempts and impulsivity. Suicidal tendencies may resolve along with remission of the bulimic symptoms (Lehoux et al., 2000).

Little is known of personality trait risk factors – apart from impulsivity- for suicide attempts among those with ED (Youssef et al., 2004). SA have been found to be more obsessive than non-attempters (Favaro & Santonastaso, 1997). A higher level of *obsessive behavior* has been found in both bulimic and anorexic SA compared to non-attempters, and in suicide repeaters compared to non-repeaters (Favaro & Santonastaso, 1996). Patients diagnosed with an ED have high rates of comorbid Axis I and/or II disorder (Braun et al., 1994; Herzog et al., 1996; Milos et al., 2003). The high rates of comorbidity may contribute to increase the risk of suicide attempts or suicide in patients with an ED (Milos et al., 2004). These authors found that the most common Axis I and II comorbid diagnoses in their sample of patients with an ED were anxiety and affective disorders, and cluster C PDs, respectively. They found that 72.9% of patients showed at least any other Axis I disorder and 68.1% at least any Axis II disorder. Moreover, when HAS was present, comorbidity with an Axis I and Axis II was more frequent. Wonderlich & Swift (1990) reported an association between ED and BPD. Yamaguchi et al. (2000) also found that more suicidal individuals had a PD (62.5%) compared to non-suicidal subjects (20.0%), but no significant differences were found in specific PDs. Moreover, SA scored higher in unstable self-image, frantic efforts to avoid abandonment, affective instability and perfectionism. They conclude that the first three personality traits reported in BPD, and the last one in obsessive personality, may be associated with suicide. Unfortunately, they did not analyze whether any personality trait differences among the different types of ED were present. Finally, they reported a higher presence of overprotective attitudes in the parents of SA with an ED. From a clinical point of view, the diagnosis of BPD seems to be much more associated with purgative ED, while obsessive personalities seem to be more frequent among AN-restrictive type.

Bulimia Nervosa (BN)

BN is the most prevalent of the ED. Between 1% to 3% of young and adolescent females have this diagnosis (APA, 1994). BN patients have frequently comorbid diagnosis on Axis I and II (Suzuki et al., 1993; Nagata et al., 2000). Suicide attempts are more frequent when BN is comorbid with mood disorders, or alcohol or drug abuse (Hatsukami et al., 1986; Suzuki et al., 1994; Wiederman & Pryor, 1996). In recent studies, HAS is found in 18% to 49% of patients with BN (Fichter et al., 1994; Wiederman & Pryor, 1996; Favaro & Santonastaso, 1998). HAS and BPD diagnosis are linked with inpatient experience (Spindler & Milos, 2004). Unfortunately, these authors did not study the relationship between BN, BPD and suicide attempts.

Bulimic symptoms seem to be closely associated with impulsivity. Lacey & Evans (1986) used the term `multi-impulsivity´ to refer to patients diagnosed of BN who displayed more than one type of impulsive behavior. Fichter et al. (1994) defined *multi-impulsivity* according to the existence of at least three of the following six behaviors: self-harm; suicide attempts; shoplifting; alcohol abuse; drug abuse; or sexual promiscuity. They compared 32 women diagnosed with multi-impulsivity to 32 bulimic women with no evidence of the six impulsive behaviors, and found that the multi-impulsivity group displayed greater comorbid psychopathology and lower psychosocial functioning. However, multi-impulsivity was not associated with greater severity of the ED itself, suggesting that impulsivity and ED are two independent problems, although there could be a link between BN and self-mutilation (Fichter et al., 1994; Welch & Fairburn, 1996; Nagata et al., 2000). The important question is whether impulsivity in patients with an ED is secondary to underlying disorders such as a multi-impulsive PD (Lacey, 1993). Nagata et al. (2000) studied the presence of multi-impulsivity in 60 patients with AN-restricting type (AN-R), 62 patients with AN-binge-eating/purging type (AN-BP), 114 patients with BN-purging type (BN) and 66 control subjects, and found that multi-impulsivity was more frequent in the BN group (18%). Moreover, BN patients with multi-impulsivity showed impulsive behaviors before ED developed and eighty percent of these patients had a HAS or self-mutilation history prior to the onset of BN, being the patients younger when self-mutilation and suicide attempts took place than in BN patients without multi-impulsivity. This result clearly suggests that impulsivity is not a consequence of chaotic eating behaviors. They also found that multi-impulsivity was significantly associated with childhood parental loss – only marginally- and the presence of BPD - 27% of multi-impulsive bulimics met the BPD criterion-, concluding that multi-impulsivity was probably multi-factorial.

Regarding other personality traits different of impulsivity, Youseff et al. (2004) found that in a subgroup of BN-purgative type (BN-P), some personality traits measured with the MMPI-2 were associated with a higher risk of suicidal behavior. The traits were `Psychastenia´ - it includes obsessive ideation, compulsive rituals and exaggerated fears-, `Anger´ - these subjects tend to be irritable and stubborn, to lose control easily and may be physically violent- and `Fears´ - the subject has particular phobias-. These patients "tend to have obsessive ideation and compulsive rituals, as well as rigorous moral principles, an excessive sense of responsibility and self-accusation, making important efforts in a rigid way to control their impulsivity" (Youssef et al., 2004).

Thompson et al. (1999) suggested that the presence of both ED and aggressive behavior – which is particularly frequent in Cluster B PD- indicated a higher risk of suicide attempt.

Anorexia Nervosa (AN)

The mortality rate of AN is approximately 5.6% per decade, suicide being the second cause of death in them, only after complications of the ED (Sullivan, 1995; Herzog et al., 2000). Milos et al. (2004) found that the rate of suicide ideation was higher in patient with AN than patients with BN. They hypothesized that starvation is a form of chronic self-harming behavior that lead to considerable distress and might contribute to higher levels of suicidal ideation in these patients.

Youseff et al. (2004) found that some personality traits measured with the MMPI-2 were associated with a higher risk of suicidal behavior and that these personality traits were different in the AN-restrictive type (AN-R) and the AN-Purgative type (AN-P). The AN-R subgroup who attempted suicide scored higher in the `Depression´ trait – this trait reflects not only feelings of pessimism, despair or discouragement, but also an excessive sense of responsibility, exaggerated self-demands and a tendency to self-punishment, among others- and `Antisocial practices´. The AN-P subgroup was characterized by higher scores in `Hysteria´, `Psychopathic deviate´, `Shyness/Self-consciousness´, `Antisocial practices´, `Obssesiveness´ and `Low self-esteem´.

Schizophrenia

Patients diagnosed of *psychosis* are at a higher risk for suicide (Harris & Barraclough, 1997). Risk factors for suicide in *schizophrenia* include being male, young and in the early years of illness, and having a history of substance misuse or suicide attempts (Drake et al., 1985; Verodoux et al., 2001). Schizophrenics represent the highest-risk group of in-patient suicide (Spiessl et al., 2002).

There has been little research regarding suicidal behavior among psychotic patients with a comorbid PD (Moran et al., 2003). Schizophrenics with comorbid *antisocial PD* (APD) represent a high-risk subgroup vulnerable to more severe substance abuse, psychiatric impairment, aggression, and legal problems (Mueser et al., 1997). Young male schizophrenics who have antisocial traits and depressive symptoms must be considered a group with special risk of suicide, and some particular interventions must be taken (Evren & Evren, 2003).

Moran et al. (2003) found in a sample of 670 psychotics that the presence of a comorbid PD was associated with an increased risk of suicidal behavior after controlling for several confounding variables. Moreover, they found that not only BPD and dissocial PD were associated with an increased risk of suicidal behaviors but that the association between any co-morbid PD and suicidal behavior remained statistically significant after excluding BPD, and impulsive and dissocial PDs. In an ulterior work, Moran & Hodgins (2004) examined the correlates of APD among 232 men with schizophrenic disorders, three-quarters of whom had committed at least one crime. Comparisons of the men with and without APD revealed no differences in the course or symptoms of schizophrenia. However, multivariate models confirmed strong associations of comorbid APD with substance abuse, attention/concentration problems, and poor academic performance in childhood; and with alcohol abuse or dependence and `deficient affective experience´ (a personality style characterized by lack of remorse or guilt, shallow affect, lack of empathy, and failure to accept responsibility for one's own actions) in adulthood.

Other Disorders

PDs are frequent among *pathological gamblers*. Blaszczynski & Steel (1998) found that 92% met criteria for at least one PD, mainly cluster B PDs, with an average of 4.6 PDs per subject. The high rate of PDs obtained in this study stand in contrast to the findings of Specker et al. (1996), who reported substantially lower levels of PD with only 25% of a sample of 40 volunteer gamblers. These high figures may reflect that the former authors used the self-report PDQ-R, which is associated with higher level of case identification compared to structure interviews (Hyler et al., 1990). Moreover, antisocial PD and narcissistic PD subjects displayed a greater severity of problem gambling (Blaszczynski & Steel, 1998).

In a retrospective study of a sample of 119 patients with Axis I adjustment disorder was found that patients with *adjustment disorders* seemed significantly more suicidal at admission than patients without adjustment disorders. Moreover, among the sample group with suicide attempts in the past, 67% had at least one PD -38% were diagnosed of a BPD and 25% of an antisocial PD- (Kryzhanovskaya & Canterbury, 2001).

2.7.3. OUR RESEARCH

The main objective of our study was to describe potential comorbidity between specified PDs and Axis I diagnosis. We carried out an analysis to determine whether or not there are significant associations between the two Axis. We expected to find, particularly, associations between *borderline PD,* and *depressive disorders* and/or *substance abuse* and *dependence.* See chapter 2.1.3 for information with regard to methodology of our research.

Results

We found that 57.3% of our sample of SA was diagnosed with a MDD and 74.2% with at least one PD. The only PD where no significant associations with Axis I disorders were found was *OCPD*. The following significant associations in our sample of SA were found:

- *Paranoid PD* with alcohol abuse (Fisher's exact test (FET) p= 0.014), with current psychotic disorder (FET p= 0.024), and with stress posttraumatic disorder (FET p= 0.042).
- *Schizoid* PD with agoraphobia (FET p= 0.029) and risk of suicide (X^2 7.291, gl= 2, p= 0.026).
- *Schizotypal PD* with social phobia (FET p= 0.001), and current psychotic disorder (FET p= 0.009).
- *Histrionic PD* with life-persistent anxiety disorder (FET p= 0.047), and substance (no alcohol) abuse (FET p= 0.041).
- *Antisocial PD* with past manic episode (FET p= 0.036), and substance (no alcohol) dependence (FET p= 0.004). Moreover, associations with substance (no alcohol) abuse, alcohol dependence, and suicide risk nearly reached significance (FET p= 0.067; FET p= 0.063; X^2 = 1.271, gl= 2, p= 0.530, respectively).
- *Narcissistic PD* with substance (no alcohol) dependence (FET p= 0.010). Moreover, associations with substance (no alcohol) abuse (FET p= 0.073), and antisocial PD (FET p= 0.057) nearly reached significance.
- *Borderline PD* with MINI general score (FET p= 0.038), major depressive episode (MDE) (FET p= 0.026), major depressive disorder (MDD) (FET p= 0.027), life-persistent anxiety disorder (FET p= 0.018), social phobia (FET p= 0.029), alcohol dependence (FET p= 0.015), and anorexia nervosa (FET p= 0.011).
- *Dependent PD* with MINI general score (FET p= 0.018), MDD (FET p= 0.046), social phobia (FET p= 0.000), current psychotic disorder (FET p= 0.039), and affective disorder with psychotic symptoms (FET p= 0.050).
- *Avoidant PD* with social phobia (FET p= 0.001).

Discussion

Paranoid PD was related to alcohol abuse, to current psychotic disorder, and to stress postraumatic disorder. It is traditionally accepted that subjects diagnosed with paranoid PD do not usually try to attempt suicide, as they usually project aggressiveness externally. However, some authors have found that paranoid PD is one of the most frequents PDs among SA and completers (Foster et al., 1997; Maj-Liz et al., 1999; Foster et al., 1999; Hawton et al., 2003). This is in agreement with our finding that paranoid PD is the third most frequent PD in our sample of SA (21.5%) – and the most frequent in cluster A-, only following BPD and avoidant PD.

With regard to the associations with Axis I we found, it is possible that Axis I disorders operate as precipitant factors. Regarding *alcohol abuse*, the majority of studies have focused on the relationship between BPD and antisocial PD, and substance abuse. This is probably because the majority of information available on PD is focused on these two PDs, and because "substance abuse" is one of the DMS-III criteria for both PDs (Frances A et al., 1986). Subjects with paranoid PD are not considered impulsive in nature, and indeed are not classified in the cluster B. However, we found that in our sample of SA those subjects diagnosed with paranoid PD were characterized by high impulsivity (high BIS) (Blasco-

Fontecilla, 2006). As alcohol has an initial disinhibitory effect, it may precipitate suicide attempts in these subjects.

With regard to the association with *current psychotic disorder*, a familial link between paranoid PD and delusional disorder has been found (Kender et al., 1985; Winokur, 1985). Moreover, it has been suggested that paranoid PD belongs to the delusional disorder spectrum, and that it may be an attenuated version of delusional disorder (Rogers & Winokur, 1988).

With regard to the association with *stress posttraumatic disorder*, we suggest that paranoid PD may be a defensive outcome after trauma.

Schizoid PD was associated with agoraphobia and risk of suicide. *Agoraphobia* is not usually considered closely associated to suicide (Beck et al., 1991). It is possible that agoraphobia is a severity factor for schizoid individuals, so that, those with both diagnosis would have a greater risk for suicide attempts. Those schizoid subjects diagnosed with agoraphobia would be more impaired in social situations. As we will report later, recent social life events have important roles as precipitating factors of suicide attempts.

Schizotypal PD was related to *social phobia* and current *psychotic disorder*. Regarding the latter association, schizotypal PD belongs to the schizophrenia spectrum. It has been suggested that schizotypal PD may be an attenuated version of schizophrenia (Rogers & Winokur, 1988) or a type of schizophrenia (WHO, 1993). It could be suggested that those schizotypal subjects who are also diagnosed with a current psychosis are probably showing the psychotic symptoms associated with suicide attempts (e.g. paranoid delusions). Moreover, comorbidity with social phobia, in the same way as agoraphobia in schizoid subjects, may also be a marker of severity of the disorder, posing those subjects affected by both diagnoses to a greater risk of suicide behavior.

Histrionic PD was associated with *life-persistent anxiety disorder*, and *substance (no alcohol) abuse*. Some other PDs, mainly antisocial PD and BPD have been associated with suicide behavior in subjects diagnosed with anxiety disorders (see above). However, no particular relationship has been described between life-persistent anxiety disorder and histrionic PD in SA. A comorbid diagnosis of life-persistent anxiety disorder seems to be a precipitating or aggravating factor in SA diagnosed with histrionic PD. Moreover, subjects diagnosed with histrionic PD are prone to fluctuations in mood in response to stress and use drugs (Kendell, 1983). Substance abuse may facilitate suicide attempts in subjects diagnosed with histrionic PD.

Antisocial PD (APD) was significantly associated with *past manic episode,* and with *substance (no alcohol) dependence.* Moreover, associations with *substance (no alcohol) abuse, alcohol dependence,* and *suicide risk,* nearly reached significance. It is possible that the manic episode was in the context of a SUD. APD is associated to an increased risk of suicide attempts and completed suicide (Buglass & Horton, 1974; Morgan et al., 1976; Black et al., 1996; Verona et al., 2001). The risk for a serious suicide attempt is 3.7 times higher in subjects diagnosed with an APD, and it is 9 times more likely in men aged 30 or younger (Beautrais et al., 1996). Men with APD are up to 12 times more likely to attempt suicide than those without antisocial PD (Mulder et al., 1994; Martens, 2000). There is a close relationship between SUD and PDs, particularly BPD and APD. It seems that, those antisocial individual who have a comorbid substance abuse, and particularly substance dependence, are at a higher risk of attempted suicide. Our finding of a relationship with alcohol dependence was expected, as an association between these two disorders has been found in SA evaluated in the ER (Lejoyeux et al., 2000).

Narcissistic PD (NPD) was significantly associated with *substance (no alcohol) dependence*. Associations with *substance (no alcohol) abuse*, and *antisocial PD* nearly reached significance. Not surprisingly, the pattern of comorbidity of NPD and APD was very similar. We, as several other authors, are of the opinion that both PD are very closely related. The main differences between both disorders might be the level of intelligence, and/or behavior/impulse control, but this hypothesis needs empirical confirmation (Blasco-Fontecilla, 2006; 2007). Description of narcissistic subjects clearly resembles that of the classical concept of psychopath. Narcissistic subjects, compared to antisocial subjects, would be more intelligent, and able to control more efficiently impulses so that, their antisocial acts would be more difficult to detect and not so clearly deviant from a social point of view. This hypothesis is theoretically supported by the similar pattern of comorbidity of both PD we found. As it happened with antisocial subjects, comorbidity with substance dependence seems to increase suicide risk in narcissistic subjects.

BPD was significantly related to *MINI general score, MDE, MDD, life-persistent anxiety disorder, social phobia, alcohol dependence, AN,* and *risk of suicide*. Regarding the relationship between MDE/MDD and BPD, it must be said that although traditionally is assumed that the diagnosis of a comorbid PD impacts negatively on the course of unipolar major depression, there is a lack of good empirical data to support this asseveration (Brieger et al., 2002). Patients with early-onset MDD have a significantly higher prevalence of PDs (Fava et al., 1996). Non-melancholic MDD is associated with a higher prevalence of comorbid PD (Hansen et al., 2003), increasing the risk of suicide. In other study, patients diagnosed with MDD and a comorbid cluster A or B PD reported more suicide attempts than patients with a cluster C PD (Brieger et al., 2002).

Our finding that BPD is significantly associated with MDD in SA is consistent with previous research. Subjects with a diagnosis of BPD and comorbid MDD are associated with a higher risk of suicide behavior than patients diagnosed with MDD alone (Malone et al., 1995a). Depressed patients with comorbid BPD showed more suicidal behaviors (Rothschild & Zimmerman, 2002). The diagnosis of a cluster B PD can lower the threshold for suicidal behaviors in patients diagnosed with MDD (Oquendo et al., 1997). Moreover, suicidality is also associated to cluster B personality traits even if the patients does not fully meet diagnostic criteria (Corbitt et al., 1996).Corbitt et al. (1996) studied a sample of 102 psychiatric inpatients with MDD. They found that the presence and severity – expressed by the number of criteria patients met- of a cluster B diagnosis and, particularly BPD, were positively correlated with the number and lethality of previous suicide attempts.

Regarding the reverse relationship, that is, the role of MDD in subjects diagnosed with BPD, depressed mood, but not comorbid affective disorder, was found to be associated with a history of suicidal behavior in BPD patients (Soloff et al., 1994). Similarly, severity of depressed mood may be a better predictor of suicide behavior than the MDD diagnosis in subjects diagnosed with a PD (Yen et al., 2003). However, further studies are needed to state whether or not MDD remains a significant risk factor in BPD patients.

Moreover, it is still not clear whether comorbidity between BPD and MDD increases or not the patient's risk for suicide attempts beyond the effect of each of these disorders independently. Generally, retrospective studies have found that patients with comorbid BPD and MDD have a closer relationship with suicidality than those diagnosed with just one disorder (Corbitt et al., 1996; Kelly et al., 2000). However, Chioqueta & Stiles (2004) found in an outpatient sample, that both cluster A and cluster B PDs were associated with suicide attempts even after controlling for lifetime depressive disorder, and severity of depression. Probably, the best study carried out in this area is the one of Soloff et al. (2000). They compared 81 inpatients with BPD, 49 patients with BPD and comorbid MDE, and 77 inpatients with a MDE alone. Patients with both diagnoses had the greater number of suicide attempts and the highest level of objective planning. Impulsivity and hopelessness predicted lethality in all three groups. Moreover, hopelessness predicted objective planning in the group with both diagnoses. Suicidal behaviors were more frequent in the sample of patients with BPD – particularly with comorbid MDE but also without MDE- compared with the sample of individuals with MDE with no comorbidity. The number of lifetime attempts was predicted by the presence of BPD diagnosis and comorbidity, level of hopelessness and history of aggression. No differences were found in lethality as rated by the Suicide Intent Scales but the global sample of patients with BPD showed a greater lifetime level of medically lethal suicidal behaviors compared with the sample of individuals diagnosed with MDE without comorbidity. They concluded that patients with comorbidity had a higher risk for suicidal behavior, and that suicidal behavior in inpatients with BPD should not be considered "less serious" than the one of inpatients with MDE.

Our finding that BPD and *lifespan anxiety disorder* are associated in SA is consistent with previous research. Several authors have found that, when patients diagnosed with panic disorder had a comorbid BPD, they had an increased risk for suicide behavior (Friedman et al., 1992; Warshaw et al., 2000). Anxiety states may trigger suicide behavior in subjects like those diagnosed with BPD, characterized by emotional instability, and lack of inner resources to manage anxious states, among others.

Regarding the relationship we found between *social phobia* and BPD in SA, it must be said that social phobia is usually comorbid – up to a 66%- with other disorders like substance misuse or other phobias, but it is of particular importance the one with MDD, and may increase suicide risk (Weisman et al., 1996; Roca, 2002). Nelson et al. (2000) found a common genetic background between social phobia and MDD. They also reported an increased risk of suicide in comorbidity.

We also found a significant association between BPD, and *alcohol dependence*. Some subjects diagnosed with a PD are substance abusers and *vice versa*. The rate of comorbid substance abuse in subjects diagnosed with BPD is very low as patients get older (Paris & Zweig-Frank, 2001). Patients with alcohol and/or drug use disorders often have comorbid PDs (Bourgeois et al., 1999; van den Bosch et al., 2001). The rate of alcohol dependence in suicides is between 7 to 41% (Roy & Linnoila, 1996; Suominen et al., 1997; Inskip et al., 1998; Lejoyeux et al., 2000). Henriksson et al. (1993) found that *alcohol dependence* was associated with a diagnosis of PDs in 36% of suicide victims. Some authors have found that alcohol dependence is especially frequent among multiple SA examined in the emergency room. Koller et al. (2002) found in their sample of 182 detoxified alcohol-dependent subjects that they scored higher in different measures of impulsivity or aggressiveness, thus suggesting that impulsive and aggressive personality traits might be important factors in the pathogenesis of suicide attempts in alcoholics. However, they found no interaction between increased impulsive-aggressive behavior and, concurrent BPD or APD.

Finally, with regard to the significant relationship between BPD and *AN* in SA, Wonderlich & Swift (1990) reported an association between ED and BPD but, little is known of personality trait risk factors –apart of impulsivity- for suicide attempts among those with ED (Youssef et al., 2004). From a clinical point of view, BPD seems to be much more associated with purgative ED, while obsessive personalities seem to be more frequent among AN-restrictive type. A higher level of *obsessive behavior* has been found in both bulimic and anorexic SA compared to non-attempters, and in suicide repeaters compared to non-repeaters (Favaro & Santonastaso, 1996). Yamaguchi et al. (2000) also found that SA scored higher in unstable self-image, frantic efforts to avoid abandonment, affective instability and perfectionism, the first three personality traits in borderline personality, and the last one in obsessive personality, appear to be related to suicide. Unfortunately, they did not analyze whether there were any personality trait differences among the different eating disorders types, probably due to their small number of cases.

Dependent PD was significantly associated with *MINI general score, MDD, social phobia, current psychotic disorder,* and *affective disorder with psychotic symptoms.* Although a relationship with MDD was expected, we cannot say the same with psychotic disorders. This, somewhat may be explained by dependent PD being secondary to very invalidating states, like psychotic ones. Alternatively, a comorbid diagnosis of dependent PD in SA diagnosed with this entire Axis I disorders may increase the risk of a suicide attempt under stressful situations for them, like a problem with the caregiver. A great comorbidity between cluster C PDs and depression in outpatient samples has been found (Farmer & Nelson-Gray, 1990; Shea et al., 1992). Chioqueta & Stiles found that 90% of outpatients diagnosed with dependent PD were also diagnosed with lifetime depressive disorder but fail to find a significant association between dependent PD and suicide attempts after controlling for lifetime depressive disorder. This suggests that depression might be a confounding factor.

Finally, *avoidant PD* was significantly associated with the diagnosis of *social phobia*. Taking into account the current poor and somewhat artificially generated differentiation between both disorders, we were not surprised at this finding.

Chapter 2.8.

RECENT LIFE EVENTS AS PRECIPITANT FACTORS OF SUICIDE BEHAVIOR IN SUBJECTS WITH PERSONALITY DISORDERS*

H. Blasco-Fontecilla, E. Baca-García and J. Sáiz-Ruiz

2.8.1. INTRODUCTION

Recent life events (RLE) are related to the onset and re-emergence of mental disorders (Paykel & Dowlatshahi, 1988). They might increase suicidal risk in those patients at risk (Welch & Linehan, 2002; Pompili et al., 2004). It is not known whether RLE are specific suicide risk factors or their action is mediated by the different psychopathological conditions (Heikkinen et al., 1997). They seem to be more central as precipitators of suicidal behavior in depressive patients when compared to schizophrenics (Baca-García et al., 2005). Furthermore, RLE may be precipitating factors for suicide in subjects diagnosed with a personality disorder (PD), but few is known (Heikkinen et al., 1997). Those patients diagnosed with a PD might have an increased suicidal risk due to a higher rate of RLE (Seivewright et al., 2000). There is no clear answer to whether subjects with a PD have more RLE because of their inner pathological behavior, which in turn might increase their risk of suicidal behavior, but exposure to RLE is not ramdom (Heikkinen et al., 1997). Furthermore, there is increasing evidence that some RLE are associated with certain personality traits (Poulton & Andrews, 1992) and PD (Samuels et al., 1994), particularly BPD (Horesh et al., 2003). Studies addressing the role of RLE in those subjects with a PD – apart from BPD- that show suicidal behavior are sparse (Kelly et al., 2000).

The main objective of this chapter is to explore whether some specific RLE might precipitate suicide attempts in particular PD.

2.8.2. OUR RESEARCH

See chapter 2.1.3 for information with regard to methodology of our research.

Results

Our first hypothesis was that RLE would be significantly more frequents in the sample of suicide attempters (SA) when compared to non-SA. Compared to both control groups, SA had significantly more "death of a close relative" (X^2= 12.629, gl= 2, p < 0.002), "an important change in food habits" (X^2=26.846, gl= 2, p < 0.001), "an important change in personal habits" (X^2= 67.736, gl= 2, p< 0.001), "minor law problems" (X^2= 9.586, gl= 2, p< 0.008), "problems with political family" (X^2=16.865, gl= 2, p< 0.001), "an important change in economic situation" (X^2 = 49.275, gl= 2, p< 0.001), "a new member in the family" (X^2= 111.834, gl= 2, p< 0.001), "son/daughter leaving home" (X^2= 13.208, gl= 2, p< 0.001), "separation from spouse" (X^2= 116.404, gl= 2, p< 0.001), "being fired" (X^2= 22.435, gl= 2, p< 0.001), "an important change in the number of discussion with spouse" (X^2= 223.478, gl= 2, p< 0.001), "an important disease/injury" (X^2= 145.020, gl= 2, p< 0.001), and "an important change in social activities" (X^2= 39.963, gl= 2, p< 0.001). Furthermore, social readjustment index (SRI) was also higher in SA.

Secondly, we looked at whether or not those SA who had a PD had more RLE than those without such a diagnosis. The only significant differences found were that those SA diagnosed with a PD had more frequently "separation from spouse" (Fisher's Exact Test (FET) p= 0.009), and "an important change in social activities" (FET p= 0.089). No significant differences were found with regard to the SRI.

Finally, we explored whether or not there were clinical significant associations between specified RLE and specified PD. We were of the opinion that some RLE might be precipitants of suicidal behavior in subjects with a certain PD but not to other PD –e.g. social situations in schizoid subjects, law problems in subjects with an antisocial PD or being fired in narcissistic individuals-. This would have to do with the specific vulnerabilities of each PD. Significant associations were found between *paranoid PD* and "important changes in social activities" (FET p= 0.029) and "social disputes" (FET p= 0.055); *schizoid PD* and "modification in personal habits" (X^2= 6.914; df= 2; p=0.032) and "important personal success" (FET p= 0.012); *schyzotypal PD* and "important changes in social activities" (FET p= 0.019) and "important change in health or behavior of a member of the family" (FET p= 0.058); *narcissistic PD* and "being fired" (FET p= 0.005). Suicide attempts in *antisocial PD* were related to "arrest" (FET p= 0.020), "minor law problems" (FET p= 0.039) and "death of partner" (FET p= 0.047). *Histrionic PD* was close to statistical significance with "problems with political family" (FET= 0.089) and "change of residence" (FET= 0.076). Furthermore, *obsessive-compulsive PD* was marginally associated with "reconciliation with partner" (FET p= 0.086) and evitative PD with "separation from spouse" (FET p= 0.076) and "beginning/ending studies" (FET p= 0.077). No significant associations were found for borderline PD.

Discussion

Every subject has a threshold which, if emotionally of physically exceed, renders existence intolerable (Gold, 1987). A landmark of subjects diagnosed with a PD is their difficulty to cope with stressful situations and a lack of flexibility (Millon, 1969). They also have several interpersonal difficulties. Furthermore, their inner lack of resources to create adaptative solutions to stressful situations may put them on risk to attempting suicide. RLE – usually adverse, but not necessarily- may be precipitating factors for suicide in subjects with a PD. Moreover, particular life events may be more harmful in specified PD, depending on the core weaknesses of each particular PD. However, in spite of the strong associations between PD and suicidal behavior, few studies have examined the relationship between RLE, suicide attempts, and PDs (Heikkinen et al., 1997; Yen et al., 2005). Despite being the best studied of all PD, this is also de case of BPD (Kelly et al., 2000). It is still not known whether RLE are precipitants of suicidal behavior or not (Yen et al., 2005). Moreover, RLE impact on suicidal behavior may depend on disorder's severity in a particular subject (Yen et al., 2005). In the context of stress-diathesis model, the stronger the diathesis, the lower threshold for RLE becoming precipitants of suicidal behavior. However, suicide completers with non-severe mental disorder are the ones who also referred the presence of RLE (Cooper et al., 2002).

RLE and Suicide Attempts

Consistently with previous research (Paykel et al., 1975; Insherwood et al., 1982; Kelly et al., 2000), we found that SA had more RLE than non-attempters. Suicidal behavior was significantly associated with "death of a close relative", "an important change in food habits", "an important change in personal habits", "minor law problems", "problems with political family", "an important change in economic situation", "a new member in the family", "son/daughter leaving home", "separation from spouse", "being fired", "an important change in the number of discussion with spouse", "an important disease/injury", and "an important change in social activities". Furthermore, the SRI was also higher in the sample of SA, giving an idea of the important role of social relationships in suicidal behavior. SA have four times more RLE than general population (Payel et al., 1975). However, other authors have found no significant differences when comparing depressive SA with depressive non-SA by using the *St. Paul Ramsay Life Experience Scale* (Malone et al., 2000). This suggests that RLE might be more related to psychopathological conditions than to suicidal behavior itself.

The following RLE have been associated with suicidal behavior: personal loses (Cheng et al., 2000; Heikkinen et al., 1997), financial and work problems (Heikkinen et al., 1997), interpersonal loses (Cavanagh et al., 1999; Heikkinen et al., 1997; Weyrauch et al., 2001) and health problems (Cavanagh et al., 1999). After controlling for BPD, MDE, substance abuse disorder, and childhood sexual abuse, the only RLE related to suicidal behavior were love/marriage problems and legal/criminal problems (Yen et al., 2005). Regarding love/marriage problems, these authors found not a single specific event related to suicidal behavior, while some legal problems – i.e. being arrested, go to jail- were related. As the authors stressed, some of these events had to do with some of the typical characteristics of subjects with a cluster B PD – i.e. impulsivity or aggressiveness-.

RLE, PD and Suicide Attempts

When we compared SA-PD with SA-non PD patients, only "separation from spouse" and "an important change in social activities" were associated to the diagnosis of a PD. Heikkinen et al. (1997) found that some RLE – problems at work and family discord- in the week and three months before were associated to an increased risk of suicide. Differences between both studies might have to do with methodological differences. In a three years, prospective longitudinal study was found that subjects diagnosed with a PD who attempted suicide were more probable to have RLE in the previous month (Yen et al., 2005).

It would be interesting to know whether subjects with a PD generate more RLE, which in turn and due to their inner lack or resources to adequately manage stressful situations and to cope with interpersonal problems, might precipitate suicidal behavior, ending in a vicious circle. Heikkinen et al. (1997) said that subjects with a PD have a limited insight on their inner behavior and they tend to externalize their responsibilities instead of assuming their conflictive behavior. They stressed that they usually have higher rates of problems at work, which might be related to their difficulties in social relationships. Some other authors have found RLE associated to the presence of certain personality traits (Fergusson & Horwood, 1987; Poulton & Andrews, 1992; Seivewright, 1987). Heikkinen et al. (1997) found a higher proportion of subjects with a PD -when compared to non-PD subjects- showing RLE, particularly familial problems, interpersonal loses, problems at work, financial problems and being jobless. They suggested that RLE might precipitate suicide attempts in those patients with a PD.

RLE, Specific PDs and Suicide Attempts

Every specified PD is characterized by their inner weakness. For the majority of people, RLE are not followed by suicidal behavior. If a pre-existent vulnerability is activated by a specified RLE, and what is worse, these subjects lack the inner resources to cope with stressful situations, a suicidal behavior might happen. RLE might be shown as the last straw. We hypothesized that specified RLE could be specific precipitants of suicide attempts in specified PD. Unfortunately; few works have been carried out in this area. Heikkinen et al. (1997) found a tendency in patients diagnosed with a cluster B PD to experience separations and interpersonal loses when compared to cluster C PD subjects. We found the following significant associations:

Suicide attempts in *paranoid PD* were associated with "important social changes". Paranoid patients are characterized, among others, by suspiciousness and a rigid minded style, lacking the inner resources to cope with changing social situations. On the other hand, we expected to find significant associations with problems at work and marital problems. It is our opinion that, information reported by those subjects in the emergency room might be biased due to their core suspiciousness.

Suicide attempts in subjects diagnosed with *schizoid PD* were related to "an important success". Schizoid subjects are characterized by their avoidance of social situations. They usually work at places where social contact is limited. Thus, "an important success" might oblige them to having social relationships, which could be experienced as a stressful situation. Researchers usually have only investigated the relationship of adverse RLE with suicidal behavior, not taking into account that neutral or even positive RLE might also precipitate suicidal behaviors. Holmes & Rahe (1967) suggested that a change from any state, more than value judgement of social desirability is what determine perceived stress – *general quantitative hypothesis-*, and what would eventually precipitate suicide attempts. The study by Kelly et al. (2000) gave support to this hypothesis. In their study with 80 patients - 34 diagnosed of MDE, 22 of BPD, and 24 with both diagnosis-, those who attempted suicide reported more RLE, even those coded as "neutral" or socially desirable, than non-SA (Kelly et al., 2000). They concluded that any change experienced as stressful, independently of social desirability, might precipitate suicidal behavior. However, Yen et al. (2005) found no association between positive RLE and suicide attempts. It can be hypothesized that positive RLE might have an impact only in certain personalities, like we found – i.e. schizoid PD-. On the other hand, the *general qualitative hypothesis* suggests that the non-desirability of an event is what would precipitate suicidal behaviors. This hypothesis is backed by the study by Paykel et al. (1975), who found no association between positive RLE and suicide attempts. It might be concluded that it is not clear the impact of neutral and positive RLE on suicidal behavior (Yen et al., 2005).

Suicide attempts in *schizotypal PD* were significantly associated with "important change in health or behavior of a member of the family" and with "important social changes". We expected to find the same precipitants of schizophrenics. We cannot guarantee that the relative who was sick was the caregiver, but this would explain suicidal behaviors in those subjects as, based on clinical grounds, some schizophrenics are very dependent on other family members, which they may live as a stressful situation. The same explanation applies for social support.

It was particularly striking to us not to find a single precipitant of suicide attempts in subjects diagnosed with *BPD*. The main reason for subjects with BPD to attempt suicide is to escape from a very anxious situation or to feel relieve (Boergers et al., 1998; Varadaraj et al., 1986; Holden et al., 1998). Runeson & Beskow (1991) found that RLE were related to suicides in adolescents diagnosed with BPD. The presence of RLE at home or familial environment and financial problems are related to suicidal behavior in subjects diagnosed with MDD, BPD or both (Kelly et al., 2000). The risk of suicidal behavior of patients with BPD was 16 times higher than the one of depressive patients. Separation from spouse/partner, sexual problems, law problems and changes in social activities and habits, job instability, financial problems and lack of a stable residence have also been associated with suicidal behavior in subjects with BPD (Lesage et al., 1994; Runeson & Beskow, 1991). Being discharged is a risk factor for suicidal behavior in them (Links et al., 2003). They also have an increased risk of suicidal behavior in the weeks following discharge (Kullgren, 1988), particularly after violating therapeutical contract (Kjelsber et al., 1991). Consistently with revised literature and with the fact that impulsive subjects attempt suicide when feeling rejected (Yen et al., 2005), we expected to find a significant association between some RLE and suicidal behavior, particularly problems with partner. However, not all the authors have found that interpersonal problems precede suicide behavior. Thus, in a case-control study comparing 21 suicides with 21 life controls was found no association between important personal losses and suicide (Kjelsberg et al., 1991). In our opinion, the lack of associations in our study may have to do with our stringent definition of suicide attempt (O'Carroll).

With regard to *antisocial PD*, suicide attempts were significantly associated with "arrest", "minor law problems", and "death of partner". The first two stressors might precipitate instrumental suicide attempts in an attempt to avoiding or delaying the legal consequences of their antisocial behavior. The last association ("death of partner") might be due to this situation being very stressful situation to antisocial subjects. In fact, a successful marriage is the only good prognosis factor of antisocial PD (Zocolillo et al., 1992).

Suicide attempts in subjects diagnosed with a *narcissistic PD* were associated with "being fired". Narcissistic subjects are characterized by personality fragility and hierarchical relationships, among others. We hypothesized that narcissistic injuries may precipitate suicide attempts in them. "Being fired" is a clear narcissistic injury. This might have to do with the emotional or economic implications related to being fired. Furthermore, rage reactions after being fired are not usual to take place at work so that it can be directed to them. We also expected to find an association with "love break-ups" or "separation", but a possible hetero-aggressive reaction toward the partner might decrease the risk of suicide attempts. In addition, suicide attempts might be interpreted as a way of the SA to dominating those who have fired them.

Suicide attempts in subjects with an *histrionic PD* were close to statistical significance with "problems with political family" and "change of residence". The first association might have to do with instrumental attempts as a way of being the centre of every situation. The second one might be related to difficulties to managing stress. On the other hand, we expected to find that problems with partner, like separation or divorce, were going to be precipitants of suicide attempts. We think that by using O'Carroll's definition of suicide attempt we probably not considered their manipulative drug overdoses as suicide attempts but as parasuicides.

SA status in *dependent PD* was associated with "being fired" and "change to a new job". Feeling rejected in these situations might precipitate suicide attempts. Curiously, both events were related to work, where they might have close relationships based on their dependence needs.

Suicide attempts in *obsessive-compulsive PD* were marginally associated with "reconciliation with partner". It is possible that this situation will be a stressful situation to these individuals, as they have to change they rigid-minded life style.

Finally, suicide attempts in *evitative PD* were nearly related to "separation from spouse" and "beginning/ending studies". To avoiding conflicts – like separating from spouse- and to having fear of unknown are typical characteristics of evitative people. They may be experienced as very stressful and precipitate suicide attempts.

Chapter 2.9.

SUICIDAL BEHAVIOR:
FROM PERSONALITY TRAITS TO ENDOPHENOTYPES

P. Courtet, F. Jollant, S. Guillaume, D. Castelnau and A. Malafosse

The WHO estimated that nearly one million people committed suicide in 2000 worldwide. Even though the epidemiological data vary from country to country, it is clear that this phenomenon has become a major public health problem in all industrialized countries. Suicide prevention strategies necessitate the identification of therapeutic targets. However, the number of risk factors and the complex nature of their interactions do not allow sufficiently accurate prediction of whether a given individual is likely to try to commit suicide. More than 90 % of people who commit suicide suffered from a psychiatric disorder, mostly a mood disorder (Mann 2003). Nevertheless, even in psychiatric groups with the highest risk, most individuals never attempt suicide. To account for this fact, it was suggested that stress factors may trigger a suicidal act only in vulnerable individuals (Mann et al. 1999). Major vulnerability factors are: a previous history of suicide attempt, a family history of suicidal behavior, impulsive aggression, and pessimism (Mann et al. 1999, Oquendo et al. 2004). Progress in the field of genomics should improve our understanding of the complex role of the aetiopathogenic factors that are involved in the development of psychiatric disorders, and particularly in suicidal behavior. Psychiatrists would also benefit from genetic and genomic tools that can help to characterize and to define suicidal phenotypes (Merikangas & Risch, 2003).

Since a dozen of years, molecular genetic studies have been applied to SB, after the prior necessary demonstration in epidemiological genetics studies that there is a genetic basis to SB. Even if real progresses are ongoing in the identification of genes that affect the suicidal risk, much more questions raised from these issues. As it is observed for other psychiatric disorders, not surprisingly, "as is the case with most complex traits, success tends to plateau at a point where good candidate genes are identified but conclusive causal inferences remain elusive because of replication failures" (Savitz et al. 2006). Faced with these frustrations, the use of intermediate phenotypes and endophenotypes is considered nowadays to represent the most promising avenue to help in identifying susceptibility genes.

The demonstrated evidence that personality disorders are largely associated with suicidal behavior stimulates the research works using personality dimensions as intermediate phenotypes. Moreover, the observation of a correlation between a serotonergic dysfunction, the vulnerability to SB, and impulsive aggression, paved the way for the investigation of more biologically based traits underlying these complex traits, that will generate endophenotypes in the aim to facilitate the identification of susceptibility genes.

2.9.1. THE GENETIC BASIS FOR SUICIDAL BEHAVIOR

The existence of a genetic component in predisposition to SB is generally accepted. Indeed, family, twin and adoption studies have all demonstrated that predisposition to SB involves genetic factors and this, in a specific manner (Brent & Mann 2005). Some studies, including the most recent ones, have suggested that genetic predisposition to SB is independent from genetic predisposition to psychiatric disorders that are generally associated with a risk of suicide, including mood disorders, schizophrenia and substance abuse. The heritability may be high, about 55% for serious suicide attempts (Statham et al. 1998).

The observation that SB has a genetic element has led to a number of molecular biology studies since the middle of the 1990s, the aim of which was to identify the genes responsible for susceptibility to SB. Since the involvement of abnormalities of the serotonin function in the pathophysiology of SB has been largely reproduced after the seminal works of Mary Asberg, exactly thirty years ago (Asberg et al. 1976), it is now well established that a serotonergic dysfunction is a trait marker associated with the vulnerability to SB independently of the psychiatric diagnoses (Mann 2003). Consequently, the hypothesis made was that genetic factors affecting suicide risk may operate through effects on serotonergic activity, because of the heritability of serotonin function. Thus, the candidate genes that have been studied first in association studies are those coding for the proteins involved in the serotonin metabolism: the tryptophan hydroxylase (TPH), which is the synthesis enzyme of serotonin, the serotonin transporter (5-HTT), MAOA and other serotonin receptors. The results of several studies and meta-analyses suggested that serotonin-related genes were associated with the vulnerability to SB in various psychiatric populations (Courtet et al. 2005a, Bondy et al. 2006). Moreover, the multiplication of these studies also makes it possible to refine the phenotype - genotype relationship, and exclude that the genetic component is manifested only for the most severe phenotypes. Indeed, it is possible that *TPH1* is associated with SB in general, that *5-HTT* is associated with violent and repeated suicide attempts, and *MAOA* is associated with a shift in the suicidal phenotype towards a violent act (Courtet et al. 2004, 2005a, 2005b).

We are currently led to believe that SB, like other psychiatric disorders, is a complex disorder, and that susceptibility is determined by the action of several genes that interact with environmental factors. In their famous recent cohort study, Caspi et al. (2003) showed that environmental stress increases the risk of depression and SB only in subjects with certain genotypes. Consequently, the complex interplays between genes and environment, the genetically and phenotypically heterogeneous samples, the small effect sizes of the putative loci explain the unequivocal identification of genes of susceptibility to SB.

2.9.2. FUTURE NEEDS TO GO BEYOND
THE CLINICAL HETEROGENEITY

Candidate gene association studies in SB have suffered from difficulties in replication. We are at a stage where research into the genetics of SB must not end in disappointment because not all the genes involved were identified: we must progress with further studies based on innovative strategies. The existence of discordant results is inherent to association studies and the methodological pitfalls should be addressed adequately in ongoing studies (Sullivan et al. 2001). One of the crucial issues in the field of psychiatric genetics in general, is particularly serious in studies on SB: how can we define the phenotypes under study, and what are the heritable phenotypes? The lack of an unambiguous definition of suicidal acts considered by some as « self-destructive behaviors with at least some intent to end one's life » explains why we can only talk about "a spectrum of suicidal behaviors", where completed suicide can be considered the most severe outcome (Mann 2003). This vast clinical spectrum may explain the heterogeneous nature of study populations and thus the heterogeneity of the results obtained in both biological and genetics studies. Indeed, as the definition of suicidal behaviors is evidently not as clear-cut as the geneticist would desire, this may lead to spurious findings due to ill-defined phenotypes. It is clear that both the exact clinical definitions of SB, suicides and suicide attempts, and the demonstration of biological dysfunction associated with these clinical entities remain unsatisfactory and are a source of confusion (Muller Oerlinghausen & Roggenbach 2002, Astruc et al. 2004).

One of the current strategies in the molecular genetics of psychiatric disorders in the aim to facilitate the identification of susceptibility genes requires the use of endophenotypes, defined as "quantitative traits that lie intermediate between the genes and the disease itself" (Gottesman & Gould 2003). If SB are polygenic and are caused by numerous genes, each contributing a small effect and conferring susceptibility to the phenotype, then it is difficult to identify the influence of each of these genetic contributions to the phenotype. Endophenotypes are hypothesized to be more elementary traits, that may be influenced by a smaller number of genes and may be more easily associated with a genotype, and that are tightly correlated with SB. By identifying measurable characteristics that reflect an underlying genotype or are more closely related to that genotype than to the diagnostic category itself, the opportunity to unravel pathophysiological pathways involving specific candidate genes as well as environmental influences on their expression becomes a more feasible possibility.

2.9.3. PERSONALITY TRAITS AS INTERMEDIATE PHENOTYPES

As largely reviewed in this book, personality disorders (PDs) increase the risk of SB independently of the presence of any comorbid axis I diagnosis (Cheng et al. 2000, Hansen et al. 2003). Given the evidence that PDs and particularly borderline personality disorders (BPD) are associated with the risk of SB, some key dimensions underlying these disorders were hypothesized to be associated with SB. Indeed, studies in BPD have shown that one of its core psychopathological features, impulsive aggression, increases the risk of SB (Hawton et al. 2003). Based on a large amount of evidence, it is now largely assumed that impulsive aggression may act as a transnosological vulnerability trait affecting the suicide risk (Mann et al. 1999, Oquendo et al. 2004, Turecki 2005).

More than two decades of clinical and biological studies led to the conclusion of a strong link between a complex clinical dimension linking impulsivity and aggression, a serotonergic dysfunction, and SB (Mann 2003). The general hypothesis of vulnerability to SB is that serotonergic dysfunction in the orbitofrontal cortex prevents subjects from controlling aggression, which may in turn increase the probability of suicide attempts when faced with stress factors. The association between impulsive aggression and the serotonin function, known to be stable over time, and the results from longitudinal studies linking this psychobiological trait with the future occurrence of suicidal acts (Roy et al. 1989, Fergusson et al. 2000) support the notion that it would act as a trait marker involved in the vulnerability to SB. Thus, impulsive aggressive dimensions may be considered to be intermediate phenotypes, in other words to be intermediate between the complex phenotype studied (SB) and genetic factors (Leboyer *et al.* 1998). The possibility that impulsive aggressive traits may carry the genetic vulnerability to SB is strengthen by the demonstration of their heritability, and because the transmission of impulsive aggression in the families may explain the familial transmission to SB (Brent & Mann 2005). First, impulsive aggression has been clearly shown to be at least partially heritable, as suggested by both twin and adoption studies, with suggested heritability estimates ranging from 20-62% (Coccaro et al. 1993, Coccaro et al. 1994, Coccaro et al. 1997). Seroczynski et al. (1999) reported that genetic and environmental influences contributing to impulsivity are shared with those contributing to irritability. One of the more common impulsive behaviors evidenced by the people who realized suicidal acts are expressions of anger or reactive aggression. Anger has also been demonstrated to be under a genetic influence (Cates et al. 1993). Second, using sophisticated methodologies Brent et al. (1996, 2003) reported that the familial transmission of suicidal ideation is related to the transmission of psychiatric disorder, whereas the familial transmission of SB may be mediated by the transmission of impulsive aggression. Kim et al. (2005) reported an increase prevalence of aggression in the first-degree relatives of suicide victims compared with controls. These recent data tend to confirm initial assumption by Kety (1986) who suggested that genetic predisposition to SB results from an inability to control impulsive behavior, which can be expressed in the presence or absence of psychiatric disorders.

Other personality dimensions or behavioral traits have been demonstrated to play a role in the vulnerability to SB: neuroticism and anxiety-related traits, hopelessness, self-esteem, problem-solving and decision making (Baud 2005).

Neuroticism, considered to reflect a propensity to experience negative affect, anger, anxiety, depression, and other negative emotions / cognitions have been involved in the vulnerability to SB, ranging from suicidal ideation to suicide attempts and completed suicides (Fergusson et al. 2000, Statham et al. 1998, Beautrais et al. 1999). Roy (2002) suggested that neuroticism may act as a inherited trait that would account for the familial transmission of SB. Very close to neuroticism is harm-avoidance, an anxiety-related temperamental trait according to the concept proposed by Cloninger et al. (1993). Heritability of harm avoidance is about 50%, and this dimension has been also linked to the serotonin system activity. Hopelessness, as assessed with the Beck's scale, is a component of the pessimistic dimension involved in the vulnerability (Oquendo et al. 2004), and it has been per se associated with the risk of SB in various populations. van Heeringen et al. (2003) reported that suicide attempters exhibited higher levels of hopelessness and harm avoidance than controls, that these levels were correlated together and negatively correlated with the prefrontal 5-HT2A receptor binding.

When considering the results of association studies in SB, molecular genetic studies logically begun to investigate the association between the same serotonin related genes and a constellation of personality traits, particularly impulsive aggressive ones. *TPH1* has been associated with anger related traits in suicide attempters as well as in healthy volunteers (Manuck et al. 1999, Rujescu et al. 2002). The serotonin transporter genotypes has been reported to influence impulsivity in suicide attempters (Courtet et al. 2004), and a large number of studies on personality revealed an association between *5-HTT* and neuroticism or harm avoidance (Reif & Lesch 2003, van Gestel & van Broeckhoven 2003). *MAOA* was first reported to be linked with impulsive aggressive behaviors in families (Brunner et al. 1993), and has been shown to interact with a history of childhood abuse on the subsequent risk of antisocial behaviors in a longitudinal study (Caspi et al. 2002).

Thus, the same functional polymorphisms of several serotonin related genes have been implicated with a serotonin system dysfunction, a constellation of personality traits, and SB. As a whole these associations raise the possibility that the genes contributing to the shaping of personality traits are involved in the transmission of vulnerability factors to SB (Baud 2005). However, the demonstration that SB and personality traits share some common genetic vulnerability factors is not sufficient to consider that these so complex dimensions represent useful candidate endophenotypes that may enhance significantly success in the identification of susceptibility genes to SB. In a recent review Savitz et al. (2006) stated that "the endophenotypic approach to gene identification has perhaps been too easily accepted as a panacea for the ills of modern genetics". This assumption warrants some comments: the use of such a strategy is likely to be promising whereas considering personality traits as good candidate endophenotypes remains problematic. Indeed, personality traits are defined according to various still debated concepts, the results from studies using a diversity of phenotypic assessment tools suggested the multidimensional structure of these traits, and logically it is far to be proven that these traits are genetically simpler than the phenotype under study, SB it self. For instance, in a recent meta-analysis of 26 studies the existence of an association between anxiety-related traits and the *5-HTT* depends on the instrument or on the concept that have been used to assess the personality trait: a positive effect appear for neuroticism while no association was found for harm avoidance (Schinka et al. 2004). The contribution of genetic factors to personality and temperamental traits and to SB is now well established by many convergent studies, although the precise links between any particular gene variant and each of these multi-determined clinical traits are still to be discovered (Ebstein 2006). Indeed, in a recent feature review on the molecular genetic architecture of human personality, Ebstein (2006) stated that "small effect sizes characteristic of non-Mendelian traits, polygenic patterns of inheritance and true heterogeneity between studies confound attempt to reach a consensus regarding the role of common polymorphisms in contributing to personality domains".

In conclusion, we can argue that it would be more promising to move from intermediate phenotypes, such as personality dimensions defined at the level of the psychopathology, to more subtle traits. These traits may represent more biologically based endophenotypes underlying these clinical dimensions, that may help to unravel the various components of the genetic predisposition to SB, as well as complex personality dimensions. For each dimension Siever (2005) proposes in an heuristic model for the identification of the promising genotypes, a cascade from the phenotypic syndrome under study (here SB) to the genes with different steps: syndrome - mediating dimension / trait - self-report measure / clinical interview - laboratory behavioral task performance - cognitive task performance - psychophysiological task performance - functional, structural, and neurochemical imaging - postmortem neurochemistry, structure, mRNA expression - genotype. Rather than subjects would be evaluated for clinical phenotypic by self-report measures, they could be assessed using new experimental paradigms including including neuropsychological, psychophysiological, or laboratory behavioral tests, to define potentially heritable endophenotypes. These complementary approaches to identifying endophenotypes in SB and personality traits may provide convergent validity for the most promising endophenotypes (Leboyer et al. 1998, Gottesman & Gould 2003, Siever 2005). A complementary approach is to identify such endophenotypes in suicide attempters, and demonstrate a specific increase in these endophenotypes compared with normal control or psychiatric comparison groups. To be considered as a marker trait, it must be possible to measure an endophenotype in an objective and cost-effective manner in clinically unaffected relatives of patients, before the onset of illness. State independence or longitudinal stability could be established in longitudinal studies with repeated measures of the endophenotypic tests of interest. Finally, genetic studies of clinically identified samples could be used to determine whether the endophenotypic measure cosegregates with the suicidal behavior in family members, and is also found in nonaffected family members at a higher rate than in the general population. The endophenotype should therefore run in families and be associated with an increased risk of clinical illness. In a growing number of publications are proposed the criteria for evaluating the validity and the utility of putative endophenotype markers, some of these criteria being universally agreed whereas others are more controversial (Bearden & Freimer 2006). Particularly, whereas some considered that endophenotypes should be specific to discrete disorders, others suggest that the possibility exists that endophenotypes may be shared by several disorders, reflecting common existing genetic factors. According to the latter opinion, considering that serotonergic dysfunction and impulsive aggression underlie the vulnerability to both borderline personality disorders and SB, putative endophenotypes extensively reviewed as useful in BPD may also be applicable in investigating SB (New & Siever 2003, Siever 2005).

2.9.4. CANDIDATE ENDOPHENOTYPES IN SUICIDAL BEHAVIOR

Neuropsychology

Neuropsychology provides an opportunity to investigate the prefrontal cortex *in vivo*. Investigations of suicide attempters may provide insight into the involvement of divergent systems in the brain in the pathogenesis of suicidal behavior, provided that neuropsychological tests are available that may demonstrate abnormalities that are specific to defined areas. Measures of neurocognitive function are widely considered to be valuable endophenotypes in large part because of their demonstrated reliability and stability over time, and because the demonstration of their heritability (Bearden & Freimer 2006, Coolidge et 2004). The neuropsychological study of SB remains in its infancy, but a growing interest is emerging at first to determine whether specific deficits may be associated with SB independently from the effect of a depression. Keilp et al. (2001) reported that as compared with low-lethality suicide attempters, high-lethality suicide attempters performed more poorly on all tests of executive functions than did clinical and control groups. Moreover, high-lethality suicide attempters were the only group to perform more poorly than healthy controls on tests of intellect, attention, and memory. Thus, high-lethality suicide attempters were differentiated by their executive functions, whereas depressed patients differed from the healthy control group on attention and memory. This suggests that executive impairment in suicide attempters exists beyond depression or depression severity.

In a recent review of the 7 published studies on the neuropsychological correlates of suicidal behavior and BPDs, LeGris & van Reekum (2006) proposed that a specific trait-like cognitive vulnerability for SB involve two different dysregulatory dishinibiting pathways. Low verbal fluency and slower information processing on Trails and Stroop tests indicated impaired executive functions and disinhibitory processes associated with dorsolateral prefrontal cortex regions. The motivational inhibitory pathway involves conflictual, affective and reflexive decision-making processes associated with the orbitofrontal brain regions.

In a recent study, Raust et al. (2007) investigated prefrontal cortex related functions in euthymic suicide attempters and controls, using executive function and working memory (cognitive functions mostly depending on the dorsolateral prefrontal cortex) and reward sensitivity tests (affective functions depending on medial and orbitofrontal cortex areas). Multivariate comparisons demonstrated significant executive function deficits in patients with suicidal behavior, where all the identified deficits (impairments in N-Back, Hayling, Stroop and Go-noGo tests) were related to the dorsolateral prefrontal cortex, rather than the orbitofrontal cortex. However, in the absence of imaging data, it cannot be asserted that a given deficit is due to dysfunction in a particular area of the brain or to neural networks mediated by multiple areas. This emphasizes the need of investigations combining neuropsychological performance and structural and functional neuroimaging to localize the underlying neural pathways and biological mechanisms involved (Keefe 1995; LeGris & van Reekum 2006).

Decision-making

We hypothesized that decision-making, an executive function more and more extensively investigated in psychiatric disorders (Dunn et al. 2006), would be of particularly relevance in SB and that it may represent a putative endophenotype in SB.

Results from post-mortem studies suggested that the serotonergic input to the ventromedial prefrontal cortex of suicide victims might modulate the vulnerability to suicidal behavior, independently of the psychiatric illness that might have triggered the suicidal act (Mann et al. 2000). Interestingly, Damasio et al. (1994) showed that the orbitofrontal cortex (OFC) region plays a key role in decision-making. Decision-making relies on the ability to make choices in life, notably in situations of uncertainty when several choices are available and contingencies underlying each choice are not explicit. Decision-making was modeled in the Iowa Gambling Task (IGT), a computerized card game where participants have to learn to sacrifice immediate reward for long-term gain. Contingencies underlying each deck are unknown leading to a feeling of uncertainty. Our group has recently studied this cognition in suicide attempters on the basis that decision-making, 1) is related to the ventromedial prefrontal cortex (Ernst et al. 2002), 2) is modulated by the serotonergic system (Rogers et al. 2003), and 3) is relevant for suicidal behavior if one considers suicide to be a bad choice.

We found decision-making performance to be significantly altered in suicide attempters in comparison to healthy controls and to patients with a past history of affective disorders but no history of suicidal acts (Jollant et al. 2005). Of note, all patients were euthymic at the time of assessment to exclude the effect of the depressive state. This result suggested that decision-making impairment might be a neuropsychological trait of vulnerability to suicidal behavior, independently of the vulnerability to affective disorders. Interestingly, the way that nonviolent suicide attempters choose was different from that of violent suicide attempters: the former seemed to switch from high-risk to low-risk decks in indecision, whereas the latter, after a first period when they seemed to explore all decks like the other groups, turned toward the disadvantageous decks. This way of making decisions was very similar to those of patients with OFC lesions or with substance abuse problems (Bechara 2003). Importantly, a recent analysis of more than 300 psychiatric patients suggested that suicidal behavior was significantly associated with decision-making impairment independently from the psychiatric diagnoses of the patients (Jollant et al. in press).

We investigated in a subgroup of suicide attempters the life events that occurred during the last year before the suicidal act. We found decision-making abilities to be negatively correlated with interpersonal difficulties in the family and marital domain, whereas no correlation was found with any other life events (Jollant et al., 2007a). Thus, people with decision-making impairment may be more prone to choose suicide as a solution to problems and may be at higher risk to engage or be involved in problematic relationships which are known triggers of suicidal acts. Vulnerability and stress therefore seem to interact in a reciprocal way.

Impairments in neuronal circuits involving orbitofrontal cortex may mediate the abnormal emotional information processing. Bechara et al. (1996) suggested that emotion-based biasing signals arising from the body are integrated in the OFC to regulate decision-making in situations of complexity. Evidence for that famous "somatic marker hypothesis" is largely based on performance on the IGT linking anticipatory skin conductance responses (SCR) to successful performance on decision-making in healthy controls, whereas these "marker" signals were absent in patients with OFC lesions and were associated with poorer IGT performance. When investigating this hypothesis by measuring the SCR when the subjects (suicide attempters and controls) were making decisions during the IGT, we observed that anticipatory SCR were generated only in healthy controls and not in suicide attempters (Guillaume et al. 2006). In healthy controls, SCR activities were significantly higher before picking a card from the risky decks than for low risk decks. Particularly, the difference in anticipate SCR amplitudes was correlated with IGT performances. This preliminary result provides some support that decision-making is guided by emotional signals, which are generated in anticipation of future events. Suicide attempters do not receive such a signal and exhibit poor IGT performances.

Investigating the influence of serotonin related genes that have been associated with SB, we reported 4 serotonergic genetic polymorphisms to modulate the learning process of decision-making in suicide attempters (Jollant et al., 2007b). Two of them (*5-HTTLPR* and *TPH1*) have been previously associated with a higher risk of suicidal behavior and one (*MAOA*) with violent behavior. Patients with "high-risk" alleles are those unable to learn to avoid the disadvantageous decks during the game. This inability to learn to switch away from immediately rewarding but long-term deleterious choices could notably have to do with the cognitive rigidity described in suicide attempters (Pollock & Williams 2004). Thus, it could be hypothesized that some genetic polymorphisms may alter the efficiency of the neurotransmission involved in the learning process necessary for advantageous decision-making in uncertain conditions and consequently increase the risk of suicidal acts. The measure of learning ability in a decision-making task could represent an endophenotype in SB that may help to identify the genes, the gene-gene interactions and the physiological mechanisms associated with the vulnerability to suicidal behavior.

Much questions remain around decision-making and suicidal behavior. One of them concerns the prevalence of a decision-making impairment in the nonaffected family members of suicide victims or attempters. In a recent study, a decision-making impairment has been reported in healthy relatives of alcoholic patients (Lovallo et al. 2006). In conclusion, decision-making should be an attractive candidate endophenotype with a plausible neurobiological basis, as this cognitive impairment would reflect a serotonergic dysfunction related to the ventromedial PFC. This cognitive function appears to be an interesting tool to study the link between different levels (genetic, environmental, anatomical) of understanding of a complex behavior.

Psychophysiology

Psychophysiological assessment allows an objective and quantifiable measure of conscious and non-conscious cognitive and emotional processes. Two methods have been used in the study of suicidal behavior namely electrodermal activity and event-related potentials. The electrodermal activity measures a change in the electrical resistance of the skin and is sensitive to numerous psychological states. Edman et al. (1986) were the first to report a higher frequency of fast habituation (lowering of the electrodermal response following repetitive tone stimuli) in violent suicide attempters compared to non violent suicide attempters and to suicidal ideators whereas the skin conductance level was only marginally decreased in violent suicide attempters. Moreover, the 4 patients who died by (violent) suicide in a one-year follow-up were all fast habituators. Keller et al. (1991) replicated this result including the observation of 4 fast habituators among 5 later suicide completers. Thorell (1987) found a lower electrodermal responsiveness in attempters than in non suicidal patients independently of the delay since the last suicidal act. Interestingly, the skin conductance level was linked to the depressive state in contrast to the responsivity which was associated with a past history of suicidal behavior. Finally, Wolfersdorf et al. (1994) showed a higher frequency of fast habituators in violent suicide attempters and completers in comparison to non suicidal depressed patients. However, comparison of the suicide - whether violent or non-violent - group with the other groups was not significant suggesting that the faster electrodermal habituation was more associated with the violent characteristics of the acts than with suicide itself. Therefore, electrophysiological hyporesponsivity may represent a trait marker of violent suicidal acts may they lead to death or not. Violence in turn could be underlied by emotional dysregulation (Davidson et al. 2000). It may be suggested that a rapid habituation may be related to inadequate information processing and "premature closure", i.e. allowing too little processing time to generate alternative solutions.

Event-related potentials (ERP) are electroencephalographic responses to specific events or stimuli. Hansenne et al. (1996) reported a significant difference in several ERP between depressive patients with or without a past history of suicidal behavior. Interestingly, one of these ERP called P300 was significantly correlated with a scale of suicidal risk and with hopelessness. Other studies (Juckel & Hegerl, 1994) also reported modifications of different ERP in suicide attempters in comparison to non-attempters. Though the interpretation of ERP may be difficult, these results suggest differences in brain activity in response to the environment in individuals with a vulnerability to suicidal behavior.

Neuroimaging

Since 70% of all genes are expressed in the brain, many functional polymorphisms can potentially influence how the brain processes information (Hasler et al. 2004). Structural, functional and molecular brain mapping have the potential to bridge the gap between SB and genes.

Structural magnetic resonance imaging findings suggest that gray and white matter hyperintensities might represent brain abnormalities associated with suicide attempts in unipolar depressed patients (Ahearn et al. 2001, Ehrlich et al. 2004). A recent study reported was the first to report fronto-limbic anatomical brain abnormalities in suicidal adult female patients with unipolar depression when compared with non-suicidal unipolar depressed and healthy subjects (Monkul et al. 2007)). Suicidal patients had smaller OFC gray matter volumes compared with healthy comparison subjects, and they had larger right amygdala volumes than non-suicidal patients.

Functional magnetic resonance imaging, positron-emission tomography and single photon-emission tomography, can be used to study functional abnormalities *in vivo* in the prefrontal cortex and the subcortical structures, and thus demonstrate functional and biochemical changes associated with SB. Since functional imaging has the capacity to assay within individuals information processing in discrete brain circuits, it has the potential to provide endophenotypes for SB. The observation that lower serotonergic activity correlates with high-lethality suicide attempts in major depression, and that postmortem studies of serotonin receptors in suicides localize changes to the ventral prefrontal cortex (PFC), led Oquendo et al. (2003) to study serotonergic response in ventral PFC in depressed high-lethality suicide attempters. Brain responses after a single-blind placebo and after fenfluramine hydrochloride administration (a serotonin-releasing agent) were measured by positron emission tomography imaging of fludeoxyglucose F 18. Depressed high-lethality suicide attempters had lower rCMRglu in ventral, medial, and lateral PFC compared with low-lethality attempters, this difference being more pronounced after fenfluramine administration. Lower ventromedial PFC activity was associated with lower lifetime impulsivity, higher suicidal intent (planning), and higher-lethality suicide attempts. These first results suggested that prefrontal localized hypofunction and impaired serotonergic responsivity are proportional to the lethality of the suicide attempt and may mediate the effects of suicide intent and impulsivity on lethality. Similar results have been obtained in a study comparing glucose metabolism following fenfluramine and placebo in personality disordered patients. Normal controls showed increased metabolism in the orbitofrontal cortex and adjacent ventromedial frontal cortex as well as the cingulated and inferior parietal cortex following fenfluramine compared to placebo, and impulsive aggressive patients appear to show significant increases only in the inferior parietal lobe (Siever et al. 1999, Soloff et al. 2000). Using another serotonergic probe (meta-chlorophenylpiperazine, mCPP), the same group found in male borderline patients with aggression a reduced baseline activity, and reduced mCPP responses as compared with placebo responses, in anterior cingulate gyrus (New et al. 2002). Moreover, it was suggested that correlations between amygdala and anterior cingulate gyrus were disrupted in patients with impulsive aggression.

As proposed by Oquendo et al. (2003), positron emission tomographic neuroreceptor studies are needed to determine whether postmortem serotonin receptor findings are also present in vivo and contribute to the abnormal rCMRglu responses. Recently, Frankle et al. (2005) evaluated regional serotonin transporter distribution in the brain of individuals with impulsive aggression by using positron emission tomography with the serotonin transporter PET radiotracer [(11)C]McN 5652. Serotonin transporter availability was significantly reduced in the anterior cingulate cortex of individuals with impulsive aggression compared with healthy subjects, whereas in other regions examined, serotonin transporter density was nonsignificantly lower in individuals with impulsive aggression compared with healthy subjects. The authors concluded that impulsive aggression may be associated with lower serotonergic innervation in the anterior cingulate cortex, a region that plays an important role in affective regulation.

The demonstration that anterior cingulate and orbitofrontal cortex are implicated in impulsive aggression, and that serotonergic agents may modulate specific regional brain glucose metabolism in both suicide attempters and in impulsive aggressive patients, provide help to improve the understanding of the pathophysiology of intermediate phenotypes involved in the vulnerability to SB. Siever (2005) suggested that these data are in favor of a reduced serotonergic facilitation via 5-HT2A receptors of prefrontal cortical inhibitory regions, particularly anterior cingulated and orbitofrontal cortex, which serves to "brake" the amygdala. Thus, reduced serotonergic activity may result in disinhibited aggression generated in response to aversive stimuli. This pathophysiological model could in part emerge from alterations in serotonergic activity, primarily reduced integrity of prefrontal inhibitory centers, or exaggerated responsiveness of amygdala and related limbic structures. Endophenotypes that reflect reduced serotonergic activity, altered frontal activation, or enhanced limbic reactivity thus might serve to characterize specific vulnerabilities of this functional circuitry in SB. They may be used in conjunction with candidate genes of the serotonergic system, in association studies. Number of data is accumulating in the new field of "imaging genetics", where serotonin transporter genotypes were reported to influence the amygdala response to fearful stimuli in healthy volunteers (Hariri et al. 2002b), the amygdala - ventromedial prefrontal cortex coupling or the prefrontal cortex activity itself (Heinz et al. 2005, Graff-Guerrero et al. 2005, Fallgatter et al. 2004).

These studies of SB, as well as personality disorders, suggest an approach that includes enhancing the phenomenological study of these phenotypes with biochemical, neuroimaging and neuropsychological characterization of dimensions related to the underlying disorder. This approach will help to identify endophenotypes, which will make genetic studies in this complex area much more powerful. These accumulating data illustrate the use to investigate endophenotypes that are basic components underlying complex personality dimensions such as anxiety-related traits or impulsive aggression, and that may facilitate the establishment of genotype – phenotype correlations, and improve our knowledge of the pathophysiological modalities of SB. Suicide prevention strategies including the identification of "at-risk" subjects and the development of new pharmacological as well as psychotherapeutic interventions should emerge from these innovative research strategies. We are entitled to being full of hope for our patients.

ACKNOWLEDGEMENTS

Dr. P. Courtet was funded by the Unité de Recherche Clinique of Montpellier University Hospital (PHRC UF 7653).

PERSONALITY DISORDERS IN A SAMPLE OF SUICIDE ATTEMPTERS: AGE MATTERS*

H. Blasco-Fontecilla, E. Baca-García and J. Sáiz-Ruiz

2.10.1. INTRODUCTION AND OBJECTIVES

The Role of Age in Suicide

Suicide risk is closely related to age in industrialized countries (La Veccia et al., 1994). Apart from Poland, Scotland, England and Wales, in the remaining industrialized countries, men older than 65 are the ones at greater risk of suicide (Pearson & Convell, 1995; Kennedy & Tanenbaum, 2000). The rate of suicide in men aged 75 or over is 8-12 times the one of the same age women population and the highest in all ages (Pearson & Convell, 1995). The rate of suicide in white men aged 85 or older is 53 to 1 compared to women in the US (Canetto, 1992; Hoyert et al., 1999). Whereas the ratio suicide attempt/suicide is 200/1 in young adults, it is of 4/1 in old people (Conwell et al., 1998; Langley & Bayatti, 1984). The increased risk of suicide is attributable to White and Asian races (CDC, 2000).

Paradoxically, in spite of suicide rates being higher in the elderly (López García et al., 1993), suicide studies carried out in younger populations are 7 times more frequent, which might be due to the reported increase of suicide rates in them (CDC, 2000). Moreover, there is a certain degree of greater social tolerability – even understanding- to suicide in the elderly. Furthermore, the relative importance of suicide as a cause of death is not as important as in younger people, as suicide is between the 10 to the 20th cause of death among the older (Harris & Barraclough, 1997). The high rates found in the elderly are probably due to old people planning suicide, giving fewer cues about their intentions and using more lethal methods –e.g. firearms, hanging- (Carney et al., 1994; Frierson, 1991; McIntosh & Santos, 1985). Moreover, old people are more usually socially isolated, have worse health and are more death-determined (Conwell et al., 1998). Harwood & Jacoby (2000) suggested that it was plausible that "older people who are less adaptable will cope poorly with inevitable changes that ageing brings, and may be at increased risk of suicide". The diagnosis more closely related to suicide in the elderly is depression (Frierson, 1991). In the aged people with major depressive disorder, suicide attempts might be related to the subjective feeling of being depressed more than to objective measures of depression (Szanto et al., 2001).

Whereas the prototype of subject who suicide is an old man, the prototype of person who attempt suicide is a young female. Reversely to suicide, suicide attempts are more frequent in young females (López García et al., 1983), particularly between those aged between 15 to 24, followed by women of 25-24 years old and 35 to 44 years old; in men, the highest rates are found in those aged 25 to 34, followed by those with 35-44 and 15-24 years old (Schmidtke et al., 1996). *Suicide behavior* is very infrequent before puberty. The rate of suicide behaviors increases in the adolescence and it is calculated that 7% of people aged 25 or younger will attempt suicide (Garrison, 1989). This author reports a rate of 3% of suicide attempts in primary school, 11% at High school, and 15-18% at College or other superior studies. In spite of the 150% reported increase of suicide deaths between 1960 to 1980 in young people (Klerman, 1987), suicide data of the US, France and Holland in the first decades of the 20th century demonstrates elevated rates of suicide among young populations that eventually decreased to increase again in the seventies (López García et al., 1993). Suicide is the second cause of death independently of gender in the group of people aged 15 to 24 – in Denmark and Japan is the commonest death cause among adolescents- and the second cause of death in European males aged 15 to 44.

Age, Personality Disorders (PDs) and Suicide

Factors associated with suicide behavior are different with regard to age. In younger populations, suicide is related to low socioeconomic class, to previous treatment in a psychiatric inpatient unit, to a significant substance abuse, to a diagnosis of a PD and to previous suicide attempts (Hawton et al., 1993). It has also been associated with being jobless and social isolation (Appleby et al., 1999). In the elderly, it has been related to stressful life events (Harwood & Jacoby, 2000). The role of PDs seems to be of lesser importance in the elderly (Szanto et al., 2001), where the prevalence of PDs is lower when compared to younger populations (Henriksson et al., 1993; Isometsa et al., 1996).

The rate of suicide in younger populations has increased in the nineties (Houston et al., 2001). In those aged 30 or younger, it has been related to the diagnosis of *substance abuse* and *personality disorders*, while in those aged 30 or older is more closely associated with *cognitive problems* or *affective disorders* (Rich et al., 1986). The diagnosis of borderline PD is particularly associated with suicide in different group of ages (Cheng et al., 1997; Foster et al., 1999).

The influence of personality traits or PDs in suicidal behaviors might be different with regard to age. It is not clear whether there is or not gender or age differences in the distribution of each specified PDs in those who attempt suicide or suicide (Szanto et al., 2001). It is possible that the personality traits and PDs frequently associated with suicide behavior in young people are not the same in the elderly, but little research has been carried out in this area (Duberstein et al., 1994). Cheng et al. (1997) found no differences in the rate of PDs in their sample of 116 suicides: 66% of those aged 35 or younger were diagnosed with a PD, while 59% of those older than 35 had this diagnosis. *Shyness, social isolation, hypocondriasis, hostility* and a *rigid-independent style* have been associated with suicide in the elderly (Clark, 1993; Farberow & Schneidman, 1963). People aged 50 or older who suicide scores high in *Neuroticism* and low in *Openess to experience* (Duberstein et al., 1994). These authors suggested that those people showing these traits would lead them to lower resilience, and to problems to cope with stressful life events. *Anankastic* and *anxious personality traits* have been related to suicide in subjects aged 60 or older (Harwood et al., 2001). Unfortunately, the relationship of those personality traits with depressive disorders has not been studied (Conwell et al., 2002). On the other hand, impulsivity decreases with age (Vaillant, 1977), a process that might reflect biological maturation.

The role of PDs in the elderly has been neglected (Agronin & Maletta, 2000). These authors said that old subjects with a PD "are vulnerable to the re-emergence or exacerbation of maladaptive traits or to the development of secondary Axis I psychopathology as a result of acute stress or the accumulation of age-related losses and other stressful experiences" which may pose them at risk of suicidal behavior. Despite the general assumption that the diagnosis of a PD is rare in the elderly, the prevalence of PDs in a community sample ranged between 5 to 10% (Agronin, 1994), which is similar to the 10 to 13% reported in all age groups in community samples (Depue, 1996; De Girolano & Reich, 1993). The most frequent PD were *obsessive-compulsive PD (OCPD)*, *dependent PD* and *mixed/unespecified PD*. Abrams & Horowitz (1996) found a rate of 10% of DSM-III PD in people aged 50 or older, both in clinical and non-clinical samples, in their meta-analysis. Thus, the diagnosis of PD in the elderly might be infra-evaluated (Fishbain, 1991). Furthermore, the only PD that has been longitudinally studied is *antisocial PD*. It seems there is a tendency to improvement with age, which might be due to the previously reported decreased impulsivity (Weiss, 1973). It also seems that subjects with *borderline PD* might improve with age, but little data are available in older populations (McGlashan, 1986; Paris et al., 1987; Rosowsky & Gurian, 1991). As it happens in younger populations, those subjects diagnosed with a PD have elevated rates of axis I disorders, particularly *major depressive disorder* (Agronin & Maletta, 2000).

Our main objective of our research with regard to age was to determine the prevalence of each specific PD in a sample of 446 suicide attempters (SA) and to explore the role of PDs in SA in the different group of ages. We expected to find that the distribution of specific PD in SA aged 50-65 years and 65 years or older is completely different to that of younger populations. Particularly, we expected to find that OCPD was the most frequent PD in SA 66 years or older, in contrast of the previously described pre-eminence of *borderline PD* or *antisocial PD* in younger SA.

2.10.2. OUR RESEARCH

See chapter 2.1.3 for information with regard to methodology of our research.

Results

The mean age of our total sample of SA was 36.61 years (SD= 14) (see Figure 4).

296 subjects (66.36%) were female. 74.2% of the SA and 48.8% of our inpatient control group had at least one PD (X^2 = 27.976, gl= 4, p < 0.001). By using an adjusted cut-off point of the IPDE-SQ, each subject was diagnosed with 0.81 PD (Standard Deviation= 1.07). The distribution of suicide attempts by age is as showed in Figure 5).

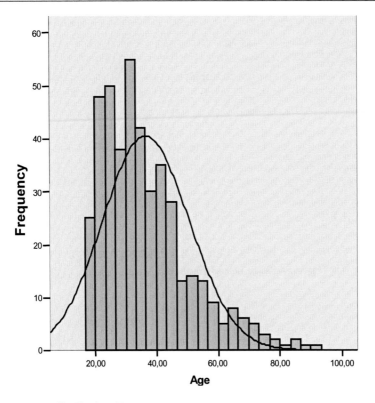

Figure 4. Age distribution (I).

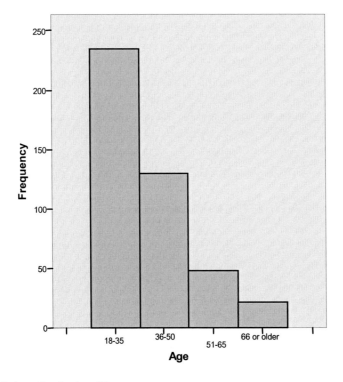

Figure 5. Age distribution (II).

234 SA were aged 18 to 35 years (80.3% diagnosed with a PD), 130 aged 36 to 50 years (72.3% diagnosed with a PD), 48 aged 51 to 65 years (64.6% diagnosed with a PD), and 22 SA were 66 or older (36.4% diagnosed with a PD) (see Table 16).

The proportion of SA was nearly a half in each subsequent age group. The prevalence of each specified PD is available in Table 17.

Table 16. Prevalence of PD in a sample of SA (n= 434)*

PD	Age			
	18-35	36-50	51-65	> 66
Paranoid PD	55/234 (23.5%)	30/130 (23.1%)	7/48 (14.6%)	1/22 (4.5%)
Schizoid PD	29/234 (12.4%)	21/130 (16.2%)	10/48 (20.8%)	1/22 (4.5%)
Schizotypal PD	12/234 (5.1%)	12/130 (9.2%)	1/48 (2.1%)	0/22 (0%)
CLUSTER A	*96/234 (41.0%)*	*63/130 (48.5%)*	*18/48 (37.5%)*	*2/22 (9.1%)*
Histrionic PD	44/234 (18.8%)	12/130 (9.2%)	8/48 (16.7%)	0/22 (0%)
Antisocial PD	14/234 (6.0%)	5/130 (3.8%)	4/48 (8.3%)	2/22 (9.1%)
Narcissistic PD	12/234 (5.1%)	4/130 (3.1%)	1/48 (2.1%)	0/22 (0%)
Borderline PD	94/234 (40.2%)	45/130 (34.6%)	7/48 (14.6%)	2/22 (9.1%)
CLUSTER B	*164/234 (70.1%)*	*66/130 (50.8%)*	*20/48 (41.7%)*	*4/22 (18.2%)*
Obsessive-compulsive PD	30/234 (12.8%)	19/130 (14.6%)	4/48 (8.3%)	4/22 (18.2%)
Dependent PD	52/234 (22.2%)	23/130 (17.7%)	1/48 (2.1%)	1/22 (4.5%)
Avoidant PD	88/234 (37.6%)	45/130 (34.6%)	10/48 (20.8%)	3/22 (13.6%)
CLUSTER C	*170/234 (72.6%)*	*87/130 (66.9%)*	*15/48 (31.2%)*	*8/22 (36.4%)*
TOTAL (n)	234	130	48	22

* Note that some SA may have more than one PD. Also, although the total sample of SA was n= 446, the diagnosis of PDs were available only in 434 subjects.

The first set of analysis was carried out in order to find the proportion of specified PD in each sub-group of the SA. We expected to find that PD characterized by a high impulsivity level – e.g. *borderline PD* or *antisocial PD*- would be more frequent in younger SA, while those characterized more by a rigid-minded cognitive style – e.g. *paranoid PD* or *obsessive-compulsive P*D (OCPD)- would be more frequent in the older groups of SA. As expected, the proportion of SA diagnosed with borderline PD was decreasing with age. Thus, 40.2% of SA aged 35 or younger had this diagnosis, while only 9.1% of those older than 65 had the same diagnosis. However, this was not the case of *antisocial PD*, as the prevalence of this diagnosis was quite stable across the different age groups. As expected, we found that the diagnosis of OCPD was the commonest among SA aged 66 or older. However, despite our hypothesis, the prevalence of paranoid PD decreased with age, although differences were not significant. *Schizoid PD* was more frequently diagnosed in the group between 50 to 65 years old. *Schizotypal PD* was more frequently diagnosed in the group of SA between 35 to 50 years. Curiously, *histrionic PD* showed a bimodal distribution, peaking in the groups of 18-35 and 50-65 years old. *Narcissistic PD* was one of the PD with lowest prevalence in all groups of ages. *Dependent PD* was more common in those SA aged 50 or younger. *Avoidant PD* was the second commonest PD in those SA aged 18 to 35 and in those aged 66 or over. It was also de commonest PD in those aged 35 to 50 – with the same percentage than borderline PD

(34.6%)- and in the group between 50 to 65 years old –with the same percentage than schizoid PD (20.8%)-.

When analysing data by each sub-group of age, it was striking to find that two of the PD which are more difficult to differentiate in the clinical arena – *schizoid PD* and *avoidant PD*-, were the commonest (20.8%) among SA aged between 50 to 65 years old. In those SA aged between 18 to 50 years old, the commonest PD were *borderline PD* and *avoidant PD*. In the group of older SA (aged 65 or older), the commonest PD were *obsessive-compulsive PD* (18.2%) and *avoidant PD* (13.6%).

When analysing data with regard to the different clusters, it was found that cluster C PDs were the commonest in three of the sub-groups, while cluster B PDs were only the commonest diagnosis only in the group of SA aged 50 to 65. Furthermore, the C cluster was the only cluster where the tendency to lowering percentages with age was broken in the group of older SA.

Table 17. Prevalence of specified PD

	N[1]	Adjusted Cut-off[2]	Prevalence of specified PD in the general population (Cooke & Hart, 2004)	Prevalence in the healthy control group (n= 515)	Prevalence in our sample of Suicide Attempters[3] (n=446)	Prevalence in the inpatients control group (n= 86)
Paranoid PD	4 (out of 7)	5	0.5-2.5%	0.6% (3/515)	21.52% (96/446)	10.5% (9/86)
Schizoid PD	4 (out of 7)	5	0.4-1.7%	0.8% (4/515)	14.12% (63/446)	8.1% (7/86)
Schyzotypal PD	5 (out of 9)	7	0.1-5.6%	0% (0/515)	5.82% (26/446)	2.3% (2/86)
Histrionic PD	5 (out of 8)	6	2-3%	2.7% (14/515)	14.79% (66/446)	8.1% (7/86)
Antisocial PD	3 (out of 7)	5	0.6-2%	0.4% (2/515)	6.05% (27/446)	1.2% (1/86)
Narcissistic PD	5 (out of 9)	7	> 1%	1.6% (8/515)	3.81% (17/446)	2.3% (2/86)
Borderline PD	5 (out of 9)	7	0.7-2%	0.6% (3/515)	34.08% (152/446)	8.1% (7/86)
OCPD	4 (out of 8)	6	1.7-2.2%	4.5% (23/515)	13.45% (60/446)	12.8% (11/86)
Dependent PD	5 (out of 8)	6	1.0-1.7%	0.2% (1/515)	17.93% (80/446)	11.6% (10/86)
Avoidant PD	4 (out of 7)	5	0.5-5%	8.2% (42/515)	34.08% (152/446)	16.3% (14/86)

[1] Number of criteria to diagnosing a "screening" PD with IPDE-SQ.
[2] Number of criteria we used to diagnosing specified PD (with our adjusted cut-off).
[3] The sum of all PD percentages might be higher than 100% due to comorbidity in axis II.

Discussion

Consistent with previous research, the prevalence of PD in our sample of SA was lower in the groups of older SA (Henriksson et al., 1995; Isometsa et al., 1996). The prevalence of PD (74.2%) that we found and the distribution of specified PD are consistent with data reported by Dirks (1998), who found a rate of 56.6% PD in their study of parasuicide, and others. Up to 77% of subjects who attempt suicide are diagnosed with at least one PD (Casey, 1989; Clarkin et al., 1984; Suominen et al., 1996; Nimeus et al., 1997; Engström et al., 1997, Ferreria de Castro et al., 1998). Dirks et al. (1998) found the following prevalence by using the *Standardized Assessment of Personality* in a consecutive sample of 120 inpatients evaluated in the emergency room whose reason to be hospitalized was parasuicide: *paranoid PD* (30.8%) [compared to our 21.5%], *schizoid PD* (3.3%) [compared to our 14.1%] , *dissocial PD* (6.6%) [compared to our 6.1%], *impulsive emotionally unstable PD* (28.3%), *borderline PD* (22.5%) [compared to our 34.1%], *histrionic PD* (16.6%) [compared to our 14.8%], *anankastic PD* (13.3%) [compared to our 13.5% in the OCPD], *avoidant PD* (30.0%) [compared to our 34.1 %] and, *dependent PD* (9.1%) [compared to our 17.9%]. The only PD where these authors found a great difference compared to our results was schizoid PD. This might be explained by the well-known tendency of IPDE-SQ to over-diagnosing this PD (Egan & McCarthy, in press). Moreover, it must be taken into account that as we used DSM-IV classification, we could not differentiate between impulsive *emotionally unstable PD* and *borderline PD*, as it is the case of the study by Dirks et al. (1998).

We found a rate of 36.4% PD in those SA aged 66 or older, compared to the 80.3% found in the group between 18 to 35 years. The 36.4% found is far greater than the reported 5-10% rate of late-life PD in the community (Agronin, 1994), and to the 10-13% reported rate in all age groups in the community (De Girolano & Reich, 1993). On the other hand, a rate of 44% of PD (16%)/personality trait accentuation (28%) has been reported in suicides (López García et al., 1993). As previously said, it is not clear whether some differences exist with regard to age or gender in the prevalence of the different personality styles that are considered as risk factor for suicidal behavior (Szanto et al., 2001). It is possible that the personality traits and PD associated with suicidal behaviors in young people are not the same in older populations.

Our main hypothesis that those PD characterized by an *elevated impulsivity* would be more frequent in younger SA was partially supported. As expected, the prevalence of *borderline PD* (BPD) decreased with age. Thus, 40.2% of our SA aged 35 or younger had this diagnosis, while only 9.1% of those SA aged 66 or older received the same diagnosis. This might be explained by the previously reported decrement of impulsivity – a nuclear dimension of borderline PD- with age (Vaillant, 1977). Indeed, it has been suggested that the relationship between aggressive impulsivity and serotonin dysfunction might be specific of young populations (Duberstein et al., 1994). This is compatible with the idea that BPD "burns out", clinical "symptoms" improving beyond the fourth decade (Stevenson et al., 2003). These authors found that the only personality dimension associated to this improvement was impulsivity. However, other personality characteristics as affective instability, interpersonal difficulties or cognitive distortions did not improve with age. Similar findings were previously reported by Stone (1990). Thus, it might be hypothesized that affective instability and interpersonal difficulties and not impulsivity are the nuclear characteristics of BPD. Regarding *antisocial PD (APD)*, it must be stressed that this is the only PD that has been studied in the long term. Some authors have reported a tendency to improve with age (Weiss,

1973; Black et al., 1995). As it was the case of BPD, this might have to do with the so-referred decrease of impulsivity with age. However, we found that the prevalence of APD was stable in the different age sub-groups. Thus, while 6.0% of our SA younger than 35 had this diagnosis, 9.1% of those aged 66 or older retained this diagnosis. This might be explained by the limited number of SA aged 66 or older (n= 22) in our sample. It must also be taken into account that both BPD and APD might be infra-represented in samples of aged people due to excess of mortality when young (Fishbain, 1991). In fact, 10% and 5% of those with BPD and APD will respectively suicide. As suggested by Solomon (Solomon, 1981), prevalence of *narcissistic PD* decreased with age. The bimodal distribution of *histrionic PD* – it was more frequent in the groups of SA aged 18-35 and 50-65- might be explained by the particular milestones at these ages – i.e. marriage, separation, menopause or *empty nest syndrome*- that those subjects have to face.

Some personality traits like obssesiveness or shynes might have a more important role in suicidal behavior in older populations. Those who suicide in the elderly score higher in `conscientiousness´ when compared to young completers, suggesting that the role of impulsivity in suicide is weaker in the elderly (Duberstein et al., 1994). Our hypothesis that subjects diagnosed with a PD characterized by a *rigid cognitive style, overcontrol of affect* and *impulses* (e.g. *paranoid PD, schizoid PD, schizotypal PD* and, *obsessive-compulsive PD*) which either remain clinically similar or worsen in late life, showing persistent rigidity and suspiciousness (Solomon, 1981) would be relatively more frequent in older populations of SA was only partially supported. Contrary to our expectations, the prevalence of *paranoid PD* decreased with age. We think that this may be the result of an artefact: as paranoid subjects get older, they could be more suspicious and less prone to give some information in the emergency room, thus providing biased information. As expected, the prevalence of *schizoid PD* increased with age and peaked in the group of SA aged between 50 to 65 (20.8%), being the most prevalent PD in this group of age with avoidant PD. Solomon (1981) said this PD worsened with age. However, there was a sharp decrease in the prevalence of schizoid PD in those SA aged 66 or over. Subjects diagnosed with a schizoid PD who attempt suicide might do so when in social situations related to work environment, which might trigger suicidal behavior. In the elderly, after job retirement, they could avoid social situations associated with work that they may live as stressful situations. This might explain the decrease on suicide behavior. With regard to *schizotypal PD*, it peaked in the group aged 35 to 50. We considered this PD as a type of schizophrenia – as it is coded in the ICD-10 (WHO, 1993)-. Thus, the risk of suicidal behavior is higher when they have paranoid delusions and extreme suspiciousness. It is possible that, as they grow older, the emergence of negative symptoms may protect them, thus explaining the lowering risk in the elderly. Finally, as expected, *OCPD* was the most prevalent PD (18.2%) in the group of SA aged 66 or older. Agronin (1994) found that OCPD, dependent PD and mixed PD were the most prevalent PD in the elderly. In a study of suicides of people aged 60 or over, OCPD and avoidant personality traits – qualitatively similar to the concept of low Openness to experience of the *NEO personality inventory*- were associated to the group of suicides (Harwood et al., 2001). A *low Openness to experience* and a *high neuroticism* have been related to suicide in people aged 50 or older (Duberstein et al., 1994). These authors also stressed that stubbornness was prominent in suicides in the elderly populations when compared to the suicides in younger populations and suggested that a rigid cognitive style may lead to a lack of resilience, problems to cope with stressful life events and make anxiety more difficult to be detected.

Moreover, the relationship of these personality traits with depressive disorders is still not studied (Conwell et al., 2002). Older suicide completers are more likely to have low scores on the `openness to experience' of the NEO-PR – a dimensional method of measuring personality- (Duberstein et al., 1994), characterised by lack of adaptability, constricted affect and cognitive rigidity, which overlaps to some extent with ICD-10 anankastic PD (Harwood et al., 2001).

Finally, when analysing data cluster by cluster, we found that the most prevalent cluster was C cluster in all the groups, with the exception of SA aged 50 to 65, where B cluster was the most frequent. Moreover, the C cluster was the only one where the tendency to a lowering prevalence of the diagnosis of PD with age reversed, as it was more frequent in the older group of SA (36.4%) when compared to the SA aged 50 to 65 (31.2%). It is generally accepted that the subjects diagnosed with a cluster C PD have not the same risk of suicidal behavior than those diagnosed with a cluster B PD (Rubio Larrosa, 2004). However, some authors have found high rates of avoidant PD among SA (Dirks, 1998; Hawton et al., 2003). Hawton et al. (2003) suggested that the lower rate of emotionally unstable PD they found was the result of the exclusion of subjects with repetitive minor self-mutilating behavior, but not real suicide attempts. It is possible that our findings have the same explanation, as we used O'Carroll's stringent definition of suicide attempt. Most remarkably, as predicted by Solomon (1981), those subjects diagnosed with a PD characterized by affective and behavior dysregulation (cluster B PDs, avoidant PD and dependent PD) would have lower levels of impulsivity and aggressiveness as they get older, so the tendency would be to improve when older, being a common outcome depression and hypochondriasis. In agreement with this, we found that cluster B PDs, avoidant PD and dependent PD were less frequent in the older subgroups of SA. Dependent PD was more frequent in the group of older SA (4.5%) when compared to the sub-sample of SA aged 50 to 65 (2.1%). This slight increase might be reflecting the more frequent dependent behaviors in older populations. Indeed, Agronin (1994) reported that the most prevalent late-life PD were *OCPD, dependent PD* and *"mixed" PD.*

Conclusion

Consistently with previous research (Isometsa et l, 1996), we found that the prevalence of PDs in SA is lower in old people when compared to young people. Moreover, as expected, OCPD and avoidant PD, 18.2% and 13.6% respectively, were the most prevalent PD among older SA. Finally, compared to OCPD and avoidant PD, the prevalence of BPD and APD was lower. This may be secondary to impulsivity decreasing with age (Vaillant, 1977). Moreover, the relationship between aggressive impulsivity and serotonin dysfunction in suicide may be specific to younger populations, if at all (Duberstein et al., 1994). However, the rate found of APD was surprisingly high.

Chapter 2.11.

SUICIDE IN PERSONALITY DISORDERS: THE ROLE OF PROTECTIVE FACTORS

M. M. Pérez-Rodriguez, N. Cuervo,
E. Baca-García and M. A. Oquendo

2.11.1. INTRODUCTION TO PROTECTIVE FACTORS FOR SUICIDAL BEHAVIORS

Psychological autopsy studies have consistently reported that around 90% of the victims of completed suicide had been diagnosed with a mental disorder (Lonnqvist et al., 1995; Arsenault-Lapierre et al., 2004). However, most individuals with psychiatric disorders do not commit suicide. For example, it has been estimated that only around 10% of patients with schizophrenia will die because of suicide (Radomsky et al., 1999). Moreover, although a high proportion of the general population suffer significant stressors and major depressive episodes, only a small percentage of subjects will carry on suicidal acts. This has prompted clinicians to search for other risk and protective factors for suicidal behavior (Mann et al., 1999; Malone et al., 2000; Phillips et al., 2002).

Suicidal behavior is complex and is probably caused by a combination of factors (Mann et al., 1999). According to the stress-diathesis model, the risk for suicidal acts is determined not only by a state-dependent trigger domain related to stressors (life events, states of depression or psychosis) but also by a threshold domain (diathesis), or trait-like predisposition to suicidal acts (Mann et al., 1999; Malone et al., 2000). Neither single domain determines suicidality. It is the combination of risk factors across domains what increases the likelihood of suicidal acts, either by a decrease in internal restraint against suicide or by an increase in the suicidal impulse caused by excess stress (Mann et al., 1999; Malone et al., 2000). Protective factors act in the opposite way, decreasing the probability of suicidal behaviors.

While the majority of studies investigating variables associated with suicidal behaviors have focused on risk factors, only a small number of studies have examined protective factors (Oquendo et al., 2005). The Practice Guideline for the Assessment and Treatment of Suicidal

Behaviors published by the American Psychiatric Association (APA, 2003) lists ten factors with protective effects for suicide: children in the home; sense of responsibility to family; pregnancy; religiosity; life satisfaction; reality testing ability; positive coping skills; positive problem-solving skills; positive social support; and positive therapeutic relationship.

In studies that compare suicide attempters with nonattempters, protective factors against suicidal behaviors are generally the opposite of risk factors. Non-suicidal individuals are more likely to be younger, of female sex, non-white, and tend to have extensive social contacts, access to effective treatments (particularly antidepressants), proper sleep, exercise, diet, and are less likely to have guns in their homes or a psychiatric disorder (Maris, 2002). However, these factors do not explain why certain individuals that share many of these characteristics attempt suicide, while others (the majority) do not.

The construct of Reasons for Living (assessed with the Reasons for Living Inventory, RFLI) (Linehan et al., 1983) was conceived as an instrument to assess protective factors for suicidal behaviors. It is based on a cognitive-behavioral theory of suicidality that hypothesizes that individuals who do not act on their suicidal urges or feelings have different expectations, beliefs, and adaptive ways of thinking (which help them resist the suicidal urges) than individuals who yield to suicidal impulses and perform suicidal acts (Molock et al., 2006). The RFLI (Linehan et al., 1983) measures six factors: survival and coping beliefs; responsibility to family; child-related concerns; fear of suicide; fear of social disapproval; and moral objections to suicide. In several samples, individuals who had attempted suicide had significantly lower total scores on the RFLI than nonattempters (Mann et al., 1999; Malone et al., 2000).

The protective role of social and cultural factors on suicidal behaviors has been observed in many studies with different designs. The influence of sociocultural factors on suicide may partially explain the large differences in suicide rates that have been observed among different countries. The highest annual rates are in Eastern Europe, with several countries with more than 30 suicides per 100,000 individuals. The lowest rates are found in most Latin American and Muslim countries, with fewer than 6.5 per 100,000 individuals (WHO, 2005).

Religion may be one of the sociocultural protective factors influencing suicide rates (Neeleman et al., 1997). Suicide rates are lower in religious countries than in secular ones (Breault, 1986; Stack, 1983), and religion has been reported to have a protective effect against suicide ideation (a risk factor for suicide attempts) (Stack & Lester, 1991; Dervic et al., 2004). Participation in religious activities has been reported to reduce the odds of committing suicide (Nisbet et al., 2000), even after controlling for the frequency of social contact. Dervic et al. (2004) found that individuals who reported having no religious affiliation were significantly more likely to have attempted suicide in their lifetime (the strongest predictor of future suicide attempts) (Leon et al., 1990) and had significantly more first-degree relatives who had committed suicide than individuals who belonged to one specific religion (Catholicism, Protestantism, Judaism, or other). Subjects with religious affiliation reported more reasons for living (measured with the RFLI) (Linehan et al., 1983), were significantly more often married, significantly more often had children, and reported a more family-oriented social network. This is consistent with reports that religious commitment increases social ties and decreases alienation (Koenig et al., 2001). All these variables have been identified as protective factors for suicide attempts, and might confound the relationship between religious affiliation and suicide attempts. However, in a logistic regression, neither marital status, nor parental status, nor time spent with family were significantly associated with suicide attempter status (Dervic et al., 2004). Religious affiliations have also been associated with lower levels of aggressiveness, which may contribute to the decreased suicide risk (Dervic et al., 2004).

Dervic et al. (2004) observed that moral objections to suicide mediated the association between religious affiliation and suicide attempts. They concluded that the presence of religious affiliation may be more relevant as a protective factor for suicidal behavior than specific religious denominations (Catholic, Protestants, etc.). This is consistent with data from several studies that suggests that it is the strength of the religious beliefs and not the specific religious affiliation what decreases suicide risk (APA, 2003; Hilton et al., 2002). Malone et al. (2000) found that religious persuasion (catholic or non-catholic) did not differ significantly between suicide attempters and nonattempters, while the scores for moral objections to suicide strongly differentiated attempters and nonattempters. They suggested that reasons for living may be a more sensitive index of moral/religious beliefs than "religion of origin". They cited as an example the rise of suicides in Ireland, which is associated with a decline in religious practices without any change in the religion of origin (Department of Health and Children, 1998).

Malone et al. (2000) observed that the patients with major depression who had not attempted suicide had more feelings of responsibility towards their family, more fear of social disapproval, more moral objections to suicide, more survival and coping beliefs, and more fear of suicide (measured with the RFLI) (Linehan et al., 1983) than depressed individuals who had attempted suicide. The authors hypothesized that reasons for living "may reflect a cultural or environmental component in the suicide threshold and may contribute to variation in suicide rates among different cultures" (Malone et al., 2000). Other authors have also found that high scores on the moral objections to suicide (Oquendo et al., 2005; Dervic et al., 2004), responsibility to family (Oquendo et al., 2005; Dervic et al., 2004), and survival and coping beliefs (Oquendo et al., 2005) subscales of the RFLI were protective factors for suicide attempts.

Data from several studies suggest that having children has a protective effect against suicidal behaviors, particularly in women (Hoyer & Lund, 1993; Warshaw et al., 2000). Qin & Mortensen (2003) found that having young children had protective effects against suicide. In another study by the same group they found that having a child less than 2 years old significantly decreased the suicide risk in women, but not in men. However, Malone et al. (2000) found that child-related concerns measured with the RFLI did not differ significantly between suicide attempters and nonattempters. In women, pregnancy and the puerperium also seem to be protective for suicidal behaviors (Harris & Barraclough, 1994).

The presence of a social support system has also been reported as a protective factor for suicidal behaviors (APA, 2003; Nisbet, 1996; Turvey et al., 2002). Donald et al. (2006) found that social connectedness, problem solving confidence, and an internal locus of control were protective factors for medically serious suicide attempts in young adults, although immediate family support was not a significant protective factor.

Other factors like education (Agerbo et al., 2002; Lorant et al., 2005), being married (APA, 2003; Warshaw et al., 2000; Heikkinen et al., 1995; Mortensen et al., 2000), being employed (APA, 2003; Mortensen et al., 2000), involvement in physical activity (Simon et al., 2004), and physical health (Maris, 2002) have been reported to be inversely related to completed suicide. Lorant et al. (2005) observed that being married had a protective effect that alleviated the negative impact of low socioeconomic status on suicide. However, some of the associations reported may be confounded, since some of the variables that protect against suicidal behaviors may be inversely related to factors that truly increase suicide risk. For example, individuals with severe mental disorders (a very strong risk factor for suicidal behaviors) (Harris & Barrraclough, 1997) may be more likely to be single or unemployed (APA, 2003), and less likely to complete higher education than individuals without severe mental illnesses; and the lack of involvement in physical activity may be caused by symptoms of a depressive disorder that also increases the suicide risk. After controlling for other risk factors, many of these associations may disappear.

Some of the observed differences in the rates of suicidal behaviors across ethnic groups may be partially mediated by protective factors that are more common in certain ethnic groups. Oquendo et al. (2005) observed that Latinos had significantly higher total scores in the RFLI than non-Latinos. They scored significantly higher on the "Survival and coping beliefs", "Responsibility to family", and "Moral objections to suicide" subscales. Latinos were significantly more likely to be Catholic. Religion and extended family networks have also been identified as protective factors for suicidal behaviors in African Americans, and may explain the very low rates of suicide in African American women (Nisbet, 1996; Gibbs, 1997).

2.11.2. PROTECTIVE FACTORS FOR SUICIDAL BEHAVIORS IN PERSONALITY DISORDERS

Very few studies have investigated the role of protective factors for suicidal behaviors in patients with personality disorders. Dervic et al. (2006) found that depressed individuals with comorbid cluster B personality disorders (PDs) had significantly lower total scores in the RFLI and significantly lower scores in the "survival and coping beliefs" and "moral objections to suicide/religious beliefs" RFLI subscales than depressed subjects without comorbid cluster B PDs. They found that moral objections to suicide, survival and coping beliefs, and aggression were independently associated with suicide attempts after controlling for age, religious affiliation, survival and coping beliefs, aggression, and cluster B PD. Dervic et al. (2006) also found that subjects with cluster B PDs were less likely to be married, less likely to have children, and less likely to report religious affiliation. They hypothesized that some specific traits of patients with cluster B PDs (like the grandiosity of narcissistic PD or the propensity for rule-breaking of antisocial PD) may make it difficult for them to commit to clear rules and adhere to moral principles such as those inherent in religiosity.

Rietdijk et al. (2001) reported that only one subscale of the Reasons for Living Inventory (Survival and coping beliefs) significantly predicted suicidal behaviors during a six-month follow-up period in patients with borderline PD. They suggested that the predictive role of this subscale could be explained by the fact that it reflected maladaptive coping strategies and depressive personality traits, which are factors associated with suicide risk.

Some characteristics of certain PDs (such as the devotion to ethics, morals, values and rules characteristic of obsessive-compulsive PD patients) might be associated with decreased suicide risk. However, there are no data available on this subject, which should be further investigated.

Chapter 2.12.

THERAPEUTIC APPROACH TO ATTEMPTED SUICIDES IN SUBJECTS WITH PERSONALITY DISORDERS

E. García-Resa, J. C. García Álvare and D. Braquehais Conesa

Far from being able to be considered as recent or isolated behavior, suicide is a universal phenomenon that has accompanied the human condition throughout its history. On occasions condemned, at other times tolerated and admired, never ignored, suicide has supposed an inexhaustible fountain of doubts, reflections and worries that have been manifested across the distinct religions, cultures and political structures of human evolution. The simple consideration of suicide causes discomfort overwhelms the conscience. Perhaps because its enigmatic character points to the center of the human condition, or as happens with all of the large enigmas of existence, its authentic nature and understanding is seen as unattainable.

In the last decades, the world in general and the West in particular, found itself confronting a new problem of enormous importance, as much sociocultural as sanitary. Suicide and its associated behavior has become one of the principle causes of demand on the emergency services, besides being one of the main causes of mortality. Thus, some authors have come to consider this type of conduct as an indirect measurement of the mental health of a society (Geijo et al., 1997; López García et al., 1993). The growing interest in this problem has become consolidated in a way parallel to the repercussion that is presented in current societies. In 1976, the WHO estimated that suicide was the tenth cause of death (Ramos-Brieva & Cordero-Villafáfila, 1989, responsible for the death of a thousand people a day. Since then multiple analyses and investigations have been developed in this respect, showing us in such an unmistakable form that there have been hardly any changes in this tendency in spite of the various calls and initiatives of analysis and prevention. Recent studies vouch for this affirmation and they consider that the prevalence of suicide in the community is maintained between 0.04 and 4.6%. These studies also produce data such as that suicide is the direct cause of approximately 30,000 annual deaths in the USA (which constitutes the eighth cause of death) (Oquendo et al., 2000) and of more than 150,000 in Europe, a figure that would be situated above the deaths associated to chronic infections and other illnesses such as HIV/AIDS (Oquendo et al., 1999).

Such are the repercussions and the importance that this phenomenon has received that, Governments and institutions such as the WHO or the American Public Health Service (OMS, 1986; US Public Health Service, 1999) have begun to recognise suicide as a health priority. In 1984, in their program "Health for all in the year 2000", the WHO included in their twelfth objective the purpose to obtain "for the year 2000, the present growing tendencies of suicides and attempted suicides are reversed". As of that moment they initiated diverse programmes and studies, oriented towards the understanding and prevention of suicidal behavior, these being reinforced through the national and international development of programmes (some of them legislated by the Governments) for the approach to said behavior. Nevertheless, far from reaching such objectives and, in spite of having been a point of inflection in the consideration of the suicidal phenomenon as a priority in public health, the WHO currently recognizes (2005) suicidal behavior as the tenth cause of "burden" for society, produced by illness measured in DALYs (disability adjusted life years) and that reflects the incapacity as much as the mortality that conveys the illness.

Likewise, it affirms that nine of the ten countries with higher rates of suicide are found in Europe (WHO, 2005), where the rates of suicide vary between six suicides per 100,000 inhabitants in Malta to 52 suicides per 100,000 inhabitants in Lithuania. Special mention must be given to the case of adolescents and young adults between 15 and 34 years of age, where suicide is the second highest cause of death in Europe (WHO, 2002) and the third in the USA (Mann, 2002).

In spite of all said and perhaps seeming a frivolous attitude with such a dramatic issue, suicide and related behaviors carry not only an enormous family and social impact, but its economic repercussion is from time to time incalculable. In the US, an approximate economic cost of $111 billion in relation to the attempts of suicide is calculated ($3.7 billion because of the medical care, $27.4 billion due to loss of productivity and some $80.2 billion derived from the loss in quality of life). Analyzing the evolution of the statistics of suicide in the US in the period from 1994 to 2000, Kashner et al. (2000) estimated for the year 2000 a figure of 30,027 suicides, with 1,096,075 potential years of life lost, a price of 978,000 dollars per person/year, and some 700,000 annual consultations related to these behaviors. This prediction was exceeded by the 31,655 documented suicides in the US in 2002 (Mann et al., 2005).

Far beyond appreciating the importance of suicide in present Western society, we cannot avoid the relevance that also keeps the suicidal frustrated or the attempted suicide incomplete. This relevance is directly related as much with the consumption of medical resources as with the morbidity that they are able to involve, but it is more, they are also the principal risk factors for suicide that we know. Nearly 10% of the patients with one attempted suicide eventually commit suicide, with 1-2% doing it in the following year (Nordentoft et al., 1993). Likewise, it is estimated that the risk of suicide in these patients is 100 times over that of the general population (Hawton & Fagg, 1988), and 50% of people who commit suicide have records of previous attempts (Roy, 1989).

For all this, attending to aspects such as the character of repeated suicidal behavior, frequent records of the same in patients that commit suicide and the possibility of prevention that this brings, the importance must be understood of the first contact made by these patients with the health system.

2.12.1. CLINICAL MANAGEMENT OF SUICIDE

Though it is certain that suicide is not an absolutely predictable behavior, an adequate evaluation and intervention at the moment of crisis can help to change the attitude of the patient about his intention to die, as well as to appraise and to delimit the cases in which there persists a serious risk of suicide. Nevertheless, it is no less certain today as there exists a great ignorance about which aspects to keep in mind and the distinct attitudes that relatives, acquaintances or doctors should do well to suspect with regard to the existence of a suicidal risk in an apparently healthy individual.

The reasons that a person decides to end their life are multiple. Behind a decision so dramatic, emerge multiple personal factors, both socio-cultural and demographic. These factors can well act as underlying or as precipitates of the behavior, and will be the ones that guide what attitude to take with a suicidal patient. The suicidal act, including when the ending is not fatal, supposes an enormous impact upon the environment of the patient. Family and friends become victims, with a feeling of deep discomfort and impotence. The appropriate approach, the family position and the establishment of support networks, will help in the task of acceptance and confrontation of the situation.

A great deal more serious is the case of successful suicides, in these it is frequent to describe the feelings of guilt apparent among relatives and acquaintances, almost always aggravated by the fact that the patient had communicated their intentions at some point, and that leads to the complex development of grief, to the breakdown of family relations and can include mimicry behavior. Once more, this has made necessary the establishment of adequate supports, the derivation to centers of help and it sets in motion social and personal resources, along with specialized help from the emergency services.

2.12.2. EVALUATION OF THE SUICIDAL PATIENT

The Clinical Interview

It is often the case that the first contact with the suicidal patient occurs in the Emergency Services of different hospitals and Health Centres, generally as a consequence of a tentative unsuccessful suicide attempt or at the patients own request, who describes feelings and occasional desires of death that cause him surprise or distress. In these situations, and before all potentially suicidal patients, the intervention of the doctor or psychiatrist should be directed in the first place to define and to identify the problem, evaluating the possible existence of a diagnostic psychiatric concomitant and the risk factors of suicide. It will be possible to establish a specific therapeutic attitude depending on the prior data and of the different health, family, and personal resources that can be arranged.

Among the diverse types of suicidal patient that we can meet, we can distinguish the following (Hyman, 1987):

1. Patients that have survived a suicide attempt.
2. Patients that come to emergency departments suffering from conception or suicidal impulses.

3. Patients that come to emergency departments referring you to other complaints, but during the interview, they are recognized to have suicidal thoughts.
4. Patients that deny having suicidal intentions who however, behave in such a way that shows they are potentially suicidal (usually they are accompanied by relatives and have come at the relative's request).

In all cases, the first contact with the suicidal patient should be carried out in a tranquil environment, avoiding any possible interruptions, and adopting an attitude of actively listening and understanding.

Beyond the basic fact to pursue death, the suicidal act always supposes a form of communication. The suicidal patient expresses their discomfort, their desperation or hostility and it is possible that, before an adequate interlocutor, they can tackle the motives that have caused them to take the decision to die. The psychiatrist should facilitate the expression of feelings and to avoid a moralizing or critical attitude, since this can provoke deterioration in the feelings of guilt and insufficiency in the patient, exercising the action of strengthening their suicidal behavior.

In those patients who have not carried out a suicidal act and whose motive for consultation differs from this, they will have to be asked about the conception of suicide. This approach should be carried out in a progressive way. Initially they can be interrogated about the existence of feelings of distaste, desperation or disillusionment and, when the answer is affirmative, it needs to be ascertained if they understand this situation as something insuperable. The vision of death as a solution is somewhat frequent in these situations and it is necessary to investigate the attitude of the patient before this last act. It is possible that the patient describes a passive and unspecific experience of "desire of death" or that on the contrary, they maintain an active attitude and have contemplated the possibility of leaving life and have even realized a plan to do so.

When the patient has been denied the possibility to carry out a suicidal act, it is convenient to investigate the reasons that stopped them from committing it, be these religious, family or cultural. If on the contrary, he recognizes the possibility of completing the act, the means at their disposal should be considered, the degree of planning, the prior existence of any intent and any other risk factors (Ros Montalbán, 1998).

Besides the information obtained from the patient, it is convenient to interview relatives and people close to the patient. The data contributed by these people can help to confirm a diagnostic impression, to clarify doubts about what has happened or to contradict information given by the patient. In this respect, it is frequently discovered that the suicidal patient has communicated their intentions in a direct or indirect way to close friends in the weeks prior, and on other occasions that the patient's behavior in the family environment manifests an intention that is potentially suicidal, contrary to those maintained during the interview with the psychiatrist. On the other hand, he will be able to value the degree of support or of containment existing in the family environment and to decide the appropriate attitude to take.

The interview with the patient and their family is not only a good instrument to obtain information, but what is more, it is a therapeutic intervention and the first step in the approach and orientation of the suicidal patient.

Table 18. What not to do with a suicidal patient

- Do not question in an inadequate way. It is better that the question should be not asked, rather than do it in too invasive a manner
- Do not undervalue suicidal behavior. Especially in the "chronically" suicidal, those with previous suicide attempts or with more manipulative gestures and less lethal acts.
- Do not have an inappropriate attitude. Adopting a critical attitude, moralizing, trying to convince to the patient or to discuss his thinking or attempted suicide
- Do not minimize the situations of stress or recent vital events.
- Over-involvement, leading us to invade the feelings of pessimism in the patient or the anguish of the relatives.

Table 19. Characteristics and objectives of the interview of the suicidal patient

Technique	Objectives
Empathy	Helps communication
Privacy	
Ask about the suicidal thinking	To evaluate the conception, the plans and attempted suicide
To check the information given by the patient with those close to the patient	
	To value the external and internal controls of the patient
	To carry out the most complete clinical history possible
	To try to arrive at a psychiatric diagnosis
	To produce a plan of help and control that should be accepted by the patient and by the family

It always must remember that, before taking any psychiatric therapeutic decision, a medical evaluation of the patient must be carried out. A correct medical evaluation must include a complete physical examination, measurement of vital signs, analysis of emergencies and an electrocardiogram. We should point out that 92% of suicide attempts are carried out by means of poisoning using prescribed drugs, such as tranquillizers, anti-depressants and analgesics. The advisable course of action is medical observation during the first 24 hours. Afterwards, a psychiatric assessment can be carried out.

The Assessment of Suicidal Risk

One of the problems that confront all medical professionals, and especially psychiatrist, consists in evaluating, and predicting the potential risk of a suicidal patient. Just as previously described, the motives that carry a person to commit suicide are multiple and do not respond to an established rule. The suicidal phenomenon covers all ranges of behavior, that go from the simple conception to the completed suicidal act and its explanation extends far beyond any philosophical, exclusively sociological or existential explanation. Nevertheless, we cannot obviate that there are clear indicators associated with a greater probability of execution of attempted and completed suicides. Thus, within *ethiopathogenic models*, those that consider suicide because of the interaction of diverse environmental and personal variables of type prevail. To this respect, Blumenthal & Kupfer (1986) proposed an ethiopatogenic model according to which, the probability to carry out a suicidal act increases depending on the distinct factors of risk present in the subject and of the interaction that is given between the same in each subject (see Figure 6).

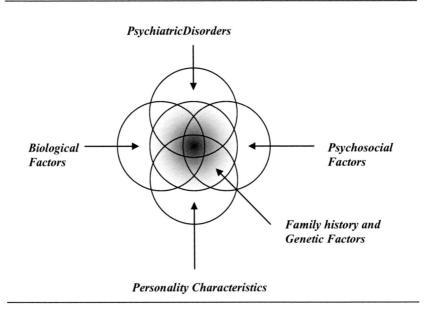

Figure 6. Model of overlapping suicide risk factors (Blumenthal & Kupfer, 1986). (Taken from Ros Montalbán, S. The suicidal conduct, 1998)

Without intention to thoroughly study this aspect, and given that the factors of suicidal risk have already been extensively reviewed previously, we simply consider opportune to name some of them:

- *Personal Factors*
  - *Race*
  - *Age*
  - *Gender*
  - *Civil state (married, single, separated, widowed)*
  - *Medical illnesses*
  - *Existance of previous stress factors*
- *Socio-cultural Factors*
  - *Social class*
  - *Employment situation*
  - *Emigration*
  - *Housing (urban, rural)*
- *Previous attempted suicides*
- *Psychiatric disorders*
  - *Affective disorders*

- *Disorders due to substance abuse*
- *Schizophrenia*
- *Mood disorders*

It is worthwhile to stress the importance of affective disorders. Several studies support strong links between affective disorders and suicide behavior. Some symptoms and personality traits that deserve a careful evaluation are sadness, desperation, desertion, hostility, guilt, dependence, shame and uselessness. Two aspects which are fundamental in the assessment of suicidal risk in patients with mood disorders are, firstly, that when evaluating repetitive suicide attempts in the same patient there might be a tendency to minimize the importance of the current suicide attempt, and secondly, that revolving-door patients can generate feelings of rejection and hostility in the mental health professional. Both processes may interfere with the correct evaluation of the potential risk of suicide. To avoid this, it is necessary to stress that mental health professionals must be neutral, and have calm, listening and understanding attitude, avoiding at all times a judgemental or prejudiced attitude.

Characteristics of Attempted Suicide

Those patients evaluated because of a suicide attempt in the emergency room at Hospitals must be correctly assessed. The characteristics of the unsuccessful attempt should be thoroughly investigated. The degree of motivation to die, the planning, the notes of farewell, the attitude before it happened, the method utilized or the personal, and physical circumstances in which it was carried out, are different topics that will help to judge the magnitude and immediate risk (Diaz-Sastre, 2000). The following topics should always be extensively evaluated:

- *Potential lethality of the method: although* poisoning, mainly by medical drugs, is usually considered as a non-violent method, the real lethality lies on the subjective knowledge of the patient about the substances used.
- *Effective awareness of the attempt:* from time to time, erroneous beliefs exist with regard to the lethality of the suicide attempt.
- *Degree of planning*: the absence of precipitating factors, the existence of a farewell note, making will/life insurance add gravity to the suicide attempt.
- *Accessibility to the rescue.*
- *Purpose:* sometimes suicide behavior is used as a way to communicating distress, and it is not a real suicide attempt as defines by O'Carroll. The possibility of secondary gains should always be taken into account.
- *Attitude after the attempt:* once the patient is stabilized, feelings of relief or frustration may arise and give and idea of the real intention and criticism of the attempt.

Instruments to Appraising Suicidal Risk

Several instruments can be used in order to complement a careful clinical anamnesis of the patient:

Sad Persons Scale (SAS)

It includes socio-demographic, psychiatric, medical and other variables related to the present or past suicide attempts. The authors proposed several courses of action depending on the obtained score:

- (0-2): mild outpatient follow-up.
- (3-4): close outpatient follow-up.
- (5-6): extreme outpatient follow-up with 24 hours family vigilance or inpatient care at a Psychiatric Unit.
- (7-10): inpatient care at a Psychiatric Unit.

**Table 20. Scale of values for suicidal risk appraisal SAD PERSONS
(Patterson et al., 1983)**

Item	Scoring
Sex	1 male
Age	1 3ª age
Depression	1 present
Previous attempt	1 yes
Ethanol abuse	1 present
Rational thinking loss	1 present
Social supports lacking	1 present
Organised plan	1 present
No spouse	1 present
Sickness	1 present

Scale of Risk/recovery

It is useful in helping to give a risk estimation of a potential future suicide attempt. It is considered that risk exists when scores are over 44-50 points. Each item of the following classification scores from 1 to 3.

Scoring for Risk:	*Scoring for Recovery:*
- (5-6): low risk	- (14-15): high recovery
- (7-8): low-moderate	- (12-13): moderate-high
- (9-10): moderate	- (10-11): moderate
- (11-12): high-moderate	- (8-9): low-moderate
- (13-15): high risk	- (5-7): low recovery

Table 21. Scale of risk/recovery (Weisman & Worden, 1972)

Risk factors	Recovery factors
Method used 1. Ingestion, cuts, stabbing. 2. Drowning, asphyxia, strangulation. 3. Jumping, shooting.	Location 1. Remote 2. Not familiar, not remote 3. Familiar
Inadequate conscience 1. Not observed 2. Confusion, coma, semi-coma. 3. Coma, deep coma.	**Person who suggested the recovery** 1. Untrained person 2. Professional 3. Key person or family (or the patient)
Lesions/toxicity 1. Light 2. Moderate. 3. Strong.	**Probability of discovery** 1. Accidental 2. Uncertain 3. Certain
Reversability 1. Good, complete recovery. 2. Medium, recovery with time. **3.** Bad, residual effects.	**Accessability for rescue** 1. Does not request aid 2. Leaves tracks 3. Requests aid
Necessary treatment 1. First aid, emergency unit. 2. Hospital admittance. 3. Intensive care	**Delay until discovery** 1. More than 4 hours 2. Less than 4 hours 3. Immedeate

Suicide Intent Scales (SIS) (Beck et al., 1974)

Its main purpose is to evaluating the severity of the suicide attempts.

Table 22. Suicide Intent Scale, SIS (Beck et al., 1974)

1. Isolation 0. Someone present 1. Someone nearby 2. No one present
2. Time 0. Intervention probable 1. Intervention improbable 2. Intervention almost impossible
3. Precautions against discovery/intervention 0. Without precautions 1. Passive precautions 2. Active precautions
4. Acts to obtain help during or after the attempt 0. To request assistance from a person who is potentially collaborating, telling them of the intent 1. Contact with someone without asking specifically for help 2. No contact or asking for assistance from a potentially colaborating person

Table 22. Continued

5. Final acts, anticipating death (e.g.. : will, insurance, ...)	
0.	None
1.	To think about it or to make some arrangements
2.	To have final plans or to have completed the arrangements
6. Active preparation for the attempt	
0.	None
1.	Minimum and moderated
2.	Intensive
7. Suicide note	
0.	Absent
1.	Note written although destroyed; to think about the note
2.	Note present
8. Communication of the intention before the attempt	
0.	None
1.	Ambiguous communication
2.	Unambiguous communication
9. Purpose of the attempt	
0.	To manipulate the environment, a cry for help, revenge
1.	Between 0 and 2
2.	Escape, to solve problems
10. Expectations about the mortal result	
0.	Thinks that death is impossible
1.	Thinks that death is possible but improbable
2.	Thinks that death is probable or certain
11. Understanding of the deadliness of the method	
0.	Was certain that the procedure was not lethal
1.	Was not certain if the procedure could be lethal
2.	Was certain that the procedure could be lethal
12. Seriousness of the attempt	
0.	Is not a serious attempt to put an end to their life
1.	Uncertainty about the seriousness to put an end to their life
2.	Serious attempt to put an end to their life
13. Attitude with regard to life/death	
0.	Does not want to die
1.	Between 0 and 2
2.	Wants to die
14. Conception of the medical intervention	
0.	It is thought that death was improbable if the patient received medical attention
1.	It is thought uncertain that medical attention could save their life
2.	It thought that the death was certain even if medical aid was recieved
15. Degree of premeditation	
0.	None, impulsive
1.	Thought about suicide in the three hours prior to the attempt
2.	Thought about suicide more than three hours before the attempt

2.12.3. THERAPEUTIC MANAGEMENT

According to the risk present in the patient, and the arranged measures of protection, the subjects should be send home or been hospitalized (See fig. 1).

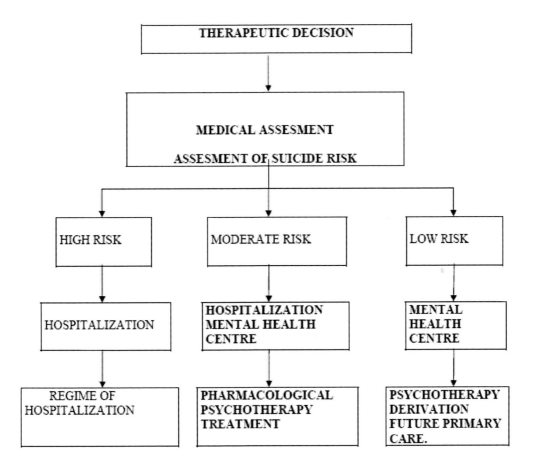

Figure 7. Algorithm of therapeutic decision.

Sending Home the Suicide Attempter

This might be the better choice in the subjects with low suicidal risk, and/or with family support. Clear instructions should be given to the responsible relatives for the treatment and control of the patient. A new outpatient assessment should be carried out as soon as possible, being the maximum time adviceable of 72 hours.

In those subjects diagnosed with a PD, the suicide behavior has frequently an instrumental intention or is the subject´s abnormal impulsive way of dealing with stressful recent life events. Those subjects lack the inner resources to cope with stressful situations. In these occasions, admission should be avoided unless there is no other way of handling this. A brief hospitalisation can be useful.

Psychiatric Hospitalisation

Subjects at a high suicidal risk should be hospitalized. The patient diagnosed with a personality disorder should be in agreement with the hospitalisation. If this is not the case, we will seek the support of the family to the suicidal patient. In the event of a competent patient who does not agree with hospitalisation, a request should be made to the patient or a family member to state in writing their refusal to the offered hospitalization. There are several situations where hospitalisation should be recommended:

- In adolescents, especially if it is the first attempt.
- Presence of serious psychiatric disorders.
- A serious suicide attempt – e.g. planned, using high lethality methods, etc.-.
- The subject is not competent – e.g. the patient is under the effects of drugs-.
- Repeated suicide attempts or recent history of serious self-harming behavior.
- Severe conflicting situations and/or social circumstances of broad risk that might precipitate a suicide attempt in a disturbed subject.
- When expectations of hospitalisation cannot be modified on the patient.
- When the suicide attempt is the answer to a "vital crisis" and, after carrying out a crisis intervention, this has failed.
- The therapist is not capable to handle the situation in an outpatient setting.

Advantages of Hospitalization

We should always bore in mind that hospitalisation does not prevent suicidality totally. Some potential benefits of hospitalisation are:

- A better assessment of the patient can be achieved, and a better understanding of the global situation is more probable.
- A more specific and targeted treatment can be applied.
- It limits the patient's access to violent methods, providing him with time to recover from his previous suicidal impulses or plans.
- A better referral to outpatient resources can be achieved, thus favouring better monitoring.

Conditions of Hospitalization

- The patient should be accommodated in a room where he can be permanently view by the staff.
- The staff must be notified of the risk of the patient.
- Frequent evaluation by psychiatrist should be carried out to monitoring improvement.

2.12.4. AFTERCARE

This term was coined by E. Sheneidman in 1971, to refer to the support that is needed by one who attempts suicide, and to the relatives of someone who has committed suicide. It is a way to prevent pain, reducing the traumatic impact upon the life of the survivors, with the objective of helping them to live longer, in a more productive way and with less discomfort (Shneidman, 2001).

When a loved one suicide, mourning on relatives has several functions: to accept the reality of the loss, to work the emotions and the consequent pain, to adapt to the new situation without the loved one, to establish a new emotional equilibrium, and to continue living (Worden, 1997).

According to Sheneidman (2001), aftercare should begin as early as possible, taking advantage of the little resistance of the family during this period. The mental health professional should:

- Be willing to support the relatives.
- Show empathy, be receptive, and favour the expression of feelings.
- Explore the negative emotions towards their deceased loved one.
- Work as a therapist.
- Stimulate involvement in the activities of everyday life.
- Help in the orientation of the immediate future.
- Carry out an overall appraisal seeking signs of physical or psychological deterioration.

Chapter 2.13.

ETHICAL AND LEGAL IMPLICATIONS OF FORCED ADMISSION BECAUSE OF CHRONIC SUICIDALITY IN PERSONALITY DISORDER. WHAT WOULD DARWIN SAY?

J. D. Molina Martín

"…I am not obliged to do a small good to society at the expence of a great harm to myself;
why then should I prolong a miserable existence, because of some frivolous advantage which
the public may perhaps receive from me?"
David Hume (1711-1776)

2.13.1. INTRODUCTION

We believe that the evolutionatory theory is a privileged one to reflect on the healthy-sick distinction, and on the problems of the individual's autonomy that the topic of PDs poses. From this point of view, personality disorders are not diseases, but stable evolutionary strategies. Chronic suicidality is inherent to the diagnosis of borderline personality disorder (BPD). From this evolutionary perspective, we hypothesize that PDs have to do with a pattern of behavior which, if somewhat abnormal, would be useful for the species' survival, and paradoxically, for the survival of some individuals dwelling on ecological niches in which such behavior could achieve biological advantage. It is within this framework that we approach the main questions met in the clinical arena: Which degree of responsibility do BDP patients have on their own suicidal behavior? Do they have the same autonomy as any other citizen? Are we bound to respect their decisions? These issues were raised by the case prompting this review: the clinical, ethical and legal aspects of involuntary admission of a BDP patient in a long-term facility because of chronic suicidality.

2.13.2. PERSONALITY DISORDERS
FROM AN EVOLUTIONARY PERSPECTIVE

From early works on inheritance of different evolutionary strategies, such as Millon's (1990), which applied the model of evolution to the study of personality, to most recent publications like the one by Paris (2003), clinical literature on psychiatry has increasingly approached personality disorders from a darwinian perspective. This model offers an appealing framework to deal with the concept of personality disorder, a stimulus to reflection on suicide as a phenomenon, and a way to tackle clinical, ethical and legal issues raised by these patients.

In 1983, Fodor proposed the hypothesis that adaptation of man to his environment takes place by selecting neural modules responsible for behavior strategies which aim at solving specific evolutionary problems. Some of them are organized as innate premotor patterns, incorporating genetic information and experience-derived information.

McGuire and Troisi proposed the concept of *stable evolutionary strategy* in 1998, referring to behaviors which do not seem amenable to change by the subject's learning in his immediate circumstance. A stable evolutionary strategy is adaptive when it achieves its *biological goals*, even though emotions are not "comfortable". Darwinian psychiatry holds that anxiety disorders are strategies conserved because of their adaptive significance (Marks and Nesse, 1994).

At the present time, American conceptualization prevails. It considers personality disorders as diagnostic entities conformed by a set of stable perceptions, emotions and behaviors causing significant malaise and biographic problems (APA 2000). Critics argue that these entities have been grouped using different models (from schizotypal of medical-psychiatric nosology to histrionic personality according to psychoanalysis). Consensus clinical criteria do not explain etiology or pathophysiology. Thus, we think it might be useful to consider personality disorders as stable evolutionary strategies serving adaptation. An evolutionary framework and our knowledge on etiology can be used to approach suicide.

2.13.3. SURVIVAL STRATEGIES, AGGRESION AND
SUICIDE IN PERSONALITY DISORDERS

From a zoologist's point of view, the survival system of human beings comprises both strategies for acquiring food and shelter and for competing with fellow beings for the enjoyment of resources (food, mating or territory). This scientist would make this question: Why have been conserved personality disorders, conceived as stable evolutionary strategies, given their dysfunctional character?

McGuire et al. (1997) would answer that *heterosis* (the adaptive use of abnormal traits) can be an advantageous method of adaptation under certain circumstances. For instance, schyzotypal individuals are overrepresented in homeless population (Mc Glasham, 1986). This condition organizes their survival avoiding competition and confers them advantage in an isolated niche (Millon and Davis, 1996). We would dare to add: as long as these deviant traits are not so strong as to suppress the possibility of reproduction.

The rapid changes our species has experienced have rendered maladaptive several useful evolutionary strategies in our present environment. Particularly, aggression has intensively been studied by ethologists as part of survival strategies. Although fighting rituals ensure fair distribution of resources among animals while preventing the elimination of the individual, in advanced human societies, where survival is guaranteed, aggressive behavior turns into a negative value for species conservation (López-Ibor et al.., 1982).

Schneider's heartless psychopathic and explosive personality subtypes (Schneider, 1980) are most prone to pathological aggression, and they correspond to antisocial personality disorder and emotionally unstable personality disorder, impulsive type or borderline personality disorder (Huertas, 2005). It is known that antisocial and borderline personality disorders have higher mortality rates because of risk-taking and suicidal behaviors (Martin, 1985, Paris, 2003). However, "minor" or sub-threshold types of these disorders achieve certain advantages. People with antisocial traits accumulate resources (Martin, 1985), and among women with borderline features predominate those who guarantee their survival as years go by (Paris, 2003).

It is difficult to determine the number of instincts present in human beings. However, instinctive life seems to center around two: conservation of the individual and conservation of the species. Biological egoism and altruism, respectively. Or, according to Dawkins' (1994) formulation: individual's egoism versus gene's egoism. Conservation instinct drives survival of man by defending his own unity and the one of the world surrounding him, species survival leads to aggression and defense instinct.

The big issue around suicide is elucidating whether all instincts center on individual's or species' conservation. Studies on human aggression show that self-destructive behaviors are widespread. If we consider suicide as a stable behavior strategy (even though abnormal) serving species' survival, we will be able to understand some "reckless" behaviors that have allowed human beings to expand within their ecosystem –the Earth – and its surroundings.

The DSM-IV-TR criteria of BPD (*APA 2000*) include a list of symptoms. We can appreciate that along unstable and intense interpersonal relationships, impulsivity, affective instability, anger, identity disturbance, feelings of emptiness, fear of abandonment and episodes of loosing reality testing, suicidal behaviors are inherent to this diagnosis.

If we regard personality disorders not as disease, but as stable evolutionary strategies, chronic suicidality of BPD represents a behavioral pattern that, although deviant from the norm, serves species' survival and paradoxically, individual's survival in those ecological niches in which this behavior carries advantages.

This leads us to the main clinical issues: which degrees of responsibility do BPD patients have on their own suicidal behavior? Do they have the same autonomy as every other citizen? Are we bound to respect their decisions? (*Charland, 2004*). This is the starting point for the following presentation: clinical ethical and legal aspects of involuntary hospitalization of a BPD patient in a long stay facility because of chronic suicidality.

2.13.4. CASE REPORT

A 33 year-old woman spends 3 years hospitalized in a Long Stay Unit because of chronic suicidality. She has suffered from mental disorders since childhood. Since age 18 she has received several different psychiatric and psychological therapies, mainly under the diagnostic label of "neurotic depression".

Antecedents and Biography

Pregnancy and delivery were uneventful. Since infancy, she has displayed tantrums. She started attending school at four, finding difficulties in socialization. Thus, she showed herself withdrawn and with adaptability problems. Quiet and introverted, she performed poorly. However, she completed college at 21. She changed of school serveral times due to adaptability difficulties.

She said that she was sexually abused by her father in the puberty. At the age of 18 she engaged in a homosexual relationship. During some time she worked while studying. She was socially and financially independent.

After breakuping up her partner, the failure of an examination, the loss of her job and multiple family disputes, she slashed her wrist, which was followed by her first admission. A diagnosis of major depression was established, and treated accordingly. After discharge she was followed-up at a Mental Health Center, with six admissions in the Short Stay Unit of public Mental Health Services and two further admissions in private hospitals.

At last she was admitted in an Intermediate Stay Unit eight months later. While hospitalized she progressed poorly. Several approaches were tried, but she attempted suicide six times (two slashing her wrists, three taking pills and one throwing herself in front of a car), some of them while on temporary leave. Her family reported that she concealed medication with the intention of attempting suicide.

After 14 months of her stay in hospital, she was proposed for Long Stay Unit inpatient management.

Hospitalization

First Part of Hospital Admission

Clinical course was poor. Attempts to build up coping strategies for responding to frustrating situations, keeping within limits or wait, were unsuccessful. These quandaries prompted many suicide attempts (6 during the first year). Most of them were superficial cuts in the wrists, after which she asked for help. Attending physicians felt that in most of these behaviors she tried to draw attention. Only a minority were related to anxious depressive signs with chronic feelings of emptiness, but she achieved secondary gain (attention and care to avoid suicide) which reinforced such conducts.

Early in her stay she wavered among attitudes of self-pity, opposition and passive-aggressive. Apathy, thoughts of death and suicide were the focus of her reasoning. She gradually withdrew from other patients and won autonomy and preferential treatment by the attending staff (she could even use one of the hospital computers). She mixed more with the therapeutic staff. She established a relationship with her psychologist (a female) in which infatuation was evident. Therapeutic limits were experienced as abandonment.

During this time, family management became complicated. On the one hand, the therapeutic team attempted that the patient spent increasingly more time out of the unit, with longer leave permissions, and making the patient responsible for her behaviors, thus trying that she found coping strategies other than inhibition and suicidal gestures. On the other hand, the family threatened lawsuit against the team in case she would commit suicide. While the relationship with her psychologist hampered therapy, and the psychiatrist felt under increasing pressure of being sued for her hypothetical suicide, more responsibility to the patient was demanded. One relative claimed that science had tried everything and put down the failure to a divine punishment because of her homosexuality. Permissions were limited by the team, and after more than one and a half year, a change of therapeutic team was proposed, attempting to break the deadlock.

Change of Therapeutic Team

The new team gathered and planned an intensive rehabilitation program. If externalization was to succeed, three aspects needed clarification and decision making. First, the *splitting* in communication among staff. Second, leave policy in case of future suicidal behaviors (establishing the roles of the team, the patient and the family – and their persistent threats of suing the team). And third, the main diagnosis, the risk/benefit ratio of maintaining inpatient therapy – which at the time was involuntary – and the ethical and legal aspects of the prospect of possible suicide and its interference on the therapeutic indication.

Regarding splitting, the therapeutic team consisted of a psychiatrist, a psychologist, a female tutor, a clinical assistant, a nurse and a social worker. Every member would routinely be informed of decisions and contingencies, to stop manipulation and disruptions of the therapeutic team as the patient tried to distinguish between "good" (those listening and giving) and "evil" (those setting limits) members. Therapeutic failure through distorted communication and rivalries were to be avoided. These frame tried to prevent the reproduction in the team of the very disease they were treating.

As to leave policy, the team had the goal of increasing demands and making the patient responsible for her behaviors. Leaves were progressively extended, encouraging out-of-hospital activities suited to her autonomy level. It was proposed to maintain leaves despite suicidal gestures, since this was a coping-style perpetuating hospitalization.

The family was gathered and explained that many different therapeutic approaches had failed because of fear of suicide experienced both by the family and the staff. It was stated that if an improvement was to be achieved, the risk of suicide had to be taken. In the team's view the age and autonomy level of the patient warranted the attempt. The alternative was unlimited hospitalization to prevent suicide, not to carry out any other therapeutic goal. It was made clear that suicide could, however, be attempted outside or in the hospital.

Finally, the main diagnosis was revised, working with the diagnosis of borderline personality disorder.

At first, the course as a whole was satisfactory. Leaves were re-established, and the patient participated in lectures far away from the hospital. She felt motivated, excited and began mixing with other patients. Anxiety and depression improved. She went on vacation on her own for one week. Lastly, she started a close relationship with another female patient.

After this first "honeymoon", the patient was attended in the Emergency Room of another hospital because of a manipulative suicidal attempt while on a weekend permission. Difficulties with family management resurfaced, and through the relation of family members with different members of the team, the split between "good ones" and "evil ones" started once again, spoiling interdisciplinary work.

Ethics Committee was consulted in order to assess whether chronic suicidality belongs to the autonomy sphere of the patient. Although it was formally assumed work had to be done along this line, the committee were asked several questions:

Can chronic suicidality be grounds for unlimited hospitalization in a Long Stay Unit in this case? In addition, in other cases? If it cannot, are we empowered to deny future admission with this profile?

If improvement continues with progressive externalization, can we take the risk of suicide versus limiting leaves and foreseeable return to unlimited hospitalization with the aim of avoiding suicide in the hospital?

Is it ethical to maintain a situation we consider iatrogenic because of family pressure and threats of a lawsuit in case of suicide while on leave?

Therapeutical Attidudes and Management Decisions

Ethical Attitude: Autonomy versus Paternalism

Probably, the most significant ethical controversy stems from the clinical conceptualization: whether BPD is better understood as a mood disorder or a personality disorder. Even the most widespread diagnostic guidelines mention this possibility: "The fact that BPD shares features with mood disorders – apparent in family history, follow-up and pharmacological research – suggests that it could be a chronic form of mood disorder" (Frances et al., 1997)

In fact, we were dealing with a 43-year-old patient who had been living autonomously despite behavior disorders due to her personality, which were diagnosed as severe depression at a precise moment. Once it became clear that the main diagnosis was emotionally unstable personality disorder (borderline type) – ICD 10 (F60.31) – one could conclude that this patient was autonomous in deciding her preferred lifestyle. In fact, it seemed that the patient expressed her desire to come back home.

After reviewing the case, the therapeutic team considered that the process of progressive externalization of the patient should continue. The choice between leaving and not leaving belonged to the personal sphere. It could be considered ethical or non-ethical, but it was the autonomous subject's decision. The alternative therapeutic measure, imprisonment, was considered iatrogenic; in fact, it was proved that the patient persisted in suicidal behavior in restricted environments, and that, during the already initiated externalization process, positive changes had taken place.

Taken together, the data allow drawing the conclusion that, in this particular case, the possibility of future suicide should not interfere in therapeutic decision-making. Hence, suicide possibility should not restrict the possibility of recovery. If it did, treatment would be conditioned by suicide.

Clinical Attitude: Incorporating Patient's Autonomy

It was explicitly decided to involve the patient in the therapeutic process by signing a therapeutic contract. The measures to be taken to face different possible behaviors on the part of the patient, specifically mentioning the risk of suicide attempts, were written down. In this sense, a change from involuntary to voluntary hospitalization was promoted. The patient was asked to sign an informed consent of this change of status, with the purpose of showing it to her family, the main opposition to the externalization process.

Therapeutic alternatives to accompany the externalization process were analyzed. The need of intensive and long-term support was anticipated, and it was considered that this support had to be guaranteed within the means at our disposal. Along with the externalization process, the participation of a community Mental Health Clinic and a Psychosocial Rehabilitation Center were enlisted.

Legal Attitude: Institutional Involvement and Lawsuit Prevention

Apart from the Ethics Committee analysis of the case, the management of the hospital had a meeting with the family. They showed their determination to sue the family for threats and pressure on the staff to hinder discharge. Such attitude was notified in writing.

Attitude on Team Management: Ecosystem

Several authors have proposed psychodynamic psychotherapeutic approaches within an evolutionary frame (Gilbert and Bayley, 2000). We prefer the point of view of McGuire and Troisi (1998), who consider evolutionary psychotherapy more as a frame than a technique. Psychoanalysis has emphasized transference, frame of bond and styles of attachment. It can make great contributions to management of reciprocity among fellow human beings. Interaction strategies with fellow beings have decisively influenced human evolution (at this time, they are far more important than physical environmental pressure).

Symbolically, our therapeutic team has become an alter-family, experiencing the separation-individuation process of a borderline personality disorder. The biological family have put their confidence on this alter-family (and welfare network) to avoid suicide. Flexibility of the team becomes tested; progressive increase in patient's autonomy and externalization demand gradual withdrawal of support, active adaptation and tolerance to autonomy and frustration in face of the risk of failure. For this process to occur, the team has to anticipate the *splitting* phenomenon, in which the members of the therapeutic team project on the patients all non-healthy parts of themselves. Transmission of professional rivalries or work stress to the patient (or being vehicles of her projective identifications) is to be avoided.

Discussion

Regarding relative risk of suicide, after reviewing 170 publications and 15 years or longer follow-ups, *Paris (2002)* states that one in ten BPD patients commits suicide, a rate akin to that showed by schizophrenia or major mood disorders. He considers its prevention a difficult task. Suicide not always happens during treatment, and in outpatient therapy, chronic suicidal behavior can best be seen as a way of communicating distress.

This author considers that psychiatric hospitalization has not established efficacy in suicide prevention and may have deleterious effects. He explicitly states that fear of threats to litigation should not be the reason for psychiatric hospital admission and that suicide risk does not contraindicate management in day hospital.

Psychological autopsies have revealed that less than a third of patients were on therapy as they committed suicide, less than half had seen their therapist in the last year and one third had never been assessed (*Lesage, 1994*). Only a minority of BPD completed suicides were on therapy (*Paris, 1987*).

Published research has not established that clinical interventions are effective in suicide prevention. Prediction algorithms have so many false positive results that are useless in care (*Maris et al., 2000*). So, reasons for hospitalization are restricted to those showed onTable 23.

Table 23. Reasons for Hospital admission in BPD (Paris, 2002c)

- Psychotic episodes
- Severe suicide attempts
- Threats of suicide
- Self-injury behaviors
- A first admission is followed by a second one

The clinician caring a patient with chronic suicidality has to estimate acute risk. However, if a patient frequently expresses suicidal thoughts and repeatedly threatens to commit suicide, when exactly should the clinician worry? There is no clear distinction between acute and chronic suicidality. Clinical judgment depends at the same extent on clinician's anxieties and on objective risk.

William (1998) reports the clarifying statement of a patient: "The most important thing is, do not hospitalize a person with borderline personality disorder for any more than 48 hours. My self-destructive episodes—one leading right into another—came out only after my first and subsequent hospital admissions, after I learned the system was usually obligated to respond. Nothing that had happened to me before being admitted to a psychiatric unit for the first time could even approach the severity of the episodes that followed" and "What I did after I entered the system was to survive using maladaptive tools as a result of knowledge I acquired in the hospital. The least amount of ill-placed reinforcement kept me going. It prevented me from having to make a choice to get well or even finding out that I wasn´t as helpless as I believed myself to be".

**Table 24. Advantages and drawbacks of
hospitalization in chronic suicidality (Paris, 2002c)**

Advantage: Increased surveillance
Drawbacks:
- Preventive procedures in acute suicidality are counterproductive in chronic suicidality
- Escalating mechanisms
    - If social support is scarce, suicidal gestures draw more attention.
    - If there is suicide risk, the patient draws more attention from nurses.

Finally, *Gunderson (2001)* has provided us with a reasonable sequence of resource utilization whenever a treatment is available.

Regarding prevention of litigation, we should bear in mind that anyone can sue another for almost any reason, that a lawsuit can be fully warranted or caused by definitely psychotic reasons, and that, the variability of appreciation in the legal world, feeling innocent does not imply that one will be found not guilty.

50% of psychiatrists and 20% of psychologists have experienced the completed suicide of a patient (Chemtob, 1988). In the United States, 20% of lawsuits against mental health professionals are due to suicide Kelley (1996). Twenty percent of such lawsuits end with a decision against the practitioner. These malpractice litigations, even when they end in acquittal, are a source of enormous stress (docks penalty).

In any case, legal reasoning needs to answer two questions: was the accident foreseeable? Was it avoidable? (See Table 25)

Table 25. Components of professional liability (Gutheil & Appelbaum, 2000)

- Existence of a duty of care
- Deviation from "lex artis"
- Existence of objective damage
- Causal link between deviation from "lex artis" and damage.
- Was the accident foreseeable?
- Was it avoidable?

Conclusion

Through this case presentation we have tried to show how ethics articulates with legal and clinical psychiatry. Evolutionary perspective is a privileged point of view to reflect on the health-disease distinction and the problems of individual's autonomy. A question underlies this difficult case: When there is a borderline personality disorder, is unlimited hospitalization in a Long-Stay Unit because of chronic suicidality warranted?

The autonomy based approach to our patient is a turning point in therapeutic intervention by the Long-Stay therapeutic team, after years of different therapies. Thus, the subject changes from a passive position (paternalism, principle of beneficence) to an active position, in which she is listened to.

In this case, autonomy centers in the issues of informed consent, of involuntary admission and of the acceptance or rejection of treatments and therapies by the family, without listening to the patient. The main conclusion we drew is the breakdown of "incapacity presumption". In this way there follows a subsequent change from an involuntary to voluntary hospitalization and the introduction of a therapeutic contract under which the patient becomes involved in her treatment.

Suicidal behavior is considered within patient's autonomy sphere, regardless of the consideration of an ethical or non-ethical behavior. So a different therapeutic approach (externalization) becomes possible. Such an approach was hindered as long as the boundary between disease and being mentally healthy was based upon social dysfunction of her behaviors (suicidal attempts), leading to unlimited and involuntary Long-Stay Unit hospitalization with the custodial goal of avoiding suicide.

Maybe the Gordian knot underlying this case, and our clinical practice as well, is reconciling our personal values with those of the subject and with those of the society we are living in. We should not forget that the main purpose of psychotherapy is increasing patient's *autonomy*, integration and adaptation based on self-knowledge (Holmes, 2001). Success would be that the patient develops a personal system of values, and behaves accordingly (Drane, 1986).

Our team, and certainly the staff previously involved in the case, suffered multiple ups and downs. Our patient can be viewed as the surfacing of difficulties of working with severely ill patients in the ecosystem of a Long-Stay Unit. The countertransference such a deeply damaged patient triggers in the therapeutic team reveals personal styles of "attachment" to the patient in the staff. The team has to manage the reactions of its members to failure of our work (often unavoidable given our position in the mental health network), professional self-esteem, and hostility towards the patient, avoidance of care, inadequate containment measures or excessive involvement.

As Guimon (2002) puts it, wherever tension in the therapeutic team increases, its members feel the pressing need giving the impression of perfect understanding between them, looking as an ideal family in which patients could believe. This need of showing themselves as a happy family pushes them to firmly pursue an egalitarian and anti-authoritarian ideal, in which every member of the team is an equal, denying obvious differences in professional qualification and personality. It is not rare that such pseudo-egalitarianism be spread to the patients, which are considered able to assume their responsibilities, even though in practice, and covertly, the team behaves as if they were not. A "pseudotherapeutic community", as Sacks and Carpenter (1974) say, arises, close to Winnicott's concept of "false self".

Building therapeutic teams in such units of severely affected patients is a long-term endeavour, with high personal cost for their members. Institutions should bear this in mind. The key for a change process to succeed in the patient is an ability to contain and elaborate the different moments gone through by the therapeutic process. They have to be integrated in the personality of this "proxy family of the patient".

Finally, regarding litigations in the case of suicide, we want to emphasize that, besides the suicide itself, there are several elements important to establish professional liability in such cases:

- Gross clinical misjudgments
- Grave errors in clinical judgment
- Failure to assess patients carefully
- Absence of adequate records
- Absence of a management plan

REFERENCES

Abramowitz, E.S., Baker, A.H., Fleischer, S.F. (1982). Onset of depressive psychiatric crises and the menstrual cycle. *American Journal of Psychiatry*, 139(4), 475-8.

Abrams, R.C & Horowitz, S.V. (1996). Personality disorders after age 50: a meta-analysis. *Journal of Personality Disorders*, 10, 271-82.

Adam, K.S. (1990). Environmental, psychosocial and psychoanalitic aspects of suicidal behavior. In: *Suicide over the life cicle*, ed. S.J. Blumenthal, & D.J. Kupfer. Washington: American Psychiatric Press.

Addington, D.E., Addington, J.M. (1992). Attempted suicide and depression in schizophrenia. *Acta Psychiatrica Scandinavica*, 85(4), 288-91.

Agerbo, E., Nordentoft, M., Mortensen, P.B. (2002). Familial, psychiatric, and socioeconomic risk factors for suicide in young people: nested case-control study. *British Medical Journal*, 325, 74.

Agren, H. (1983). Life at risk: markers of suicidality in depression. *Psychiatric Development*, 1, 87-104.

Agronin, M.E. (1994). Personality disorders in the elderly: an overwiew. *Journal of Geriatric Psychiatry*, 27, 151-91.

Agronin, M.E., Maletta, G. (1999). Personality disorders in late life. *Am J Geriatr Psychiatry* 2000;8:4-18; Appleby L, Cooper J, Amos T et al. Psychological autopsy study of suicides by people aged under 35. *British Journal of Psychiatry*, 75, 168-174.

Ahearn, E.P., Jamison, K.R., Steffens, D.C., et al. (2001). MRI correlates of suicide attempt history in unipolar depression. *Biological Psychiatry,* 50(4), 266-70.

Ahrens, B., Haug, H.J. (1996). Suicidality in hospitalized patients with a primary diagnosis of personality disorder. *Crisis*, 17(2), 59-63.

Ahrens, B., Linden, M., Zaske, H., et al. (2000). Suicidal behavior--symptom or disorder? *Comprehensive Psychiatry*, 41(2 Suppl 1), 116-21.

Aidjacic-Gross, et al. (2003). Are seasonalities in suicide dependent on suicide methods? A reappraisal. *Social Science and Medicine*, 57, 1173-81.

Akhart, S. (1989). Narcissistic personality disorder: descriptive features and differential diagnosis. *Psychiatric Clinics of North America*, 12, 505-30.

Akhart, S. (1990). Paranoid personality disorder: a synthesis of developmental, dynamic, and descriptive features. *American Journal of Psychotherapy*, 44(1), 5-25.

Akiskal, H.B. (1981). Subaffective disorders : Dysthymic, cyclothymic and bipolar II disorders in the "borderline" realm. *Psychiatric Clinics of North America*, 4, 25-6.

Akiskal, H.S., Akiskal, K. (2005). Epiloque. The renaissance of the ancident concept of temperament (with a focus on affective temperaments). In: *Personality disorders.* Chichester, M. Maj, H.S. Akiskal, J.E. Mezzich,, A. Okasha, pp. 479-500. Wiley.

Akiskal, H.S., Bourgeois, M.L., Angst, J., et al. (2000). Re-evaluating the prevalence of and diagnostic composition within the broad clinical spectrum of bipolar disorders. *Journal of Affective Disorders,* 59(Suppl.1), S5-S30

Akiskal, H.S., Chen, S.E., Davis, G.C., et al. (1985). Borderline: an adjective in search of a noun. *Journal of Clinical Psychiatry*, 46, 41-8.

Alexander, G.M., Peterson, B.S. (2001). Sex steroids and human behavior: implications for developmental psychopathology. *CNS Spectrums*, 6(1), 75-88.

Allebeck, P., Allgulander, C., Fisher, LD. (1988). Predictors of completed suicide in a cohort of 50,465 young men: role of personality and deviant behaviour. *British Medical Journal,* 297(6642), 176-8.

Allebeck, P. & Allgulander, C. (1990a). Psychiatric diagnoses as predictors of suicide: a comparision of diagnoses at conscription and in psychiatric care in a cohort of 50465 young men. *British Journal of Psychiatry*, 157, 339-44.

Allebeck, P., Allgulander, C. (1990b). Suicide among young men: psychiatric illness, deviant behaviour and substance abuse. *Acta Psychiatrica Scandinavica*, 81(6), 565-70.

Allebeck, P., Allgulander, C., Henningsohn, L. et al. (1991). Causes of death in a cohort of 50465 young men: validity of recorded suicide as underlying cause of death. *Scandinavian Journal of Soccial Medicine*, 19(4), 242-7.

Allebeck,, P., Varla, A., Kristjansson, E., et al. (1987). Risk factors for suicide among patients with schizophrenia. *Acta Psychiatrica Scandinavica*, 76(4), 414-9.

Allgulander, C. (1994) Suicide and mortality patterns in anxiety neurosis and depressive neurosis. *Archives of General Psychiatry*, 51(9), 708-12.

Allgulander, C., Fisher, L.D. (1990). Clinical predictors of completed suicide and repeated self-poisoning in 8895 self-poisoning patients. *European Archives of Psychiatry Neurology Sciences*, 239(4), 270-6.

Allport, G.W. (1937). *Personality: a psychological interpretation.* New York: H. Holt and Company

Allport, G.W. (1961). *Pattern and growth in personality.* New York: Holt, Rinerhart and Winston

Amador, X.F., Friedman, J.H., Kasapis, C., et al. (1996). Suicidal behavior in schizophrenia and its relationship to awareness of illness. *American Journal of Psychiatry*, 153(9), 1185-8.

American Foundation for Suicide Prevention. (1998). *Fact about suicide.*

American Psychiatric Association (1980). *Diagnostic and statistical manual of mental disorders,* 3rd edn. (DSM-III) Washington, DC: American Psychiatric Association.

American Psychiatric Association (1987). *Diagnostic and Statistical manual of mental disorders*, 3rd edn, revised, (DSM-III-R). Washington, DC: American Psychiatric Association.

American Psychiatric Association. (1994) *Diagnostic and Statistical manual of mental disorders,* 4th edn, (DSM-IV). Washington, DC: American Psychiatric Association.

American Psychiatric Association. (1995). *Diagnostic and Statistical manual of mental disorders,* 4th edn, (DSM-IV). DSM-IV breviario. Criterios diagnósticos. Barcelona: Masson

American Psychiatric Association. (2000). *Diagnostic and statistical manual of mental disorders,* 4th edn, (DSM-IV). Washington, DC: American Psychiatric Association.

American Psychiatric Association. (2002) *Diagnostic and Statistical manual of mental disorders*, 4th edn, revised, (DSM-IVTR). Washington, DC: American Psychiatric Association.

American Psychiatric Association. (2003). Practice guideline for the assessment and treatment of patients with suicidal behaviors. Arlington (VA): American Psychiatric Association. Available online at: *http://www.psych.org/psych_pract/treatg/pg/ SuicidalBehavior_05-15-06.pdf*

Angst, J., Angst, F., Stassen, H.H. (1999). Suicide risk in patients with major depressive disorder. *Journal of Clinical Psychiatry*, 60 Suppl 2, 57-62.

Angst, J. & Clayton, P. (1986). Premorbid personality of depressive, bipolar, and schizophrenic patients with special reference to suicidal issues. *Comprehensive Psychiatry*, 27, 511-32.

Angst, J., Clayton, P.J. (1998). Personality, smoking and suicide: a prospective study. *Journal of Affective Disorders*, 51(1), 55-62.

Angst, J., Preisig, M. (1995). Outcome of a clinical cohort of unipolar, bipolar and schizoaffective patients. Results of a prospective study from 1959 to 1985. *Schweiz Archives of Neurologic Psychiatry*, 146(1), 17-23.

Anguelova, M., Benkelfat, C., Turecki, G. (2003). A systematic review of association studies investigating genes coding for serotonin receptors and the serotonin transporter: I. Affective disorders. *Molecular Psychiatry*, 8, 574–91.

Antikainen, R., Hintikka, J., Lehtona, J., et al. (1995). A prospective three-year follow-up study of borderline personality disorder inpatients. *Acta Psychiatrica Scandinavica*, 92, 327-35.

Apter, A., Bleich, A., King, R.A., et al. (1993). Death without warning? A clinical postmortem study of suicide in 43 Israeli adolescent males. *Archives General Psychiatry*, 50, 138-42.

Apter, A., Kotler, M., Sevy, S., et al. (1991). Correlates of risk of suicide in violent and nonviolent psychiatric patients. *American Journal of Psychiatry*,148, 883-7.

Apter, A., Plutchik, R., Sevy, S., et al. (1989). Defense mechanisms in risk of suicide and risk of violence. *American Journal of Psychiatry*, 146, 1027-31.

Arranz-Marti, B., Ros-Montalbán, S., San-Molina, L. (2004). Impulsividad, agresividad y suicidio. In: *Impulsividad*, ed. S. Ros-Montalbán, M.D. Peris-Díaz & R. Gracia-Marco, pp. 195-210. Barcelona: Psiquiatría Editores, S.L.

Arsenault-Lapierre G, Kim C, Turecki G. (2004). Psychiatric diagnoses in 3275 suicides: a meta-analysis. *BMC Psychiatry*, 4, 37.

Asberg, M., Thoren, P., Traskman, L., et al. (1976). "Serotonin depression"--a biochemical subgroup within the affective disorders? *Science*, 191(4226), 478-80.

Asberg M, Traskman L, Thoren P. (1976). 5-HIAA in the cerebrospinal fluid. A biochemical suicide predictor? *Archives General Psychiatry*, 33(10), 1193-7.

Astruc, B., Torres, S., Jollant, F., et al. (2004). The influence of past major depressive disorder on the intent to die in suicide attempters. *Journal of Clinical Psychiatry*, 65(5), 690-5.

Ateneo. (2004). *El Pensamiento. Tipos de pensamiento. Origen del pensamiento. El pensamiento y el cuerpo.* Conferencia impartida en el "Ateneo de Psiquiatría" del Área de Psiquiatría y Psicología Médica. Granada: Facultad de Medicina de Granada.

Axelsson, R., Lagerkvist-Briggs, M. (1992). Factors predicting suicide in psychotic patients. Eur *Archives of Psychiatry Clinical Neuroscience*, 241(5), 259-66.

Audenaert, K., Peremans, K., Goethals, I., et al. (2005). Functional imaging of the suicidal brain. *Nuclear Medicine Communications*, 26(5), 391-3.

Austin, E.J., Deary I.J. (2000). The "four As": a common framework for normal and abnormal personality? *Personality Individual Diferences*, 28, 977-95.

Ayuso Gutierrez, J.L. (1999). Recidiva esquizofrenica: causas y prevencion. In: *Esquizofrenia. Enfermedad del cerebro y reto social, ed.* J. Saiz, pp. 149-157. Barcelona: Masson.

Baca Baldomero, E., Roca Bennasar, M. (2004) Personalidad y trastorno de la personalidad: historia y evolución de los conceptos. In: *Trastornos de Personalidad*, pp. 3-32. Barcelona: ArsXXI.

Baca-García, E. Diaz-Sastre, C., Saiz-Ruiz J, et al. (2002). How safe are psychiatric medications after a voluntary overdose? *European Psychiatry*, 17,466-70.

Baca-Garcia, E., Diaz-Sastre, C., Basurte, E., et al. (2001). A prospective study of the paradoxical relationship between impulsivity and lethality of suicide attempts. *Journal of Clinical Psychiatry*, 62 (7), 560-4.

Baca-Garcia, E., Diaz-Sastre, C., Ceverino, A., et al.(2003). Association between the menses and suicide attempts: A replication study. *Psychosomatic Medicine*, 65(2), 237-44.

Baca-García, E., Vaquero, C., Diaz-Sastre C., et al. (2002). A gender-specific association between the serotonin transporter gene and suicide attempts. *Neuropsychopharmacology*, 26 (5), 692-5.

Baca-Garcia, E., Perez-Rodriguez, M.M., Diaz Sastre, C., et al. (2005). Suicidal behavior in schizophrenia and depression: a comparison. *Schizophrenia Research*, 75(1), 77-81.

Baca-Garcia, E., Vaquero, C., Diaz-Sastre, C., et al. (2003). A pilot study on a gene-hormone interaction in female suicide attempts. *European Archives Psychiatry Clinic Neuroscience*, 253(6), 281-5.

Ballenger, J.C., Davidson, J.R.T., Lecrubier, Y., et al. (1998). Consensus statement on social anxiety disorder from the Internacional Consensus Group on Depresion and Anxiety. *Journal of Clinical Psychiatry*, 59 (17 Suppl), 54-60.

Balon R. (1987). Suicide: can we predict it? *Comprehensive Psychiatry*, 28(3), 236-41

Bancroft, J.H., Skrimshire, A.M., Simkin, S. (1976). The reasons people give for taking overdoses. *British Journal of Psychiatry*, 128, 538-48.

Barber, M.E., Marzuk, P.M., Leon, A.C., et al. (1998). Aborted suicide attempts: a new classification of suicidal behavior. *American Journal of Psychiatry*, 155(3), 385-9

Barner-Rasmussen, P. (1986). Suicide in psychiatric patients in Denmark. *Acta Psychiatrica Scandinavica*, 73(4), 449-55.

Barraclough, B., Bunch, J., Nelson, B., et al. (1974). A hundred cases of suicide: clinical aspects. *British Journal of Psychiatry*, 125, 355-73.

Barrat, E.S. (1994). Impulsiveness and aggression. In: *Violence and mental disorder*, ed. J. Monahan & H.J. Steadman, pp. 285-302. Development in risk assesssmnet. Chicago: The university of Chicago Press.

Barrat, E.S., Stanford, M.S., Kent, T.A., et al. (1997). Neuropsychological and cognitive psychophisiological substrates of impulsive aggression. *Biological Psychiatry*, 41, 1045-61.

Battaglia, M., Togersen, S. (1996). Schizotipical disorder: At the crossroads of genetics and nosology. *Acta Psychiatrica Scandinavica*, 94, 303-10.

Bateson, G. (1992). Las categorías lógicas del aprendizaje y la comunicación. In: *Pasos hacia una ecología de la mente, pp. 309-336.* Buenos Aires: Planeta.

Baxter, D. & Appleby, L. Case register of suicide risk in mental disorders. (1999). *British Journal of Psychiatry*, 175, 322-6.

Baud, P. (2005). Personality traits as intermediary phenotypes in suicidal behavior: genetic issues. *American Journal of Medical Genetics,* 133(1), 34-42.

Bayon, C., Hill, K., Svrakic, D.M., et al. Dimensional assessment of personality in an outpatient sample: Relations of the systems of Millon and Cloninger. *Journal of Psychiatric Research*, 30, 341-52.

Beaumont, G., Hetzel, W. (1992). Patients at risk of suicide and overdose. *Psychopharmacology*, 106 Suppl, S123-S126.

Beautrais, A.L. (2004). Further suicidal behavior among medically serious suicide attempters. *Sucide & Life Threatening Behavior*, 34 (1), 1-11.

Beautrais, A.L., Joyce, P.R., Mulder, R.T., et al. (1996). Prevalence and comorbidity of mental disorders in persons making serious suicide attempts: a case-control study. *American Journal of Psychiatry*, 153, 1009-14.

Bearden, C.E. & Freimer, N.B. (2006). Endophenotypes for psychiatric disorders: ready for primetime? *Trends in Genetics*, 22(6), 306-13.

Beautrais, A.L., Joyce, P.R., Mulder, R.T. (1999). Personality traits and cognitive styles as risk factors for serious suicide attempts among young people. *Suicide & Life Threatening Behavior*, 29(1), 37-47

Bechara, A. (2003). Risky business: emotion, decision-making, and addiction. *Journal of Gambling Studies*, 19(1), 23-51.

Bechara, A., Damasio, H., Damasio, A.R., et al. (1999). Different contributions of the human amygdala and ventromedial prefrontal cortex to decision-making. *Journal of Neuroscience*, 19, 5473-81.

Bechara, A., Tranel, D., Damasio, H., et al. (1996). Failure to respond autonomically to anticipated future outcomes following damage to prefrontal cortex. *Cerebral Cortex*, 6(2), 215-25.

Beck, A.T. (1986). Hopelessness as a predictor of eventual suicide. *Annals of New York Academy of Science,* 487, 90-6.

Beck, A.T. (1996). Personality disorders (and their relationship to syndromal disorders). Cited by Pretzer JL & Beck AT. A cognitive theory of personality disorders. In: *Major theories of personality disorder*, ed. J.F. Clarkin & M.F. Lenzenweger, pp. 36-105. New York: Guildford Press

Beck, A.T., Beck, R., Kovacs, M. (1975). Classification of suicidal behaviors: I. Quantifying intent and medical lethality. *American Journal of Psychiatry*, 132 (3), 285-7.

Beck, A.T., Kovacs, M., Weissman, A (1979). Assessment of suicidal intentation: The Scale for Suicide Ideation. *Journal of Consulting Clinical Psychology*, 47(2), 343-52.

Beck, A.T., Resnik, H.L.P., Lettieri, D.J. (1974). *The Prediction of Suicide.* Charles Press Plublishers.

Beck, A.T., Steer, R.A., Kovacs, M., et al. (1985). Hopelessness and eventual suicide: a 10-year prospective study of patients hospitalized with suicidal ideation. *American Journal of Psychiatry*, 142(5), 559-63.

Bellivier, F., Chaste, P., Malafosse, A. (2004). Association between the TPH gene A218C polymorphism and suicidal behavior: A meta-analysis. *American Journal of Medical Genetics Part B-Neuropsychiatric Genetics*, 124B(1), 87-91.

Bellivier, F., Szoke, A., Henry, C., et al. (2000). Possible association between serotonin transporter gene polymorphism and violent suicidal behavior in mood disorders. *Biological Psychiatry*, 48(4), 319-22.

Benjamin, L.S. (1996). *Interpersonal Diagnosis and Treatment of Personality Disorders* (2nd ed.). New York: Guildford Press.

Benjaminsen, S., Krarup, G., Lauritsen, R. (1990). Personality, parental rearing behaviour and parental loss in attempted suicide: a comparative study. *Acta Psychiatrica Scandinavica*, 82(5), 389-97.

Berglund, M., Nilsson, K (1987). Mortality in severe depression. A prospective study including 103 suicides. *Acta Psychiatrica Scandinavica*, 76(4), 372-80.

Berglund, M., Ojehagen, A. (1998). The influence of alcohol drinking and alcohol use disorders on psychiatric disorders and suicidal behavior. *Alcohol Clinical Experimental Research*, 22(7 Suppl), 333S-345S.

Bertolote, J.M., Fleischmann, A. (2002). A global perspective in the epidemiology of suicide. *Suicidology*, 7(2), 6-8

Beskow J, Runeson B, Asgard U. (1990). Psychological autopsies: methods and ethics. *Suicide Life Threaten Behavior*, 20, 307-323.

Bilban, M., Skibin, L. (2005). Presence of alcohol in suicide victims. *Forensic Science International*, 147S: S9-S12.

Bille-Brahe, U., & Jessen, G. (1994). Suicide in Demark, 1922-1991: the choice of method. *Acta Psychiatrica Scandinavica*, 90, 91-6.

Birtchnell, J. (1981). Some familial and clinical characteristics of female suicidal psychiatric patients. *British Journal of Psychiatry*,138, 381-90

Black, D.W., Winokur, G., Nasrallah, A. (1987). Is death from natural causes still excessive in psychiatric patients? A follow-up of 1593 patients with major affective disorder. *Journal of Nervous Mental Disorders*, 175(11), 674-80.

Black, D.W., Winokur, G., Nasrallah, A. (1988). Effect of psychosis on suicide risk in 1,593 patients with unipolar and bipolar affective disorders. *American Journal of Psychiatry*, 145(7), 849-52.

Blacker, D., Endicott, J. (2000). Psychometric porperties: concepts of reliability and validity. In: *Handbook of Psychiatric Measures*, pp. 7-14. Washington DC: American Psychiatric Association.

Blasco-Fontecilla, H., Leira-Sanmartin, M., Baca-García E, et al. ¿Hay trastornos de la personalidad que protegen de la conducta suicida? IV Congreso Nacional de Trastornos de la Personalidad, 2002. *http//: www.seetp.com*

Blasco Fontecilla, H. (2006). *Suicidio y trastornos de personalidad*. Alcalá de Henares, Madrid (Spain): Alcalá de Henares University.

Blasco Fontecilla, H. (2007). Introducción conceptual: ¿Se pueden diferenciar el trastorno de personalidad antisocial y la psicopatía? *Monografías de psiquiatría*, 1, 3-13.

Blashfield, R.K., Breen, M.J. (1989). Face validity of the DSM-III-R personality disorders. *American Journal of Psychiatry*, 146(12), 1575-9.

Blaszczynski, A., Steel, M., McConaghy, N. (1997). Impulsivity in pathological gambling: The antisocial impulsivist. *Addiction*, 92, 75-87.

Blumenthal, S.J., Kupfer, D.J. (1986). Generalizable treatment strategies for suicidal behaviour. *Annals of the New York Academy of Sciences*, 487, 327-40.

Boardman, A.P. & Healy, D. (2001). Modelling suicide risk in affective disorders. *European Psychiatry*, 16, 400-5.

Bobes-Garcia, J., Saiz-Martinez, P.A., Gonzalez Garcia-Portilla, M.P., et al. (1997). Depresion y conducta suicida. In: *Depresion. Vision actual*, ed. J.L. Ayuso JL, J. Saiz J, pp. 79-95. Madrid: Aula Medica.

Boergers, J., Spirito, A., Donaldson, D. (1998). Reasons for adolescent suicide attempts: associations with psychological functioning. *Journal of American Academy of Child and Adolescent Psychiatry*, 37(12), 1287-93.

Bondy, B., Buettner, A., Zill, P. (2006). Genetics of suicide. *Molecular Psychiatry*, 11, 336-51.

Bonner, R.L. (1992). Isolation, seclusion and psychosocial vulnerbility as risk factors for suicide behavior. In: *Assessment and Prediction of Suicide*, ed. R.W. Marris, A.L. Berman, J.T. Maltsberger, R.I. Yufit. New York: Guilford Press.

Borg, S.E., Stahl, M. (1982). Prediction of suicide. A prospective study of suicides and controls among psychiatric patients. *Acta Psychiatrica Scandinavica*, 65(3), 221-32.

Bosnar, A., et al. (2004). Suicide rate after the 1991-1995 war in Southwestern Croatia. *Archives of Medical Research*, 35: 344-7.

Bostwick, J.M., Pankratz, V.S. (2000). Affective disorders and suicide risk: a reexamination. *American Journal Psychiatry*, 157(12), 1925-32.

Boudewyn, A.C., Liem, J.H. (1995). Childhood sexual abuse as a precursor to depression and self-destructive behavior in adulthood. *Journal of Trauma Stress*, 8(3), 445-59.

Bowlby, J. (1973). *Attachment and Loss*, Vol 2, Separation: anxiety and anger. Basic Books: New York.

Bowly, J. (1993). Attachment and Loss, II: Separation, Anger, and Loss, cited by Cloninger CR, Svrakic DM, Przybeck TR. A psychobiological model of temperament and character. *Archives of General Psychiatry,* 50(12), 975-90.

Bradvik, L., Berglund, M. (2001). Late mortality in severe depression. *Acta Psychiatrica Scandinavica*, 103(2), 111-6.

Braquehais, M.D. (2006). *El papel de la impulsividad y la agresividad en los intentos de suicidio*. Alcalá de Henares: Alcalá de Henares University.

Breault, K.D. Suicide in America: a test of Durkheim's theory of religious and family integration, 1933-1980. *AJS*, 92, 628-56.

Brent, D.A. (1987). Correlates of the medical lethality of suicide attempts in children and adolescents. *Journal of American Academy of Child Adolescent Psychiatry*, 26(1), 87-91.

Brent, D.A., Bridge, J., Johnson, B.A., et al. (1996). Suicidal behavior runs in families. A controlled family study of adolescent suicide victims. *Archives of General Psychiatry*, 53(12), 1145-52.

Brent, D.A., Mann, J.J. (2005). Family genetic studies, suicide, and suicidal behavior. *American Journal of Medical Genetics C Seminars of Medical Genetics*, 133(1), 13-24.

Brent, D.A., Oquendo, M., Birmaher, B., et al. (2003). Peripubertal suicide attempts in offspring of suicide attempters with siblings concordant for suicidal behavior. *American Journal of Psychiatry*, 160(8), 1486-93.

Brent, D.A., Perper, J.A., Goldstein, C.E., et al. (1988). Risk factors for adolescent suicide. A comparison of adolescent suicide victims with suicidal inpatients. *Archives of General Psychiatry*, 45(6), 581-8.

Brent, D.A., Perper, J., Moritz, G., et al. (1993). Suicide in adolescents with no apparent psychopatholgy. *Journal of American Academy of Child and Adolescent Psychiatry*, 32, 494-500.

Brieger, P., Ehrt, U., Bloeink, R., et al. (2002). Consequences of comorbid personality disorders in major depression. *Journal of Nervous Mental Disorder*, 190, 304-9.

Brodsky, B.S., Malone, K.M., Ellis, S.P., et al. (1997). Characteristics of borderline personality disorder associated with suicidal behavior. *American Journal of Psychiatry*, 154, 1715-19.

Brodsky, B.S., Oquendo, M., Ellis, S.P., et al. (2001). The relationship of childhood abuse to impulsivity and suicidal behavior in adults with major depression. *American Journal of Psychiatry*, 158, 1871-7.

Bronisch, T. (1996). The relationship between suicidality and depression. *Archives of Suicide Research*, 2, 235-54.

Bronish, T., Mombour, W. (1998). The modern assessment of personality disorders. Part 2: reliability and validity of personality disorders. *Psychopatology,* 31, 293-301.

Bronisch, T., Wittchen, H.U., Krieg, C., et al. (1985). Depressive neurosis. A long-term prospective and retrospective follow-up study of former inpatients. *Acta Psychiatrica Scandinavica*, 71(3), 237-48.

Brown, M., Barraclough, B. (1997). Epidemiology of suicide pacts in England and Wales, 1988-92. *British Medical Journal*, 315(7103), 286-7.

Brown, M., Barraclough, B. (1999). Partners in life and in death: the suicide pact in England and Wales 1988-1992. *Psychological Medicine*, 29(6), 1299-1306.

Brown, G.K., Beck, A.T., Steer, R.A., et al. (2000). Risk factors for suicide in psychiatric outpatients: a 20-year prospective study. *Journal of Consulting Clinical Psychology*, 68, 371-7.

Brown, G.L., Goodwin, F.K., Ballenger, J.C., et al. (1979). Aggression in humans correlates with cerebrospinal fluid amine metabolites. *Psychiatry Research*, 1(2), 131-9.

Brown, M., King, E., Barraclough, B. (1995). Nine suicide pacts. A clinical study of a consecutive series 1974-93. *British Journal of Psychiatry*, 167(4), 448-51.

Brown, L.K., Overholser, J., Spirito, A., et al. (1991). The correlates of planning in adolescent suicide attempts. *Journal of American Academy of Child and Adolescent Psychiatry*, 30(1), 95-9.

Brown, A.S., Susser, E.S., Lin, S.P., et al. (1995). Increased risk of affective disorders in males after second trimester prenatal exposure to the Dutch hunger winter of 1944-45. *British Journal of Psychiatry*, 166(5), 601-6.

Brunner, H.G., Nelen, M., Breakefield, X.O., et al. (1993). Abnormal behavior associated with a point mutation in the structural gene for monoamine oxidase A. *Science*, 262(5133): 578-80.

Brzustowicz, L.M., Hodgkinson, K.A., Chow, E.W., et al. (2000). Location of a major susceptibility locus for familial schizophrenia on chromosome 1q21-q22. *Science*, 288(5466), 678-82.

Buchholtz-Hansen, P.E., Wang, A.G., Kragh, S.P. (1993). Mortality in major affective disorder: relationship to subtype of depression. The Danish University Antidepressant Group. *Acta Psychiatrica Scandinavica*, 87(5), 329-35.

Buckley, N.A., Whyte, I.M., Dawson, A.H., et al. (1995). Correlations between prescriptions and drugs taken in self poisoning: implications for prescribers and drug regulation. *The Medical Journal of Australia*, 62, 194–7.

Bueno, G. (1991). *El reino de la Cultura y el reino de la Gracia, pp. 53-56.* Oviedo: El Basilisco, 2ª época.

Bueno, G. (1996). *El mito de la cultura – Ensayo de un filosofía materialista de la cultura.* Barcelona: Editorial Prensa Ibérica.

Bulik, C.M., Carpenter, L.L., Kupfer, D.J., et al. Features associated with suicide attempts in recurrent major depression. *Journal of Affective Disorder*, 18(1), 29-37.

Bullman, T.A., Kang, H.K., Thomas, T.L. (1991). Posttraumatic stress disorder among Vietnam veterans on the Agent Orange Registry. A case-control analysis. *Annals Epidemiology*, 1(6), 505-512.

Burton, R. (1998). *Anatomia de la melancolía.* Madrid: Asociación Española de Neuropsiquiatría. Historia.

Buss, A.H., Durkee, A. (1957). An inventory for assessing different kinds of hostility. *Journal of Consulting Psychology*, 21, 343-9.

Buss, A.H. & Plomin, R. (1975). A temperament theory of Personality development. New York: Wiley.

Buss, A. H. & Plomin, R. (1986). The EAS approach to temperament. In: *The study of temperament: Changes, continuities and challenges*, ed. R. Plomin, & J. Dunn, pp. 67-77. Hillsdale, NJ: Lawrence Erlbaum.

Butcher, J.N., Megargee, E.I. (1989). In: Hathaway, S.R., McKinley, J.C., editors. *Minnesota Multiple Personality Inventory-2^{TM}*. University of Minnesota Press.

Butterfield, M.I., Stechuchak, K.M., Connor, K.M., et al. (2005). Neuroactive steroids and suicidality in posttraumatic stress disorder. *American Journal of Psychiatry*, 162(2), 380-2.

Caldwell, C.B., Gottesman, I.I. (1990). Schizophrenics kill themselves too: a review of risk factors for suicide. *Schizophrenia Bulletin*, 16(4), 571-89.

Canetto, S.S. (1992). Gender and suicide in the elderly. *Suicide Life Threatening Behaviour*, 22, 80-97

Cantor, N., Genero, N. (1986). Psychiatric diagnosis and natural categorization: a close analogy. In: *Contemporary directions in psychopathology. Toward the DSM-IV,* ed. T. Millon, G.L. Klerman, pp. 233-256. New York: Guilford.

Carney, S.S., Rich, C.L., Burke, P.A., et al. (1994). Suicide over 60: The San Diego Study. *Journal of American Geriatric Society*, 42, 174-80

Casey, P.R. (1989). Personality disorder and suicide intent. *Acta Psychiatrica Scandinavica*, 79, 290-5.

Casey, P. (1998). Personality disorders. In: *Seminars in General Adult Psychiatry*, Vol 2, ed. G. Stein & G. Wilkinson, pp. 753-814. London: Gaskell.

Caspi, A. (2000). The child is father of the man: personality continuities from childhood to adulthood. *Journal of Personality and Social Psychology,* 78(1), 158-72.

Caspi, A., McClay, J., Moffitt, T.E., et al. (2002). Role of genotype in the cycle of violence in maltreated children. *Science,* 297 (5582), 851-4.

Caspi, A., Moffit, T.E. (2006). Gene-environment interactions in psychiatry: joining forces with neuroscience. *Natural Review of Neuroscience,* 7(7), 583-90.

Caspi, A., Sugden, K., Moffit, T.E., *et al.* (2003). Influence of life stress on depression: moderation by a polymorphism in the 5-HTT gene. *Science,* 301(5631), 386-9.

Casson, R.W. (1983). Schemata in Cognitive Anthropology. *Annual Review of Anthropology,* 12, 429-62.

Cates, D.S., Houston, B.K., Vavak, C.R., et al. (1993). Heritability of hostility-related emotions, attitudes, and behaviors. *Journal of Behavior Medicine,* 16(3), 237-56.

Cavanagh, J.T.O., Owens, D.G.C., Johnstone, E.C. (1999). Life events in suicide and undetermined death in southeast Scotland: A case-control study using the method of psychological autopsy. *Social Psychiatry Psychiatric Epidemiology,* 34, 645-50.

Centers for Disease Control's Web-based Injury Statistics Query and Reporting System (WISQARS) website and "Fatal Injury Reports" [homepage on the Internet] [cited 2006 Aug 9]. Available from: http://webappa.cdc.gov/sasweb/ncipc/mortrate10_sy.html. Accessed August 2006

Centers for disease control and prevention: deaths: final data for 1998 (CDC). (2000). National vital statistic reports, 48(11)

Ceverino, A. (2000). Aspectos medicolegales de la esquizofrenia. In: *Guia Terapeutica de las Esquizofrenias,* ed. A. Chinchilla Moreno, pp. 219-229. Barcelona: Masson.

Chance, S.E., Reviere, S.L., Rogers, J.H., et al. (1996). An empirical study of the psychodynamics of suicide: a preliminary report. *Depression,* 4(2), 89-91.

Chandrasena, R., Beddage, V., Fernando, M.L. (1991). Suicide among immigrant psychiatric patients in Canada. *British Journal of Psychiatry,* 159, 707-9.

Chanoit, P.F. (1985). Raices psicopatológicas de los actos suicidas. *Psicopatología,* 5(2), 115-20.

Charland, L.C. (2004). Character: Moral treatment and the personality disorders. in: Radden, J. *The Philosophy of Psychiatry.* New York: Oxford University Press.

Chastang, F., Rioux, P., Dupont, I., et al. (1998). Risk factors associated with suicide attempt in young French people. *Acta Psychiatrica Scandinavica,* 98(6), 474-79.

Chastang, F., Rioux, P., Dupont, I., et al. (1999). Tentativas de suicidio e inseguridad laboral: una asociacion compleja. *European Psychiatry,* 6, 173-80.

Chemtob, C.M., Hamada, R.S., Bauer, G., et al. (1988). Patient´suicides: frequency and impact on psychiatrists. *American Journal of Psychiatry,* 54(5), 254-62.

Cheng, A.T.A. (1995). Mental illness and suicide: a case-control study in East Taiwan. *Archives of General Psychiatry,* 52, 594-603.

Cheng, A.T.A., Chen, T.H.H., Chen, C.C., et al. (2000). Psychosocial and psychiatric risk factors for suicide: Case-control psychological autopsy study. *British Journal of Psychiatry,* 177, 360-5.

Cheng, T.A., Hsu, M.A. (1992). A community study of mental disorders among four aboriginal groups in Taiwan. *Psychological Medicine,* 22, 255–63.

Cheng, K.K., Leung, C.M., Lo, W.H., et al. (1990). Risk factors of suicide among schizophrenics. *Acta Psychiatr Scandinavica,* 81(3), 220-4.

Cheng, A.T., Mann, A.H., Chan, K.A. (1997). Personality disorder and suicide. A case-control study. *British Journal of Psychiatry,* 170, 441-446.

Child, I.L. (1968). Personality in culture. In: *Handbook of personality theory and research,* eds. E.F. Borgatta & W.W. Lambert, pp. 82-83. Chicago: Rand McNally.

Chinchilla Moreno, A. (1997). *Tratamiento de las depresiones.* Barcelona: Masson.

Chotai, J., Serretti, A., Lattuada, E., et al. (2003). Gene-environment interaction in psychiatry disorders as indicated by season of birth variations in tryptophan hydroxylase (TPH), serotonin transporter (5-HTTPLR), and dopamine receptor (DRD4) gene polymorhisms. *Psychiatry Research,* 119(1-2), 99-111.

Clark, L.A. (1993). *Manual for the Schedule for Non-adaptive and Adaptive Personality.* Minneapolis: University of Minnesota Press.

Clark, L.A., Harrison, J.A. (2001). Assessment instruments. In : *Handbook of Personality Disorders:Theory, Research and Treatment.* New York, Guildford.

Clark, L.A., Livesley, W.J., Morey, L. (1997). Personality disorder assessment: The challenge of construct validity. *Journal of Personality Disorders,* 11: 205-231.

Clarke, L., Ungerer, J., Chahoud, K., et al. (2002). Attention deficit hyperactivity disorder is associated with attachment insecurity. *Clinical Child Psychology & Psychiatry,* 7(2), 179-98.

Clarkin, J.F., Abrams, R. (1998). Personality disorder in the elderly. *Current Opinion in Psychiatry,* 11 (2), 131-5.

Clarkin, J.F., Friedman, R.C., Hurt, S.W., et al. (1984). Affective and character pathology of suicidal adolescents and young adults in patients. *Journal of Clinical Psychiatry,* 45, 19-22.

Clayton, P.J. (1985). Suicide. *Psychiatry Clinics of North America,* 8(2), 203-14

Cleckey, H. The mask of sanity. St Louis, MO: C.V. Mosby Co, 1941.

Clements, C.D., Bonacci, D., Yerevanian, B., et al. (1985). Assessment of Suicide Risk in Patients with Personality Disorder and Major Affective Diagnosis. *Quality review bulletin,* 5, 150-4.

Cloninger, C.R. (1987) A systematic method for clinical description of personality variants. *Archives of General Psychiatry,* 44, 573-588

Cloninger, C. R. (1988). A unified biosocial theory of personality and its role in the development of anxiety states. *Psychiatric development,* 6(2), 83-120.

Cloninger, C. R. (1994). Temperament and personality. *Current Opinion in Neurobiology,* 4(2), 266-73.

Cloninger, C.R. (2002). Implications of comorbidity for the classification of mental disorders: the need for a psychobiology of coherente. In: *Psychiatric Diagnosis and Classification,* ed. M. Maj, W. Gaebel, J.J. López-Ibor, N. Sartorius N, pp. 79-105. Chichester: Wiley.

Cloninger, C.R., Bayon, C., Svrakic, D.M. (1998). Measurment of temperament and character in mood disorders: a model of fundamental states as personality types. *Journal of Affective Disorders,* 51, 21-32.

Cloninger, C.R., Przybeck, T.R., Svrakic, D.M. (1991). The Tridimensional Personality Questionnaire: US normative data. *Psychology Reports,* 69, 1047-57.

Cloninger,C.R., Przybeck, T.R., Svrakic, D., et al. (1994). *The Temperament and Character Inventory (TCI): A guide to its development and use.* St Louis, MO: Center for Psychobiology of Personality, Washington University.

Cloninger, C.R., Svrakic, D.M. (1997). *Integrative psychobiological approach to psychiatric assessment and treatment. Psychiatry*, 60, 120-141.

Cloninger, C.R., Svrakic, D.M., Przybeck, T.R. (1993). A psychobiological model of temperament and character. *Archives of General Psychiatry*, 50, 975-90.

Coccaro, E.F., Bergeman, C.S., McClearn, G.E. (1993). Heritability of irritable impulsiveness: a study of twins reared together and apart. *Psychiatry Research*, 48(3), 229-42.

Coccaro, E., Siever, L.J., Klar, H.M. (1989). Serotonergic studies in patients with affective and personality disorders: correlates with suicidal and impulsive-aggressive behavior. *Archives of General Psychiatry*, 46, 587-99.

Coccaro, E.F., Silverman, J.M., Klar, H.M., et al. (1994). Familial correlates of reduced central serotonergic system function in patients with personality disorders. *Archives of General Psychiatry*, 51(4), 318-24.

Coccaro, E.F., Bergeman, C.S., Kavoussi, R.J., et al. (1997). Heritability of aggression and irritability: a twin study of the Buss-Durkee aggression scales in adult male subjects. *Biological Psychiatry*, 41(3), 273-84.

Coderch, J. (1987). Psiquiatría dinámica. Barcelona: Herder.

Cohen, J. (1986). Statistical approaches to suicidal risk factor analysis. *Annals of New York Academy of Sciences*, 487, 34-41.

Cohen, S., Lavelle, J., Rich, C.L., et al. (1994). Rates and correlates of suicide attempts in first-admission psychotic patients. *Acta Psychiatrica Scandinavica*, 90(3), 167-71.

Cohen, D., Llorente, M., Eisdorfer, C. (1998). Homicide-suicide in older persons. *American Journal of Psychiatry*, 155(3), 390-6.

Coid, J.W. (1999). Aetiological risk factors for personality disorders. *British Journal of Psychiatry*, 174, 530-38.

Coid, J. (2003a). Epidemiology, public health and the problem of personality disorder. *British Journal of Psychiatry* 44, S3-10.

Coid, J.W. (2003b). Formulating strategies for the primary prevention of adult antisocial behaviour: "high risk" or "population strategies? In: *Early Prevention of Adult Antisocial Behabiour*, ed. D.P. Farrington & L.W. Coid, pp. 32-78. Cambridge: Cambridge University Press.

Collins FS, Green ED, Guttmacher AE, et al. (2003). A vision for the future of genomics research. *Nature*, 422(6934), 835-847.

Conner, K.R. (2004). A call for research on planned vs. unplanned suicidal behavior. *Suicide & Life Threaening Behavior*, 34(2), 89-98.

Conner, K.R., Duberstein, P.R., Conwell, Y., et al. (2001). Psychological vulnerabiliyt to completed suicide: a review of empirical studies. *Suicide & Life Threatening Behavior*, 31, 367-85.

Conner, K.R., Duberstein, P.R., Conwell, Y., et al. (2003). Reactive agression and suicide. Theory and evidence. *Agression and Violent Behavior*, 8, 413-32.

Conwell, Y., Duberstein, P.R., Caine, E.D. (2002). Risk factors for suicide in later life. *Biological Psychiatry*, 52, 193-204.

Conwell, Y., Duberstain, P.R., Cox, C., et al. (1998). Age differences in behaviors leading to completed suicide. *American Journal of Geriatric Psychiatry*, 6, 122-6.

Cooke DJ, hart SD. Personality disorders. Personality Disorders. In Johnstone, E. V. et al. (Eds.), *Companion to Psychiatric Studies* (8th Edition). Edinburgh: Churchill

Livingstone, 2004. Avalaible at: *http://www.fleshandbones.com/readingroom/pdf/1010.pdf*

Coolidge, F.L., Thede, L.L., Jang, K.L. (2004). Are personality disorders psychological manifestations of executive function deficits? Bivariate heritability evidence from a twin study. *Behavior Genetics*, 34(1), 75-84.

Cooper, J., Appleby, L., Amos, T. (2002). Life events preceding suicide by young people. *Social Psychiatry Psychiatric Epidemiology*, 37, 271-5.

Cooper, P.N., Milroy, C.M. (1994). Violent suicide in South Yorkshire, England. *Journal of Forensic Science*, 39, 657-67.

Corbella, J. (2005). Suicide. In: *Legal Medicine and Toxicology*, ed. Gisbert Calabuig, pp. 325-6. Barcelona: Villanueva.

Corbitt, E.M., Malone, K.M., Haas, G.L., et al. (1996). Suicidal behavior in patients with major depression and comorbid personality disorders. *Journal of Affective Disorders*, 39, 61-72.

Cornelius, J.R., Salloum, I.M., Mezzich, J., et al. (1995). Disproportionate suicidality in patients with comorbid major depression and alcoholism. *American Journal of Psychiatry*, 152(3), 358-64.

Corruble, E., Damy, C., Guelfi, J.D. (1999). Impulsivity: a relevant dimension in depression regarding suicide attempts? *Journal of Affective Disorder*, 53(3), 211-5.

Coryell, W., Andreasen, N.C., Endicott, J., et al. (1987). The significance of past mania or hypomania in the course and outcome of major depression. *American Journal of Psychiatry*, 144(3), 309-15.

Coryell, W., Tsuang, M (1982). Primary unipolar depression and the prognostic importance of delusions. *Archives of General Psychiatry*, 39, 1181-4.

Costa, P.T., McCrae, R.R. (1992). *Revised NEO Personality Inventory (NEO-PI-R) and NEO Five-Factor Inventory (NEO-FFI) professional manual.* Odessa, FL: Psychological Assessment Resources.

Costa, P.T., Widiger, T.A. editors. (1994). *Personality disorders and the five-factor model of personality.* Washington DC; American Psychological Association.

Cote, T.R., Biggar, R.J., Dannenberg, A.L. (1992). Risk of suicide among persons with AIDS. A national assessment. *Journal of the American Medical Association*, 268(15), 2066-8.

Courtet, P., Buresi, C., Abbar, M., et al. (2003). No association between non-violent suicidal behavior and the serotonin transporter promoter polymorphism. *American Journal of Medical Genetics*, 116, 72–6.

Courtet, P., Franc, N., Picot, M.C., et al. (2006). Season of birth variations as risk factor of suicide attempts and interaction with the serotonin transporter gene. *Psychiatric Danubia,* 18 suppl 1, 75.

Courtet, P., Jollant, F., Castelnau, D. (2005). Suicidal behavior: relationship between phenotype and serotonergic genotype. *American Journal of Medical Genetics*, 133, 25–33.

Courtet, P., Jollant, F., Buresi, C., et al. (2005b). The MAOA gene may influence the means used in suicide attempts. *Psychiatric Genetics*, 15 (3), 189-193.

Courtet, P., Torres, S., Picot, M.C., et al. (2004). The serotonin transporter gene may be involved in the short-term risk of subsequent suicide attempt. *Biological Psychiatry*, 55, 46-51.

Crumley, F. (1979). Adolescent suicide attempts. *Journal of American Medical Association*, 241, 2404-7

Damasio, H., Grabowski, T., Frank, R., et al. (1994). The return of Phineas Gage: clues about the brain from the skull of a famous patient. *Science*, 264 (5162), 1102-5.

Davidson, R.J., Putnam, K.M., Larson, C.L. (2000). Dysfunction in the neural circuitry of emotion regulation--a possible prelude to violence. *Science*, 289 (5479), 591-4.

Davidoff, L.L. (1984). Introducción a la psicología, 2ª edn. México: McGraw-Hill.

Davis, A.T., Schrueder, C. (1990). The prediction of suicide. *Medical Journal of Australia*, 153, 552-4.

Dawkins, R. (1994). *El gen egoísta. Las bases biológicas de nuestra conducta.* Barcelona: Salvat.

Dawkins, R. (1999). *The Extended Phenotype: The Long Reach of the Gene.* Oxford: Oxford University Press.

De Girolano, G. & Reich, J.H. (1993). *Epidemiology of Mental Disorders and Psychosocial Problems.: Personality Disorders.* Geneva: World Health Organization.

De la Cruz, C., Corominas, A., Sarró, B. (1988). El suicidio en la profesion medica: revision bibliografica. *JANO*, 2(9), 45-52.

De Lara, C.L., Dumais, A., Rouleau, G., et al. (2006). STin2 variant and family history of suicide as significant predictors of suicide completion in major depression. *Biological Psychiatry*, 59(2), 114-20.

De Leo, D. et al. (1999). *Hanging as a means to suicide in young Australians: a report to the Commonwealth Ministry of Health and Family Services.* Brisbane, Australian Institute for Suicide Research and Prevention.

De Moore, G.M., Robertson, A.R. (1999). Suicide attempts by firearms and by leaping from heights: a comparative study of survivors. *American Journal of Psychiatry*, 156(9), 1425-31.

Department of Health and Children, National Task Force on Suicide: *Report of the National Task Force on Suicide* (abstract). Dublin: Stationery Office; 1998, pp 5-84.

Depue, R.A. (1996). A Neurobiological Framework for the Structure of Personality and Emotion: Implications for Personality Disorders. In: *Major Theories of Personality Disorder*, ed. F. Clarkin & M.F. Lenzenweger, pp. 36-105. New York: Guildford Press.

Dervic, K., Oquendo, M.A., Grunebaum, M.F., et al. (2004). Religious affiliation and suicide attempt. *American Journal of Psychiatry*, 161, 2303-8.

Dervic, K., Oquendo, M.A., Currier, D., et al. (2006). Moral objections to suicide: Can they counteract suicidality in patients with cluster B psychopathology? *Journal of Clinical Psychiatry*, 67, 620-5.

Devereux, G. (1973). *Ensayos de Etnopsiquiatría General, pp. 103-124.* Barcelona: Barral Editores.

Deykin, E.Y., Alpert, J.J., McNamarra, J.J (1985). A pilot study of the effect of exposure to child abuse or neglect on adolescent suicidal behavior. *American Journal of Psychiatry*, 142(11), 1299-1303.

Dhossche, D.M. (2000). Suicidal behavior in psychiatric emergency room patients. *South Medical Journal*, 93(3),310-4.

Diaz, F.J., Baca-Garcia, E., Diaz-Sastre, C., et al. (2003). Dimensions of suicidal behavior according to patient reports. *European Archives of Psychiatry Clinics Neuroscience*, 253(4), 197-202.

Díaz Marsá, M., Carrasco, J.L., López Ibor, J.J., et al. (1998). Un estudio de la personlidad en los trastornos de la conducta alimentaria. *Actas Luso Españolas de Neurología Psiquiatría y Ciencias Afines*, 26, 288-96.

Díaz-Sastre, C. (2000). *Valoración del intento de suicidio en urgencias.* I Congreso Virtual de Psiquiatría.

Diekstra, R.F. (1989). Suicidal behavior in adolescents and young adults: the international picture. *Crisis*, 10(1), 16-35.

Diekstra, R.F.W. (1990). An international perspective of the epidemiology and prevention of suicide. In: *Suicide over the life cicle*, ed. S.J. Blumenthal, D.J. Kupfer DJ. Washington: American Psychiatric Press, 1990.

Diekstra, R.F. (1993). The epidemiology of suicide and parasuicide. *Acta Psychiatrica Scandinavica*, 37(Suppl), 9-20.

Diekstra, R.F., Garnefski, N. (1995). On the nature, magnitude, and causality of suicidal behaviors: an international perspective. *Suicide Life Threatening Behavior*, 25(1), 36-57.

Diekstra, R.F., Gulbinat, W. (1993). The epidemiology of suicidal behavior: a review of three continents. World Health Statistics Quarterly. *Rapport Trimestriel de Statistiques Sanitaires Mondiales*, 46, 52-68.

Dirks, B. (1998). Repetition of parasuicide: ICD-10 personality disorders and adversity. *Acta Psychiatrica Scandinavica*, 98, 208-13.

Dodge, K.A., Coie, J.D. (1987). Social-information-processing factors in reactive and proactive aggression in children´s peer groups. *Journal of Personality and Social Psychology*, 53, 1146-58.

Dolan, M. (2004). Psychopathic personality in young people. *Advances in Psychiatric Treatment*, 10, 466-73.

Donald, M., Dower, J., Correa-Velez, I., et al. (2006). Risk and protective factors for medically serious suicide attempts: a comparison of hospital-based with population-based samples of young adults. *Australian New Zealand Journal of Psychiatry*, 40, 87-96.

Dorpat, T.L., Ripley, H.S. (1967). The relationship between attempted suicide and committed suicide. *Comprehensive Psychiatry*, 8(2), 74-9.

Douglas, J. et al. (2004). "Near-fatal" deliberate self-harm: characteristics, prevention and implications for the prevention of suicide. *Journal of Affective Disorders*, 79, 263-8.

Dowson, J.H., Grounds, A.T. (1995). *Personality disorders: Recognition and Clinical Management.* Cambridge: Cambridge University Press

Drane, J.F. (1986). Ética y psicoterapia. Perspectiva filosófica. In: *Ética y valores en psicoterapia*, ed. M. Rosenbaum. México: Fondo de Cultura Económica.

Drake, R.E., Gates, C., Cotton, P.G., et al. (1984). Suicide among schizophrenics: who is at risk? *Journal of Nervous Mental Disorders*, 172, 613-8.

Drake, R.E., Gates, C., Whitaker, A., et al. (1985). Suicide among schizophrenics: a review. *Comprehensive Psychiatry*, 26(1), 90-100.

Du, L., Faludi, G., Palkovits, M., et al. Frequency of long allele in serotonin transporter gene is increased in depressed suicide victims. *Biological Psychiatry*, 46(2), 196-201.

Duberstein, P.R., Conwell, Y. (1997). Personality disorders and completed suicide: a methodological and conceptual review. *Clinics Psychology Science Practice*, 4, 359-76.

Duberstein, P.R., Conwell, Y., Caine, E.D. (1994). Age differences in the personality characteristics of suicide completers: preliminary findings from a psychological autopsy study. *Psychiatry*, 57, 213-24.

Duffy, J. & Kreitman, N. (1993). Risk factors for suicide and undetermined death among in-patient alcoholics in Scotland. *Addiction*, 88(6), 757-66.

Dumais, A., Lesage, A.D., Alda, M. (2005). Risk factors for suicide completion in major depression: a case-control study of impulsive and aggressive behaviors in men. *American Journal of Psychiatry*, 162, 2116-24.

Dunn, B.D., Dalgleish, T., Lawrence, A.D. (2006). The somatic marker hypothesis: a critical evaluation. *Neuroscience Biobehavior Review*, 30(2), 239-71.

Durkheim, E. (1982). *El suicidio*. Madrid: Akal Universitaria.

Earls, F. (1989). Sex differences in psychiatric disorders: origins and developmental influences. *Journal of Clinical Psychiatry*, 50 Suppl., 4-7.

Eaves, J.L. (2006). Genotype x Environment interaction in psychopathology: fact or artifact? *Twin Research Human Genetics*, 9(1), 1-8.

Ebstein, R.P. (2006). The molecular genetic architecture of human personality: beyond self-report questionnaires. *Molecular Psychiatry*, 11(5), 427-45.

Edman, G., Asberg. M., Levander, S., et al. (1986). Skin conductance habituation and cerebrospinal fluid 5-hydroxyindoleacetic acid in suicidal patients. *Archives of General Psychiatry*, 43(6), 586-92.

Eddleston, M. et al. (2006). Choice of poison for intentional self-poisoning in rural Sri Lanka. *Clinical Toxicology of Philadelphia*, 44 (3), 283-6.

Egan, V., Austin, E.J., Elliot, D., et al. (2003). Personality traits, personality disorders and sensational interests in mentally disordered offenders. *Legal Criminological Psychology, 8,* 51-62.

Egan, V., McCarthy, I. (in press) Personality disordered offenders. A research treatment programme. II. Assessment, selection and evaluation. Forensic Psychology in Europe.

Ehrlich, S., Noam, G.G., Lyoo, I.K., et al. White matter hyperintensities and their associations with suicidality in psychiatrically hospitalized children and adolescents. *Journal of American Academy of Child and Adolescent Psychiatry*, 43(6), 770-6.

Ernst, M., Grant S.J., London, E.D., et al. (2002). Decision-making in a risk-taking task: a PET study. *Neuropsychopharmacology, 26,* 682-91.

Ekselius, L., Lindström, E., von Knorring, L., et al. (1994). SCID II interviews and the SCID screen questionnaire as diagnostic tools for personality disorders in the DSM-III-R. *Acta Psychiatrica Scandinavica*, 90, 120-3.

Eley, T., Sudgen, K., Corsico, A., et al. (2004). Gene-environment interaction analysis of serotonin system markers with adolescent depression. *Molecular Psychiatry*, 9(10), 908-15.

Elliot, A.J., Pages, K.P., Russo, J., et al. (1996). A profile of medically serious suicide attempts. *Journal of Clinical Psychiatry*, 57(12), 567-71.

El-Rufaie, O.E.F., Al-Sabosy, M., Abuzeid, M.S.O., et al. (2002). Personality profile among primary care patients: experienting with the Arabic IPDE ICD-10. *Acta Psychiatrica Scandinavica*, 105, 37-41.

Engstrom, G., Alling, C., Gustavsson, P., et al. (1997). Clinical characteristics and biological parameters in temperamental clusters of suicide attempters. *Journal of Affective Disorder*, 44(1), 45-55.

Ernst, C., Lalovic, A., Lesage, A., et al. (2004). Suicide and no axis I psychopathology. *BMC Psychiatry*, 4, 7

Ettlinger, R. (1964). Suicides in a group of patients who had previously attempted suicide. *Acta Psychiatrica Scandinavica*, 40, 363-78.

Evenden, J.L. (1999). Varieties of impulsivity. *Psychopharmacology*, 146(348), 361.

Ewing, J.A. (1984). Detecting alcoholism. The CAGE questionnaire. *Journal of American Medical Association*, 252(14), 1905-7.

Eyman, jr. & Eyman, S.K. (1992). Personality assessment in suicide prediction. In: *Assessment and Prediction of Suicide*, cited by by Abdel-khalek, A., & Lester, D. (2002). Can personality predict suicidality? A study in two cultures. *International Journal of Social and Personality*, 48(3), 231-9.

Eysenck, H.J. (1967). *The Biological Basis of Personality*. Springfield: Charles C. Thomas.

Eysenck, H.J. & Eysenck S.B.G. (1975) The EPQ. London: University London Press.

Fabrega, H, et al. (1991). On the homogeneity of personality disorder clusters. *Comprehensive Psychiatry*, 32, 373-85.

Fallgatter, A.J., Herrmann, M.j., Roemmler, J., et al. (2004). Allelic variation of serotonin transporter function modulates the brain electrical response for error processing. *Neuropsychopharmacology*, 29, 1506-11.

Farberow, N.L., & Schneidman, E.S., Leonard, C.V. (1971). An eight year survey of hospital suicides. *Suicide Life Threatening Behavior*, 1, 198-201.

Farmer, R.D.T., Rohde, J.R. (1980). Effect of availability and acceptability of lethal instruments on suicide mortality: an analysis of some international data. *Acta Psychiatrica Scandinavica*, 62, 436-46.

Farrington, D., Loeber, R. & Van Kammen, W.B. (1990). Long-term criminal outcomes of hyperactivity-impulsivity-attention deficit and conduct problems in childhood. In: *Straight and Devious Pathways from Childhood to Adulthood,* ed. L.N. Robins & M. Rutter. Cambridge: Cambridge University Press; 1990.

Fava, M., Alpert, J.E., Borus, J.S., et al. (1996). Patterns of personality disorder comorbidity in early-onset versus late-onset major depression. *American Journal of Psychiatry*, 153, 1308-12.

Fawcett, J., Busch, K.A., Jacobs, D., et al. (1997). Suicide: a four-pathway clinical-biochemical model. *Annals of New York Academy of Science*, 836, 1971-81.

Fawcett, J., Scheftner, W., Clark, D., et al. (1987). Clinical predictors of suicide in patients with major affective disorders: a controlled prospective study. *American Journal of Psychiatry*, 144(1), 35-40.

Fergusson, D.M. & Horwood, L.J. (1987). Vulnerability to life events exposure. *Psychology Medicine*, 17(3), 739-49.

Fergusson, D.M., Woodward, L.J., Horwood, L.J. (2000). Risk factors and life processes associated with the onset of suicidal behaviour during adolescence and early adulthood. *Psychological Medicine*, 30(1), 23-39.

Ferrada, N.M., Asberg, M., Ormstad, K., et al. Definite and undetermined forensic diagnoses of suicide among immigrants in Sweden. (1995). *Acta Psychiatrica Scandinavica*, 91(2), 130-5.

Ferreira de Castro, E., Cunha, M.A., Pimenta, F., et al. Parasuicide and mental disorders. *Acta Psychiatrica Scandinavica*, 97, 25-31.

Ferro, T., Klein, D.N., Schwartz, J.E., et al. (1998). 30-Month stability of personality disorders diagnoses in depressed outpatients. *American Journal of Psychiatry*, 155, 653-9.

First, M.B., Gibbon, M.., Spitzer, R.L., et al. (1997). *Structured Clinical Interview for DSM-IV axis II Personality Disorders (SCID-II) (Version 2.0)*. Washington. American Psychiatric Press.

First, M.B., Pincus, H.A., Levine, J.B., et al. (2004). Clinical utility as a criterion for revising psychiatric diagnosis. *American Journal of Psychiatry*, 161(6), 946-54.

Fishbain, D.A. (1991). Personality disorder in old age. *Journal of Clinical Psychiatry*, 52, 477-8.

Flisher, A., Parry, C.D., Bradshaw, D. et al. (1997). Seasonal variation of suicide in South Africa. *Psychiatry Research*, 66, 13–22.

Fodor, J. (1983). *The Modularity of Mind*. Cambridge: MIT Press.

Fonagy, P., Gergely, G., Jurist, E.L. et al. (2002). *Affect Regulation, Mentalisation and the Development of the Self*. New York: Other Press.

Foster, T., Gillespie, K., McClelland, R., et al. (1999). Risk factors for suicide independent of DSM-III-R Axis I disorder. Case-control psychological autopsy study in Northern Ireland. *British Journal of Psychiatry*, 175, 175-9.

Fountoulakis, K.N., Kaprinis, G.S. (2006). Personality disorders: new data versus old concepts. *Current Opinion of Psychiatry*, 19(1), 90-4.

Fowler, R.C., Rich, C.L., Young, D. (1986). San Diego Suicide Study. II. substance abuse of young men. *Archives of General Psychiatry*, 43, 962-5.

Frances, A., Clarkin, J.F., Gilmore, M., et al. (1984). Reliability of criteria for borderline personality disorder: A comparison of DSM-III and the diagnosis interview for borderline patients. *American Journal of Psychiatry*, 141, 1080-84.

Frances, A., First, M.B, Pincus, H.A.(1997). *DSM-IV Guía de uso*. Barcelona: Masson.

Frances, R.J., Franklin, J., Flavin, D.K. (1987). Suicide and alcoholism. *American Journal of Drug Alcohol Abuse*, 13(3), 327-41.

Frances, A., Fyer, M., Clarkin, J. (1986). Personality and suicide. *Annals of New York Academy of Science*, 487, 281-93.

Frank, E., Dingle, A.D. (1999). Self-reported depression and suicide attempts among U.S. women physicians. *American Journal of Psychiatry*, 156(12), 1887-94.

Frankle, W.G., Lombardo, I., New, A.S., et al. (2005). Brain serotonin transporter distribution in subjects with impulsive aggressivity: a positron emission study with [11C]McN 5652. *American Journal of Psychiatry*, 162(5), 915-23.

Frick, P.J. (1998). Callous-unemotional traits and conduct problems: applying the two-factor model of psychopathy to children. In: *Psychopathy: Theory, Research and Implications for Society*, ed. D. Cooke, A. Forth & R. Hare R, pp. 161-89. Dordrecht: Kluwer, 1998.

Friedman, R.C., Aronoff, M.S., Clarkin, J.F., et al. (1983). History of suicidal behavior in depressed borderline inpatients. *American Journal of Psychiatry*, 140, 1023-26.

Friedman, S., Smith, L., Fogel, A. (1999). Suicidality in panic disorder: a comparison with schizophrenic, depressed, and other anxiety disorder outpatients. *Journal of Anxiety Disorders*, 13(5), 447-61.

Frierson, R.L. (1991). Suicide attempts by the old and the very old. *Archives of Internal Medicine*, 151, 141-4.

Fyer, M.R., Frances, A.J., Sullivan, T., et al. (1988). Suicide attempts in patients with borderline personality disorder. *American Journal of Psychiatry*, 145(6), 737-9.

Fulton, M., Winokur, G. (1993). A comparative study of paranoid and schizoid personality disorders. *British Journal of Psychiatry*, 150, 1363-7.

Gabbard, G. (1989). Two subtypes of narcissistic personality disorder. *Bulletin Menninger Clinic*, 53, 527-32.

García Resa, E., Braquehais, D., Blasco, H., et al. Aspectos sociodemográficos de los intentos de suicidio. *Actas Españolas de Psiquiatría*, 30 (2), 112-9.

Garpenstrand, H., Annas, P., Ekblom, J., et al. (2001). Human fear conditioning is related to dopaminergic and serotonergic biological markers. *Behavior Neuroscience*, 115, 358-64.

Garrison, C.Z.(1989). The study of suicidal behavior in the schools. *Suicide Life Threatening Behavior*, 19(1), 120-30.

Garrison, C.Z., Jackson, K.L., Addy, C.L., et al. (1991). Suicidal behaviors in young adolescents. *American Journal of Epidemiology*, 133(10), 1005-14.

Geijo MS, Franco MA. (1997). Suicidio. In: *Manual del residente de Psiquiatria*, ed. S. Cervera, V. Conde, A. Espino, et al., pp. 1269-81. Madrid.

Geertz, C. (2000). *La interpretación de las culturas, pp. 19-117*. Barcelona: Gedisa.

Gibbs, J.T. (1997). African-American suicide: a cultural paradox. *Suicide Life Threatening Behavior*, 27, 68-79.

Guillaume, S., Jollant, F., Jaussent, I., et al. (2006). Emotional reactivity and decision making in suicide attempters. Presented at the CINP: Chicago.

Geijer, T., Frisch, A., Persson, M.L.. (2000). Search for association between suicide attempt and serotonergic polymorphisms. *Psychiatric Genetics*, 10, 19–26.

Geijo, M.S., Franco, M.A. (1997). Suicidio. In: *Manual del residente de Psiquiatria, ed.* S. Cervera, V. Conde, A. Espino, 1269-81. Madrid.

Geiser, F. & Lieberz, K. (2000). Schizoid and narcissistic features in personality structure diagnosis. *Psychopathology*, 33, 19-24.

Geller, J.L. (1986). In again, out again: Preliminary evaluation of state hospital`s worst recidivists. *Hospital Community Psychiatry*, 1305-8.

Gerson, J., Stanley, B. (2002). Suicidal and self-injurious behavior in personality diosrder: controversies and treatment directions. *Current Psychiatry Reports*, 4, 30-8.

Gibson, P. (1986). Gay male and lesbian youth suicide. In: *U. S. Department of Health and Human Services. Report of the Secretary's task force on youth suicide*, ed. M.D. Rockville, pp. 3110-42. Alcohol, Drug Abuse, and Mental Health Administration.

Gilbert, P., Bailey, K.G. (2000). Genes on the coach. Filadelfia: Taylor and Francis Group.

Gili Planas, M., Roca Bennasar, M. (2004). Modelos sobre los trastornos de la personalidad. En: Trastornos de Personalidad. Barcelona: ArsXXI

Gillespie, N.A., Whitfield, J.B., Williams, B., et al. (2005). The relationship between stressful life events, the serotonin transporter (5-HTTLPR) genotype and major depression. *Psychological Medicine*, 35(1), 101-11.

Giner, J., Leal, C. (1982). Conducta suicida. In: *Psiquiatría*, ed. A. López-Ibor, O. Ruiz, S. Barcia, pp. 1120-30. Barcelona: Toray.

Giner, J., Seoane, J., Jimenez, R. (1974). Diferentes constelaciones dentro de la conducta suicida. *Folia Neuropsiquiatrica*, 123-33.

Goffman, E. (1981). *La presentación de la persona en la vida cotidiana, pp. 33-42*. Buenos Aires: Amorrortu.

Gold, D.D. Jr.(1987). Suicide attempt: one diagnosis, multiple disorders. *South Medical Journal*, 80(6), 677-82

Goldring, N., Fieve, R.R. (1984). Attempted suicide in manic-depressive disorder. *American Journal of Psychotherapy*, 38(3), 373-83.

Goodyer, I.M. (2006). Continuities and discontinuities from childhood to adult life. In: *Seminars in Child & Adolescent Psychiatry, e*d. S.G. Gowers, pp. 40-58. London: Gaskell

Goodall, J. (1986). *The Chimpanzees of Gombe: Patterns of Behavior.* Cambridge, MA: The Belknap Press of Harvard University Press.

Goldman, R.G., Skodol, A.E., McGrath, P.J., et al. (1994). Relationship between the Tridimensional Personality Questionnaire and DSM-III-R personality traits. *American Journal of Psychiatry*, 151, 274-6.

Goldney, R.D. (2002). A global view of suicidal behaviour. *Emergence Medicine*, 14, 24-34.

Goldsmith, H.H., Buss, A.H., Plomin, R., et al. (1987). Roundtable: what is temperament? Four Approaches. *Child Development*, 58(2), 505-29.

Gómez, A., Barrera, A., Jaar, E., et al. (1995). Comorbilidad psiquiátrica en mujeres con intento de suicidio. *Revista de Psiquiatría de la Facultad de Medicina de Barcelona*, 22(1), 10-7.

Gomez, A., Lolas, F., Martin, M., et al. (1992). The influence of personality on suicidal behaviour. *Actas Luso Españolas de Neurología Psiquiatría y Cincencias Afines*, 20, 250-6.

Goodwin, F.K. & Jamison, K.R. (2001). Manic-depressive illness, cited by Boardman AP, Healy D. Modelling suicide risk in affective disorders. *European Psychiatry*, 16, 400-5.

Gordon, G., Akhtar, S. (1990). The literature on personality disorders, 1985-1988: trends, issues and controversies. *Hospital Community Psychiatry*, 41, 39-51.

Gorwood, P., Batel, P., Ades, J., et al. (2000). Serotonin transporter gene polymorphisms, alcoholism, and suicidal behavior. *Biological Psychiatry*, 48(4), 259-64.

Goto, H., Nakamura, H., Miyoshi, T. (1994). Epidemiological studies on regional differences in suicide mortality and its correlation with socioeconomic factors. *Tokushima Journal of Experimental Medicine*, 41(3-4), 115-132.

Gottesman, I.I. &, Gould, T.D. (2003). The endophenotype concept in psychiatry: etymology and strategic intentions. *American Journal of Psychiatry*, 160(4), 636-45.

Gould, M.S. (1990). Suicide cluster and media exposure. In: *Suicide Over the Life Cycle,* ed. S.J. Blumenthal, D.J. Kupfer. Washington: American Psychiatric Press.

Grabe, H., Lange, M., Wolff, B., et al. (2005). Mental and physical distress is modulated by a polymorphism in the 5-HT transporter gene interacting with social stressors and chronic disease burden. *Molecular Psychiatry*, 10, 220-34.

Gracia-Marco, R., Cejas, M.R., Ros-Montalbán, S. (2004). Suicidio: ¿una entidad nosológica independiente? In: *Diagnóstico diferencial y racionalización del tratamiento farmacológico*, ed. P. Pichot, J. Ezcurra, A. González-Pinto, M. Gutiérrez-Fraile, pp. 457-82. Madrid: Aula Médica, S.A.

Graff-Guerrero, A. De la Fuente-Sandoval, C., Camarena, B., et al. (2005). Frontal and limbic metabolic differences in subjects selected according to genetic variation of the SLC6A4 gene polymorphism. *Neuroimage,* 25, 1197-1204.

Grant, B.F., Hasin, D.S., Stinson, F.S., et al. (2004). Prevalence, correlates, and disability of personality disorders in the United States: results from the national epidemiologic survey on alcohol and related conditions. *Journal of Clinical Psychiatry*, 65(7):948-58.

Gray, J.A. (1981). A critique of Eysenck´s theory of personality. In: *A model for personalit,* ed. H.J. Eysenck, pp. 246-76. New York: Springer-Verlag.

Gray, J.A. (1983). Anxiety, personality and the brain. In: *Physiological Correlates of Human Behaviour: Individual Differences and Psychopathology*, ed. A. Gale & J.A. Edwards. New York: Academic Press, 1983.

Green, J. & Goldwyn, R. (2002). Annotation: Attachment disorganisation and psychopathology: new findings in attachment research and their potential implications for developmental psychopathology in childhood. *Journal of Child Psychology and Psychiatry and Allied Disciplines*, 43 (7), 835-46.

Grilo, C.M., McGlashan, T.H., Skodol, A.S. (2000). Stability and course of personality disorders: the need to consider commorbidities and continuities between Axis I psychiatric disorders and Axis II personality disorders. *The Psychiatric quarterly*, 71, 291-307.

Grunebaum, M.F., Galfalvy, H., Russo, S., et al. (2004). Melancholia and the probability and lethality of suicide attempts. *British Journal of Psychiatry*, 184, 534-5.

Gruzca, R.A., Pryzbeck, T.R., Spitznagel, E.L., et al. (2003). Personality and depressive symptoms: a multi-dimensional analysis. *Journal of Affective Disorders*, 74, 123-30.

Guimon, J. (2002). The Loving Therapeutic Team. *Advances in Relational Mental Health*, 1, 3.

Gunderson, J.G. (1984). *Borderline Personality Disorder*. Washington, DC, American Psychiatric Press.

Gunderson, JG. (2001). *Borderline personality disorder: a clinical guide*. Washington, DC: American Psychiatric Press.

Gunderson, J.G., Kolb, J.E., Austin, V. (1981). The Diagnostic Interview for Borderline Patients. *American Journal of Psychiatry*, 138, 896-903.

Gunderson, J.G., Ronningstam, E. (2001). Differentiating narcissistic and antisocial personality disorders. *Journal of Personality Disorders*, 15(2), 103-9.

Gunderson, J.G., Ronningstam, E., Bodkin, A. (1990). The Diagnostic Interview for Narcissistic Patients. *Archives of General Psychiatry*, 47, 676-80.

Gunderson, J.G., Ridolfi, M.E. (2001). Borderline personality disorder: suicidality and self-mutilation. *Annual New York Academy of Science*, 932, 61-73; discussion 73-77

Gunderson, J.G., Zanarini, M.C., Kisiel, C.L. (1995). Borderline personality disorder, ed. W. Livesley. *The DSM-IV personality disorders*. New York: The Guilford Press

Gunnell, D., & Frankel, S. (1994). Prevention of suicide: aspirations and evidence. *British Medical Journal*, 308, 1227-33.

Gunnell, D., Middleton, N., Frankel, S. (2000). Method availability and the prevention of suicide - a re-analysis of secular trends in England and Wales 1950-1975. *Social Psychiatry Psychiatric Epidemiology*, 35, 437-43.

Gutheil, T.G., Appelbaum, P.S. (2000). *Clinical Handbook of Psychiatry and the Law*.Philadelphia: Lippincott Williams & Wilkins.

Guthrie, P.C., Mobley, B.D. (1994). A comparison of the differential diagnostic efficiency of three personality disorder inventories. *Journal of Clinical Psychology*, 50, 656-665.

Gutiérrez-García, J.M. (1998). Predominance of urban suicides over rural suicides in Spain. *Actas Luso Españolas Neurología Psiquiatría Ciencicas Afines*, 26(2), 111-5.

Guze, S.B., Robins, E. (1970). Suicide and primary affective disorders. *British Journal of Psychiatry*, 117, 437-8.

Hackett, T.P., Stern, T.A (1994). Suicidio y otros estados destructivos. In: *Psiquiatría de Enlace en el Hospital Genera,* ed. N.H. Cassem, pp. 345-78. Madrid: Díez de Santos, S.A.

Hakko, H., Rasanen, P., Tiihonen, J. (1998). Secular trends in the rates and seasonality of violent and nonviolent suicide occurrences in Finland during 1980–95. *Journal of Affective Disorders,* 50, 49–54.

Halbreich, U., Endicott, J., Nee, J. (1983). Premenstrual depressive changes. Value of differentiation. *Archives of General Psychiatry,* 40(5), 535-42.

Hall, R.C., Platt, D.E. (1999). Suicide risk assessment: a review of risk factors for suicide in 100 patients who made severe suicide attempts. Evaluation of suicide risk in a time of managed care. *Psychosomatics,* 40(1), 18-27.

Hansen, P.E., Wang, A.G., Stage, K.B., et al. (2003). Danish University Antidepressant Group. Comorbid personality disorder predicts suicide after major depression: a 10-year follow-up. *Acta Psychiatrica Scandinavica,* 107(6), 436-40.

Hansenne, M., Pitchot, W., Gonzalez Moreno, A., et al. (1996). Suicidal behavior in depressive disorder: an event-related potential study. *Biological Psychiatry,* 40(2), 116-22.

Hare, R.D. (1991). *The Hare Psychopathy Checklist-Revised.* Toronto: Multi Health Systems.

Hare, R.D., Hart, S.D., Harpur, T.J. (2001). Psychopathy and the DSM-IV criteria for antisocial personality disorder. *Journal of Abnormal Psychoogy,* 100(3), 391-8.

Hariri, A.R., Mattay, V.S., Tessitore, A., et al. (2002). Dextroamphetamine modulates the response of the human amygdale. *Neuropsychopharmacology,* 27(6), 1036-40.

Hariri, A.R., Mattay, V.S., Tessitore, A., et al. (2002b). Serotonin transporter genetic variation and the response of the human amygdala. *Science,* 297(5580), 400-3.

Harkavy, F.J., Restifo, K., Malaspina, D., et al. (1999). Suicide behavior in schizophrenia:characteristics of individuals who had and had not attempted suicide. *American Journal of Psychiatry,* 156 (8), 1276-78.

Harris, M. (1998). *Introducción a la Atropología General.* Madrid: Alianza Editorial – Colección Manuales.

Harris, M (2004). *Teorías sobre la cultura en la era postmoderna.* Barcelona: Crítica-Biblioteca de Bolsillo.

Harris, E.C., Barraclough, B.M. (1994). Suicide as an outcome for medical disorders. *Medicine,* 73, 281-96.

Harris, E.C., Barraclough, B. (1997). Suicide as an outcome for mental disorders. *A meta-analysis. Brithish Journal of Psychiatry,* 170, 205-228.

Harris, E.C., Barraclough, B. (1998). Excess mortality of mental disorder. *British Journal of Psychiatry,* 173, 11-53.

Harwood, D., Hawton, K., Hope, T., et al. (2001). Psychiatric disorder and personality factors associated with suicide in older people: A descriptive and case-control study. *Internal Journal of Geriatric Psychiatry,* 16, 155-65.

Harwood, D., Jacoby, R. (2000). Suicidal behaviour among the elderly. In: *The International Handbook of Suicide and Attempted Suicide,* ed. K.E. Hawton & Van Herringen. New York: Wiley, John & Sons.

Hasler, G., Drevets, W.C., Manji, H.K., et al. (2004). Discovering endophenotypes for major depression. *Neuropsychopharmacology,* 29(10), 1765-81.

Haw, C., Hawton, K., Houston, K., et al. (2003). Correlates of relative lethality and suicidal intent among deliberate self-harm patients. *Suicide Life Threatening Behavior*, 33, 353-64.

Hawton, K. (2001). Studying Survivors of Nearly Lethal Suicide Attempts: An Important Strategry in *Suicide Research. Suicide Life Threatening Behavior*, 32 (Suppl), 76-84.

Hawton, K., Fagg, J. (1988). Suicide,and other causes of death, following attempted suicide. *British Journal of Psychiatry*, 152, 359-366.

Hawton, K., Fagg, J., Platt, S., et al. (1993). Factors associated with suicide after parasuicide in young people. *British Medical Journal*, 306, 1641-4.

Hawton, K., Fagg, J., Simkin, S., et al. (1997). Trends in deliberate self-harm in Oxford, 1985-1995. Implications for clinical services and the prevention of suicide. *British Journal of Psychiatry*, 171, 556-60.

Hawton, K., Harris, L., Simkin, S., et al. (2000) Effect of death of Diana, princess of Wales on suicide and deliberate self-harm. *British Journal of Psychiatry*, 177, 463-6.

Hawton, K., Houston, K., Haw, C., et al. (2003). Comorbidity of axis I and axis II disorders in patients who attempted suicide. *American Journal of Psychiatry*, 160(8), 1494-500.

Hawton, K., Houston, K., Shepperd, R. (1999). Suicide in young people. Study of 174 cases, aged under 25 years, based on coroners' and medical records. *British Journal of Psychiatry*, 175, 271-6.

Healy, D., Langmaak, C., Savage, M. (1999). Suicide in the course of the treatment of depression [see comments]. *Journal of Psychopharmacology*, 13(1), 94-9.

Heikkinen, M., Aro, H., Lonnqvist, J. (1992a). Recent life events and their role in suicide as seen by the spouses. *Acta Psychiatrica Scandinavica*, 86(6), 489-94.

Heikkinen, M., Aro, H., Lonnqvist, J. (1992b). The partners' views on precipitant stressors in suicide. *Acta Psychiatrica Scandinavica*, 85(5), 380-4.

Heikkinen, M., Aro, H., Lonnqvist, J. (1994). Recent life events, social support and suicide. *Acta Psychiatrica Scandinavica Suppl*, 377, 65-72.

Heikkinen, M.E., Henriksson, M.M., Isometsa, E.T., et al. (1997). Recent life events and suicide in personality disorders. *Journal of Nervous Mental Disorders*, 185(6), 373-81.

Heikkinen, M.E., Isometsa, E.T., Marttunen, M.J., et al. (1995). Social factors in suicide. *British Journal of Psychiatry*, 167, 747-53.

Heinz, A., Braus, D.F., Smolka, M.N. (2005). Amygdala-prefrontal coupling depends on a genetic variation of the serotonin transporter. *Natural Neuroscience*, 8, 20-1.

Helgason, T., Magnusson, H. (1989). The first 80 yeras of life: a psychiatric epidemiological study. *Acta Psychiatrica Scandinavica*, 79 (Supp. 348):85-94.

Helzer, J.E., Pryzbeck, T.R. (1988). The co-occurrence of alcoholism with other psychiatric disorders in the general population and its impact on treatment. *Journal of Stud Alcohol*, 49(3), 219-24.

Hempel, C.G. (1961). Introduction to problems of taxonomy. In: *Field Studies in the Mental Disorders,* ed. J. Zubin, pp. 3-22. New York: Grune & Stratton.

Henderson, J.M., Ord, R.A (1997). Suicide in head and neck cancer patients. *Journal of Oral Maxillofacial Surgery*, 55(11), 1217-21.

Hendin, H., Haas, A.P. (1991). Suicide and guilt as manifestations of PTSD in Vietnam combat veterans. *Amercian Journal of Psychiatry*, 148(5), 586-91.

Henriksson, M.M., Aro, H.M., Marttunen, M.J., et al. (1993). Mental disorders and comorbidity in suicide. *American Journal of Psychiatry*, 150(6), 935-40.

Henriksson, M.M., Marttunen, M.J., Isometsa, E.T., et al. Mental disorders in elderly suicide. *Internal Psychogeriatry*, 7(2), 275-86.

Henry, C., Lacoste, J., Bellivier, F., et al. (1999). Temperament in bipolar illness: impact on prognosis. *Journal of Affective Disorders*, 56, 103-8.

Heuman, K., Morey, L. (1990). Reliability of categorical and dimensional judgments of personality disorder. *American Journal of Psychiatry*, 147, 498-500.

Hill, J. (1984). Disorders of personality. In: *Child Psychiatry: Modern approaches*, ed. M. Rutter & L. Hersov, pp. 723-36. London: Blackwell.

Hill, J. (2002). Disorders of Personality. In: *Child and Adolescent Psychiatry*, ed. M. Rutter & E. Taylor, pp. 723-36. Oxford: Blackwell Publishing.

Hilton, S.C., Fellingham, G.W., Lyon, J.L. (2002). Suicide rates and religious commitment in young adult males in Utah. *American Journal of Epidemiology*, 155, 413-9.

Holden, R.R., Kerr, P.S., Mendonca, J.D., et al. (1998). Are some motives more linked to suicide proneness than others? *Journal of Clinical Psychology*, 54(5), 569-76.

Holmes, J. (2001). Aspectos éticos de las psicoterapias. In: *La ética en Psiquiatría,* ed. S. Bloch, P. Chodoff, S. A. Green, pp. 218-234. Madrid: Triascastela.

Holmes, T.H. & Rahe, R.H. (1967). The social readjustment rating scale. *Journal of Psychosomatic Research*, 11, 213-8.

Holmes, V.F., Rich, C.L. (1990). Suicide among physician. In: *Suicide over the life cicle*, ed. S.J. Blumenthal, D.J. Kupfer. Washington: American Psychiatric Press.

Hoppe, S.K., Martin, H.W. (1986). Patterns of suicide among Mexican Americans and Anglos, 1960-1980. *Social Psychiatry*, 21(2), 83-8.

Horesh, N., Orback, I., Gothelf, D., et al. (2003). Comparison of the suicidal behavior of adolescent inpatients with borderline personality disorder and major depression. *Journal of Nervous Mental Disorder*, 191(9), 582-8.

Hori, M., Shiraishi, H., Koizumi, J. (1993). Delusional depression and suicide. *Japanese Journal of Psychiatry Neurology*, 47(4), 811-7.

Houston, K., Hawton, K., Shepperd, R. (2001). Suicide in young people aged 15-24: a psychological autopsy study. *Journal of Affective Disorders*, 63, 159-70.

Hoyert, D.L., Kochanek, K.D., Murphy, S.L. (1999). Deaths: final data for 1997. *National Vital Statistics Reports*, 47, 1-104.

Hoyer, G., Lund, E. (1993). Suicide among women related to number of children in marriage. *Archives of General Psychiatry*, 50(2), 134-7.

Hyler, S.E. (1994). *Personality Diagnostic Questionnaire-IV (PDQ-IV)*. New York: New York State Psychiatric Institute.

Hyman, S.E. (1987). *Manual of Psychiatry Emergencies*. Little Brown.

Huertas, D. (2005). *Agresividad en las disfunciones cerebrales*. In: D. Huertas, J.J. López Ibor Aliño JJ, & M.D. Crespo Hervás, pp. 78-99. Barcelona: Ars Médica.

Hueston, W.J., Werth, J., Matinous, A.G. (1999). Personality disorder traits: prevalence and effects on heltah status in primary care patients. *Intern Journal of Psychiatry Medicine*, 29, 63-74.

Hunter, E.M. (1991). An examination of recent suicides in remote Australia. *Australian and New Zealand Journal of Psychiatry*, 25, 197–202.

Inskip, H.M., Harris, E.C., Barraclough, B. (1998). Lifetime risk of suicide for affective disorder, alcoholism and schizophrenia. *British Journal of Psychiatry*, 172, 35-7.

Irfani, S. (1978). Personality correlates of suicidal tendency among Iranian and Turkish students. *Journal of Psycholgoy*, 99 (2d Half), 151-3.

Isherwood, J., Adam, K.S., Hornblow, A.R. (1982). Life event stress, psychosocial factors, suicide attempt and auto-accident proclivity. *Journal of Psychosomatic Research*, 26, 371-83.

Isometsa, E.T., Henriksson, M.M., Aro, H.M., et al. (1994). Suicide in bipolar disorder in Finland. *American Journal of Psychiatry*, 151(7), 1020-4.

Isometsa, E.T., Henriksson, M.M., Aro, H.M., et al. (1994a). Suicide in major depression. *American Journal of Psychiatry*, 151(4), 530-6.

Isometsa, E., Henriksson, M., Aro, H., et al. (1994b). Suicide in psychotic major depression. *Journal of Affective Disorders*, 31(3), 187-91.

Isometsa, E., Henriksson, M., Heikkinen, M., et al. (1996). Suicide among subjetcs with personality disorders. *American Journal of Psychiatry*, 153(5), 667-73.

Isometsa, E., Henriksson, M., Marttunen, M., et al. (1995). Mental disorders in young and middle aged men who commit suicide. *BMJ*, 310, 1366-7.

Jablensky, A. (2002). The classification of personality disorders: critical review and need for rethinking. *Psychopathology*, 35(2/3), 112-6.

Jablensky, A., Kennedy, R.E. (2002). Criteria for assessing a classification in psychiatry. In: *Psychiatric diagnosis and classification*, ed. M. Maj, W. Gaebel, J.J. López-Ibor, N. Sartorius, pp. 1-24. Chichester: Wiley, 2002, pp 1-24.

Jackson, H.J. & Burgess, P.M. (2004). Personality disorders in the community: results from the Australian National Survey of Mental Health and Well-being Part III. Relationships between specific type of personality disorder, Axis 1 mental disorders and physical conditions with disability and health consultations. *Social Psychiatry Psychiatric Epidemiology*, 39(10), 765-6.

Jaspers, K. (1963). General psychopathology. Chicago: University of Chicago Press

Johnson, J., Horwarth, E., Weissman, M.M. (1991). The validity of major depression with psychotic features based on a community study. *Archives of General Psychiatry*, 48, 1075-81.

Jollant, F., Bellivier, F., Leboyer, M., et al. (2005). Impaired decision making in suicide attempters. *American Journal of Psychiatry*, 162(2), 304-10.

Jollant, F., Buresi, C., Guillaume, S., et al (2007b). The influence of four serotonin-related genes on decision-making in suicide attempters. *American Journal of Medicine Genetic Neuropsychiatric Behavior*, 144(5), 615-24

Jollant, F., Guillaume, S., Jaussent, I., et al. (2007a). Impaired decision-making in suicide attempters may increase the risk of problems in affective relationships. *Journal of Affective Disorders*, 99(1-3), 59-62

Jollant, F., Guillaume, S., Jaussent, I., et al. Psychiatric diagnoses and personality traits associated with disadvantageous decision-making. *Eur Psychiatry* (in press)

Juckel, G., Hegerl, U. (1994). Evoked potentials, serotonin, and suicidality. *Pharmacopsychiatry,* 27 Suppl 1, 27-9.

Jones, P.B., Rantakallio, P., Hartikainen, A.L., et al. (1998). Schizophrenia as a longterm outcome of pregnancy, delivery, and perinatal complications: a 28-year follow-up of the 1966 north Finland general population birth cohort. *American Journal of Psychiatry*, 155(3), 355-64.

Josepho, S.A. & Plutchik, R. (1994). Stress, coping and suicide risk in psychiatric inpatients. *Suicide Life Threatening Behavior*, 24, 48-57.

Kagan, J., Reznick, J.S., Snidman, N. (1987). The physiology and psychology of behavioral inhibition in children. *Children Deviance,* 58(6), 1459-73.

Kaplan, S., Lester, D. (1994). Depression, mania, and suicidal preoccupation. *Psychology Reports*, 3(1), 974-5.

Kaplan H.J. & Sadock, B.J. (1998). *Synopsisf of psychiatry*, 8th ed. Baltimore: Williams and Wilkins.

Kardiner, A. (1939). *The individual and his society*. New York: Columbia University Press.

Kashner, T.M., Shoaf, T., Rush, A.J. (2000). The economic burden of suicide in the United States in the year 2000. *The Economics of Neuroscience*, 2(3), 44-8.

Kaslow, N.J., Reviere, S.L., Chance, S.E., et al. (1998). An empirical study of the psychodynamics of suicide. *Journal of American Psychoanalitic Associaton*, 46(3), 777-96.

Kaufman, J., Yang, B.Z., Douglas-Palumberi, H., et al. (2004). Social supports and serotonin transporter gene moderate depression in maltreated children. *Procedings Natural Academy of Science*, 101, 17316-21.

Kavka, J. (1998). The suicide of Richard Corey: an explication of the poem by Edwin Arlington Robinson, cited by Ronningstam, E.F., Maltsberger, J.T. (1998). Pathological narcissism and sudden suicide-related collapse. *Suicide Life Threaten Behavior*, 28, 261-71.

Kavoussi, R., Armstead, P., Coccaro, E. (1997). The neurobiology of impulsive aggression. *Psychiatric Clinics of North America*, 20(2), 395-403.

Keefe, R. S. The contribution of neuropsychology to psychiatry. (1995). *American Journal of Psychiatry*, 152(1), 6-15.

Keilp, J. G., Sackeim, H. A., Brodsky, B. S., et al. (2001). Neuropsychological dysfunction in depressed suicide attempters. *American Journal of Psychiatry*, 158(5), 735-41.

Keller, F., Wolfersdorf, M., Straub, R., et al. (1991). Suicidal behaviour and electrodermal activity in depressive inpatients. *Acta Psychiatrica Scandinavica*, 83(5), 324-8.

Kelly, T.M., Soloff, P.H., Lynch, K.G., et al. (2000). Recent life events, social adjustment, and suicide attemtps in patients with major depression and borderline personality disorder. *Journal of Personality Disorders*, 14, :316-26.

Kendler, K.S., Kessler, R.C., Walters, E.E., et al. (1995). Stressful life events, genetic liability, and onset of an episode of major depression in women. *American Journal of Psychiatry*, 152(6), 833-42.

Kendler, K., Khun, J., Vittum, J., et al. (2005). The interaction of stressful life events and a serotonin transporter polymorphism in the prediction of episodes of major depression. *Archives of General Psychiatry*, 62 (5), 529-35.

Kendler, K.S., Masterson, C.C., Davis, K.L. (1985). Psychiatric illness in first-degree relatives of patients with paranoid psychosis, schizophrenia and medical illness. *British Journal of Psychiatry*, 147, 524-1.

Kendler, K.S., Masterson, C.C., Ungaro, O.R., et al. (1984). A family history study of schizophrenic related personality disorders. *American Journal of Psychiatry*, 141, 424-7.

Kennedy, G.J., & Tanenbaum, S. (2000). Suicide and aging: international perspectives. *Pyschiatry*, 71, 345-59.

Kernberg, O.F. (1967). Borderline personality organization. *Journal of American Pschoanalitic Association*, 15, 641-85.

Kernberg, O. (1984). *Severe personality disorders*. New Haven, CT: Yale University Press

Kernberg O. (1992). *Aggressions in personality disorders and perversions*. New Haven, CT: Yale University Press.

Kernberg, O.F. (1993). Suicidal behavior in borderline patientes: diagnosis and psychotherapeutic considerations. *American Journal of Psychothery*, 47, 245-54.

Kernberg, O.F. (1996). A Psychoanalitic Theory of Personality Disorders. In: Major theories of personality disorder, ed. J.F. Clarkin & M.F. Lenzenweger, pp. 36-105. New York, Guildford Press.

Kessler, R,C,, Borges, G,, Walters, E.E. (1999). Prevalence of and risk factors for lifetime suicide attempts in the National Comorbidity Survey. *Archives of General Psychiatry*, 56(7), 617-26.

Kety, S. (1986). Genetic factors in suicide. In: *Suicide*, ed. A. Roy A. Baltimore: Williams & Wilkins.

Kim, C.D., Seguin, M., Therrien, N., et al. (2005). Familial aggregation of suicidal behavior: a family study of male suicide completers from the general population. *American Journal of Psychiatry*, 162(5), 1017-9.

King, E. (1994). Suicide in the mentally ill. An epidemiological sample and implications for clinicians. *British Journal of Psychiatry*, 165(5), 658-63.

Kjellander, C., Bongar, C., King, A. (1998). Suicidality in borderline personality disorder. *Crisis*, 19, 125-35.

Kjellsberg, E., Eikeseth, P.H., Dahl, A.A. (1991). Suicide in borderline patients –predictive factors. *Acta psychiatrica Scandinavica*, 84, 283-7.

Klerman, G.L. (1987). Clinical epidemiology of suicide. *Journal of Clinical Psychiatry*, 48 Suppl, 33-8.

Koen, L. et al. (2004). Violence in male patients with schizophrenia: risk markers in a South African population. *Australian New Zealand Journal of Psychiatry*, 38, 254–9.

Koenig, H.G., McCullough, M.E., Larson, D.B. (2001). *Handbook on Religion and Health*. New York: Oxford University Press.

Kolb, J., Gunderson, J.G. (1980). Diagnosing borderline patients with a semi-structured interview. *Archives of General Psychiatry*, 37, 37-41.

Koller, G., Preub, U.W., Bottlender, M., et al. (2002). Impulsivity and aggression as predictors of suicide attempts in alcoholics. *European Archives of Psychiatry Clinics Neuroscience*, 252:155-60.

Kotler, M., Iancu, I., Efroni, R., et al. (2001). Anger, impulsivity, social support and suicide risk in patients with postraumatic stress disorder. *Journal of Nervous Mental Disorders*, 189, 162-7.

Korn, M.L., Plutchik, R., Van Praag, H.M. (1997). Panic-associated suicidal and aggressive ideation and behavior. *Journal of Psychiatric Research*, 31(4), 481-7.

Kotler, M., Barak, P., Cohen, H. (1999). Homicidal behavior in schizophrenia associated with a genetic polymorphism determining low catechol-Omethyltransferase (COMT) activity. *American Journal of Medical Genetics*, 88, 628–33.

Kottack, C.P. (1994). *Antropología – una exploración de la diversidad humana con temas de la cultura hispana*. Madrid: McGraw-Hill.

Kraepelin, E. (1899). *Psychiatrie*. Leipzig: Barth.

Kraepelin, E. (1921). Manic-Depressive Insanity and paranoia, cited by Henry et al. (1999).

Kraus, J. (1975). "Suicidal behaviour" in New South Wales. *British Journal of Psychiatry*, 126, 313-8.

Kreitman, N., Philip, A.E. (1969). Parasuicide. *British Journal of Psychiatry*, 115, 746-7.

Kreitman, N., Schreiber, M. (1979). Parasuicide in young Edinburgh women, 1968-75. *Psychological Medicine*, 9(3), 469-79.

Kretschmer, E. (1936). *Physique and Character. An Investigation of the Nature of Constitution and of the Theory of Temperament.* London: P. Kegan & T. Trench & Co., LTD.

Kretschmer E (1954). Constitución y carácter, cited by Baca Baldomero, E., Roca Bennasar, M. Personalidad y trastorno de la personalidad: historia y evolución de los conceptos. En: *Trastornos de Personalidad*, ArsXXI, Barcelona, 2004

Kroeber, A.L., Kluckhohn, C. (1952). *Culture: A Critical Review of Concepts and Definitions. Papers of the Peabody Museum* (Harvard University), 47 (1)

Krueger, R.F. (2005). Continuity of axes I and II: toward a unified modelo f personality, personality disorders, and clinical disorders. *Journal of Personality Disorder*, 19(3), 233-61.

Krug, E.G., Dahlberg, L.L., Mercy, J.A., et al. (2002). *World Report on Violence and Health.* Geneva, World Health Organization

Kullgren, G. (1988). Factors associated with completed suicide in borderline personality disorder. *Journal of Nervous Mental Disorder*, 176, 40-4.

Kumar, C.T.S., Mohan, R., Ranjith, G., et al. (2006). Characteristics of high intent suicide attempters admitted to a general hospital. *Journal of Affective Disorders*, 91, 77-81.

Kupfer, D.J., Carpenter, L.L., Frank, E. (1988). Is bipolar II a unique disorder? *Comprehensive Psychiatry*, 29(3), 228-36.

Laín-Entralgo, P. (1978). *Historia de la medicina.* Barcelona: Masson, S.A.

Lambert, M.T. (2003). Suicide risk assessment and management: focus on persoanlity disorders. *Current Opinion in Psychiatry*, 16, 71-6.

Lander, E.S. (1996). The new genomics: global views of biology. *Science*, 274, 536-539.

Langley, G.E., Bayatti, N.N. (1984). Suicides in Exe Vale Hospital, 1972-1981. *British Journal of Psychiatry*, 145, 463-7.

La Vecchia, C., Lucchini, F., Levi, F. (1994). Worldwide trends in suicide mortality, 1955-1989. *Acta Psychiatrica Scandinavica*, 90(1), 53-64.

Leal, C., Crespo, M.D. (1999). Introduccion. In: *Trastornos depresivos en la mujer*, ed. C. Leal. Barcelona: Masson, 1999: 1-7.

Leboyer, M. (2003). Searching for alternative phenotypes in psychiatric genetics. *Methods of Molecular Medicine*, 77: 145-61.

Leboyer, M., Bellivier, F., Nosten-Bertrand, M., et al. (1998). Psychiatric genetics: search for phenotypes. *Trends in Neuroscience*, 21(3), 102-5.

Lecubrier, Y. (2001). The influence of comorbidity on the prevalence of suicidal behavior. *European Psychiatry*, 16, 395-9.

LeGris, J., van Reekum, R. (2006). The neuropsychological correlates of borderline personality disorder and suicidal behaviour. *Canadian Journal of Psychiatry*, 51(3), 131-42.

Leibenluft, E., Fiero, P.L., Rubinow, D.R. (1994). Effects of the menstrual cycle on dependent variables in mood disorder research [published erratum appears in *Arch Gen*

Psychiatry 1995 Feb;52(2):144] [see comments]. *Archives of General Psychiatry*, 51(10), 761-81.

Lejoyeux, M., Leon, E., Rouillon, F. (1994). Prevalence and risk factors of suicide and attempted suicide. *Encephale*, 20(5), 495-503.

Lenzenweger, M.F., Loranger, A.W., Korfine, L., et al. (1997). Detecting personality disorders in a nonclinical population: Application of a 2-stage procedure for case identification. *Archives of General Psychiatry*, 54, 345-351.

Leon, A.C., Friedman, R.A., Sweeney, J.A., et al. (1990). Statistical issues in the identification of risk factors for suicidal behavior: the application of survival analysis. *Psychiatry Research*, 31, 99-108.

Lesage, A.D., Boyer, R., Grunberg, F., et al. (1994). Suicide and mental disorders: a case-control study of young men. *American Journal of Psychiatry*, 151, 1063-68.

Lesch, K.P., Bengel, D., Heils, A., *et al.* (1996). Association of anxiety-related traits with a polymorphism in the serotonin transporter gene regulatory region. *Science*, 274, 1527-31.

Lester, D. (1969). Suicidal behavior in men and women. *Mental Hygiene*, 53(3), 340-5.

Lester, D. (1988). A physiological theory of sex differences in suicide. *Medical Hypotheses*, 25(2), 115-7.

Lester, D. (1993). Suicidal behavior in bipolar and unipolar affective disorders: a meta-analysis. *Journal of Affective Disorder*, 27(2), 117-21.

Lester, D. (1998). Suicide and homicide after the fall of communist regimes. *European Psychiatry*, 5(6), 392-6.

Lester, D. (2001). The epidemiology of suicide. In: *Suicide prevention: Resources for the Millennium*. Philadelphia, PA: Brunner & Routledge, cited by Abdel-khalek A & Lester D. (2002). Can personality predict suicidality? A study in two cultures. *IJSP*, 48(3):231-9.

Lester, D. (1998). *Suicide in African Americans*. Commack, NY, Nova Science.

Lin, P.Y., Tsai, G. (2004). Associaton between serotonin transporter gene promoter polymorphism and suicide: results of a meta-analysis. *Biological Psychiatry*, 55(10), 1023-30.

Lester, D., Abe, K. (1989). The effect of controls on sedatives and hypnotics on their use for suicide. *Clinical Toxicology*, 27, 299-303.

Lester, D., Beck, A.T., Steer, R.A. (1989). Attempted suicide in those with personality disorders. A Comparison of Depressed and Unsocialized Suicide Attempters. *European Archives of Psychiatry and Neurology Sciences*, 239, 109-12

Lester, D., Leenars, A. (1993). Suicide rates in Canada - before and after tightening firearms control laws. *Psychology Reports*, 72, 787-90.

Lester, D., Yang, B. (1991). The relationship between divorce, unemployment and female participation in the labour force and suicide rates in Australia and America. *Australian New Zealand Journal of Psychiatry*, 25(4), 519-23.

Levav, I., Lima, B.R., Somoza Lennon, M., et al. (1989). Salud mental para todos en América Latina y el Caribe. Bases epidemiológicas para la acción. *Boletín de la Oficina Sanitaria Panamericana*, 107, 196-219.

Levine, R.A. (1973). *Culture, Behaviour, ad Personality*. London: Hutchinson..

Lewis, G., Appleby, L. (1988). Personality disorder: the patients psychiatrists dislike. *British Journal of Psychiatry*, 153, 44-9.

Lewis, G., Hawton, K., Jones, P. (1997). Strategies for preventing suicide. *British Journal of Psychiatry*, 171, 351-4.

Li, D.W., He, L. (2006). Further clarification of the contribution of the tryptophan hydroxylase (TPH) gene to suicidal behavior using systematic allelic and genotypic meta-analyses. *Human Genetics*, 119(3), 233-40.

Li, X.Y., Philips, M.R., Wang, Y.P., et al. (2003). The comparison of impulsive and non-impulsive attempted suicide (in Chinese). *Chinese Journal of Psychiatry*, 29, 27-31. Ref Type: Abstract

Lin, P.Y., Tsai, G.C. (2004). Association between serotonin transporter gene promoter polymorphism and suicide: Results of a meta-analysis. *Biological Psychiatry*, 55(10), 1023-30.

Linehan, M.M., Goodstein, J.L., Nielsen, S.L., et al. (1983). Reasons for staying alive when you are thinking of killing yourself: the reasons for living inventory. *Journal of Consulting Clinical Psychology*, 51, 276-86.

Linkowski, P., de M.V, Mendlewicz, J. (1985). Suicidal behaviour in major depressive illness. *Acta Psychiatrica Scandinavica*, 72(3), 233-8.

Links, P.S., Gould, B., Ratnayake, R. (2003). Assessing suicidal youth with antisocial, borderline, or narcissistic personality disorder. *Canadian Journal of Psychiatry*, 48(5), 301-10.

Links, P.S. & Stockwell, M. (2002). The role of couple therapy in the treatment of narcissistic personality disorder. *American Journal of Psychotherapy*, 56, 522-38.

Lipe, H., Schultz, A., Bird, T.D. (1993). Risk factors for suicide in Huntingtons disease: a retrospective case controlled study. *American Journal of Medical Genetics*, 48(4), 231-3.

Litman, R.E. (1992). Predicting and preventing hospital and clinic suicides. In: *Assessment and prediction of suicide*, ed. R.W. Marris, A.L. Berman, J.T. Maltsberger JT, R.I. Yufit. New York: Guilford Press.

Livesley, W.J., Jackson, D.N. (1986). The internal consistency and factorial structure of behaviors judged to be associated with DSM-III personality disorders. *American Journal of Psychiatry*, 143, 1473-4.

Livesley, W.J., Jackson, D.N., Schroeder, M.L. (1989). A study of the factorial structure of personality pathology. *Journal of Personality Disorders*, 3, 292-306.

Livesley, W.J., Jang, K.L. (2000). Toward an empirically based classification of personality disorder. *Journal of Personality Disorders*, 14(1), 137-51.

Livesley, W.J., Jang, K.L., Jackson, D.N., et al. (1993). Genetic and environmental contributions to dimensions of personality disorders. *American Journal of Psychiatry*, 150, 1826-31.

Livesley, W.J., Jang, K.L., Vernon, P.A. (1998). Phenotypic and genetic structure of traits delineating personality disorder. *Archives of General Psychiatry*, 55(10), 941-8.

Livesley, W.J., Schroeder, M.L., Jackson, D.N., et al. (1994). Categorial distinctions in the Study of Personality Disorder: Implications for Classification. *Journal of Abnormal Psychology*, 103(1), 6-17

Lonnqvist, J.K., Henriksson, M.M., Isometsa, E.T., et al. (1995). Mental disorders and suicide prevention. *Psychiatry and Clinical Neurosciences*, 49, S111-6

Lopez-Garcia, M.B., Hinojal-Fonseca, R., Bobes-García, J. (1993). El suicidio: aspectos conceptuales, doctrinales, epidemiologicos y juridicos. *Revista de Derecho Penal y Criminologia*, 3, 309-411.

Lopez-Ibor Aliño, J.J., Chinchilla Moreno, A., Fuentes Alvarado, P. (1982). *Etología de la agresividad humana*. In: C. Ruiz Ogara, D. Barcia Salorio, J.J. López Ibor, pp. 324-331. Barcelona: Toray.

Loranger, A.W. (1988). *Personality Disorders Examination (PDE) Manual*. Yonkers, NY: DV Communications.

Loranger, A.W. (1990). The impact of DSM-III on diagnostic practice in a university hospital. *Archives of General Psychiatry*, 47, 672-5.

Loranger, A.W. (1992). Are current self-report and interview measures adequate for epidemiological studies of personality disorders? *Journal of Personality Disorders*, 6, 313-25.

Loranger, A.W. (1995). International Personality Disorder Examination Manual: ICD-10 Module. Washington, DC: American Psychiatric Press.

Loranger, A.W. (1996). Dependent personality disorder. *Journal of Nervous Mental Disorder*, 184, 17-21.

Loranger, A.W. (2001). *OMNI Personality Inventories. Professional manual. OMNI Personality Inventory. OMNI Personality Disorders Inventory*. Florida. Psychological Assessment Resources.

Loranger, A., Hirschfeld, R.M.A., Sartorious, N., et al. (1991). The WHO/ADAMHA International Pilot Study of Personality Disorders: Background and purpose. *Journal of Personality Disorders*, 5, 296–306.

Loranger, A.W., Lenzenweger, M.F., Gartner, A.F., et al. (1991). Trait-State artefacts and the diagnosis of personality disorders. *Archives of General Psychiatry*, 48, 720-8.

Loranger, A., Sartorious, N., Andreoli, A. (1994). The International Personality Disorders Examination. The WHO/ADAMHA International Pilot Study of Personality Disorders. *Archives of General Psychiatry,* 51, 215–24.

Lorant, V., Kunst, A.E., Huisman, M., et al. (2005). The EU Working Group. A European comparative study of marital status and socio-economic inequalities in suicide. *Social Sciences of Medicine*, 60, 2431-41.

Lovallo, W.R., Yechiam, E., Sorocco, K.H., et al. (2006). Working memory and decision-making biases in young adults with a family history of alcoholism: studies from the Oklahoma family health patterns project. *Alcohol Clinical Experimental Research*, 30(5), 763-73.

Lynam DR, Caspi A, Moffitt TE, Loeber R, Stouthamer-Loeber M. (2007). Longitudinal evidence that psychopathy scores in early adolescence predict adult psychopathy. *Journal of Abnormal Psychology,* 116, 155-65.

Madoz-Gúrpide, A., Baca-García, E., Díaz-Sastre, C., et al. (1999). Attempted suicide and previous contact with health system. *Actas Españolas de Psiquiatría*, 27(5), 329-33.

Maes, M., Cosyns, P., Meltzer, H.Y., et al. (1993). Seasonality in violent suicide but not in nonviolent suicide or homicide. *American Journal of Psychiatry*, 150, 1380–5.

Magnusson, P.K.E., Rasmussen, F., Lawlor, D.A., et al. (2006). Association of body mass index with suicide mortality: A prospective cohort study of more than one million men. *American Journal of Epidemiology*, 163(1), 1-8.

Main, M. & Solomon, J. (1986). Discovery of a new, insecure-disorganised / disorientated attachment pattern. In: *Affective Development in Infancy,* ed. M. Yogman & T.B. Brazelton TB, pp. 95-124. Norwood: Ablex.

Maier, W., Lichtermann, D., Klinger, T., et al. (1992). Prevalences of personality disorders (DSM-III-R) in the community. *Journal of Personality Disorders*, 6, 187-96.

Mairer, W. & Minges, J., Lichtermann, D., et al. Personality disorders and personality variations inrelatives of patients with bipolar affective disorders. *Journal of Affective Disorder*, 53, 173-81.

Malinowski, B (2001). *Sex and Repression in Savage Society*. London: Routledge.

Malone, K.M., Corbitt, E.M., Li, S., et al. (1996). Prolactin response to fenfluramine and suicide attempt lethality in major depression. *British Journal of Psychiatry*, 168, 324-9.

Malone, K.M., Haas, G.L., Ellis, S.P., et al. (2000). Protective factors against suicidal acts in major depression: reasons for living. *American Journal of Psychiatry*, 157(7), 1084-88.

Malone, K.M., Haas, G.L., Sweeney, J.A., et al. (1993). Major depression and the risk of attempted suicide. *Journal of Affective Disorders*, 34(3), 173-85.

Malone, K.M., Oquendo, M.A., Haas, G.L., et al. (2000). Protective factors against suicidal acts in major depression: reasons for living. *American Journal of Psychiatry*, 157(7), 1084-8.

Maltsberger, J.T. (1994). Calculated risks in the treatment of intractable suicidal patients. *Psychiatry*, 57, 199-212.

Maltsberger, J.T. (1997). Ecstatic suicide. *Archives of Suicide Research*, 3, 283-301.

Mann, J.J. (1993). Psychobiologic predictors of suicide. *Psychiatric Q*, 64(4), 345-58.

Mann, J.J. (1995). Violence and aggression. In: *Psychopharmacology: The fourth generation of progress*, ed. F.E. Bloom & D.J. Kupfer DJ, pp. 1919-28. Nueva York: Raven Press.

Mann, J.J. (1998). The neurobiology of suicide. *Natural Medicine*, 4(1), 25-30.

Mann, J.J. (2002). A Current Perspective of Suicide and Attempted Suicide. *Annals of Internal Medicine*, 136, 302-11.

Mann, J.J. (2003). Neurobiology of suicidal behaviour. *Natural Review of Neuroscience*, 4, 819–28.

Mann, J.J. (2004). Searching for triggers of suicidal behavior. *American Journal of Psychiatry*, 161, 395-8.

Mann, J.J. (2005). Suicide Prevention Strategies. A Systematic Review. *Journal of American Medical Association*, 294(16), 2064-74.

Mann, J.J., Arango, V. (1992). Integration of neurobiology and psychopathology in a unifed model of suicidal behabior. *Journal of Clinical Psychopharmacology*, 12(2 Suppl), 2-7.

Mann, J.J., Currier, D., Stanley, B., et al. (2006). Can biological tests assist prediction of suicide in mood disorders? *International Journal of Neuropsychopharmacology*, 9(4), 465-74.

Mann, J.J., Huang, Y.Y., Underwood, M.D., et al. (2000). A serotonin transporter gene promoter polymorphism (5-HTTLPR) and prefrontal cortical binding in major depression and suicide [see comments]. *Archives of General Psychiatry*, 57(8), 729-38.

Mann, J.J., McBride, P.A., Malone, K.M., et al. (1995). Blunted serotonergic responsivity in depressed inpatients. *Neuropsychopharmacology*, 13, 53-64.

Mann, J.J., Malone, K.M., Nielsen, D.A., et al. (1997). Possible association of a polymorphism of the tryptophan hydroxylase gene with suicidal behavior in depressed patients. *American Journal of Psychiatry*, 154, 1451–53.

Mann, J.J. & Malone, K.M. (1997). Cerebrospinal fluid amines and higher-lethality suicide attempts in depressed inpatients. *Biological Psychiatry*, 41(2), 162-71.

Mann, J.J., Marzuk, P.M., Arango, V. (1989). Neurochemical studies of violent and nonviolent suicide. *Psychopharmacology Bulletin*, 3, 407-13.

Mann, J.J., Oquendo, M., Underwood, M.D., et al. (1999a). The neurobiology of suicide risk: a review for the clinician. *Journal of Clinical Psychiatry*, 60 Suppl. 2: 7-11.

Mann, J.J., Waternaux, C., Haas, G.L., et al. (1999b). Toward a clinical model of suicidal behavior in psychiatric patients. *Amercian Journal of Psychiatry*, 156(2), 181-9.

Mann, J.J., Huang, Y.Y., Underwood, M.D., et al. (2000). A serotonin transporter gene promoter polymorphism (5-HTTLPR) and prefrontal cortical binding in major depression and suicide (see comments). *Archives of General Psychiatry*, 57, 729–38.

Mann, J.J., Malone, K.M. (1997). Cerebrospinal fluid amines and higher lethality suicide attempts in depressed impatients. *Biological Psychiatry*, 41, 162-71.

Mann, J.J., Apter, A., Bertolote, J., et al. (2005). Suicide Prevention Strategies. *Journal of American Medical Association*, 294 (16), 2064-74.

Manuck, S.B., Flory, J.D., Ferrell, R.E, et al. (1999). Aggression and anger-related traits associated with a polymorphism of the tryptophan hydroxylase gene. *Biological Psychiatry*, 45(5), 603-14.

Maris, R.W. (2002). Suicide. *Lancet*, 360, 319-26.

Maris, R.W., Berman, A.L., Silverman, M.M. (2000). *Comprehensive textbook of suicidology*. Londres, Guilford.

Martín, R.L., Cloninger, C.R., Guze, S.V., et al. (1985). Mortality in a follow-up of 500 psychiatric outpatients:1. Total mortality. *Archives of General Psychiatry*, 42, 47-54.

Martos- Rubio, A. (2000). *Historia de la Psiquiatría*. Barcelona: Temis Pharma, S.L.

Marzuk, P.M., Tardiff, K., Hirsch, C.S. (1992). The epidemiology of murder-suicide. *Journal of American Medical Association*, 267(23), 3179-83.

Maser, J.D., Akiskal, H.S., Schettler, P., et al. (2002). Can temperament identify affectively ill patients who engage in lethal or non-lethal suicidal behavior? *Suicide Life Threateing Behavior,* 32, 10-32.

Massing, W., Angermeyer, M.C. (1985). The monthly and weekly distribution of suicide. *Social Science & Medicine*, 21, 433–41.

Mattia, J.I., Zimmerman, M. (2001). Epidemiology. In: *Handbook of personality disorders: Theory, practice & research*, ed. J. Livesley, pp. 107-23. New York: Guildford Press

Marks, I.M., Nesse, R.M. (1994). Fear and fitness: an evolutionary analysis of anxiety disorders. *Ethology sociobiology*, 15, 247-61.

Marttunen, M.J., Aro, H.M., Henriksson, M.M., et al. (1991). Mental disorders in adolescent suicide : DMS-III-R axes I and II diagnoses in suicides among 13- to 19-years-olds in Finland. *Archives of General Psychiatry*, 48, 834-9.

McGlashan, T.H. (1986). The Chesnut Lodge Follow-up Study III: long term otucome of borderline personalities. *Archives of General Psychiatry*, 43, 20-30.

McGuire, M.T., Marks, I., Nesse, R.M., et al. (1997). Evolutionary biology: a basic science for psychiatry. In: *The Maladapted Mind.,* ed. S. Barón-Cohen S, pp. 23-38. Sussex: Psychology Press.

McGuire M., Troisi A. (1998). *Darwinian Psychiatry*. Nueva York Oxford University Press.

Mc Hugh, P.R., Slavney, P.R. (2001). *Las perspectivas de la Psiquiatría*. Zaragoza: Prensas Universitarias de Zaragoza.

McIntire, M.S., Angle, C.R. The taxonomy of suicide and self-poisoning: a pediatric perspective. In: *Self-destructive behavior in children and adolescents*. ed. C.F. Wells & I.R. Stuart, pp. 224-49. New York, NY, Van Nostrand Reinhold.

McIntosh, J.L., Santos, J.F. (1985-86). Methods of suicide by age: sex and race differences among the young and old. *International Journal of Aging Human Development*, 22, 123-39.

McIntosh, J.L., Santos, J.F., Hubbard, R.W., et al. (1994). *Elder suicide: research, theory and treatment*. Washington, DC, American Psychological Association

McKusick, V.A. (2001). The anatomy of the human genome: a neo-Vesalian basis for medicine in the 21st century. *Journal of American Medical Association*, 286(18), 2289-95.

Medina, A., Moreno, M.J. (1998). *Los trastornos de la personalidad. Un estudio médico-filosófico*. Córdoba: producciones S.L., Novartis

Mehlum, L., Friis, S., Vaglum, P., et al. (1994). The longitudinal pattern of suicidal behaviour in borderline personality disorder: a prospective follow-up study. *Acta Psychiatrica Scandinavica*, 90, 124-30.

Meltzer, H.Y., Okayli, G. (1995). Reduction of suicidality during clozapine treatment of neuroleptic-resistant schizophrenia: impact on risk-benefit assessment. *American Journal of Psychiatry*, 152(2), 183-90.

Merikangas, K.R. & Risch, N. (2003). Will the genomics revolution revolutionize psychiatry? *American Journal of Psychiatry*, 160(4), 625-35.

Merson, S., Tyrer, P., Duke, P., et al. (1994). Interrater reliability of ICD-10 guidelines for the diagnosis of personality disorders. *Journal of Personality Disorders*, 8, 89-95.

Mehryar, A.H., Hekmat, H., Khajavi, F. (1977). Some personality correlates of contemplated suicide. *Psychology Reports*, 40(3), 1291-4.

Mendez, M.F., Doss, R.C. (1992). Ictal and psychiatric aspects of suicide in epileptic patients. *International Journal of Psychiatry Medicine*, 22(3), 231-237.

Micciolo, R., Williams, P., Zimmermann-Tansella, C., et al. (1991). Geographical and urban–rural variation in the seasonality of suicide: Some further evidence. *Journal of Affective Disorders*, 21, 39–43.

Michaelis, B.M. ,et al. (2003). Characteristics of a first suicide attempts in single versus multiple suicide attempters with bipolar disorder. *Comprehensive Psychiatry*, 44 (1), 15-20.

Mieczkowski, T.A., Sweeney, J.A., Haas, G.L., et al. (1993). Factor composition of the Suicide Intent Scale. *Suicide Life Threatening Behavior*, 23(1), 37-45.

Miles, C.P (1977). Conditions predisposing to suicide: a review. *Journal of Nervous Mental Disorder*, 164(4), 231-46.

Milin, R., Turgay, A. (1990). Adolescent couple suicide: literature review. *Canadian Journal of Psychiatry*, 35(2), 183-6.

Millon T. (1967). *Theories of psychopathology*. Philadelphia: Saunders.

Millon T. (1969). *Modern psychopathology: A Biosocial approach to maladaptive learning and functioning*. Philadelphia: Saunders.

Millon T. (1977). *Millon Clinical Multiaxial Inventory Manual*. Minneapolis: National Computer Systems.

Millon T. (1981). *Disorders of Personality*. DSM-III: Axis II. New York: John Wiley & Sons.

Millon T. (1987). *Millon clinical multiaxial inventory manual II.* Minneapolis: National Computer Systems.

Millon, T. (1990). *Towards a new personology: an evolutionary model.* Nueva York: John Wiley.

Millon, T. (1991). Classification in Psychopathology: rationale, alternatives, and standards. *Journal of Abnormal Psychology*, 100, 245-61.

Millon, T. (1993). *La personalidad y sus trustornos.* Barcelona: Martínez Roca

Millon, T. (1998). Teorías de la personalidad: históricas, modernas y contemporáneas. In: *Trastornos de la personalidad*, ed. T. Millon, R. Davis, pp. 37-84. Más allá del DSM-IV. Barcelona: Masson, S.A.

Millon Th., Davis R.D. (1996) *Trastornos de la personalidad.* Más allá del DSM-IV. Barcelona: Masson, 1998.

Millon, T., Disenhaus, H. (1972). *Research Methods in Psychopathology.* New York: Wiley.

Millon, T., Davis, R. (1996). An Evolutionary Theory of Personality Disorders. In: *Major theories of personality disorder*, ed. J.F. Clarkin & M.F. Lenzenweger, pp. 221-346. New York, Guildford Press.

Millon, T, Davis, R.C. (1998). *Trastornos de la personalidad.* Más allá del DSM-IV. Barcelona: Masson, S.A.

Millon, T., Davis, R. (2001). *Trastornos de la personalidad en la vida moderna.* Barcelona, Masson.

Millon, T., Meagher, S.E., Grossman, S.D. (2001). Theoretical perspectives. In: *Handbook of personality disorders : theory, research and treatment*, pp. 39-59. New York: Guildford.

Millon, T., Millon, C., Davis, R.D. (1994). *Millon Clinical Multiaxial Inventory-III.* Minneapolis: Nacional Computer Systems.

Milos, G., Spindler, A., Buddeberg, C., et al. (2003). Axes I & II comorbidity and treatment experiences in eating disorder subjects. *Psychotherapy Psychosomatics*, 72, 276-85.

Miniño, A.M., Arias, E., Kochanek, K.D., Murphy, S.L., Smith, B.L. (2002). Deaths: final data for 2000. *National Vital Statistics Reports*, 50(15). Hyattsville, MD: National Center for Health Statistics

Mirnics, K., Middleton, F.A., Stanwood, G.D., et al. (2001). Disease-specific changes in regulator of G-protein signalin 4 (RGS4) expression in schizophrenia. *Molecular Psychiatry*, 6(3), 293-301.

Minkoff, K., Bergman, E., Beck, A.T., et al. Hopelessness, depression, and attempted suicide. *American Journal of Psychiatry*, 130(4), 455-9.

Miron, C.J., Saenz, G.M., Blanco, M.L., et al. (1997). Descriptive epidemiology of suicide in Spain (1906-1990). *Actas Luso Españolas de Neurología Psiquiatría y Ciencias Afines*, 25(5), 327-31.

Mittendorfer-Rutz, E., Rasmussen, F., Wasserman, D. (2004). Restricted fetal growth and adverse maternal psychosocial and socioeconomic conditions as risk factors for suicidal behaviour of offspring: a cohort study. *Lancet*, 364(9440), 1135-40.

Modestin, J., Kopp, W. (1988). Study on suicide in depressed inpatients. *Journal of Affective Disorder*, 15(2), 157-62.

Moeller, F.G., Barrat, E.S., Schmitz, J.M., et al. (2001). Psychiatric aspects of impulsivity. *American Journal of Psychiatry*, 158, 1783-93.

Moffitt, T.E. (1993). Adolescence-limited and life-course persistent antisocial behavior: A developmental taxonomy. *Psychological Review*, 100, 674–701.

Moffit, T.E., Caspi, A., Rutter, M.(2005). Strategy for investigating interactions between measured genes and measured environments. *Archives of General Psychiatry*, 62(5), 473-81.

Molinari, V., Ames, A., Essa, M. (1994). Prevalence of personality disorders in two geropsychiatric inpatient units. *Journal of Geriatric Psychiatry Neurology*, 7(4), 209-15.

Molock, S.D., Puri, R., Matlin, S., et al. (2006). Relationship Between Religious Coping and Suicidal Behaviors Among African American Adolescents. *Journal of Black Psychology*, 32, 366-89.

Monkul, E.S., Hatch, J.P., Nicoletti, M.A., et al. (2007). Fronto-limbic brain structures in suicidal and non-suicidal female patients with major depressive disorder. *Molecular Psychiatry* 12(4), 360-66

Monkul, E.S., Spence, S., Nicoletti, M.A., et al. (in press). Fronto-limbic brain structures in suicidal and non-suicidal female patients with major depressive disorder. *Molecular Psychiatry*

Monras-Arnau, M. (1995). Seguimiento a cinco años de alcohólicos con antecedentes de tentativas suicidas. *Adicciones Revista de Socidrogalcohol*, 7(4), 479-94.

Monras-Arnau, M. (2000). La tentativa autolítica como indicador pronóstico en el tratamiento del alcoholismo. *I Congreso Virtual de Psiquiatría*, Conferencia 36-POS-A.

Monroe, S.M., Simons, A.D. (1991). Diathesis-stress theories in the context of life stress research: implications for the depressive disorders. *Psychological Bulletin*, 110(3), 406-25.

Moore, J. & Farmer, A (1984). Personality and illness. In: *Child Psychiatry: Modern approaches,* ed. M. Rutter & L. Hersov, pp. 711-21. London: Blackwell.

Moran, P. (1999). *Antisocial Personality Disorder. An Epidemiological Perspective.* London: Gaskell.

Moran, P. (2000). Should psychiatrists treat personality disorders? London: King's College London (Maudsley Discussion Paper No. 7)

Moran, P., Jenkins, R., Tylee, A., Blizard, R., Mann, A. (2000). The prevalence of personality disorder among UK primary care attenders. *Acta Psychiatrica Scandinava*, 102, 52-7.

Morey, L.C. (1998a). Personality disorders in DSM-III and DSM-III-R: convergence, coverage, and internal consistency. *American Journal of Psychiatry*, 145(5), 573-7.

Morey, L.C. (1998b). The categorical representation of personality disorder: a cluster analysis of DSM-III-R personality features. *Journal of Abnormal Psychology*, 97, 314-21.

Morey, L.C., Waugh, M.H., Blashfield, R.K. (1985). MMPI scales for DSM-III personality disorders: Their derivation and correlates. *Journal of Personality Assessment*, 49, 245-56.

Mortensen, P.B., Agerbo, E., Erikson, T., et al. (2000). Psychiatric illness and risk factors for suicide in Denmark. *Lancet*, 355, 9-12.

Mortensen, P.B., Juel, K. (1993). Mortality and causes of death in first admitted schizophrenic patients. *British Journal of Psychiatry*, 163, 183-9

Mortensen, P.B., Juel, K. (1990). Mortality and causes of death in schizophrenic patients in Denmark. *Acta Psychiatrica Scandinavica*, 81(4), 372-7.

Morton, M.J. (1993). Prediction of repetition of parasuicide: with special reference to unemployment. *Internal Journal of Social Psychiatry*, 39(2), 87-99.

Moscicki, E.K. (1985). Epidemiology of suicidal behavior. In: *Suicide prevention: toward the year 2000*, ed. M.M. Silverman & R.W. Maris, pp. 22-35. New York, NY, Guilford.

Moscicki, E.K. (1997). Identification of suicide risk factors using epidemiologic studies. *Psychiatric Clinics of North America*, 20(3), 499-517.

Motto, J.A., Heilbron, D.C., Juster, R.P. (1985). Development of a clinical instrument to estimate suicide risk. *American Journal of Psychiatry*, 142(6), 680-6.

Muller, P. (1989). Suicide of the schizophrenic patient and its relation to the therapeutic situation. *Psychiatric Praxis*, 16(2), 55-61.

Muller-Oerlinghausen, B. & Roggenbach, J. (2002). Concretism in biological suicide research -- are we eating the menu instead of the meal? Some thoughts on present research strategies. *Pharmacopsychiatry*, 35(2), 44-9.

Muller-Oerlinghausen, B., Roggenbach, J., Franke, L. (2004). Serotonergic platelet markers of suicidal behavior -do they really exist? *Journal of Affective Disorders*, 79(1-3), 13-24.

Murase, S., Ochiai, S., Ueyama, M., et al. (2003). Psychiatric features of seriously life-threatening suicide attempters. A clinical study from a general hospital in Japan. *Journal of Psychosomatic Research*, 55, 379-83.

Murphy, G.E., Wetzel, R.D., Robins, E., et al. (1992). Multiple risk factors predict suicide in alcoholism. *Archives of General Psychiatry*, 49(6), 459-63.

Nada-Raja, S., Skegg, K., Langley, J. et al. (2004). Self-harmful behaviors in a population-based sample of young adults. *Suicide & Life Threatening Behavior*, 34, 177-86.

Nakao, K., Gunderson, J.G., Philips, K.A., et al. (1992). Functional impairment in personality disorders. *Journal of Personality Disorders*, 6, 24-33.

National Institute for Mental Health in England (NIMHE). Personality disorder: No longer a diagnosis of exclusion, 2003. *http://www.nimhe.org.uk*

NCHS. Deaths: final data for 2003. U.S. Department Of Health And Human Services. *URL:http://www.cdc.gov/nchs/products/pubs/pubd/hestats/finaldeaths03/finaldeaths03.htm*

National injury mortality reports, 1987–1998. Atlanta, GA, Centers for Disease Control and Prevention, 2000.

Neeleman, J., Halpern, D., Leon, D., et al. (1997). Tolerance of suicide, religion and suicide rates: an ecological and individual study in 19 Western countries. *Psychological Medicine*, 27, 1165-71.

Neeleman, J., Jones, P., Van-Os, J., et al. (1996). Parasuicide in Camberwell-ethnic differences. *Social Psychiatry Psychiatric Epidemiology*, 31(5), 284-7.

Nemeroff, C.B., Compton, M.T., Berger, J. (2001). The depressed suicidal patient. Assessment and treatment. *Annals of New York Academy of Science*, 932, 1-23.

Nestadt, G., Romanoski, A.J., Chahal, R., et al. (1990). An epidemiological study of histrionic personality disorder. *Psychology Medicine*, 20, 413-22.

Neugebauer, R., Reuss, M.L. (1998). Association of maternal, antenatal and perinatal complications with suicide in adolescence and young adulthood. *Acta Psychiatrica Scandinavica*, 97(6), 412-8.

New, A.S., Hazlett, E.A., Buchsbaum, M.S., et al. (2002). Blunted prefrontal cortical 18fluorodeoxyglucose positron emission tomography response to meta-chlorophenylpiperazine in impulsive aggression. *Archives of General Psychiatry*, 59(7), 621-9.

New, A.S., Siever, L.J. (2003). Biochemical endophenotypes in personality disorders. *Methods of Molecular Medicine*, 77, 199-213.

Newman, S.C., Bland, R.C. (1991). Suicide risk varies by subtype of affective disorder. *Acta Psychiatrica Scandinavica*, 83(6), 420-6.

Nielsen, D.A., Goldman, D., Virkkunen, M., et al. (1994). Suicidality and 5-hydroxyindolacetic acid concentration associated with a tryptophan hydroxylase polymorphism. *Archives of General Psychiatry*, 51, 34-8.

Nielsen, D.A., Virkkunen, M., Lappalainen, J., et al. (1998). A tryptophan hydroxylase gene marker for suicidality and alcoholism. *Archives of General Psychiatry*, 55, 593–602.

Nieto, E., Vieta, E., Cirera, E. (1992). Suicide attempts in patients with organic disease. Intentos de suicidio en pacientes con enfermedad organica. *Medicina Clinica*, 98(16), 618-21.

Nieto Rodríguez, E., Vieta Pascual, E. (1997a). La conducta suicida en los trastornos afectivos. In: *La conducta suicida*, ed. S. Ros Montalbán, pp. 99-121. Madrid: Editorial Libro del Año, 1997.

Nieto Rodríguez, E., Vieta Pascual, E. (1997b). La conducta suicida en los trastornos bipolares. In: *Trastornos bipolares,* ed. E. Vieta Pascual, C. Gasto Ferrer, pp. 318-336. Barcelona: Springer-Verlag Iberica.

Nilsson, A., Axelsson, R. (1989). Psychopathology during long-term lithium treatment of patients with major affective disorders. A prospective study. *Acta Psychiatrica Scandinavica*, 80(4), 375-88.

Nimeus, A., Traskman-Bendz, L., Alsen, M. (1997). Hopelessness and suicidal behavior. *Journal of Affective Disorders*, 42(2-3), 137-44.

Nisbet, P.A. (1996). Protective factors for suicidal black females. *Suicide Life Threatening Behavior*, 26, 325-41.

Nisbet, P.A., Duberstein, P.R., Conwell, Y., et al. (2000). The effect of participation in religious activities on suicide versus natural death in adults 50 and older. *Journal of Nervous Mental Disorders*, 188, 543-6.

Nishimura, A., Shioiri, T., Nushida, H., et al. (1999). Changes in choice of method and lethality between last attempted and completed suicides: How did suicide attempters carry out their desire? *Legal Medicine*, 1, 150-8.

Nordentoft, M., Breum, L., Munck, L.K., et al. (1993). High mortality by natural and unnatural causes: a 10-year follow-up study of patients admitted to a poisoning treatment centre after suicide attempts. *British Medical Journal*, 306, 1637-41.

Nurnberg, H.G., Woodbury, M.A., Bogenschutz, M.P (1999). A mathematical typology analysis of DSM-III-R personality disorder classification: grade of membership technique. *Comprehensive Psychiatry*, 40, 61-71.

Nyman, A.K., Jonsson, H. (1986). Patterns of self-destructive behaviour in schizophrenia. *Acta Psychiatrica Scandinavica*, 73(3), 252-62.

O´Carroll, P.W., Berman, D.L., Haris, R.W., et al. (1996). Beyond the Tower of Babel: a nomenclature for suicidiology. *Suicide Life Threatening Behavior*, 126(3), 237-45.

O'Donnell, I., Farmer, R., Catalan, J. (1996). Explaining suicide: the views of survivors of serious suicide attempts. *British Journal of Psychiatry*, 168(6), 780-6.

Oldham, J.M. (1991). Introduction. In: Oldham JM (edit.). *Personality disorders: new perspectives on diagnostic validity*, pp. 17-20. Washington DC: American Psychiatric Press.

Oldham, J.M. (1994). Personality Disorders: current perspectives. *Journal of American Medical Association,* 272(22), 1770-6.

Oldham, J.M. (2005). Personality disorders. *Focus*, 3(3), 372-82.

Ojima, T., Nakamura, Y., Detels, R. (2004). Methods of suicide in Japan and US. *Journal of Epidemiology*, 14 (6), 187-92

OMS. (1976). El suicidio. Cuadernos de Salud Pública, num 59. Ginebra: Organización Mundial de La Salud.

OMS. (1986). El suicidio. Estrategias del Plan "Salud para todos en el año 2000". Madrid: Organización Mundial de La Salud.

Oquendo, M.A., Baca-Garcia, E. (2004). Nurture versus nature: evidence of intrauterine effects on suicidal behaviour. *Lancet*, 364(9440), 1102-04.

Oquendo, M.A., Dragatsi, D., Harkavy-Friedman, J., et al. (2005). Protective factors against suicidal behavior in Latinos. *The Journal of Nervous and Mental Disease*, 193, 438-43.

Oquendo, M.A., Ellis, S.P., Greenwald, S., et al. (2000). *Suicidio en depresión mayor y diferencias étnicas*. I Congreso Virtual de Psiquiatría.

Oquendo, M.A., Friend, J.M., Halberstan, B., et al. (2003). Association of comorbid posttraumatic stress disorder and major depression with greater risk for suicidal behavior. *American Journal of Psychiatry*, 160[3], 580-2.

Oquendo, M.A., Galfalvy, H., Russo, S., et al. (2004b). Prospective Study of Clinical Predictors of Suicidal Acts after a Major Depressive Episode in Patients with Major Depressive Disorder or Bipolar Disorder. *American Journal of Psychiatry*, 161(8), 1433-41.

Oquendo, M.A., Malone, K.M., Ellis, S.P., et al. (1999). Inadequacy of antidepressant treatment for patients with major depression who are at risk for suicidal behavior. *American Journal of Psychiatry*, 156(2), 190-4.

Oquendo, M.A., Placidi, G.P., Malone, K.M., et al. (2003). Positron emission tomography of regional brain metabolic responses to a serotonergic challenge and lethality of suicide attempts in major depression. *Archives of General Psychiatry*, 60(1), 14-22.

Oquendo, M.A., Waternaux, C., Brodsky, B., et al. (2000). Suicidal behavior in bipolar mood disorder: clinical caracteristics of attempters and non-attempters. *Journal of Affective Disorders*, 59, 101-17.

Overstone, I.M.K. & Kreitman, N. (1974). Two syndromes of suicide. *British Journal of Psychiatry*, 124, 336-45.

Pallis, D.J., Barraclough, B.M., Levey, A.B, et al. (1982). Estimating suicide risk among attempted suicides. I: the development of new clinical scales. *British Journal of Psychiatry*, 141, 37-44.

Papp, P. (1991). *El proceso del cambio, pp. 36*. Buenos Aires: Paidós.

Paris, J. (1990). Completed suicide in borderline personality disorder. *Psychiatry Annals*, 20, 19-21.

Paris, J. (2002a). Implications of long-term outcome research for the managment of patients with borderline personality disorder. *Harvard Review Psychiatry*, 10(6), 315-23.

Paris, J. (2002b). Borderline personality disorder, suicide and pharmacotherapy. *Psychiatric Services*, 53(10), 1330-1.

Paris, J.C. (2002c). Chronic suicidality among patients with borderline personality disorder. *Psychiatric Services*, 53, 738-42.

Paris, J. (2003). *Personality Disorders Over Time*. Washington: American Psychiatric Publishing.

Paris, J. (2005). Outcome and epidemiological research on personality disorders: implications for classification. *Journal of Personality Disorders*, 19(5), 557-62.

Paris, J., Brown, R., Nowlis, D. (1987). Long-term follow-up of borderline patients in a general hospital. *Comprehensive Psychiatry*, 28, 530-5.

Paris, J., Nowlis, D., Brown, R. (1989). Predictors of suicide in borderline personality disorder. *Canadian Journal of Psychiatry*, 34, 8-9.

Paris, J., Zweig-Frank, H. (2001). A 27-year follow-up of patients with borderline personality disorder. *Comprehensive Psychiatry*, 42, 482-7.

Parker, G., Hadzi-Pavlovic, D. (2001). A question of style: refining the dimensions of personality disorder style. *Journal of Personality Disorders*, 15(4), 300-18.

Parsons, T. (1964). Social structure and personality. New York: Free Press.

Patience, D.A., McGuire, R.J., Scott, A.I., et al. (1995). The Edinburgh Primary Care Depression Study: personality disorder and outcome. *British Journal of Psychiatry*, 67, 324-30.

Patterson, W.M., Dohn, H.H., Bird, J. et al. (1983). Evaluation of suicidal patients: The SAD PERSONS Scale. *Psychosomatics*, 30, 296-302.

Pavia, M., Nicotera, G., Scaramuzza, G., et al. (2005). Suicide mortality in Southern Italy : 1998-2002. *Psychiatry Research,* 134, 275-9.

Paykel, E.S. & Dienelt, M.N. (1979). Suicide attempts following acute depression. *Journal of Nervous Mental Disorder*, 153, 234-43.

Paykel, E.S., Dowlatshahi, D. *Life events and mental disorder*, city by Heikkinen, M.E., Henriksson, M.M., Isometsa, E.T., et al. (1997). Recent life events and suicide in personality disorders. *Journal of Nervous Mental Disorder*, 185(6), 373-81.

Paykel, E.S., Prusoff, B.A., Myers, J.K. (1975). Suicide attempts and recent life events. A controlled comparison. *Archives of General Psychiatry*, 32(3), 327-33.

Pearson, J.L., Conwell, Y. (1995). Suicide in late life: challenges and opportunities for research. *International Psychogeriatry*, 7(2), 131-6.

Pendse, B., Westrin, A., Engström, G. (1999). Temperament traits in seasonal affective disorder, suicide attempters with non-seasonal major depression and healthy controls. *Journal of Affective Disorders,* 54, 55-65.

Perez Urdaniz, A., Vega Fernandez, F.M., Martin Navarro, N., et al. (2005). Diagnostics discrepancies between ICD-10 and DSM-IV in personality disorders. *Actas Españolas de Psiquiatría*, 33(4), 244-53.

Perry, C.J. (1990). Personality disorders, suicide and self-destructive behavior. In: *Suicide: understanding and responding*, eds. D. Jacobs & H. Brown. Madison (CT): International Universities Press

Perry, J.C. (1992). Problems and considerations in the valid assessment of personality disorders. *American Journal of Psychiatry*, 149, 1645-53.

Perry, J.C. & Herman, J.L. (1993). Trauma and defence in the etiology of borderline personality disorder. In: Paris J, editor. *Borderline Personality Disorder: Etiology and Treatment*. Washington, DC: American Psychiatric Press.

Pfennig, A., Kunzel, H.E., Kern, N., et al. (2005). Hypothalamus-pituitary-adrenal system regulation and suicidal behavior in depression. *Biological Psychiatry*, 57(4), 336-42.

Pfohl, B., Blum, N., Zimmerman, M. (1995). *Structured Interview for DSM-IV personality (SIDP-IV)*. Iowa city. University of Iowa.

Pfohl, B., Blum, N., Zimmerman, M., et al. (1989). *Structured Interview for DSM-III-R Personality (SIDP-R)*. Iowa city. University of Iowa. Department of Psychiatry.

Pfohl, B., Coryell, W., Zimmerman, M., et al. (1986). DSM-III personality disorders: diagnostic overlap and internal consistency of individual DSM-III criteria. *Comprehensive Psychiatry*, 27(1), 21-34.

Pfohl, B., Stangl, D., Zimmerman, M. (1982). *The Structured Interview for DSM-III Personality Disorders (SIDP)*. Iowa city. University of Iowa. Hospital and Clinics.

Philip, A.E. (1970). Traits, attitudes and symptoms in a group of attempted suicides. *British Journal of Psychiatry*, 116, 475-82.

Phillips, K.A., Gunderson, J.G., Hirschfield R.M., et al. (1990). A review of the depressive personality. *American Journal of Psychiatry*, 147, 830-7.

Phillips, D.P., Lesyna, K., Paight, D.J (1992). Suicide and the media. In: *Assessment and prediction of suicide*. R.W. Marris, A.L.Berman, J.T. Maltsberger, R.I. Yufit. New York: Guilford Press.

Phillips, M.R., Yang, G., Zhang, Y., et al. (2002). Risk factors for suicide in China: a national case-control psychological autopsy study. *Lancet*, 360, 1728-36

Pierce, D.W. (1977). Suicidal intent in self injury. *British Journal of Psychiatry*, 130, 377-85.

Pirkola, S.P., Isometsa, E.T., Heikkinen, M.E., et al. (1999). Female psychoactive substance-dependent suicide victims differ from male--results from a nationwide psychological autopsy study. *Comprehensive Psychiatry*, 40(2), 101-7.

Placidi, G.P., Oquendo, M.A., Malone, K.M., et al. (2000). Anxiety in major depression: relationship to suicide attempts. *American Journal of Psychiatry*, 157 (10):1614 -8.

Platt, S. (1986). Parasuicide and unemployment. *British Journal of Psychiatry*, 149, 401-5.

Plutchik, R., Van Praag, H. (1989). The measurement of suicidality, aggressivity and impulsivity. *Progress in Neuropsychopharmacology Biological Psychiatry*,13, S23-34.

Plutchik, R., Van Praag, H.M., Conte, H.R. (1989). Correlates of suicide and violence risk: III. A two-stage model of countervailing forces. *Psychiatry Research*, 28(2), 215-25.

Pollock, L.R. & Williams, J.M. (2004). Problem-solving in suicide attempters. *Psychological Medicine*, 34(1), 163-7.

Pompili, M., Ruberto, A., Girardi, P., et al. (2004). Suicidality in DSM-IV cluster B personality disorders. An overview. *Ann Ist Super Sanità*, 40(4), 475-83.

Pope, H.G., Jonas, J.M., Hudson, J.I., et al. (1983). The validity of DSM-III borderline personality disorder : a phenomenologic, family history, treatment response, and long-term follow-up study. *Archives of General Psychiatry*, 40, 23-30.

Poulin, F., Boivin, M. (2000). Reactive and proactive aggression: evidence of a two factor-model. *Psycological Assesment*, 12, 115-22.

Poulton, R.G., Andrews, G. (1992). Personality as a cause of adverse life events. *Acta Psychiatrica Scandinavica*, 85, 35-8.

Pounder, D.J. (1985). Suicide by leaping from multistorey car parks. *Medicine Science Law*, 25, 179-88.

Preti, A., Miotto, P. (1998). Seasonality in suicides: The influence of suicide method, gender and age on suicide distribution in Italy. *Psychiatry Research*, 81, 219–31.

Prieto-Cuellar, M., López-Sánchez, J.M. (1995). Las penalidades del joven Goethe ("Werther"). Seminario N° 794 (26-I-1994). In: *Seminarios de la Unidad de Docencia y Psicoterapia* (1993-1994), ed. J.M. Lopez-Sanchez. Granada, pp. 396-417. H. Virgen de las Nieves: Junta de Andalucia.

Prins, H. (1991). Is psychopathic disorder a useful clinical concept? A perspective from England and Wales. *Internal Journal of Offending TherapyComp Crime,* 35(2), 19-125.

Pritchard, C. (1990). Suicide, unemployment and gender variations in the Western world 1964-1986. Are women in Anglo-phone countries protected from suicide? *Social Psychiatry Psychiatric Epidemiology*, 25(2), 73-80.

Qin, P., Mortensen, P.B. (2003). The impact of parental status on the risk of completed suicide. *Archives of General Psychiatry*, 60, 797-802.

Quinn, N., Strauss, C. (1994). *A Cognitive Cultural Anthropology.* In: *Assessing Cultural Anthropology*, ed. R. Borofsky. New York: McGraw-Hill.

Radomsky, E.D., Haas, G.L., Mann, J.J., et al. (1999). Suicidal behavior in patients with schizophrenia and other psychotic disorders. *American Journal of Psychiatry*, 156, 1590-5.

Roy, A. (1985a). Family history of suicide in manic-depresive patients. *Journal of Affective Disorders*, 8, 187-9.

Roy, A. (1985b). Family history of suicide in affective disorders patients. *Journal of Clinical Psychiatry*, 8, 317-9.

Roy, A. (2002). Family history of suicide and neuroticism: a preliminary study. *Psychiatry Research*, 110(1), 87-90.

Roy, A., de Jong, J., Linnoila, M. (1989). Cerebrospinal fluid monoamine metabolites and suicidal behavior in depressed patients. A 5-year follow-up study. *Archives of General Psychiatry*, 46, 609-12.

Roy, A., Schreiber, J., Mazonson, A., et al. (1986). Suicidal behavior in chronic schizophrenic patients: a follow-up study. *Canadian Journal of Psychiatry*, 31(8), 737-40.

Rujescu, D., Giegling, I., Bondy, B., et al. (2002). Association of anger-related traits with SNPs in the TPH gene. *Molecular Psychiatry*, 7(9), 1023-9.

Raja, M., Azzoni, A. (2004). Suicide attempts: differences between unipolar and bipolar patients and among groups with different lethality risk. *Journal of Affective Disorders*, 82, 437-42.

Ramberg, I.L., Wasserman, D. (2000). Prevalence of reporter suicidal behaviour in the general population and mental health-care staff. *Psychological Medicine*, 30, 1189-96.

Ramos-Brieva, J. & Cordero-Villafáfila, A. (1989). Suicide risk after attempted suicide (its incidence and predictive evaluation. *Actas Luso Españolas de Neurología Psiquiatría y Ciencias Afines*, 17(2), 119-25.

Rapeli, C.B., Botega, N.J. (2005). Severe suicide attempts in young adults: suicide intent is correlated with medical lethality. *Sao Paulo Medicine Journal*, 123 (1), 43.

Raust, A., Slama, F., Mathieu, F., et al. (2007). Prefrontal cortex dysfunctions in patients with suicidal behavior. *Psychological Medicine*, 37(3), 411-9

Reich, J. (1998). The relationship of suicide attempts, borderline personality traits, and major depressive disorder in a veteran outpatient population. *Journal of Affective Disorder*, 49, 151-6.

Reich, J.H. (1988). A family history method for DSM-III anxiety and personality disorders. *Psychiatry research*, 26, 131-9.

Reich, J.H. & Girolano, G. (1997). Epidemilogy of DSM-III personality disorders in the community and clinical populations. In: *Assesment and Diagnosis of Personality Disorders*, ed. A.W. Loranger AW, A. Janca, N. Sartorius, pp. 18-42. Cambridge: Cambridge University Press.

Reich, J.H., Thompson, W.D. (1987). Differential assortment of DSM-III personality disorder clusters in three populations. *British Journal of Psychiatry*, 150, 471-5.

Reich, J.H., Rusell, G.V. (1993). Effect of personality disorders on the treatment outcome of axis I conditions. an update. *Journal of Nervous Mental Disorder,* 181, 475-484.

Reif, A. & Lesch, K.P. (2003).Toward a molecular architecture of personality. *Behavior Brain Research*, 139 (1-2), 1-20.

Rendu, A., Moran, P., Patel, A., et al. (2002). Economic impact of personality disorders in UK primary care attenders. *British Journal of Psychiatry*, 181, 62-6.

Retterstol, N. (1998). Suicide in a cultural history perspective, part 1. *Norwegian Journal of Suicidology,* 2

Rich, C.L. (1986). Endocrinology and suicide. *Suicide Life Threatening Behavior*, 16(2), 301-11.

Rich, C.L., Fowler, R.C., Fogarty, L.A., et al. (1988). San Diego Suicide Study. III. Relationships between diagnoses and stressors. *Archives of General Psychiatry*, 45(6), 589-92.

Rich, C.L., Ricketts, J.E., Fowler, R.C., et al. (1988). Some difeerences between men and women who comit suicide. *American Journal of Psychiatry*, 145, 718-22.

Rich, C.L., Runeson, B.S. (1992). Similarities in the diagnostic comorbidity between suicide among young people in Sweden and the United States. *Acta Psychiatrica Scandinavica*, 86, 335-9.

Rich, C.L., Young, D., Fowler, R.C. (1986). San Diego suicide study. I. Young vs old subjects. *Archives of General Psychiatry*, 43(6), 577-82.

Rietdijk, E.A., van den Bosch, L.M., Verheul, R., et al. (2001). Predicting self-damaging and suicidal behaviors in female borderline patients: reasons for living, coping, and depressive personality disorder. *Journal of Personality Disorder*, 15, 512-20.

Rihmer, Z., Barsi, J., Arato, M, (1990). Demeter E. Suicide in subtypes of primary major depression. *Journal of Affective Disorder*, 18(3), 221-5.

Rihmer, Z., Belso, N., Kiss, K. (2002). Strategies for suicide prevention. *Current Opinion in Psychiatry*, 15, 83-7.

Rihmer, Z., Pestality, P. (1999). Bipolar II disorder and suicidal behavior. *Psychiatric Clinics of North America*, 22(3), 667-8.

Rihmer, Z., Rutz, W., Pihlgren, H. (1995). Depression and suicide on Gotland. An intensive study of all suicides before and after a depression-training programme for general pracgtitioners. *Journal of Affective Disorder*, 35, 147-52.

Robins, E., Gassner, J., KaSI, J., et al. (1959). The communication of suicidal intent: a study of 135 cases of successful (completed) suicide. *American Journal of Psychiatry*, 115, 724-33.

Robins, E., Guze, S.B. (1970). Establishment of diagnostic validity in psychiatric iones: its application to schizophrenia. *American Journal of Psychiatry*, 126(1), 983-7.

Robinson, D.J. (1996). *The schizoid personality*. Disordered personalities. Ontario, Canada: Rapad Psychler Press.

Roca Bennasar, M. et al. (2004). *Trastornos de la personalidad*. Barcelona: Ars Médica.

Rogers, R.D., Tunbridge, E.M., Bhagwagar, Z., et al. (2003). Tryptophan depletion alters the decision-making of healthy volunteers through altered processing of reward cues. *Neuropsychopharmacology*, 28(1), 153-62.

Ronningstam, E.F., Gunderson, J., Lyons M. (1995). Changes in pathological narcissism. *American Journal of Psychiatry*, 152, 253-7.

Ronningstam, E.F., Maltsberger, J.T. (1998). Pathological narcissism and sudden suicide-related collapse. *Suicide Life Threaten Behavior*, 28, 261-71.

Roose, S.P., Glassman, A.H., Walsh, B.T., et al. (1983). Depression, delusions, and suicide. *American Journal of Psychiatry*, 140, 1159-62.

Ros Montalbán, S. (1998). *La conducta suicida*. Madrid: Arán Ediciones, S.A.

Rose S. (2001). Moving on from old dichotomies: beyond nature-nurture towards a lifeline perspective. *British Journal of Psychiatry*, 40, s3-s7.

Rosengart, M., et al. (2005). An evaluation of state firearm regulations and homicide and suicide death rates. *Injury Prevention*, 11, 77-83.

Rossow, I. (1996). Alcohol and suicide-beyond the link at the individual level. *Addiction*, 91 (10), 1413-16.

Rosowsky, E., Gurian, B. (1991). Borderline personality disorder in late life. *Internal Psychogeriatry*, 3, 39-52.

Ross, S., Dermatis, H., Levounis, P., et al. (2003). A comparison between dually diagnosed inpatients with and without Axis II comorbidity and the relationship to treatment outcome. *American Journal of Drug Alcohol Abuse*, 29(2), 263-79.

Rothschild, L. & Zimmerman, M. (2002). Borderline personality disorder and age of onset in major depression. *Journal of Personality Disorder*, 16, 189-99.

Rothstein, A. (1980). *The narcissistic pursuit of perfection*. New York: International Universities Press.

Roy, A. (1982). Risk factors for suicide in psychiatric patients. *Archives of General Psychiatry*, 39, 1089-95.

Roy, A. (1984). Suicide in recurrent affective disorder patients. *Canadian Journal of Psychiatry*, 29(4), 319-22.

Roy, A. (1989). Suicide. In: *Comprenhesive textbook of psychiatry*, ed. H. Kaplan & B. Sadock, pp. 1414-27. Baltimore: Willians and Wilkins.

Roy, A., Lamparski, D., DeJong, J., et al. (1990). Characteristics of alcoholics who attempt suicide. *American Journal of Psychiatry*, 147(6), 761-5.

Roy, A., Mazonson, A., Pickar, D. (1984). Attempted suicide in chronic schizophrenia. *British Journal of Psychiatry*, 144, 303-6.

Roy, A., Rylander, G., Forslund, K., et al. (2001). Excess tryptophan hydroxylase 17 779C allele in surviving cotwins of monozygotic twin suicide victims. *Neuropsychobiology*, 43, 233–6.

Roy-Byrne, P.P., Post, R.M., Hambrick, D.D., et al. Suicide and course of illness in major affective disorder. *Journal of Affective Disorder*, 15(1), 1-8.

Rubio Larrosa, V. (2002). Perfil clínico del trastorno límite de la personalidad y de los trastornos del grupo A. Barcelona: Prous Science.

Rubio Larrosa V. (2004). Comportamientos suicidas y trastorno de la personalidad. In: *Comportamientos suicidas. Prevención y tratamiento,* ed. J. (Bobes García, P.A. Sáiz Martínez PA, pp. 222-31. Barcelona: Ars Médica.

Rubio Larrosa, V., Pérez Urbaniz, A. (2003). Trastornos de la personalidad. Madrid: Elsevier.

Rujescu, D., Giegling, I., Sato, T., et al. (2001). A polymorphism in the promoter of the serotonin transporter gene is not associated with suicidal behavior. *Psychiatric Genetics*, 11, 169–72.

Runeson, B. (1989). Mental disorder in youth suicide. DSM-III-R axes I and II. *Acta Psychiatrica Scandinavica*, 79, 490-7.

Runeson, B., Beskow, J. (1991). Borderline personality disorder in young Swedish suicides. *Journal of Nervous Mental Disorder*, 179, 153-6.

Ruocco, A.C. (2005). Reevaluating the distinction between axis I and axis II disorders: the case of borderline personality disorder. *Journal of Clinical Psychology*, 61(12), 1509-23.

Russell, G.F.M., Hersov, L. (1983). *Handbook of Psychiatry, vol. 4: The Neuroses and Personality Disorders*. Cambridge: Cambridge University Press.

Rutter, M. (1984). Continuities, transition and turning points in development, In: *Development through life: A handbook for clinicians*, ed. M. Rutter & D. Hays, pp. 1-25. Oxford: Blackwell, 1984.

Rutter, M. (1987). Temperament, Personality and Personality Disorder. *British Journal of Psychiatry,* 150, 443-58.

Rutter, M., Kim-Cohen, J., & Maughan, B. (2006). Continuities and discontinuities in psychopathology between childhood and adult life. *Journal of Child Psychology and Psychiatry*, 47, 276-306.

Sacks, M. H. and W. T. Carpenter. (1974). The pseudo-therapeutic community: An examination of anti-therapeutic forces on psychiatric units. *Hospital and Community Psychiatry*, 25, 315-8.

Sainsbury, P. (1982). Depression and suicide prevention. *Bibl Psychiatry*, 162(17), 32.

Saiz, J., Montejo, M.L. (1976). La tentativa de suicidio en el hospital general. *Archivos de la Facultad de Medicina de Madrid*, 4, 211-20.

Salk, L., Lipsitt, L.P., Sturner, W.Q., et al. (1985). Relationship of maternal and perinatal conditions to eventual adolescent suicide. *Lancet*, 1(8429), 624-7.

Samuels, J., Eaton, W.W., Bienvenu, O.J., et al. (2002). Prevalence and correlates of personality disorders in a community sample. *British Journal of Psychiatry*, 180, 536-42.

Samuels, J.F., Nestadt, G., Romanoski, A.J., et al. 1994. DSM-III personality disorders in the community. *American Journal of Psychiatry,* 151, 1055-62.

Samuelsson M, Jokinen J, Nordstrom AL, Nordstrom P. (2006). CSF 5-HIAA, suicide intent and hopelessness in the prediction of early suicide in male high-risk suicide attempters. *Acta Psychiatrica Scandinavica*, 113 (1), 44-7.

San Molina, L., Arranz Marti, B. (1997). Trastorno por uso de sustancias y suicidio. In: *La conducta suicida, ed.* R. Montalban, pp. 129-38. Madrid: Editorial Libro del Año.

Sansone, R.A., Gaither, G.A., Songer, D.A. (2002). Self-harm behaviors across the life cycle: a pilot study of inpatients with borderline personality disorder. *Comprehensive Psychiatry*, 43(3), 215-8.

Sarkar, J. & Adshead, G. (2006). Personality disorders as disorganisation of attachment and affect regulation. *Advances in Psychiatric Treatment*, 12, 297-305.

Satck, S. (1992). Marriage, family, religion and suicide. In: *Assessment and prediction of suicide*, ed. R.W. Marris, A.L. Berman, J.T. Maltsberger, R.I. Yufit. New York: Guilford Press.

Sarró, B., Nogue, S. (1992). Suicidios. *Medicina Clinica*, 98, 624-6.

Savitz, J.B., Cupido, C.L., Ramesar, R.S. (2006). Trends in suicidology: personality as an endophenotype for molecular genetic investigations. *PLoS Medicine*, 3(5), e107.

Schalling, D., Edman, G. (1993). *The Karolinska Scales of Personality (KSP). An inventory for assessing temperament dimensions associated with vulnerability for psychosocial deviance*. Manual. Stencil. Stockholm: The Department of Psychiatry, The Karolinska Institute.

Schinka, J.A., Busch, R.M., Robichaux-Keene, N. (2004). A meta-analysis of the association between the serotonin transporter gene polymorphism (5-HTTLPR) and trait anxiety. *Molecular Psychiatry*, 9(2), 197-202.

Schmidtke, A., Bille-Brahe, U., DeLeo, D., et al. (1996). Attempted suicide in Europe: rates, trends and sociodemographic characteristics of suicide attempters during the period 1989-1992. Results of the WHO/EURO Multicentre Study on Parasuicide. *Acta Psychiatrica Scandinavica*, 93 (5), 327-38.

Schmidkte, A., Bille-Brahe, U., De Leo, D., Kerkhof, A.D. (2004). *Suicidal behaviour in Europe: results from the WHO/EURO Multicentre Study on Suicidal Behaviour.* Gottingen: Hogrefe & Huber.

Schmidtke, A., Hafner, H. (1998). The Werther effect after television films: new evidence for an old hypothesis. *Psychological Medicine*, 18, 665–76.

Schneider, K. (1980). *Las personalidades psicopáticas.* Madrid: Morata.

Schoenfeld, M., Myers, R.H,. Cupples, L.A., et al. (1984). Increased rate of suicide among patients with Huntington's disease. *Journal of Neurology Neurosurgical Psychiatry*, 47(12), 1283-7.

Schotte, D.E., Cools, J., Payvar, S. (1990). Problem-solving deficits in suicidal patients: trait vulnerability or state phenomenon? *Journal of Consulting Clinical Psychology*, 58(5), 562-4.

Seeman, M.V. (1986). Current outcome in schizophrenia: women vs men. *Acta Psychiatrica Scandinavica*, 73(6), 609-17.

Seguí-Montesinos, J. (1989). Las tentativas autolíticas reincidentes en el servicio de urgencias de un hospital general. *Psiquis*, 10, 264-8.

Seivewright, N. (1987). Relationship between life events and personality in psychiatric disorders. *Stress Medicine*, 3, 163-8.

Seivewright, N., Tyrer, P., Ferguson, B., et al. (2000). Longitudinal study of the influence of life events and personality status on diagnostic change in three neurotic disorders. *Depression Anxiety*, 11, 105-13.

Seroczynski, A.D., Bergeman, C.S., Coccaro, E.F. (1999). Etiology of the impulsivity/aggression relationship: genes or environment? *Psychiatry Research*, 86(1), 41-57.

Serreti, A., Lattuada, E., Cusin, C., et al. (1999). Clinical and demographic features of psychotic and nonpsychotic depression. *Comprehensive Psychiatry*, 40(5), 358-62.

Shapiro, C.M., Parry, M.R. (1984). Is unemployment a cause of parasuicide? *British Medical Journal of Clinical Research Edition*, 289 (6458), 1622.

Shearer, S.L., Peters, C.P., Quaytman, M.S., et al. (1988). Intense lethality of suicide attempts among females borderline inpatients. *American Journal of Psychiatry*, 145, 1424-27.

Shedler, J., Westen, D. (2004). Refining DSM-IV personality disorder diagnosis: integrating science and practice. *American Journal of Psychiatry*, 161, 1350-65.

Shenassa, E.D., Catlin, S.N., Buka, S.L. (2003). Lethality of firearms relative to other suicide methods: a population-based study. *Journal of Epidemiology Community Health*, 57, 120-4.

Shneidman, E.S. (2001). *Comprehending suicide: landmarks in 20th-century suicidology.* Washington: American Psychological Association.

Sher, L., Oquendo, M.A., Mann, J.J. (2001). Risk of suicide in mood disorders. *Clinical Neuroscience Research,* 1, 337-44.

Sher, L., Oquendo, M.A., Grunebaum, M.F., et al. (2007). CSF monoamine metabolites and lethality of suicide attempts in depressed patients with alcohol dependence. *European Neuropsychopharmacology,* 17*(1),12-5*

Siever, L.J. (2002). Personality Disorders in Schizophrenia spectrum. In: *Review of Psychiatry,* ed. A. Tassman & M. Riba. Washington: APA.

Siever, L.J. (2005). Endophenotypes in the personality disorders. *Dialogues Clinical Neuroscience,* 7(2), 39-51.

Siever, L.J., Buchsbaum, M.S., New, A.S., et al. (1999). d,l-fenfluramine response in impulsive personality disorder assessed with [18F]fluorodeoxyglucose positron emission tomography. *Neuropsychopharmacology,* 20(5), 413-23.

Silverman, M.M. (2006). The language of suicidology. *Suicide Life Threatening Behavior,* 36(5), 519-32.

Simon, T.R., Powell, K.E., Swann, A.C. (2004). Involvement in physical activity and risk for nearly lethal suicide attempts. *American Journal of Preventive Medicine,* 27, 310-5.

Simon, T.R., Swann, A.C., Powell, K.E., et al. (2001). Characteristics of impulsive suicide attempts and attempters. *Suicide Life Threatening Behavior,* 32 (Supl.), 49-59.

Simonds, J.F., McMahon, T., Armstrong, D. (1991). Young suicide attempters compared with a control group: psychological, affective, and attitudinal variables. *Suicide Life Threatening Behavior,* 21(2), 134-51.

Singleton, N, Meltzer, H., Gatward, R. (1998). *Psychiatric Morbidity Among Prisoners in England and Wales.* London: HMSO.

Skodol, A.E., Gunderson, J.G., Pfohl, B., et al. (2002). The borderline diagnosis I: psychopathology, comorbidity, and personality structure. *Biological Psychiatry,* 51, 936-50.

Skodol, A.E., Gunderson, J.G., McGlashan, T.H., et al. (2002). Functional impairment in patients with schizotypal, borderline, avoidant, or obsessive-compulsive personality disorder. *American Journal of Psychiatry,* 159(2), 276-83.

Skodol, A.E., Gunderson, J.G., Shea, M.T., et al. (2005). The collaborative longitudinal personality disorder study (CLPS): overview and implications. *Journal of Personality Disorders,* 19(5), 487-504.

Skodol, A.E., Oldham, J.M., Bender, D.S., et al. (2005). Dimensional representations of DSM-IV personality disorders: relationships to functional impairment. *American Journal of Psychiatry,* 162(10), 1919-25.

Sleet, D., Bonzo, S., Branche, C. (1998). An overview of the National Center for Injury Prevention and Control at the Centers for Disease Control and Prevention. *Injury Prevention,* 4(4), 308-12.

Smith, D.I., Burvill, P.W. (1991). Relationship between alcohol consumption and attempted suicide morbidity rates in Perth, Western Australia, 1968-1984. *Addictive Behavior,* 16(1-2), 57-61.

Smith et al. (1995) cited by Rendu Rendu, A., Moran, P., Patel, A., et al. (2002). Economic impact of personality disorders in UK primary care attenders. *British Journal of Psychiatry,* 181, 62-6.

Snyder, M.L. (1994). Methods of suicide used by Irish and Japanese samples: a cross-cultural study from 1964 to 1979. *Psychology Reports,* 74, 127-30.

Söderberg, S. (2001). Personality disorders in parasuicide. *Nordic Journal of Psychiatry*, 55, 163-7.

Sokal, R.R. (1974). Classification: purposes, principles, progress, prospects. *Science*, 185(4157), 1115-1123.

Soloff, P.H., Meltzer, C.C., Greer, P.J., et al. (2000). A fenfluramine-activated FDG-PET study of borderline personality disorder. *Biological Psychiatry*, 47(6), 540-7.

Soloff, P.H. & Ulrich, R.F. (1981). Diagnostic interview for borderline patients: A replication study. *Archives of General Psychiatry*, 38, 686-92.

Soloff, P.H., Lis, J.A., Kelly, T., et al. (1994). Risk factors for suicidal behavior in borderline personality diosrder. *American Journal of Psychiatry*, 151, 1316-23.

Soloff PH, Lynch KG, Kelly TM, et al. (2000). Characeristics of suicide attempts of patients with major depressive episode and borderline personality disorder: a comparative study. *American Journal of Psychiatry*, 157: 601-8.

Soloff, P.H., Lynch, K.G., Kelly, T.M. (2002). Childhood abuse as a risk factor for suicidal behavior in borderline personality disorder. *Journal of Personality Disorders*, 16, 201-14.

Soloff, P.H., Fabio, A., Kelly, T.M., et al. (2005). High-lethality status in patients with borderline personality disorder. *Journal of Personality Disorders*, 19(4), 386-399.

Solomon, K. (1981). Personality disorders in the elderly. In: Personality disorders, diagnosis, and management, ed. J.R. Lion. pp. 310-338. Baltimore: Williams & Wilkins.

Somasundaram, D.J., Rajadurai, S. (1995). War and suicide in northern Sri Lanka. *Acta Psychiatrica Scandinavica*, 91(1), 1-4.

Spalletta, G.A., Troibi, A., Saracco, M, et al. (1996). Symptoms profile, axis II comorbidity and suicidal behavior in young males with DSM-III-R depressive illnesses. *Journal of Affective Disorders*, 39, 141-8.

Spiro, M.E. (1983). *Oedipus in the Trobriands*. Chicago: University Chicago Press.

Spitzer, R., Williams, J.B.W., Gibbon, M. (1987). *Structured Clinical Interview for DSM-III-R Personality Disorders (SCID-II)*. New York. Biometrics Research Department, New York State Psychiatric Institute.

Spivak, B., Shabash, E., Sheitman, B., et al. (2003). The effects of Clozapine Versus Haloperidol on Measures of Impulsive Aggression and Suicidality in Chronic Schizophrenia Patients: An Open, Non-Randomized, 6 month Study. *Journal of Clinical Psychiatry*, 64, 755-60.

Stack, S. (1983). The effect of religious commitment on suicide: a cross-national analysis. *Journal of Health Social Behavior*, 24, 362-74.

Stack, S., Lester, D. (1991). The effect of religion on suicide ideation. *Social Psychiatry Psychiatric Epidemiology*, 26, 168-70.

Stalenheim, E.G. (1997). Karolinska Scales of personality in a forensic psychiatric population: stability over time and between situations. *Nordic Journal of Psychiatry*, 51, 379-84.

Stanley, B., Gameroff, M.J., Michalsen, V., et al. (2001). Are suicide attempters who self-mutilate a unique population? *American Journal of Psychiatry*, 158, 427-32

Stark, C., Gibbs, D., Hopkins, P., et al. (2006). Suicide in farmers in Scotland. *Rural and Remote Health*, 6, 509.

Statham, D.J., Heath, A.C., Madden, P.A., et al. (1998). Suicidal behaviour: an epidemiological and genetic study. *Psychological Medicine*, 28(4), 839-55.

Steblaj, A., Tavcar, R., Dernovsek, M.Z. (1999). Predictors of suicide in psychiatric hospital. *Acta Psychiatrica Scandinavica*, 100(5), 383-8.

Stein, D., Apter, A., Ratzoni, G., et al. (1998). Association between multiple suicide attempts and negative affects in adolescents. *Journal of American Academy Child and Adolescent Psychiatry*, 37(5), 488-94.

Stenager, E.N., Stenager, E., Koch, H.N., et al. (1992). Suicide and multiple sclerosis: an epidemiological investigation. *Journal of Neurology and Neurosurgical Psychiatry*, 55(7), 542-5.

Stephens, J.H., McHugh, P.R. (1991). Characteristics and long-term follow-up of patients hospitalized for mood disorders in the Phipps Clinic, 1913-1940. *Journal of Nervous Mental Disorder*, 179(2), 64-73.

Stone, G. (1999). *Suicide and attempted suicide*. New York: Carroll &Graff Publications.

Stone, M.H., Hurt, S.W., Stone, D.K. (1987). The PI 500: DSM-III criteria: I. Global outcome. *Journal of Personality Disorder*, 1, 291-8.

Stone, M. (1989). Long-term follow-up of narcissistic personality disorder. *Psychiatric Clinics of North America*, 12, 621-41.

Stone, M.H. (1990). *The fate of borderline patients*. New York, Guilford.

Straus, M.A., Kantor, G.K. (1994). Corporal punishment of adolescents by parents: a risk factor in the epidemiology of depression, suicide, alcohol abuse, child abuse, and wife beating. *Adolescence*, 29(115), 543-61.

Stravinski, A. & Boyer, R. (2001). Loneliness in relation to suicide ideation and parasuicide. A population-wide study. *Suicide & Life Threatening Behavior*, 31, 32-40.

Sullivan Everstine, D. & Everstine, L. (1992). *Personas en crisis*. Méjico: Pax.

Sullivan, P.F., Eaves, L.J., Kendler, K.S., et al. (2001). Genetic case-control association studies in neuropsychiatry. *Archives of General Psychiatry*, 58(11), 1015-24.

Suokas, J., Lonnqvist, J. (1991). Outcome of attempted suicide and psychiatric consultation: risk factor and suicide mortality during a five-year follow-up. *Acta Psychiatrica Scandinavica*, 84, 545-9.

Suominen, K., Henriksson, M., Suokas, J., et al. (1996). Mental disorders and commorbidity in attempted suicide. *Acta Psychiatrica Scandinavica*, 94, 234-40.

Suominen, K., Isometsa, E., Henriksson, M., et al. (1997). Hopelessness, impulsiveness and intent among suicide attempters with major depression, alcohol dependence, or both. *Acta Psychiatrica Scandinavica*, 96(2), 142-9.

Suominen, K., Isometsä, E., Suokas, J., et al. (2004). Completed suicide after a suicide attempt: a 37-year follow-up study. *American Journal of Psychiatry*, 161, 562-3.

The Surgeron General's Report call to action to prevent suicide. (1999). Washington, DC. U.S.Public Health Service.

Suris, J.C., Parera, N., Puig, C. (1996). Chronic illness and emotional distress in adolescence. *Journal of Adolescent Health*, 19(2), 153-6.

Surtees, P.G., Wainwright, N.W., Willis-Owen, S.A., et al. (2006). Social adversity, the serotonin transporter (5-HTTLPR) polymorphism and major depressive disorder. *Biological Psychiatry*, 59, 224-9.

Swanson, M.C., Bland, R.C., Newman, S.C. (1994). Antisocial personality disorder. *Acta Psychiatrica Scandinavica*, 376 (suppl.), 63-70.

Swartz M, et al. (1990). Estimating the prevalence of borderline personality disorder in the comunity. *Journal of Personality Disorders*, 4, 257-72.

Szanto, K., Prigerson, H.G., Reynolds III, C.F. (2001). Suicide in the elderly. *Clinical Neuroscience Research*, 366-76.

Szerman, N. (2004). Impulsividad y trastornos de la personalidad. In: *Impulsividad*, ed. S. Ros-Montalbán, M.D. Peris-Díaz & R. Gracia-Marco R, pp. 101-18. Barcelona: Psiquiatría Editores, S.L.

Tamosiunas, A., Reklaitiene, R., Virviciute, D., et al. (2006). Trends in suicide in a Lithuanian urban population over the period 1984-2003. *BMC Public Health*, 6: 184.

Taylor, S.E., Way, B.M., Welch, W.T., et al. (2006) Early family environment, current adversity, the serotonin transporter promoter polymorphism, and depressive symptomatology. *Biological Psychiatry*, 60(7), 671-6

Tejedor, M.C., Sarró, B. (1997). Intento de autólisis. In: *Interconsulta Psiquiátrica,* ed. J.E. Rojo, E. Cirera, pp. 435-446. Barcelona: Masson.

Thorell, L.H. (1987). Electrodermal activity in suicidal and nonsuicidal depressive patients and in matched healthy subjects. *Acta Psychiatrica Scandinavica*, 76(4), 420-30.

Thornicroft, G., Sartorius, N. (1993). The course and outcome of depression in different cultures: 10-year follow-up of the WHO Collaborative Study on the Assessment of Depressive Disorders. *Psychological Medicine*, 23(4), 1023-32.

Tienari, P. (1991). Interaction between genetic vulnerability and family environment: the Finnish adoptive family study of schizophrenia. *Acta Psychiatrica Scandinavica*, 84(5), 460-5.

Tobeña, A. (2003). Aethiopathogenesis of personality disorders (from genes to biodevelopmental processes). In: *New Oxford Textbook of Psychiatry*, ed. MG. Gelder, J.J. Lopez-Ibor Jr, & N.C. Andreasen, pp. 965-70.. Oxford: Oxfors University Press.

Torgersen, S., Kringlen, E., Cramer V. (2001). The prevalence of personality disorders in a community sample. *Archives of General Psychiatry*, 58, 590-6.

Trull, T.J., Steppp, S.D., Durrett, C.A. (2003). Research on borderline personality disorder: an update. *Current Opinion in Psychiatry*, 16, 77-82.

Trull, T.J., Tragesser, S.L., Solhan, M., et al. (2007). Dimensional models of personality disorder: Diagnostic and Statistical Manual of Mental Disorder fifth edition and beyond. *Current Opinion Psychiatry*, 20(1), 52-6.

Tuckman, J. & Youngman, N. (1963). Identifying suicide risk groups among attempted suicides. *Public Health Reports*, 78, 763-66.

Turecki, G. (2005). Dissecting the suicide phenotype: the role of impulsive-aggressive behaviours. J *Psychiatry Neuroscience*, 30(6), 398-408.

Turner, S.M., Biedel, D.C., Townsley RM. (1993). Social phobia: a comparison of specific and generalized subtypes and avoidant personality disorder. *Journal of Abnormal Psychology*, 101, 326-31.

Turvey, C.L., Conwell, Y., Jones, M.P., et al. (2002). Risk factors for late-life suicide: a prospective, community-based study. *American Journal of Geriatric Psychiatry*, 10, 398-406.

Tylor, E.B. (1958). *Primitive culture: researches into the development of mythology, philosophy, religion, art, and custom*. New York: Harper Torchbooks.

Tyrer, P. (1996). Personality disorders: Diagnosis, management and course. London, UK: WrightTyrer P, Johnson T. Establishing the severity of personality disorder. *American Journal of Psychiatry,* 153(12), 1593-97.

Tyrer, P. (2005).The problem of severity in the classification of personality disorder. *Journal of Personality Disorders*, 19(3), 309-14.

Tyrer, P., Alexander, M.S. (1979). Classification of personality disorder. *British Journal of Psychiatry*, 135, 163-7.

Tyrer, P., Alexander, J. (1988). Personality assessment schedule. In *Personality Disorders: Diagnosis, Management and Course*. London: Wright.

Uña Suárez. (1985). Sociología del suicidio. Ampliaciones epistemológicas. *Psicopatologia*, 5(2), 129-136.

US Census Bureau. Statistical abstracts of the United States, cited by Gunderson, J.G., Ridolfi, M.E. (2001). Borderline personality disorder: suicidality and self-mutilation. *Annals of New York Academy of Sciece*, 932, 61-73, discussion 73-7.

U.S. Public Health Service, *The Surgeon General's Call To Action To Prevent Suicide*. Washington, DC: 1999 [cited 2006 Aug 9]. Available from: http://www.surgeongeneral.gov/library/calltoaction/calltoaction.htm. Accessed August 2006.

Vaillant, G.E. (1977). *Adaptation to life*. Cambridge, Massachusetts: Harvard University Press.

Vallejo Ruiloba, J. (1998). *Introduccion a la psicopatologia y la psiquiatria*. Barcelona: Masson, 1998.

Van Gastel, A., Schotte, C., Maes, M. (1997). The prediction of suicidal intent in depressed patients. *Acta Psychiatrica Scandinavica*, 96(4), 254-9.

Van Gestel, S. & Van Broeckhoven, C. (2003). Genetics of personality: are we making progress? *Molecular Psychiatry*, 8(10), 840-52.

Van Heeringen, C., Audenaert, K., Van Laere, K., et al. (2003). Prefrontal 5-HT2a receptor binding index, hopelessness and personality characteristics in attempted suicide. *Journal of Affective Disorder*, 74(2), 149-58.

Van Horn, E., Manley, C., Leddy, D., et al. (2000). Problems in developing an instrument for the rapid assessment of personality status. *European Psychiatry,* 15 (Suppl 1), 29-33.

Van Ijzendoorn, M.H., Schuengel, C., Bakermans-Kranenburg, M.J. (1999). Disorganised attachment in early childhood: meta-analysis of precursors, concomitants and sequelae. *Development and Psychopathology*, 11, 225-49.

Varadaraj, R., Mendonca, J.D., Rauchenberg, P.M. (1986). Motives and intent: a comparison of views of overdose patients and their key relatives/friends. *Canadian Journal of Psychiatry*, 31(7), 621-4.

Velamoor, V.R., Cernovsky, Z. (1990). Unemployment and the nature of suicide attempts. *Psychiatric Journal of University Ottawa* 15(3), 162-4.

Verheul, R. (2005). Clinical utility of dimensional models for personality pathology. *Journal of Personality Disorders*, 19(3), 283-302.

Verheul, R., Widiger, T.A. (2004). A meta-analysis of the prevalence and usage of the personality disorder not otherwise specified (PDNOS) dianosis. *Journal of Personality Disorders*, 18(4), 309-19.

Vevera, J., Fisar, Z., Kvasnicka, T., et al. (2005). Cholesterol-lowering therapy evokes time-limited changes in serotonergic transmission. *Psychiatry Research*, 133(2-3), 197-203.

Vieta, E., Nieto, E., Gasto, C., et al. (1992). Serious suicide attempts in affective patients. *Journal of Affective Disorder*, 24(3), 147-52.

Vinoda, K.S. (1966). Personality characteristics of attempted suicides. *British Journal of Psychiatry,* 112, 1143-50.

Vitiello, B., Stoff, D.M. (1997). Subtypes of aggression and their relevance to child psychiatry. *Journal of Amercian Academy Child Adolescent Psychiatry*, 36, 307-15.

Wakefield, J.C. (2006). Personality disorder as harmful dysfunction: DSM's cultural deviance criterion reconsidered. *Journal of Personality Disorders*, 20(2), 157-69.

Waldron, I. (1976). Why do women liver longer than men? *Social Science Medicine*, 2(1), 2-13.

Wang, S. (1997). Traumatic stress and attachment. *Acta Physiologica Scandinavica*, 161 (suppl. 640), 164–9.

Warshaw, M.G., Dolan, R.T., Keller, M.B. (2000). Suicidal behavior in patients with current or past panic disorder: five years of prospective data from the Harvard/Brown Anxiety Research Program. *American Journal of Psychiatry*, 157, 1876-8.

Wasserman, I.M (1992). Economy, work, occupation and suicide. In: *Assessment and prediction of suicide,* ed. R.W. Marris, A.L. Berman, J.T. Maltsberger, R.I. Yufit. New York: Guilford Press, 1992.

Wasserman, D., Cullberg, J. (1989). Early separation and suicidal behaviour in the parental homes of 40 consecutive suicide attempters. *Acta Psychiatrica Scandinavica*, 79, 296-302.

Wasserman D, Varnik A, Dankowicz M. (1998). Regional differences in the distribution of suicide in the former Soviet Union during perestroika, 1984–1990. *Acta Psychiatrica Scandinavica Supplementum,* 394, 5–12.

Watson D, Clark LA, Harkness AR. (1994). Structures of personality and their relevance to psychopathology. *Journal of Abnormal Psychology*, 103, 18-31.

Watzlawick, P., Beavin Bavelas, J., Jackson, D.D. (1997). *Teoría de la Comunicación Humana, pp. 56-60.* Barcelona: Herder.

Weeke, A., Vaeth, M. (1986). Excess mortality of bipolar and unipolar manic-depressive patients. *Journal of Affective Disorders*, 11(3), 227-34.

Weiss, J.M.A. (1973). The natural history of antisocial attitudes: what happens to psychopaths? *Journal of Geriatric Psychiatry*, 6, 236-42.

Weissman, M.M.(1993). The epidemiology of personality disorder: a 1990 update. *Journal of Personality Disorders*, 7, 44-62.

Weissman, M.M. (1993). The epidemiology of personality disorders: a 1990 update. *Journal of Personality Disorders*, 7(suppl), 44-62.

Weissman, A.N., Beck, A.T., Kovacs, M. (1979). Drug abuse, hopelessness, and suicidal behavior. *Intern Journal of Addict*, 14(4), 451-64.

Weissman, M.M., Bland, R.C., Canino, G.J., et al. (1999). Prevalence of suicide ideation and suicide attempts in nine countries. *Psychological Medicine*, 29(1), 9-17.

Weissman, M., Fox, K., Klerman, G.L. (1973). Hostility and depression associated with suicide attempts. *American Journal of Psychiatry*, 130, 450-4.

Weisman, A.D. & Worden, J.W. (1972). Risc-Rescue Rating in Suicide Assessment. *Archives of General Psychiatry*, 20, 553-60.

Welch, S.S., Linehan, M.M. (2002). High-risk situations associated with parasuicide and drug use in borderline personality disorder. *Journal of Personality Disorders*, 16(6), 561-9.

Westen, D., Arkowitz-Westen, L. (1998). Limitations of axis II in diagnosing personality pathology in clinical practice. A*merican Journal of Psychiatry*, 155(12), 1767-71.

Westen, D., Shedler, J., Bradley, R. (2006). A prototype approach to personality disorder disgnosis. *American Journal of Psychiatry*, 163(5), 846-56.

Wetzel, R.D. (1976). Hopelessness, depression, and suicide intent. *Archives of General Psychiatry*, 33(9), 1069-73.

Weyrauch, K.F., Roy-Byrne, P., Katon, W, et al. (2001). Stressful life events and impulsiveness in failed suicide. *Suicide Life Threaten behavior*, 31, 311-9.

Wheeler, M. A., Stuss, D. T. & Tulving, E. (1997). Toward a theory of episodic memory: the frontal lobes and autonoetic consciousness. *Psychological Bulletin*, 121(3), 331-54.

White, L. (1959). *The Evolution of Culture: The Development of Civilization to the Fall of Rome, pp. 3*. New York: McGraw-Hill.

Wicki, W., Angst, J. (1991). The Zurich Study. X. Hypomania in a 28- to 30-year-old cohort. *European Archives of Psychiatry Clinical Neuroscience*, 240(6), 339-48.

Widiger, T.A. (1993). The DSM-III-R categorial personality diosorder diagnoses: A critique and alternative. *Psychology Inquiry,* 4, 75-90.

Widiger, T.A. (2005). A dimensional model of personality disorder. *Current Opinion in Psychiatry*, 18, 41-3.

Widiger, T.A., Costa, P.T. (2002). Five-factor model personality disorder research. In: *Personality disorders and the five-fractor model of personality,* ed. P.T. Costa Jr, T.A. Widiger, pp. 59-87. Washington DC: American Psychological Association.

Widiger, T.A., Frances, A. (1987). Interviews and inventories for the measurement of personality disorders. *Clinical Psychology Review*, 7, 49-75.

Widiger, T.A., Frances, A.J., Harris, M., et al. (1991). Comorbidity among axis II disorders. In: *Personality disorders: new perspectives on diagnostic validity*, ed. J.M. Oldham, pp. 163-194. Washington DC: American Psychiatric Press.

Widiger, T.A., Mangine, S., Corbit, E.M., et al. (1995). *Personality Disorder Intervew-IV: A semistructured interview for the assessment of personality disorders.* Florida: Psychological Assessment Resources.

Widiger, T.A., Sanderson, C.J. (1995). Toward a dimensional model of personality disorder. In: *The DSM-IV Personality Disorders*, ed. W.J. Livesley, pp. 433-58. New York: Guilford, 1995.

Widiger, T.A., Simonsen, E. (2005). Alternative dimensional models of personality disorder: finding a common ground. *Journal of Personality Disorders*, 19, 110-30.

Widiger, T.A., Weissman, M.M. (1991). Epidemiology of borderline personality disorder. *Hospital Comunity Psychiatry*, 42, 1015-21.

Wiedenmann, A., Weyerer, S. (1993). The impact of availability, attraction and lethality of suicide methods on suicide rates in Germany. *Acta Psychiatrica Scandinavica*, 88, 364-8.

Wilhelm, K., Mitchell, P., Niven, H., et al. Life events, first depression onset and the serotonin transporter gene. *British Journal of Psychiatry*, 188, 210-5.

Wilkinson, D.G. (1982). The suicide rate in schizophrenia. *British Journal of Psychiatry*, 140, 138-41.

Williams, L. A "classic" case of borderline personality disorder. *Psychiatric Services*, 49, 173-4.

Williams, C.L., Davidson, J.A., Montgomery, I. (1980). Impulsive suicidal behavior. *Journal of Clinical Psychology*, 36(1), 90-4.

Winston, A.P. (2000). Recent developments in borderline personality disorder. *Advances in Psychiatric Treatment*, 6, 211-7.

Wintemute, G.J., Parham, C.A., Beaumont, J.J., et al. (1999). Mortality among recent purchasers of handguns. *New England Journal of Medicine*, 341, 1583-9.

Wolfersdorf, M., Straub, R. (1994). Electrodermal reactivity in male and female depressive patients who later died by suicide. *Acta Psychiatrica Scandinavica*, 89(4), 279-84.

Wolk-Wasserman, D. (1987). Contacts of suicidal neurotic and prepsychotic/psychotic patients and their significant others with public care institutions before the suicide attempt. *Acta Psychiatrica Scandinavica*, 75(4), 358-72.

Worden, J.W. (1997). Las cuatro tareas del duelo. El tratamiento del duelo, asesoramiento psicológico y terapia. Barcelona: Paidós

World Health Organization. (1992). *The ICD-10 classification of mental and behavioural disorders*. Clinical descriptions and diagnostic guidelines. Geneva: WHO.

World Health Organisation (1993). *The ICD-10 classification of mental and behavioural disorders*. Geneva: World Health Organisation.

World Health Organisation (1995). *International Personality Disorders Examination (IPDE) – DSM-IV module*, Cambrige University Press.

World Health Organisation (1996). *International Personality Disorders Examination (IPDE) –ICD 10 Module*, Cambridge University Press.

World Health Organization. (2000). World Health Organization Report 2000. Health Systems: Improving Performance. Geneva: World Health Organization: Geneva.

World Health Organization. (2000). [cited 2006 Aug 9]. Preventing suicide: A resource for general pshysicians. Geneva: World Health Organization. Available from: *http://www. who.int/mental_health/media/en/56.pdf*

World Health Organization. (2002). European monitoring survey on national suicide prevention programmes and strategies. Suicide Prevention in Europe.

World Health Organization. (2005). [cited 2006 Aug 9]. Country reports and charts Web page. Geneva: World Health Organization. Available from:
http://www.who.int /mental_health/prevention/suicide/country_reports/en/index.html.

World Health Organization. (2005). European Ministerial Conference on Mental Health. Helsinki, Finland.

World Health Organization. (2006). International Statistical Classification of Diseases and Related Health Problems 10th Revision. Geneva: World Health Organisation.

World Health Organization. (2006). [cited 2006 Aug 9]. Suicide Prevention and special programmes. Preventing suicide: a resource for general physicians. Geneva: World Health Organization. Available from: *http://www.who.int/mental_health/prevention/ suicide/suicideprevent/en/index.html*

World Health Organization. (2005). [cited 2006 Aug 9]. Country reports and charts Web page. Geneva: World Health Organization.. Available from: *http://www.who.int/ mental_health/prevention/suicide/country_reports/en/index.html.*

Yehuda, R., Southwick, S.M., Ostroff, R.B., et al. (1988). Neuroendocrine aspects of suicidal behavior. *Neurology Clinics*, 6(1), 83-102.

Yen, S., Pagano, M.E., Shea, M.T., et al. (2005). Recent life events preceding suicide attempts in a personality disorder sample: findings from the collaborative longitudinal personality disorders study. *Journal of Consulting Clinical Psychology*, 73(1), 99-105

Yen, S., Shea, T., Pagano, M., et al. (2003). Axis I and axis II disorders as predictors of prospective suicide attempts: findings from the collaborative longitudinal personality disorders study. *Journal of Abnormal Psychology*, 312, 375-81.

Yen, S., Shea, T., Sanislow, C.A., et al. (2004). Borderline personality disorder criteria associated with prospectively observed suicidal behavior. *American Journal of Psychiatry*, 161, 1296-98.

Yip, P.S.F, Tan, R.C. (1998). Suicides in Hong Kong and Singapore: a tale of two cities. *International Journal of Social Psychiatry*, 44, 267–79.

Yip, P.S.F. (2001). An epidemiological profile of suicide in Beijing, China. *Suicide and Life-Threatening Behavior*, 31, 62–70.

Yip, P., Chao, A., Chiu, C. (2000). Seasonal variation in suicides: Diminished or vanished—experience from England and Wales, 1982–1996. *British Journal of Psychiatry*, 177, 366–9.

Yip, P., Fu, K.W., Yang, K.C., et al. (2006). The effects of a celebrity suicide on suicide rates in Hong Kong. *Journal of Affective Disorders*, 93, 245-52.

Young, E.A., Coryell, W. (2005). Suicide and the hypothalamic-pituitary-adrenal axis. *Lancet*, 366(9490), 959-61.

Young, M.A., Fogg, L.F., Scheftner, W., et al. (1996). Stable trait components of hopelessness: baseline and sensitivity to depression. *Journal of Abnormal Psychology*, 105(2), 155-65.

Youssef, G., Plancherel, B., Laget, J., et al. (2004). Personality trait risk factors for attempted suicide among young women with eating disorders. *European Psychiatry*, 19, 131-9.

Yufit, R.I., Bongar, B. (1992). Suicide, stress and coping with life cicle events. In: *Assessment and prediction of suicide*, ed. R.W. Marris, A.L. Berman, J.T. Maltsberger, R.I. Yufit. New York: Guilford Press, 1992.

Zacharakis, C.A. Hadjivassilis, V., Madianos, M.G., et al. (2005). Suicide in Cyprus 1998-1999. *European Psychiatry*, 20, 110-4.

Zanarini, M.C., Frankenburg, F.R., Dubo, E.D, et al. (1998). Axis I comorbidity of borderline personality disorder. *American Journal of Psychiatry*, 155, 1733-9.

Zanarini, M.C., Frankenburg, F.R., Sickel, A.E., et al. (1996). *The Diagnostic Interview for DSM-IV Personality Disorders (DIPD-IV)*. Belmont, MA: McLean Hospital.

Zanarini, M., Frankenburg, F., Zhauncey, D., et al. (1987). The diagnostic interview for personality disorders: interrater and test-retest reliability. *Comprehensive Psychiatry*, 28, 467-80.

Zanarini, M.C., Gunderson, J.G., Frankemburg, F.R., et al. (1989). The revised Diagnostic Interview for Borderlines: Discriminating BDP from other Axis II disorders. *Journal of Personality Disorders*, 3: 10-18.

Zanarini, M.C., Gunderson, J.G., Frankenburg, F.R., et al. (1990). Discriminating borderline personality from other axis II disorders. *American Journal of Psychiatry*, 147, 161-7.

Zanarini, M.C., Skodol, A.E., Bender, D., et al. (2000). The collaborative longitudinal personality disorders study: reliability of Axis I and II diagnoses. *Journal of Personality Disorders*, 14, 291-9.

Zanarini, M.C., Williams, A.A., Lewis, R.E., et al. (1997). Reported pathological childhood experiences associated with the development of borderline personality disorders. *American Journal of Psychiatry*, 154, 1733-9.

Zhang, J., McKeown, R.E., Hussey, J.R., et al. (2005). Low HDL cholesterol is associated with suicide attempt among young healthy women: the Third National Health and Nutrition Examination Survey. *Journal of Affective Disorders*, 89(1-3), 25-33.

Zimmerman, M. (1994). Diagnosing personality disorders. A review of issues and research methods. *Archives of General Psychiatry*, 51, 225-45.

Zimmerman, M. & Coryel, W.H. (1990). Diagnosing personality disorders in the comunity. *Archives of General Psychiatry*, 47, 527-31.

Zlotnick, C., Johnson, D., Yen, S., et al. (2003). Clinical features and impairment in women with borderline personality disorder (BPD) with posttraumatic stress disorder (PTSD), BPD without PTSD, and other personality disorders with PTSD. *Journal of Nervous Mental Disorders*, 191(11), 706-13.

Zoccolillo, M., Pickles, A., Quinton, D., et al. (1992). The outcome of childhood conduct disorder: implications for defining adult personality disorder and conduct disorder. *Psychology Medicine*, 22(4), 971-86.

Zuckerman, M., Kuhlman, D.M., Joireman, J., et al. (1993). A comparison of three structural models for personality: the Big Three, the Big Five, and the Alternative Five. *Journal of Personality and Social Psychology*, 65, 757-68.

ABOUT THE AUTHORS AND CONTRIBUTORS

AUTHORS

Hilario M. Blasco-Fontecilla, MD, PhD, PgDip in child & adolescent Psychiatry, Department of Psychiatry, Acute Inpatient Unit, Dr. R. Lafora Hospital, Madrid, Spain

Enrique Baca-García, MD, PhD, Department of Psychiatry, Foundation Jiménez Diaz University Hospital, Autonoma University of Madrid, Spain, Department of Neurosciences, Columbia University Medical Center, New York

Jerónimo Saiz-Ruiz, MD, PhD, Professor of Psychiatry at Alcalá de Henares University, Head of Department, Department of Psychiatry at Ramón y Cajal Hospital, Madrid, Spain

CONTRIBUTORS

Enrique Baca-García, MD, PhD, Department of Psychiatry, Foundation Jiménez Diaz University Hospital, Autonoma University of Madrid, Spain. Department of Neurosciences, Columbia University Medical Center, 1051 Riverside Drive, New York, NY 10032, e-mail: eb2452@columbia.edu

Eduardo Barbudo del Cura, MD, Distrito Centro Mental Health Center, c/ de la cabeza, 4, Madrid, Spain, e-mail: eduardobar2000@yahoo.es

Hilario M. Blasco-Fontecilla, MD, PhD, PgDip in child & adolescent Psychiatry, Department of Psychiatry, Acute Inpatient Unit, Dr. R. Lafora Hospital, carretera de colmenar viejo km. 13,800, 28049, Madrid, Spain, e-mail: hmblasco@yahoo.es

Dolores Braquehais Conesa, MD, PhD, Horta-Guinardo Mental Health Center, avenida de virgen de montserrat, 16-18 1°, Barcelona, Spain, e-mail: dbraquehais@yahoo.es

Montserrat Caballero González, MD, Valdemoro Mental Health Center, calle Duque de Lerma s/n, Valdemoro, Madrid, Department of Psychiatry, 12 Octubre Hospital, Madrid, Spain, e-mail: montsecgg@gmail.com

Fernando Cañas de Paz, MD, Head of Department, Department of Psychiatry, Dr. R. Lafora Hospital, carretera de colmenar viejo km. 13,800, 28049, Madrid, Spain, e-mail: fcanasd@hotmail.com

Didier Castelnau, MD, Professor of Psychiatry, Head of Department, Service de Psychologie Médicale & Psychiatrie, CHU de Montpellier, Université Montpellier I, Montpellier, France

Antonio Ceverino Domínguez, MD, PhD, Hortaleza Mental Health Center, c/ Mar Caspino s/n, Madrid, Spain, Psychiatry Department, Foundation Jiménez Díaz; Madrid, Spain, e-mail: aceverino@hotmail.com

Philippe Courtet, MD, PhD, Professor of Psychiatry, Service de Psychologie Médicale et Psychiatrie, Hôpital Lapeyronie, CHU Montpellier, 34295 Cedex 5. France. Université Montpellier I, INSERM E 0361, Montpellier, France, e-mail : p-courtet@chu-montpellier.fr

Nieves Cuervo, MD, Department of Psychiatry, St. Luke's-Roosevelt Hospital Center, University Hospital of Columbia University, New York, NY, USA

Carmen Díaz Sastre, MD, PhD, Hortaleza Mental Health Center, c/ Mar Caspino s/n, Madrid, Spain

Blanca Franco, MD, Department of Psychiatry, Acute Inpatient Unit, Dr. R. Lafora Hospital, carretera de colmenar viejo km. 13,800, 28049, Madrid, Spain

Carolina Franco-Porras, MD, Vallecas Mental Health Center, c/ Peña Gorbea, 4, Madrid, Spain

Juan Carlos García Álvarez, MD, Aspe Mental Health Unit, Alicante, Spain, e-mail: jc.garcia@cmn-alicante.com

Eloy García Resa, MD, Head of the Acute Unit, Mediterranean Neuroscience Clinic, Alicante, Spain, e-mail: eloy.garcia@cmn-alicante.com

Silvia González Parra, MD, Department of Psychiatry, Acute Inpatient Unit, Dr. R. Lafora Hospital, carretera de colmenar viejo km. 13,800, 28049, Madrid, Spain, e-mail: silviagp22@hotmail.com

Sébastien Guillaume, MD, MsC, Service de Psychologie Médicale & Psychiatrie, CHU de Montpellierl Université Montpellier I, INSERM E 0361, Montpellier, France

Luis Jiménez Treviño, MD, PhD, Department of Psychiatry, Asturias Central Hospital, Oviedo, Spain, e-mail: luistrevino@eresmas.com

Fabrice Jollant, MD, MsC, Service de Psychologie Médicale & Psychiatrie, CHU de Montpellierl Université Montpellier I, Montpellierl INSERM E 0361, Montpellier, France

Monica Leira Sanmartin, MD, Rivas-Arganda del Rey Mental Health Center, c/ Juan de la Cierva, 20, Arganda del Rey, Madrid, e-mail: monicaleira@gmail.com

Alain Malafosse, MD, PhD, Professor of Psychiatry, Head of Department, Département de Psychiatrie, Hôpitaux Universitaires de Genève, Geneva, Switzerland, INSERM U 888, Montpellier, France

Juan D. Molina Martin, MD, PhD, MsC, Department of Psychiatry, Acute Inpatient Unit, Dr. R. Lafora Hospital, carretera de colmenar viejo km. 13,800, 28049, Madrid, Spain, e-mail: candrader@medynet.com; jmolina.hpmaalud.madrid.org

Maria Oquendo, MD, PhD, Department of Neurosciences, Columbia University Medical Center, 1051 Riverside Drive, New York, NY 100321, e-mail: moquendo@neuron.cpmc.columbia.edu

Maria Mercedes Pérez-Rodriguez, MD, PhD, Department of Psychiatry, Ramón y Cajal Hospital, Carretera de Colmenar Viejo, km. 9,100, Madrid, 28034, Spain, e-mail: merperez@yahoo.com

Carmen Pinto, MD, MDRCPsych, MsC, PgDip in CBT for children & adolescents, Child & Adolescent Psychiatry, Lambeth Adolescent Team & Lambeth CLAMHS, 35 Black Prince Road, London, SE11 6JJ, e-mail: Carmen.Pinto@iop.kcl.ac.uk

Jose Juan Rodríguez Solano, MD, PhD, Head of Mental Health Center, Vallecas Mental Health Center, c/ Peña Gorbea, 4, Madrid, Spain, e-mail: jrodriguez.scsm@salud.madrid.org

Jerónimo Saiz Ruiz, MD, PhD, Professor of Psychiatry at Alcalá de Henares University, Madrid, Spain, Head of Department, Department of Psychiatry, Ramón y Cajal Hospital, Carretera de Colmenar Viejo, km. 9,100, Madrid, 28034, Spain, e-mail: jsaiz@psiquiatria.com

Dolores Saiz González, MD, PhD, Department of Psychiatry, Clinico Hospital, calle Profesor Martin Lagos s/n, 28040, Madrid, Spain, e-mail: lolasaiz@yahoo.es

INDEX

B

E

J

K

L

N

O

P

Q

R

S

W

Y

Z